150 Years of South African Rugby

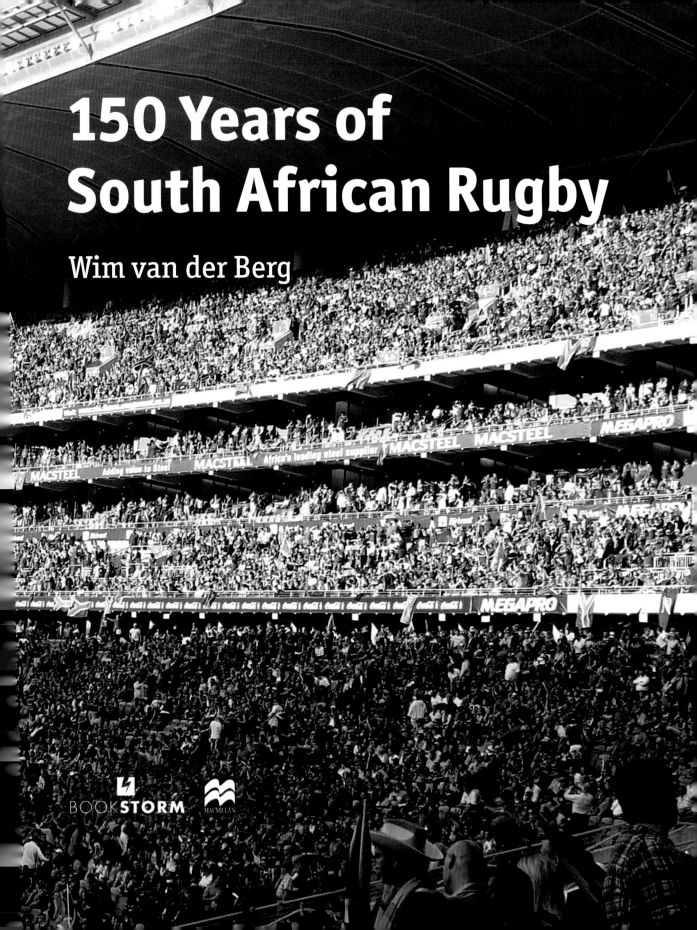

150 Years of
South African Rugby

Wim van der Berg

BOOKSTORM   MACMILLAN

Above: Springbok victory, 1995.

Half title page: Bok front row, CJ van der Linde, Chiliboy Ralepelle and Gurthrö Steenkamp against Italy, 2010.

Title page: FNB Stadium, venue for the 2010 Tri-Nations test against New Zealand.

First published jointly in 2011
by Bookstorm (Pty) Ltd
Suite # 10, Private Bag 12, Cresta, 2118
Johannesburg, South Africa
www.bookstorm.co.za

and Pan Macmillan South Africa
Private Bag X19, Northlands,
Johannesburg, 2116, South Africa
www.panmacmillan.co.za

ISBN 978-1-92043-414-4

Text © Wim van der Berg, 2011
Photographs © Christiaan Kotze, Willie Roos, Elarese
van der Bergh, Wim van der Berg, Rudolf van der Berg,
Hoërskool Monument, GLRU, BBRU, KZNRU

Editing by Patricia Botes
Proofreading by Vanessa Perlman
Design and typesetting by Triple M Design, Johannesburg
Printed and bound by Ultra Litho (Pty) Limited

Contents

Preface   **vii**
Acknowledgements   **ix**

1   **Official champions at last!** The Springboks in the World Cup   **1**

2   **The early beginnings** – Schools, clubs and soldiers pave the way   **23**

3   **Turmoil at the top – The** Woes and fortunes of 13 rugby presidents   **43**

4   **Segregation, frustration and infighting** – The history of multiracial rugby in South Africa   **65**

5   **A competition of two phases** – The Currie Cup: SA rugby's Holy Grail   **81**

6   **The struggle for the golden cup** – A new Currie Cup giant emerges   **101**

7   **Two teams dominate the nineties** – Natal and the Lions break the Currie Cup drought   **121**

8   **The pillars of South African rugby** – Craven Week, Vodacom Cup and so much more   **141**

9   **Test matches** – The grip of South African rugby loosens   **159**

10   **The SANZAR disillusion** – The reality of professionalism in rugby   **177**

Statistics   **201**
Select bibliography   **226**
Index   **228**

Preface

The biggest challenge in writing *150 Years of South African Rugby* was how to condense the rich history of the game in this country and still do justice to the great men and their deeds over 150 years.

It is a task that, ideally, needs five or six volumes. My solution was to try and tell the story of South African rugby since 1861 rather than depict the history in a definitive manner.

Having been fortunate enough to follow our game since the early 1950s – initially as a wide-eyed boy of seven, and later as player, administrator and journalist – it was a joyous task.

The research brought back many personal memories but, more importantly, opened my eyes to the rugby journey through the years – an arduous journey at times, moving through periods of hardship, political wrangling, three wars, administrative turmoil, but also a glorious one.

The most glaring shortcoming I identified during preparing and working on the book was undoubtedly the story of South Africa's rugby among the black and so-called coloured people. The records of that part of our rugby history are incomplete and fragmented. It is therefore regrettable that the chapter on the rugby outside of the IRB-recognised SA Rugby Football Board (now SA Rugby Union) is somewhat skimpy.

I nevertheless hope that the book tells enough of South Africa's rugby story to make readers proud of what has been achieved over the 150 years.

WvdB

Lwazi Mvovo, young Springbok wing of the Sharks, evades a tackle in the 2010 Super Rugby series.

Acknowledgements

Writing *150 Years of South African Rugby* has truly been a fun experience – and for that and the fact that the thought of such a book became a reality, there are many, many people to thank.

First, there are publishers, Bookstorm. To every member of staff, thank you for your support and assistance. And to publisher and CEO Louise Grantham a special thank you for the belief that the book could work; for your humour and patience; and especially for your direction.

Also a big thank you to my wife Alida. She supported, suggested, assisted and reasoned – and also did the translation into Afrikaans to, as she put it, 'let the people understand what you have written'!

There are so many others who gave of their time and knowledge. In particular, my thanks goes to former Springbok logistics manager Mac Hendricks for his input into 'coloured' rugby; and to Derek Jardine for photos he provided of that little-known but very important part of South Africa's rugby history.

You don't need too many reference books if you have friends like former rugby writers Gerhard Burger and Herman le Roux with their background of South African rugby. Thank you to them – and also to Gerhard and Collis Janse van Rensburg for their guidance on matters grammatical – both Afrikaans and English; to photographer Christiaan Kotze for the bulk of the pictures used in the book; and to rugby unions and officials for their assistance.

And lastly, thank you to all the players and officials at all levels for their contribution in growing the great game in South Africa over the past 150 years. Without them, there wouldn't have been a rugby history.

WvdB

Willem de Waal, prolific points scorer.

1

Official champions at last!

The Springboks in the World Cup

24 June, 1995. That was the unforgettable Saturday when the *Amabokoboko* became everyone's team, when everyone in South Africa from the Zimbabwean border to Cape Agulhas rejoiced over winning the World Cup. It was the day the Springboks won the World Cup at their first attempt and on home soil in a tryless final, beating the All Blacks 15–12 after extra time at Ellis Park in Johannesburg.

The triumph followed 135 years of a rugby foundation that was built on much more than mere passion and commitment. A largely solid administration; strong, effective domestic competitions such as the Currie Cup; and a strong schools rugby structure all played their part. It also followed years of disagreement and negotiations with the South African government because of its apartheid policies that did not allow players of colour to be selected at any level of South African rugby and that led to the ostracism of the Springboks by the rugby world.

These factors that had carried or clouded South African rugby over more than a century mattered little to the average fanatical, die-hard supporter that June day in 1995. To them, the World Cup win confirmed South Africa's standing as the best in the world over the past century. After all, they argued, their beloved Boks had won more matches against every single rugby-playing country than they had lost; they had beaten New Zealand at home, something the All Blacks then hadn't yet achieved in South Africa; the Boks had won four successive Grand Slams on tours to the United Kingdom and Ireland with all four Home Unions succumbing while the All Blacks and the Wallabies had recorded only one Grand Slam each. To these supporters, the Springboks had been the champions since that very first series win against the British Isles team of Mark Morrison in 1903. Only France (1958) and the British Lions (1974) with series wins

Proud Springbok fullback, Percy Montgomery, with his 2007 World Cup winner's medal.

Morné du Plessis – The forces of fortune

1971–1980: 22 tests, 15 captaincies

Springbok team manager Morné du Plessis, a man of few but always thoughtful words, said in the heat of the moment after the final whistle had gone in the 1995 World Cup final that it was if some unseen force had guided the Springboks' fortunes. And he was not far off the mark, for a string of events leading up to the final swung the title South Africa's way – and some of them could have short-circuited what was to become a wonderful occasion and year for South African rugby.

The first crisis was the removal of the Springbok coaching and management team a mere nine months and five tests before the World Cup kick-off. Springbok coach Ian McIntosh was fired by Louis Luyt after a record in charge that reflected only four wins and two draws from 12 tests. However, considering how poorly his long line of successors fared against France, England, New Zealand and Australia in the years to come, McIntosh's performance wasn't too shabby. He had only two relatively easier matches against an average Argentina, and Luyt – renowned at Transvaal and the Lions for not giving coaches time to settle in and build a team – might have been a little hasty if it hadn't been for the benefit of hindsight. The proof is in the pudding, they say. Kitch Christie's fairy-tale record with Transvaal and the Lions after being plucked from coaching Pretoria Harlequins' second team got him the top job in South African rugby 18 months later.

Turning the Springboks' performance around in nine months was one of the positive things leading up to the World Cup in a period that could have been a disaster. Then there was the injury to Springbok wing Chester Williams that forced him to withdraw from the World Cup squad. The forces Morné du Plessis referred to played another part, and Williams' replacement, Pieter Hendriks, scored a brilliant try in the Newlands opener against Australia. That set the Boks on their way. Following the suspension of Hendriks and James Dalton for their part in the punch-up against Canada, Hendriks was replaced by a fit-again Williams – who went on to score four tries in his first World Cup outing!

Another serious setback was the hand injury to fullback André Joubert. The man they called the Rolls Royce of fullbacks was very nearly eliminated from the semi-final against France and also the final against New Zealand in the Springboks' bruising quarterfinal match against Western Samoa because of a broken hand. Joubert told the story to Albert Heenop in his book on the Natal Sharks' golden era (the 1990s): 'We kicked through a grubber and I came running from the rear. Mike Umaga hit me with a stiff arm and I took the impact of it on my hand. Five minutes later, in a tackle, I realised that something bad had happened inside my hand. I tried to play on, but simply couldn't.' It was immediately clear that the hand had been broken in the contact and Joubert was replaced by Brendan Venter. Gavin Johnson moved from wing to fullback.

A crisis was on hand. Johnson, good player though he was, had come off a very average game against Western Samoa. Kitch Christie simply had no choice – and Joubert went for surgery that same night. He then spent hours in a decompression chamber, so that a week later, he took to the field against France in the semi-final in Durban with a protective (green) brace used in the Irish game of hurling around his left hand. He also wore it for the final against New Zealand the following week. Joubert admits the injury was at the back of his mind all the time.

The two suspensions after the Canada encounter very nearly cost the Springboks a place in the final. However, to get there, the Boks first had to beat France in the semi-final in Durban. And in a winter season where the rain, contrary to tradition and pattern, affected three of the five World Cup matches played in the coastal city, the semi-final day was close to being washed out. That would have seen South Africa eliminated and France would have gone through on a superior disciplinary record after South Africa's part in the infamous Battle of Boet Erasmus against Canada.

Durban looked as if it had been hit by a monsoon. The field resembled a dam and the heavy rain led to a 90-minute delay in the kick-off. Referee Derek Bevan had to decide on the safety of the players. Lightning was the most serious threat; the others were the danger of collapsed scrums; and the pools of water after such collapses and rucks that could conceivably lead to drowning when players piled on top of one another. After a lull in the rain Bevan decided that the game could go on, but ten minutes after the players took to the field, the heavens reopened!

The Boks slid and slipped to a 19–15 win. They were fortunate when big French flank Abdel Benazzi lost his footing on the wet field as he charged for the try line and what would have been the winner in the dying minutes. Had there been a TMO at that time, the try might even have been awarded!

Then came the final – and young All Blacks flyhalf Andrew Mehrtens, from right in front, missed the simplest of drop kicks with the scores tied at 9–all two minutes from normal time.

The New Zealand press openly broadcast that food poisoning had struck the New Zealand camp the day before the final. They intimated that it was an orchestrated ruse to ensure that the All Blacks were not at their best. A waitress simply identified as 'Suzie', they said, was responsible for the poisoning. However, no proof was ever provided by those pressmen or anyone else about whether it was the restaurant food – the All Blacks had eaten out – or the water used during their training session or the food in their hotel that had been responsible for the poisoning. Nor were the alleged affected players identified – and the All Blacks stayed in the same hotel two years later!

thereafter spoiled the home record of the Boks up to 1995. Yes, the Boks were the champions – and the refrain from Queen's song reverberated around the stands that remained packed with the 60 000 plus spectators long after the final whistle and the presentation of the Webb Ellis Cup that underlined the Springboks' official status.

It was also on that day in June that the magic of Madiba brought a nation together when President Nelson Mandela visited the Springboks in their change room before the match and afterwards presented the Webb Ellis Cup to victorious Bok captain Francois Pienaar. The President, wearing a Springbok cap and a No 6 Springbok jersey – Pienaar's number – presented the World Cup trophy to the South African captain with the words, 'Thank you for what you have done for South Africa'. To which Pienaar replied, 'We could never have done what you have done for South Africa'. The win and what it achieved for the country fulfilled the team's slogan throughout the World Cup campaign: 'One team, one nation'.

That clear, crisp Highveld Saturday afternoon, just more than 100 years after the SA Rugby Football Union was formed in Kimberley in 1889, became undoubtedly the greatest day in South Africa's proud rugby history. Because of its timing in the new democracy's short history, and the effect the win had on the country's people, it was arguably a much bigger happening than the World Cup title the Springboks won in France in 2007. Strangers hugged one another; spectators chanted in unison and bounced up and down as the more than 60 000 fans celebrated at Ellis Park; and in the streets throughout the country, hooters blared and the new South African flag was waved enthusiastically.

The opening thriller
The opening match, exactly four weeks before the final, set the tone for the tournament when Pienaar's Springboks, against all odds, beat defending champions Australia at Newlands. This traditional seat of South African rugby was where the Wallabies had beaten the Springboks 26–3

three years before. There are two outstanding memories of that marvellous winter's day in Cape Town: the excited crowd, overwhelmingly optimistic during an unforgettable opening ceremony; and the manner in which Pieter Hendriks rounded the Wallaby icon David Campese on his way to the try that set the stage for the tournament.

A mere three years before, in 1992, the Springboks had been allowed back into the international fold following the release of Mandela from prison and with the first democratic elections in South Africa's history in 1994 then just around the corner. There were a number of events during the tournament where the South Africans got fortuitous breaks. Not that they didn't deserve the championship, but it could so easily have been different. But more about that as the tournament progressed from that first match against Australia …

The try by Hendriks just before half-time – incidentally one he rates as only his third-most memorable – was outstanding and perhaps the clincher. It overturned a 13–9 Springbok deficit to a 14–13 lead at half-time after the Wallabies had started the match like the champions they were. The slow-starting Springboks, playing with a passion brought on by the general hype in Cape Town and South Africa and in particular by the vociferous Newlands record crowd of just over 53 000, worked their way back into the game. As had been the case for over a century, it was the Springbok scrum in particular that made the Wallabies disintegrate up front. Added to that was a resolute defence brought about by the excitement of the day that manifested in adrenaline-boosted tackles that startled the Australian side.

Errors from the yellow-clad Wallabies became more frequent just as the confidence of the South Africans grew. The Boks were more clinical, they had the patience, and they read the Wallaby attacks clearly and repelled them easily. Springbok flyhalf Joel Stransky – the first Springbok to score in all four possible ways in one match – stretched the Springboks' advantage to 27–13 when he went over for his try in the 64th minute. He scored 22 of those points through a try, a conversion, a drop goal

and four penalties. The shock of Hendriks' effort on the half-time whistle had shaken the defending champions. With the Springboks undoubtedly the stronger team after the break, the Wallabies got just reward for their last-ditch efforts in the closing few minutes when hooker Phil Kearns went over to make it a two-try-each contest.

But the better team had won and had done so convincingly after coming into the tournament with very few giving them a chance to win this first match or, indeed, the tournament. The final score of 27–18 didn't quite reflect the Springboks' dominance. While the Australian squad was gracious in defeat, they went into their second match with the realisation that their road to retaining the trophy had been made steeper by the Springbok team.

A disappointing second game

'Honeymoon-hangover' may well be the description of the Springboks' second match six days later. Lowly Romania were the opponents, and the Boks opted to give the players who hadn't featured in the first game a run under the captaincy of Adriaan Richter. They ignored the basics, didn't stick to the game plan, and the crowd – again at Newlands – saw the Springboks struggle against a committed defence by a proud side that had very little else to offer. Two grinding, scrumming tries by Richter were all the Boks could offer, added to the one conversion and three penalties by Gavin Johnson. The Romanians scored a single try by Nicolae Raceanu and a penalty for a flattering scoreline of 21–8 to the Boks. The Springboks' performance was disappointing to say the least and many fans wondered just how good South Africa's depth was. What would happen if quality replacements were needed in the case of injury?

Battle of Boet Erasmus

These questions were to be answered as the tournament went on, but the infamous Battle of Boet Erasmus which followed the Romania incompetence didn't do much as

James Dalton was suspended in the match against Canada.

André Joubert played the semi-final and final with a broken hand.

a confidence booster. When the Boet Erasmus stadium lights went out just before the kick off in Port Elizabeth, it should perhaps have been seen as an omen of what lay ahead, for it was a dark day for rugby in general and South African rugby in particular. The Springboks ran up a 17–0 lead at the break, and stretched it to 20–0 shortly thereafter. But that was it, except for a tight Springbok defence against an abrasive, aggressive team. Then, ten minutes before full time, three players were sent off. It started with a shoving match between Springbok hero of the Australia victory Pieter Hendriks and his opposite from Canada, Winston Stanley. Silly attempts to help team-mates saw an all-out brawl develop. Springbok hooker James Dalton and Canadians Rod Snow and captain Gareth Rees were given their marching orders and subsequently Hendriks and Canada's Christian Stewart – the latter rushing in to prolong the initial shoving – were cited. All five players were suspended for the duration of the competition – and the sending-off of the two Boks nearly had serious consequences later before the semi-final against France.

As an aside, Stewart was a nephew of the fine Springbok flyhalf and centre of the 1960s Dave Stewart, and he had played for Western Province before seeking international fame with Canada. Three years after the 1995 incident, he went to the UK with the Springboks in the days when players could still represent more than one country and played in three tests for South Africa.

The pool rounds had been negotiated successfully with one outstanding performance, one poor show and one filled with ignominy – but the Springboks had made it to the quarterfinals to face Western Samoa. This time, the Springboks were on the Highveld where they thrilled the large Ellis Park crowd with great running rugby founded on an impressive forward display. It was Chester Williams' first World Cup appearance and he celebrated his debut in the competition with a South African test record of four tries. Lock Mark Andrews and hooker Chris Rossouw scored two more as the Boks ran up a lead of 35–0. Tu Nu'ual'itia and Shem Tatupu scored converted tries for the visitors in the last quarter before Williams' fourth try made it 42–14. It was lovely to watch, but the match was also filled with some unacceptable stiff-arm and late tackles by the Samoans, who were lucky to

Jake White – Restoring the pride

Springbok coach 2004–2007

Jake White became Springbok coach after the infamous *Kamp Staaldraad* saga and the subsequent poor performance of the Springboks at the 2003 World Cup in Australia claimed their victims, one of whom was national coach Rudolf Straeuli. The Boks were eliminated in the 2003 quarterfinal and the introduction of White had an immediate impact.

White's tenure started in 2004 – and in that same year, the Boks were named the IRB's Team of the Year and White, Coach of the Year. Schalk Burger, barely out of the junior ranks, was the IRB's Player of the Year and the Boks had risen from number six to fourth in the world rankings. What's more, White won the Tri-Nations series at his first attempt – only the second time South Africa had won in nine years of competition. The result of this successful year was that White was appointed Springbok coach until after the 2007 World Cup.

The former Jeppe High School for Boys first team player never played any rugby of note and had never been in charge of a provincial side but was assistant coach of the Sharks in 2000. In fact, although helping at club level as director of rugby at the Golden Lions, White had never coached a club side. His provincial coaching experience was also limited to junior teams – schools, Under-19 and Under-21. He was then roped in by Springbok coach Nick Mallett to assist with video analysis for the Springboks and was a Springbok assistant coach under Harry Viljoen in 2001 before he was appointed as the national Under-21 coach. White coached that team to the Under-21 World Championship in the first edition of the new competition, and in 2004, his appointment as Springbok coach came. First the Springboks beat Ireland in a two-test home series and then Wales, also in South Africa. Then came the Tri-Nations title followed by a very average Grand Slam tour where the Boks won two (Wales and Scotland) and lost two (England and Ireland).

In 2005, after White's glorious first year in charge, the Boks moved up to number two in the world rankings following another good Tri-Nations and beating the Wallabies three times. They didn't retain the title, however,

and their performance spiralled downwards. This downward trend, slight though it was, continued in 2006. It was a poor year for Springbok rugby. In 2006, the Boks lost 49–0 to Australia – a record – and to New Zealand at home and away, and the Boks boasted only two home wins in the six Tri-Nations matches. The end-of-the-year tour produced a 32–15 loss to Ireland and a 23–31 defeat in the first test against England at Twickenham. The Boks salvaged some pride to defeat the English 25–14 in the second test. The Springboks won only five of their 12 matches. However, 2006 was also a year of thorough planning on the part of White that included sending an under-strength national side to the UK in order to rest some of his players. Consultations with world expert Prof Tim Noakes of the High Performance Centre of the Sports Science Institute of South Africa had convinced White that his players needed rest before the 2007 World Cup. Then in 2007 England were twice trounced on their tour to South Africa – and visions of a possible World Cup title started to emerge.

White also sacrificed the Tri-Nations after a win and a loss at home by selecting what was virtually a second-string Springbok side for the Australasian leg of the competition; then beat Namibia in what was hardly a proper warm-up game in Cape Town before setting off for the World Cup in France. There was a match in Galway against Connacht (won 18–3) and a six-minute blitz that put paid to Scotland (26–3) before the Boks were off to Paris for their World Cup campaign. They won the tournament and White relinquished the reins – and has never coached at any level of note since.

Overall, White's record does not make for outstanding reading. Of his 54 tests in charge, he won 36 with only five from 12 in 2006 – his worst year in charge – but in mitigation, there was the resting of his top players for the year-end tour. Three wins from nine against the All Blacks; two from four against Ireland; one from four against France; and six from 11 against Australia do not, however, do justice to the man who won the World Cup for South Africa. He also took them from number six to number one in the world.

escape with only penalties. No fewer than 20 penalties to the Springboks, who themselves conceded only eight, tell the story of the transgressions by a side that seemingly had a total disregard for the laws.

With the win, South Africa had qualified for the semifinal against France in Durban. However, the tough match against Western Samoa had taken its toll. Locks Kobus Wiese (knee) and Mark Andrews (rib), as well as flank Ruben Kruger (shoulder) and André Joubert (broken hand) were the casualties. There was also concern about scrumhalf Joost van der Westhuizen. They were, however, all passed as fit to play against France. Joubert had surgery on his hand and spent some time in a decompression chamber to make it to the semi-final.

In the first of the northern-southern hemisphere semi-final clashes South Africa had to play France at King's Park on a field saturated by torrential rain. England and New Zealand were scheduled to meet the next day at Newlands.

Weather threatens Boks' semi-final

The match going ahead in Durban was touch and go. Lightning, the danger of injury in collapsed scrums, and even the possibility of drowning in rucks with puddles of water all over the field contributed to the kick-off being 90 minutes late. Welsh referee Derek Bevan was the man who had to make the decision. Frenchman Marcel Martin was on the playing field – where he wasn't allowed to be as a World Cup director! – trying to persuade the referee to call off the game. The reason was clear: if the game wasn't played, the side with the better disciplinary record would advance to the next round, in this case, the final. Boet Erasmus could well come back to haunt the Boks.

Dr Louis Luyt, president of the SA Rugby Football Union and a member of the organising committee, was also there and said to the referee: 'Mr Bevan, you are the only person who can decide on this game, but whatever you decide, I will accept.' The semi-final went ahead in unplayable conditions, and ten minutes later the rain

Jake White.

White it was who laid the platform for the period up to the 2011 World Cup in New Zealand through his use of outside experts – including former Wallaby coach Eddie Jones – and his careful selection of players and the moulding of his squad.

came down again. But the threat of abandonment after the start was not considered.

The Boks kept their focus while waiting for the match to kick off and France tried to unnerve Joubert with their first piece of possession. Joel Stransky kicked an early penalty but then missed two attempts as the rain pelted down again. It was a matter of minimising mistakes and taking opportunities, and ten minutes before the break, Ruben Kruger was driven over by his team-mates after a forward rush. With the conversion good, the Boks were 10–0 up. Future Sharks player Thierry Lacroix then kicked over two penalty goals and the Boks edged into half-time 10–6 ahead.

The wind was against South Africa in the second half. Penalties seemed the logical way to advance the score as the teams slipped through the mud and the minutes. Stransky kicked another penalty just after the restart (13–6). Lacroix returned the compliment a minute later and then it was Stransky's turn again some seven minutes into the second half. The Boks were now 16–9 ahead but it was 16–12 after 57 minutes when the French kicker again found the target. With 11 minutes remaining, Stransky made it 19–12 and the Boks appeared to be on their way to the final with France needing two scores to win, one of which had to be a try. That seemed unlikely until Lacroix reduced the deficit to four points at 19–15 with five minutes remaining.

It was indeed far from over, and the Boks were pinned to their own territory and mostly their own try line as the French threw everything they had into the attack. It looked like they had succeeded when Benazzi slipped and was denied an otherwise certain try – the Boks had made it to the World Cup final!

The England-New Zealand semi-final

The other semi-final at Newlands was almost a mismatch – and England could blame that on the Kiwi's 20-year-old Man of the Tournament, Jonah Lomu. He scored four tries with scant respect for big names or the England defence. The All Blacks were 10–0 up after four minutes following Lomu's first try and a converted try by Josh Kronfeld. The lead stretched to 18–0 following an Andrew Mehrtens penalty and a surprise drop goal by Zinzan Brooke. The score at half-time was 25–3 after a Rob Andrews penalty. In the end, the Kiwis ran in six tries – by Lomu (four), Kronfeld and Graeme Bachop – to England's four. Mehrtens converted only three of New Zealand's tries but also kicked a penalty and a drop goal to add to Brooke's drop goal over for their 45-point tally. England scored all four of their tries in the second half, coming back from 25–3 when the game was virtually won. The closest they came to New Zealand was in fact on the whistle when wing Rory Underwood scored his second try. Rob Andrews converted to make the points difference a more respectable 16. England's other tries came from Will Carling (two), with Andrews slotting in a penalty and two conversions.

England were denied a shot at the title – and it rankled after 1991 when, as the best side in the tournament, they squandered an opportunity in the final at Twickenham against Australia. Leaving World Cup tournaments empty-handed seemed to be England's destiny as the Boks surprised them in 1999.

So it was to Ellis Park that the two old adversaries, historically the best teams up until then, went for the 1995 final. New Zealand were the outright favourites on a day of splendour. Helicopters circled the huge Ellis Park stadium, packed to its 62 000 capacity, while trailing the 16 participating nations' flags. There was a drummers' pageant of the different nations; parachutists dived from the sky; jets flew by; and shortly before the kick-off, a SA Airways jumbo jet flew low over the stadium from the southern side with the words GOOD LUCK BOKKE under its wings.

An epic final

This was real rugby: a match between the two perennial giants, the leaders of the rugby world since they

Kitch Christie – The gentleman who did the 'hospital job'

Springbok coach 1994–1996

Kitch Christie, the man who guided the Springboks to their first World Cup title in 1995, did so with fewer than three seasons at the helm of a provincial side. Ian McIntosh was fired as Springbok coach after the 1994 tour to New Zealand where the Springboks lost two and drew the third test. New president of the SA Rugby Football Union, Louis Luyt, decided that Christie was the man who should take over the reins. Luyt, who was also the Gauteng Lions Rugby Union president, had brought Christie from across the Jukskei River from Northern Transvaal to guide the Lions to their two successive Currie Cup wins in 1993 and 1994. Those were their first titles since a share in 1972 when they were still Transvaal, and under Christie and his assistant Ray Mordt – also from Pretoria Harlequins and Northern Transvaal – the Lions won the Lion Cup and the M-Net series in both seasons and the Super 10 in 1993. (Mordt was the man who guided the fortunes in the 1994 Currie Cup when Christie was moved to the Boks.) Christie's performance was good enough for South Africa's rugby supremo.

Christie, who played and coached at Pretoria Harlequins and also had a spell with Glenwood Old Boys in Durban, made his mark as club coach with these two clubs, and also with the Chicago Lions club in the United States, leading them to the

Midwest regional title in 1980. He was coaching the Quins' second team when Luyt appointed him to the Lions job, but had over the years raked in many trophies for the club. He was also a Northern Transvaal selector and assistant coach. A man of few words, Christie was pushed into the toughest coaching job in world rugby a mere nine months before the kick-off in South Africa with a demanding public clamouring for the World Cup title.

In South Africa there always has been – and still is – the belief that the Boks are the best in the world and Christie had to vindicate this perception. He first coached the Springboks to two wins over Argentina in South Africa, then clocked wins against Scotland and Wales overseas at the end of 1994. In 1995, the Boks had a single warm-up match against Western Samoa. Thereafter Christie won

the six matches in the World Cup – three in the pool round-robin, the quarterfinal, semi-final and the final. Later in 1995 he was in charge of the 40–11 win of the Springboks over Wales, a rout of Italy in Rome, and then signed off as Springbok coach with the 24–14 away win against England in November of that year.

Christie's health had deteriorated. He had leukaemia. Unbeaten as a coach in his tenure of 14 tests – a record he shared with New Zealand's Fred Allen until Nick Mallett improved upon it – Christie resigned early in 1996. He recovered to the extent that his dream of coaching Northern Transvaal was realised, but was too ill to accompany them to Australasia on their 1997 Super 12 tour. He died in April 1998.

The quiet man's contribution was perhaps immortalised by the way he identified and selected his players, and his preparedness to make use of the expertise of outsiders to assist in the technical aspects of the game. After his death, one tribute out of the many explained the bond between Christie and his players at all levels better than most. It came from then CEO of the SA Rugby Football Union, Rian Oberholzer, who said 'His knowledge of the game and the manner in which he understood and dealt with his players were key factors in his success at both national and provincial level.'

Chester Williams and Pieter Hendriks – The full circle

Chester Williams: Springbok player 1993–2000, 27 test matches

Pieter Hendriks: Springbok player 1992–1996, 14 test matches

When Chester Williams was called up to replace the suspended Pieter Hendriks after the Battle of Boet Erasmus in 1995, it was in some way justice for the winger from Cape Town. He was originally selected for the World Cup squad but had to cry off because of injury. Hendriks, on the other hand, wasn't originally selected and came into the side in Williams' place to score that wonderful try in the opening match against Australia at Newlands. When he was suspended for his part in the fighting that broke out in Port Elizabeth against Canada, the Roodepoort Rugby Club winger's World Cup had run its course after three matches.

Williams grabbed his second chance and scored four tries in his first World Cup outing against Samoa, thereby setting a new South African try-scoring record; and he played in the next two matches – the semi-final and the final. He was no newcomer to the test arena and had played in ten tests before his first World Cup outing.

All in all, Williams played 27 tests for the Springboks in which he scored 14 tries. He also played 20 tour (non-test) matches for the Springboks and scored a further 13 tries in those matches. Hendriks played in four test matches before the opener at Newlands and went on to represent South Africa in a further seven matches for a total of 14 tests in which he scored two tries. He also played seven tour matches, scoring four tries. Interestingly, he rates the try when he rounded one of the world's all-time greats David Campese at Newlands as only his third best – but he probably never scored a more important one than that try on the left wing!

Chester Williams.

Pieter Hendriks.

started playing in the 1890s. Their results were so close after their 44 years of competition and 41 tests. As they took to the field, South Africa had an edge of two tests, having won 20 and lost 18 to New Zealand. Three had been drawn. Since their first clash in Dunedin in 1921, South Africa had scored 460 points to 430. Both sides had beaten the other by 17 points, the Boks winning 17–0 in Durban in 1928 and the All Blacks beating South Africa 20–3 in Auckland in 1965. The individual records were just as close, with Naas Botha's record 20 points at Wellington in 1981 being just two more than Shane Howarth's 18 in Auckland in 1994.

Afterwards, a lot was made of the alleged poisoning of the All Blacks players in the few days leading up to the final. There are many theories and as many accusations, but the accepted 'culprit' was allegedly one 'Suzie' who was a waitress at one of the All Blacks' eating places. The possibility of interference by British bookmakers to influence the final outcome of the match was also mentioned and in fact pursued by journalists. But to this day, no comment has come from the All Blacks team management or players, and no All Blacks suffering from food poisoning have been identified. There is also no certainty about where the poisoned food was eaten or whether the water at training had been spiked. Suffice it to say that, in 1980, when the All Blacks lost the Bledisloe Cup (which they contest for against Australia annually) for the first time since 1949, food poisoning was also blamed for the All Blacks' defeat!

The Springboks were also adversely affected after eating pasta before the opening match, 'and at one point, we were afraid that they were all suffering from severe food poisoning. But we never breathed a word,' Luyt writes in his autobiography.

It was logical that New Zealand were the favourites. They were in devastating form against England and had scored 222 points in their three pool matches. Their scores were 43–19 against Ireland; 34–9 against Wales; and a massive 145–17 against Japan in a game that was not good for rugby or the World Cup. That drubbing was the highest World Cup score yet; the 21 All Blacks tries was a new record; Simon Culhane's 45 points was a new World Cup record for a single match (and the highest ever by a player on test debut); and Mark Ellis scored six tries, the most by an individual in the competition. In the quarterfinal, New Zealand beat Scotland 48–30 and ran over England 45–29 in the semi-final. They did so by playing attractive and effective rugby. The Boks, on the other hand, had stuttered through their second and third pool matches and struggled in the rain against France.

The final was not a match filled with exhilarating running rugby, although the All Blacks did try to enforce their running plan from the outset in an effort to dominate with their total rugby. It paid some early dividends when New Zealand were awarded a penalty and Mehrtens put them 3–0 up after good work from Frank Bunce, Glen Osborne and Graeme Bachop. This three-point New Zealand lead had been turned around to a Springbok lead of similar margin after flyhalf Joel Stransky had slotted two penalties in and a drop goal over to Mehrtens' two penalties for the All Blacks. The little 22-year-old from Canterbury then slotted a drop goal over 13 minutes after half-time to tie the scores, and 9–all is how it remained until the end of normal time.

Mehrtens was born in Durban. His grandfather George played for the All Blacks and his father Terry represented Natal against the 1970 All Blacks and played for the coastal province in the Currie Cup and friendlies. Young Andrew did his country of birth a favour when he missed a sitter of a drop goal two minutes before the whistle for normal time after big All Blacks centre Bunce had set up a ruck following a bullocking run.

The Boks had survived a match full of drama, uncompromisingly hard play and outstanding tackling by the Springboks who had kept the All Blacks – and the great Jonah Lomu – tryless. In fact, Lomu never scored against South Africa. The World Cup beckoned with two halves of ten minutes waiting for the adversaries.

Mehrtens atoned for his earlier mistake with a long penalty virtually immediately after the start of extra time. Stransky responded a minute before the break in extra time after a rush by Os du Randt had forced the All Blacks into a transgression. The score was 12–all. It was Stransky again, this time with a huge up-and-under that put the Springboks on attack. They were awarded the scrum after the kick. Joost van der Westhuizen passed it straight and true to Stransky – and South Africa's great moment had arrived. Stransky ignored a previously called move, and struck the ball with a clean drop kick that soared high over the northern crossbar. Stransky simply turned and ran back, well aware that there were still some six or seven minutes of playing time left. The fact that he missed a later penalty was irrelevant. South Africa had won!

And deservedly so. They came close to tries via Ruben Kruger, Joost van der Westhuizen, James Small and André Joubert; they had unsettled the All Blacks' pattern with a solid, aggressive defence that prevented the New Zealanders from playing their game of total rugby with their usual effectiveness; and they never lost their focus in what was an enthralling and very hard but unspectacular game in the true tradition of the clashes between these two great rugby nations.

Afterwards, during the presentation ceremony of the Webb Ellis Cup when President Nelson Mandela and Francois Pienaar had thanked one another for the other's contribution to the country, Pienaar further enhanced the unity brought about by the win when he said that the Springboks had won the trophy not just for the 60 000 spectators at the final at Ellis Park but for all 43 million South Africans.

SANZAR, the Tri-Nations and other changes

The 1995 Rugby World Cup was the last to be played by amateurs, or as the players were then already called, 'shamateurs'. For years, players had been paid for their efforts in contravention of the amateur laws of the game, and for years, everyone accepted it in all major rugby-playing countries – with the exception of Argentina

The 1995 World Cup winning team

The Springbok squad that won the 1995 Rugby World Cup consisted of 28 players and a team management of five (excluding the experts coach Kitch Christie called in to help with the preparation of the side). The squad was:

Player squad:
Francois Pienaar (captain)
Gavin Johnson
André Joubert
Pieter Hendriks
James Small
Brendan Venter
Japie Mulder
Christiaan Scholtz
Joel Stransky
Hennie le Roux
Joost van der Westhuizen
Johan Roux

Rudolf Straeuli
Adriaan Richter
Ruben Kruger
Robby Brink
Mark Andrews
Kobus Wiese
Hannes Strydom
Krynauw Otto
Pieter (Os) du Randt
Balie Swart
Marius Hurter
Garry Pagel
James Dalton

Chris Rossouw
Chester Williams*
Naka Drotské*

* Added to original squad after the suspension of Pieter Hendriks and James Dalton following the game against Canada in Port Elizabeth.

Team management:
Manager, Morné du Plessis
Coach, Kitch Christie
Assistant coach, Gysie Pienaar
Team doctor, Frans Verster
Physiotherapist, Evan Speechly

Joel Stransky kicks another penalty in the 1995 World Cup.

1995 World Cup – Madiba's opening of the great event

President Mandela, whose role in the Springboks' victory of the 1995 World Cup should never be underestimated, opened the third Rugby World Cup at Newlands on Cape Town on 26 May 1995 with the following words:

It is with great pride and pleasure that I welcome you to the opening of the Rugby World Cup in South Africa.

There can be no greater expression of a nation's pride, nor nobler path to universal understanding than for the cream of its youth to compete on the playing field. It is through their love of the game, their desire to succeed through skill and sacrifice, that mighty links are forged.

In this spirit of healthy rivalry, let play begin. And may the better team win!

where the fun and pleasure of the game were still regarded as paramount. The day before the World Cup final, the president of the SA Rugby Football Union, Dr Louis Luyt, rocked the rugby establishment when he announced the forming of SANZAR (an acronym for South Africa New Zealand Australia Rugby). A new Super 12 competition between the best provincial sides of the top three rugby southern hemisphere countries would kick off in 1996, and a Tri-Nations competition between the national sides would be played annually on a home-and-away basis, Luyt announced.

It followed months of back-stabbing and subterfuge dealings between officials, with the deal eventually being signed with Newscorp which was owned and run by Rupert Murdoch. Springbok captain Francois Pienaar and Hennie le Roux of the World Cup-winning Springboks had meanwhile secretly negotiated with Murdoch's great competitor Kerry Packer, and an unpleasant stand-off

between the players and Luyt ensued – especially as the Lions World Cup Boks then revolted against the SANZAR deal after signing a contract with Packer's television outfit while they were guests of SARFU at Sun City. According to Luyt, the players returned with demands for an increase in pay from the Transvaal Rugby Union, by then renamed as the Gauteng Lions Rugby Union before they became the Golden Lions.

On Luyt's instructions, the Lions team was selected without the star players who were in revolt and they played – and narrowly lost – their next Currie Cup match against Eastern Province in Port Elizabeth with their second-stringers. The players then dropped their demands, publicly apologised and returned to action – but the lure of money had already sullied the game and the camaraderie and togetherness was gone with all players now, as Luyt put it, 'jealously guarding their own financial interests'. It was, Luyt said, a case of management against

World Champions! Francois Pienaar holds the Webb Ellis Cup aloft.

Christie called it a day in 1996. Illness had caught up with him and he was replaced by André Markgraaff.

The new South African coach lost four and won one of his five games in charge against New Zealand in 1996. With three of those victories coming in a series – the last to be played between the two countries – South Africa had, for the first time, lost a series to New Zealand in South Africa.

Pienaar was dropped from the Springbok side after Markgraaff accused him of feigning an injury and Gary Teichmann took over as national captain. Neither Teichmann nor Markgraaff made it to the 1999 World Cup hosted by Wales and played in the UK and France. Markgraaff resigned after a tape-recording came to light in which he made some derogatory remarks about black players. Teichmann was axed as player and captain by Nick Mallett who became coach in November 1997 after Carel du Plessis – successor to Markgraaff – was fired following a series loss to the British Lions after only eight matches in charge.

The 1999 campaign

The 1999 World Cup campaign was marked by some strange selections by Mallett, including that of an un-fit Bob Skinstad. Mallett took with him injured players Os du Randt and Joost van der Westhuizen, the captain, who both had knee trouble. Henry Honiball pulled a hamstring before the first match against Scotland. Stuttering along, the Boks beat Scotland, Spain and Uruguay and lost Brendan Venter in the last match, who was suspended for 'recklessness'. Venter kicked at a ball that was whipped away by his captain before he could make contact with it. In its place, he made contact with the scrum cap of Uruguayan lock Mario Lame and was out for 21 days, until the day before the final – if South Africa were to reach it.

The Boks trekked to Paris for their quarterfinal match against Martin Johnson's England side at Stade de France. England were obvious favourites after their

workers, and even the workers were fighting among themselves for a larger slice of the huge new money cake.

Pienaar eventually received the $300 000 he initially sought from Packer to convince fellow players to join the TV magnate's 'rugby circus' where mixed teams made up from the best players in the world would play in a series of matches – as the cricketers had done in the Packer Series in the late 1970s. As part of the patching-up process, Pienaar's fee was paid by SANZAR via SARFU. Later, in August, the game went professional worldwide after an IRB meeting in Paris – and rugby as it had been played for well over 100 years changed forever. Pienaar remained on as captain of South Africa, but coach Kitch

World Cup history and South Africa's entry

Australia and New Zealand – later to become South Africa's partners in the two toughest international and franchise competitions respectively in the world under the future SANZAR – were the major combined driving force behind the first Rugby World Cup that was hosted by the two Antipodean countries in 1987. That tournament was a rush job – and a huge success, from a playing and spectator point of view as well as financially, considering the short lead time of 18 months in which to arrange the tournament. From the very beginning, the World Cup was run by a wholly owned subsidiary of the International Rugby Football Board (IRB) with the returns being used for the advancement of the game in general but in particular for the affiliated countries of the IRB.

The first World Cup, won by New Zealand who were the dominant and undisputed leading side in those years, saw the first open clamour for payment by the players. It was not a new concept, but it was now driven by players who realised they would play more and should start earning for their performances. Money had in the past been passed on clandestinely to players in a time that the amateur code was sneeringly referred to as 'shamateurism', and by 1987 it was obvious: professionalism was not far away.

South Africa were not allowed participation in the 1987 tournament or the subsequent 1991 Rugby World Cup – co-hosted by the Five Nations in the UK, Ireland and France – because of its government's apartheid policy. The 1987 tournament was won by co-hosts New Zealand who beat France in the final (29–9) while Australia were deservedly victorious in 1991 in a dour battle at Twickenham after subduing co-hosts England 12–6.

The 1995 tournament was awarded to South Africa in 1992. The country would be the first to host the tournament by itself and made a whopping – for those years – R28-million profit. The tournament had nine automatic qualifiers. Australia, England, New Zealand, Scotland, Ireland, Western Samoa, France and Canada had qualified by virtue of reaching the quarterfinals in the 1991 tournament, and South Africa were in as hosts for the tournament. No less than 51 countries contested the right for the remaining seven places, which went to Argentina, Tonga, Ivory Coast, Japan, Wales, Italy and Romania. The 16 teams that qualified for the World Cup finals in South Africa were drawn into pools, and after an internal round-robin the two top sides of each pool advanced to the quarterfinals.

impressive play-off win against Fiji to advance to the quarters. Courtesy of a marginal try, the Boks led 16–12 at the break. That became 16–15 shortly after half-time. Then followed one of the most amazing acts of kicking seen in a test match as Jannie de Beer kicked five drop goals between the 47th and 84th minutes. De Beer also kicked five penalties and two conversions in the 44–21 win over England and afterwards said: 'The Lord gave me the talent and the forwards gave me the ball.'

The semi-final against Australia at Twickenham was a cliff-hanger. The Springboks came back with two penalties after being 18–12 down to square it up at 18–all after full time. De Beer had again kept them in contention with two penalty kicks, the last, a pressure angled effort right on time. Once more the Springboks had to go into extra time. De Beer put the Boks ahead at 21–18 in the first ten minutes of the added period, but then South Africa suffered the fate the All Blacks did in Johannesburg four years before. Matt Burke equalised for the tiring Wallabies, and then, two minutes into the second period of extra time, Wallabies flyhalf Stephen Larkham let fly with a drop kick from wide and near the Boks' 10-metre line. Larkham, not renowned for his kicking, didn't strike it cleanly but it flew the nearly 50 metres. The Wallabies were ahead, 24–21. A hands-in offence by Van der Westhuizen – a very marginal call, one must add – saw Burke convert his eighth penalty and the Wallabies advanced to the final against France, who surprisingly beat the All Blacks a day after the first semi-final.

South Africa and New Zealand, who had played out that tense final four years earlier, had to play for third and fourth places the next week. A rather forgettable 1999 Rugby World Cup came to an 18–14 winning end for the Boks after an error-ridden performance between the two old foes. A feature of the 1999 Rugby World Cup was the few tries in the play-offs, probably brought about by the new interpretation of the laws that favoured defence. The Springboks scored only three tries in their last three (play-off) matches, and the eventual champions Australia, scored five. New Zealand scored seven and France, nine. A total of 24 tries in seven matches, of which eight came in the clash between France and New Zealand and four scored by France in the quarters against a poor Argentinian side, did little for a World Cup that really only came alive late in the competition. Australia won the final 35–12 in Cardiff to become the first country to win the World Cup twice.

The lukewarm interest in the tournament could be blamed on poor marketing and the fact that the Home Unions – with the exception of France and England – had poor tournaments.

Those criticising the slowness of transformation in the Springbok side were vindicated when only four players of colour, namely Deon Kayser, Kaya Malotana, Wayne Julies and Breyton Paulse, were included in the Springbok squad. On merit they were arguably the only four who deserved to be there, and therein lies the indictment of a lack of transformation. Whether they deserved to play in more matches out of the Springboks' six is a moot point.

The rather average showing by the Springboks in the 1999 World Cup tournament was disappointing – especially if read in conjunction with the excellent performances since Mallett had taken over the side for the 1997 year-end tour. He won 16 consecutive matches and with the win in Carel du Plessis' last test in charge, the Boks had tied the world record of 17 consecutive wins held by the All Blacks.

But then it went wrong. The Boks lost to England at the end of 1998; they beat Italy twice in South Africa, notching up scores of 74–3 and 101–0; lost to Wales for the first time ever in Cardiff; lost twice to New Zealand and once to Australia; and a Tri-Nations win against the Wallabies took them to the World Cup on a more positive note. Teichmann's axing came after the overseas leg of the Tri-Nations campaign and Joost van der Westhuizen became the World Cup captain.

The 2003 disaster

If 1999 was a disappointing World Cup, the 2003 edition in Australia was a disaster – off the field as well as on it. During the run-up to the World Cup, there was the unpleasant affair of Geo Cronje who declined to room with fellow lock Quinton Davids because of the latter's skin colour. There was also the unhappiness of the black players in the Springbok squad throughout the lead-up to the World Cup and an investigation was subsequently ordered to investigate racism in South African rugby.

And then there was the *Kamp Staaldraad* affair revealed after the Springboks' return from the 2003 World Cup campaign that ended in the quarterfinal when the Boks were thumped 29–9 by a New Zealand team hardly in second gear. Coach Rudolf Straeuli resigned after the tournament when the *Kamp Staaldraad* allegations surfaced, but probably would not have escaped the axe after a tenure that saw him win only 12 of 23 matches as national coach – against Wales (in South Africa, twice), Argentina, Samoa, Australia, Scotland in South Africa (twice), Argentina and Australia (both in South Africa), Uruguay, Georgia and Samoa (all World Cup). Before they lost the 2003 World Cup quarterfinal to New Zealand, the Boks had lost to England in a crucial pool match after tying 6–all at half-time. England went on to win 25–6 which relegated the Springboks to second place in their pool and set them up with the All Blacks as opponents.

A lack of experience was partly to blame for the poor results. However, all things considered, the World Cup

Nick Mallett – strange selections.

Kaya Malotana, the first black World Cup Bok, in 1999.

was doomed by a South African administration that over the years had done little to instil confidence in their ability to provide the necessary guidance that could have prevented much of the pre-tournament unpleasantness. *Kamp Staaldraad*, discussed elsewhere in this chapter, was not responsible for the disappointingly poor performances, as record-breaking Springbok captain John Smit tells in his autobiography.

Matters didn't improve after the tournament. Corné Krige captained the side that included Joost van der Westhuizen, captain of the previous World Cup campaign in 1999. The 2003 World Cup was the last straw for Krige who eventually bowed out after 18 tests as skipper. He had a 39% winning record, winning only seven of those matches. This poor record cannot be blamed on him. Krige led by example, but had little chance of success during a rather poor period in South Africa's rugby history, on and off the field.

The 2004 season brought in a new coach, Jake White, and also a new captain, John Smit, who had had one match as test captain in 2003 against Georgia in the World Cup. Smit was to go on to set a new world record as captain of a national team. He became only the second Springbok, after Percy Montgomery, to break the 100-test barrier when he did so in the Tri-Nations test against New Zealand at the FNB Stadium just outside Soweto in August 2010. By the end of 2010, Smit had 102 caps and had captained the side 76 times.

This duo went on to win the Springboks their second World Cup in 2007. The tournament was hosted by France but also played in Wales. It was the longest season – 44 weeks – Springbok rugby had known.

Then, after the victory, White was swiftly shunted aside as his contract had expired. Despite making the decision to retire himself, the way in which he left rankled. That was due to the breakdown with many of the country's leading administrators, and the coach also did himself no favours with his outspoken criticism in a book of what was now no longer SARFU but SARU, and its leaders.

2007: A second title

The 2007 Rugby World Cup was a strange tournament with some major surprises early on in the competition. South Africa had few problems in dispatching their opposition as the Springbok juggernaut barged on. It was made easier for the Springboks as the other five sides in the top six in the world rankings fell by the wayside. New Zealand, once again an overwhelming favourite to win the title, went out in the quarterfinal against France. Their Antipodean neighbours, Australia, also did not reach the semi-finals, while Argentina made the road ahead too difficult for France after winning the opening game of the tournament against the home side.

The rather fortuitous French win against the All Blacks was shown to be exactly what it was as the home team lost their semi-final against England following a not-too-convincing campaign. France, who played the All Blacks in Wales in the preceding quarterfinal, won only their second match in the last 12 against New Zealand in a match where the Tricolores miraculously didn't concede a single penalty in the second half! It was a match won as much through interpretations and mistakes by England referee Wayne Barnes as it was one lost by the All Blacks.

Jake White had for some time indicated that experience would be key to winning the World Cup. He proved that when he sent the most experienced team in Springbok history into battle in the final – and it could well have been with more than the 668 caps they had between them if it hadn't been for an injury to centre Jean de Villiers. He injured a biceps during the tournament and prop BJ Botha's knee forced him to the sideline. Pierre Spies had stayed at home following blood clots on his lungs. Another setback for the Boks was the suspension of fiery flanker Schalk Burger after a high tackle in the opening match against Samoa for which he was suspended for two games. But the Boks' depth, with Wikus van Heerden filling in, carried them through.

Samoa

In their first match, the Springboks led only 9–7 after 18 minutes against Samoa – an aggressive side that was inclined to tackle high and late with relative impunity from referee Paul Honiss. Two tries in the seven minutes before half-time, the first of Bryan Habana's four and one by Percy Montgomery, saw the Boks into a comfortable 21–7 lead at the break. After half-time, however, South Africa ran in six more tries, with Habana dotting down four times and Montgomery scoring a brace in the match. Fourie du Preez and JP Pietersen were the other try-scorers in a 59–7 win that didn't do justice to the Samoans' gutsy display.

It is interesting that the Boks played Samoa in their first World Cup, and again in 2003 and 2007, making it three pool encounters in four World Cup tournaments. (It would become four in five in 2011!)

England

Then followed the pool match against defending champions England, who had earlier in the year taken two huge thumpings (58–10 and 55–22) on their tour to South Africa. This time it was 36–0 to the Springboks in a win so comprehensive that England didn't even have a single kick at goal! The Boks were up 20–0 at half-time in perhaps their best performance of the World Cup campaign. They took the lead after six minutes when Fourie du Preez broke around the blind side to send Juan Smith over. It was Du Preez again who set up the second try, for JP Pietersen, after half-time. The Springboks' forwards were outstanding and controlled matters throughout. It was the Boks' fourth consecutive win over England and also the champions' biggest defeat in a World Cup, surpassing the 44–21 (a victory margin of 23 points) in the 1999 match when Jannie de Beer kicked five drop goals.

Tonga

Tonga put up a wonderful fight in their pool encounter. In the end South Africa won 30–25. The Boks' 'second' team, however, was in control virtually throughout and four missed penalties could have put them out of sight early on. The only two (brief) occasions that the Springboks trailed in the tournament were in this match, when Tonga led 3–0 early in the first half and then took the lead at 10–7 four minutes into the second spell after the Boks had led 7–3 at the break. However, three tries in six minutes followed after Jake White had brought on his first team replacements, and the Boks went out to a 27–10 lead after 65 minutes. Although the Springboks were the better side and deserved to win, there was a late scare as Tonga threatened after the siren. A try looked like a real possibility, but with the Tongans chasing for a try and glory, the ball bounced out in the South African 22 – and the match finished 30–25.

United States and Fiji

The match against the United States had a nine-try demolition overshadowed by a rather casual approach by the Springboks who didn't seem as focused as they should have been. The match was also marked by the way speedy Eagles winger Takudzwa Ngwenya feinted inside and then rounded Habana, who was judged Player of the Tournament after the final. The 64–15 win against the Eagles put the Springboks into the quarterfinal against Fiji. It was to be the Springboks' third match against a South Sea opponent in the 2007 World Cup. And again, it was no walk-over. In fact, with 21 minutes remaining the scores were tied at 20–all, and it took two tries in the last 11 minutes by Juan Smith and Butch James to put daylight between the two sides, with the Springboks running out 37–20 winners. Earlier, the Boks were well ahead at 20–6 after 51 minutes before Fiji struck back with two tries in two minutes to tie the scores. South Africa then took control and through halfbacks James and Fourie du Preez

Corné Krige – 2003 World Cup captain.

played the game in the Fiji 22 to ward off any chance of an upset.

Argentina

The surprise side of the tournament was Argentina. They twice beat France – in the opening match and again in the play-off for third place – and thoroughly deserved their semi-final berth where they were to meet the Boks. The Springboks, however, simply outclassed them. They were hit by three first-half tries by the Springboks through Fourie du Preez, Habana and Danie Rossouw. The Boks led 24–6 at half-time and the closest the Pumas came to the Springboks' score was after their early second-half try when they crept up to 24–13. Percy Montgomery,

Kamp Staaldraad – a 'boot-camp' for the Boks

Kamp Staaldraad (literally translated Camp Steel Wire) was a 'boot-camp' that Springbok coach Rudolf Straeuli implemented before the 2003 World Cup campaign as part of the Springboks' preparation. It was seen as a team-building exercise and only became public after the rather disastrous tournament where the Boks were eliminated in the quarterfinal. The public condemned the camp and it cost a number of officials their positions as they tried to defend it. Straeuli resigned in the aftermath.

Piet Heymans, chief executive of the SA Rugby Players Association (SARPA), who was in Australia at the time, (according to the website Independent Online) said player associations throughout the world condemned the practices at Staaldraad. Representatives of top rugby-playing nations had told him that, in a professional era, the idea of such a camp would never be 'entertained'. Countries such as New Zealand, Australia and England had so-called team-building sessions but these were conducted in a 'very professional, scientific, humanitarian and dignified manner'. Heymans said the goings-on at *Kamp Staaldraad* were 'clearly not dignified'.

The camp was overseen by the team's bodyguard, Adriaan Heijns, and run by five 'instructors' armed with guns. Among the things forced on the players by the instructors in what was intended as a bonding exercise were: spending a night in the cold near Thabazimbi during which they were to kill and cook chickens, but not eat them; being forced naked into a pool; spending four hours in a pit with a tarpaulin over them; being forced into fox holes where they had to sing the national anthem, listen to the England anthem and the All Blacks' Haka while

cold water was poured over them; and being deprived of sleep. Firearms were also used. It was later pointed out that the plan to gel the team into a unit by eliminating all individuality could be counter-productive as individuality could often make the difference between winning or losing on a rugby field.

However, while the condemnation was made public, many of the players said in private discussions that *Kamp Staaldraad* was not as bad as it had been made out to be; that it did bond the side to a large degree but helped little on the playing field. In fact, record-breaking Springbok captain John Smit, who captained the Springboks for the first time in a test in the 2003 World Cup, writes in his book: '"Congratulations," they (the training "commanders") said. "It's all over and there's a braai on the go for you." 'We all tucked into the lamb chops and guzzled beers – it was the best braai I ever had! There was an immense sense of relief. These okes had nearly killed us, they had broken us, and here we were having beers with them. The vibe was really good on the bus, the guys had a feeling of togetherness and felt a sense of achievement. Rugby was the last thing on our minds because we were just so amazed at ourselves and talking and telling "army" stories. We still talk and laugh about Staaldraad to this day.'

The Staaldraad exercise had a tragic sequel when the Boks' video analyst Dale McDermott committed suicide in the aftermath of the scandal. He was the man who brought the camp to the public's notice when he provided images of the camp, and he was asked to resign from his job at the South African Council for Scientific and Industrial Research from which he had been contracted out to the Boks.

---

however, struck two more penalties well and converted Habana's second try to make this another win in a match marked by some ill-tempered play in the second half. Good pressure and seizing the opportunities from resultant Argentinian mistakes made this a thoroughly professional outing by the Boks who won comfortably, 37–13, despite slacking in the second stanza.

The final against England

England, with new resolve and input from the players on how they should approach the matches as their coach Brian Ashton seemed out of his depth, helped Phil Vickery's team first eliminate Australia in the quarterfinal (12–10) and then account for France in the semi-final (14–9). They were undoubtedly a different and better side than the one beaten 36–0 by the Springboks in the pool rounds and would take some beating. However, the Boks remained the favourites. England's improvement could be gauged by the fact that the Boks had to make more tackles than the defending champions; won less ball at the breakdown; made more errors in their kicking game; and spent less time in the England 22 than their opponents did in that of the Springboks. Territory (56–44) as well as possession (55–45) belonged to England. Overall, however, the Springboks exerted more pressure.

Their six attempts at goal to the two by England tell the story of the match and also the result, with only one missed kick from the six giving South Africa a 15–6 win. England tried to avoid line-outs with the Boks putting in the ball. It didn't matter. Seven of the Springboks' 13 line-out wins came from steals on England's throw. With Victor Matfield imperious in this aspect of the game and also around the field, the Springboks were content to kick the ball out in playing for territory and won more than a quarter of England's possession in this facet.

The match – hard, tough and uncompromising – was never a spectacle but always a good contest, and had one stand-out moment of controversy. England left wing Mark Cueto in the 43rd minute scored what every England player and fan believed was a try following a break by Matthew Tait and a quick ruck. Danie Rossouw was the man who nudged Cueto into touch as he dived over. After an agonising wait, the TMO decision went the Springboks' way – and rightly so as replays show conclusively that the England winger's foot touched the line. Cueto, however, claims his foot was above and not on the line. In the end, England have themselves to blame for squandering opportunities by poor decision-making or lost line-outs. The Boks' defence, of which the covering work by Rossouw for the Cueto near-try is an example, probably did as much as anything else in securing the win for South Africa who withstood pressure when it mattered and scored when the opportunities arose.

It was nearly the end of the road for White, who took the Boks on the year-end tour to England where they

Jaque Fourie – more responsibility in the 2007 World Cup campaign after Jean de Villiers' biceps injury.

thrashed Wales 34–12, scoring five tries to two, but lost 22–5 to the Barbarians with a team much changed from the one that won the World Cup.

2

The early beginnings
Schools, clubs and soldiers pave the way

The euphoria with which the Springboks' two World Cup titles in 1995 and 2007 were greeted did not spring up in the year of the competitions, although the black community of course provided a newly found support base after the abolishment of apartheid and the development that had taken place in the game of rugby since the 1970s. Rugby, or its forerunners, was after all a sport that was first played in its primitive form in Cape Town as early as the 1860s – and had since grown to be regarded as South Africa's national, if not biggest, sport. The two wins had become the pride of a united nation.

The football played in those years was based on the so-called 'Winchester rules as adapted'. Schools were the first to try their hand at it, and as the numbers grew and greater formalisation and frequency of fixtures were sought, the first clubs were established. The very early growth was in Cape Town, but the coastal regions followed mainly because of regiments settled there, while the inland development came on the back of the discovery of gold and diamonds. A combination of this growth of the game nationally, the lack of uniform laws and increasingly better modes of transport ultimately led to the formation of the SA Rugby Football Board in Kimberley in 1889.

The man attributed with starting the early game in South Africa is George Ogilvie, MA, DLitt, who was principal of Diocesan College – better known as Bishops – in Cape Town from 1861 to 1885. That early game they played was not, however, rugby as we know it today. It was first played at the school in 1861 even before soccer had become a recognised game, but there can be little doubt that the game played at Bishops is one of two football games that developed into what we now know as rugby. The game

The oldest known rugby photograph in South Africa taken in 1878. The players are from Hamiltons – G Wrentmore, J Wiley and W Searle.

George Ogilvie, principal of Diocesan College from 1861 to 1885.

Bishops, 1882.

at Bishops was a derivative of Winchester football played under the rules of the elite Winchester school in England – just as schools like Rugby and Eton had their own rules and their own games.

The game played at Bishops was adapted according to the number of players and the size of the available ground – and also the whims of Ogilvie! It became known as Gog's game or simply gogball (the name originating from the one the boys at Bishops made up for Ogilvie by combining his initial G and the first letters of his surname, hence 'Gog'). It was as distinct from the Winchester rules football that Ogilvie had learnt as a youngster in England as the Winchester rules differed from those at Rugby, Eton and other English schools.

Rugby in South Africa, or its early predecessor(s) including Winchester football, was conceivably played elsewhere in the country and probably before 1861, but no record of such matches exists. It is therefore widely

How the rules developed

Football, in the wider sense, came to South Africa with the British who took control of the Cape in 1806. The army units spread sport in general, and the schools that learnt from them took it further afield and gradually developed the game that was played in Cape Town.

Although the first match recorded in South Africa took place in 1862 and the Diocesan College (Bishops) is credited as the place where football was first played in 1861, there can be little doubt that matches took place in the period between 1806 and 1861. And it was not rugby that they played in the 1860s, but Winchester football. Winchester, like other elite schools such as Rugby, Eton, Cheltenham and Westminster, had its own set of rules – and because the rules of a game determine the game, each of these institutions had their own game of football which was played at that particular school only.

Inter-school activities necessarily followed, and to obtain some uniformity in 1842, Cambridge took the lead to get a measure of conformity. It was only in 1863, however, that some schools and clubs undertook to adopt and play matches according to these rules. That was the beginning of soccer, where hands could initially be used 'to stop the ball'. In another link to soccer, the ball varied according to the place the game was played. Initially it was round, and many instances were reported of a match proceeding after a ball had been punctured! It must have been very difficult to dribble under those circumstances ...

According to reports of those early days, the ball could be handled only in extraordinary circumstances, as when it bounced off an opponent and was caught before it landed on the ground. Games started with what was known as a 'hot' and which is akin to the present scrum. No hooking was allowed and the aim was to shove the other side off the ball. It sometimes lasted for the duration of a match – and the rules stated that a match could last five days! Once out of the hot, the aim (and skill) of Winchester football was to dribble the ball over the opponents' line. If it missed the goals consisting of two gowns put on the grass, it was called a shit (!) and one point allowed for it. If it went over the line between the two gowns and was touched by the 'behind' (vaguely fulfilling the role of today's fullback in rugby or goalkeeper in soccer), the team was awarded two points. Without such a touch, they gained three points. When it went over the canvass – replacing the long lines of juniors at the side of the field who were regarded as the touchline – a line-out was formed. But the ball could not be caught and the line-out consisted of shouldering and fly-kicking at the ball that brought its own bruises and injuries!

George (late Canon) Ogilvie who became headmaster of Bishops in 1861, adapted the Winchester rules which were used as a basis for the game at Bishops. After all, Ogilvie was a former scholar from Winchester! His initial G and the first letters of his surname Ogilvie combined to make him known as Gog to the 18 boys at Bishops when he took over as headmaster. And the game he introduced after adapting the Winchester rules was naturally called gogball. Bishops, like the elite English schools, then also had their own set of rules. Unlike in England, handling was allowed and there was tackling. A team consisted of 22 players of whom 20 were in the hot and the other two were the behinds.

Rugby was played on a pitch that 'would not exceed 200 yards in length and 100 yards in width'. (Just imagine, with today's laws, what would happen if a player intercepted on his own try line and had to run the length of the field! A furlong race, they would've called it in the old days.) A goal was scored if it passed through the posts (which didn't have a cross-bar). You were off-side if you were in front of a kicker, the ball had to be dropped out (from 10 yards from the defending goal line) if kicked over the goal line by the opposition; tackling was allowed as in gogball; and no handling except from a fair catch or an opposing player was allowed. Importantly, a hot formed over a player who opted to run and was tackled (a crude form of today's ruck). The handling that today forms the basis of the game of rugby was thereafter gradually introduced.

South Africa's two oldest clubs, Hamiltons and Villagers, 1877.

accepted that Bishops played the first football in South Africa, although they weren't involved in the first match. The first recorded match took place in 1862 on the race course at Green Point, reported the *Cape Argus* of 21 August of that year. The match was between the Officers and the Civil Service. A series of matches between scratch sides followed and watching football became a popular pastime. (There is also mention of a match in 1860, on 23 August, between the Officers and Civilians but no supporting records could be found.)

The matches were unscheduled and were few and far between, despite being very popular. Each match was a sporting as well as a social occasion with ladies also adorning the touchlines, but the haphazard way in which the fixtures were planned was unsatisfactory – both to players and spectators. After more than a decade of these matches between informal opponents, the inevitable outflow was that football had to become more organised. The way to do that was through the establishment of clubs.

The Hamilton Rugby Club (Hamiltons), formed in March 1875, was composed mainly of men from the Sea Point area – and Green Point is where the club has remained for 136 years since! It is officially regarded as South Africa's oldest rugby club. (Claims by Swellendam that they had formed an earlier club could not be substantiated after a fire in their clubhouse destroyed all documents to that effect.) They played the Winchester game with all its derivatives implemented by Ogilvie but had only the two colleges, Bishops and SACS (South African College), as opponents. There was also no rugby home for the men from the southern suburbs. The upshot was the formation of Western Province Rugby Club in 1876. However, with the club favouring the Rugby rules but a large portion of the members not, a breakaway was inevitable. That happened just weeks later when Villagers was formed. This new club, called the Villager

Diggers won the Pirates Grand Challenge competition in 1896.

Rugby Football Club, started playing a 'code' of their own, namely rugby football. On 2 June 1876, the first of the famous derby matches between Hamiltons and Villagers took place in Rondebosch under the Winchester rules. It is fitting that the first meeting between these two sides that would become rugby foes over the next 136 years ended in a pointless draw. The two sides met again on 24 August, again under the Winchester rules and again it ended in a scoreless draw.

Breakthrough for rugby football

With members moving to play for Villagers or Hamiltons, the Western Province Rugby Club became defunct in 1877 and matches were again limited to four sides – the two colleges, Hamiltons and Villagers. However, in 1878, a former England international fullback William

H. Milton joined Villagers. He supported and taught the Rugby code and was so influential, probably because of his standing as an international, that rugby was the game played by most by the end of that year. Milton – later Sir William, the administrator of Southern Rhodesia – represented South Africa at cricket in the late 1880s.

The two colleges and two clubs extended their rivalry until 1882, when a new club, Gardens, was welcomed into the fray. This was followed a year later by the Woodstock club, and the game of rugby had truly arrived in Cape Town – and beyond it. For it was in 1878 that the famous Stellenbosch Rugby Club was unofficially born when the university, still known as Victoria College, played against and was thumped by Bishops. What was later to become the Maties consisted then, not of students, but a number of men from the town and surrounds – and they played again the following year. By 1880, Stellenbosch was an

In a fix about the fixtures

Arranging fixtures is never an easy thing – and it was an utter nightmare in 1891 when Griquas visited Natal on one of their ground-breaking tours. In this memorable year for South African rugby, the outstanding highlight for Natal – not yet really part of the bigger rugby scene – was the visit of Bill Maclagan's British side to Pietermaritzburg. It was a year after the establishment of the Natal Rugby Union.

Kimberley kicked off their tour against the Savages on 1 August 1891 and played three more games on the Agricultural Showgrounds in Pietermaritzburg – and after the last of these 'an enjoyable evening was had by all that night when an impressive list of speeches and songs were delivered at the Horseshoe Hotel,' it was reported. But their highlight would be the match against a Durban side.

The Natal side to face the British tourists was really a Maritzburg side, and all 15 players for the encounter against the tourists were from the Natal capital. The match had been arranged for 11 August and was (eventually!) duly played, with the British side running out easy winners by 25–0. However, amidst all the excitement of the tourists' match, it had slipped the administrators' minds that this day had also been scheduled for the intertown match between Pietermaritzburg and Durban to decide the fate of the Browne Cup – and at the same ground!

Maritzburg had therefore been given a double-header on the same day at as high a level as they had experienced until then!

To add to the confusion, Kimberley was to play Durban at the same venue on that same day – and the visitors from the Cape Colony simply wouldn't budge although Durban had to play in the intertown. The match was not to be postponed, said Kimberley, and they were leaving Natal on 15 August as scheduled, come what may – even if the game against Durban had to be called off. The solution came when the Association Football committee agreed to call off their match in order for three rugby matches to be played at the Agricultural grounds.

And then the strange fixtures were hastily put in place. Maritzburg won the intertown match against Durban by two tries to nil – and then a combined team was selected from the two adversaries to face Kimberley. Five Durban players had impressed in this hastily arranged intertown curtain-raiser to a match they were initially scheduled to play in themselves! They were picked for what was by then a very tired side called Combined Natal that then took the place of Durban for the match against Kimberley, which the visitors won by two tries to nil.

And only then could the match between Natal and the British side be played!

---

organised club. And this most famous of all rugby clubs in South Africa – and over the years arguably also the most noteworthy in the world – sparked rugby in the country areas to the extent that a Country Challenge competition was started. Almost needless to mention, the team now known as the Maties won it in its first year, 1885, as well as the following two years. (There was, however, an unofficial country competition before their advent in which they did not participate, but this competition was not formalised or recognised.)

Two years after Stellenbosch unofficially came into being as a rugby club in 1880, their traditional intervar-sity foes Ikeys were established as a club. The year 1882 is regarded as the establishment of the club that later, as the University of Cape Town, produced many a famous Springbok and hundreds of Western Province rugby players. The university developed from the SA College (SACS) previously mentioned.

Meanwhile the organisation of the clubs that had sprung up in Cape Town and in the country districts necessitated a body to control matters. The Western Province Rugby Football Union (WPRFU) was therefore formed on 31 May 1883 at the Masonic Hotel in Cape Town. The clubs present were Hamiltons, Villagers,

Hamiltons, 1881.

Stellenbosch, Woodstock, Rugby and United Bank. The two colleges, Bishops and SACS, were not present. With the formation of the WPRFU came the famous Grand Challenge competition, initially decided on a knock-out basis and won by Hamiltons. SACS did play, Bishops did not; and Hamiltons accounted for Villagers, Rugby and the country side Malmesbury en route to the first Western Province title. They continued to dominate, winning six of the first ten titles with three wins going to their great adversaries Villagers and one title to Gardens. Thereafter, because of the increasing number of clubs taking part, the knock-out system was replaced by a league format. A Junior Challenge for second teams of clubs was also instituted.

Because half the teams would be eliminated in the first round of the Grand Challenge, an incentive was needed for those teams knocked out (although this was frowned upon by some of the teams like Bishops for whom participation was more important than victory). Bishops and SACS, because of their youth and the fact that the game was now played by more and bigger men, didn't fare too well in the Grand Challenge. In 1892 the inter-collegiate competition was instituted. Victoria College (the forerunner of Stellenbosch University), Bishops and SACS (who were now both colleges as an extension of the schools that in earlier years had played against men) were the three contestants for the Anderson Senior Cup for first teams; Anderson Junior Cup for second teams; and the Harris Cup for third teams. The trophies for the first and second teams were donated by Henry Anderson, father of Biddy who was to become a Springbok in 1896. The trophy for the third side was the Harris Cup, donated

First Maties, 1880.

by and named after the jeweller (M Harris of Cape Town) from whom the other two trophies were bought!

The competition was not a great success – but it laid the foundation for the famous intervarsity between Stellenbosch and the University of Cape Town (UCT, who in intervarsity parlance are fondly known as the Ikeys). In 1889 the intercollegiate competition was contested for the last time.

These early years of rugby were obviously not easy. And it wasn't only the difficulty of travel! There was a shortage of funds; of grounds; of players; and also of approval by the authorities. One of the main objections of George Ogilvie to Bishops switching over to rugby was that the game was too rough for his boys. 'If you boys want to kill yourselves, do so!' he is quoted as saying when permission was sought to change to Rugby rules

because all the clubs had done so, leaving Bishops without opponents.

The man who had approached him was the captain of football at Bishops in 1879, Ryk Myburgh. His rugby career ended the year after the grudging permission to play rugby was granted by Ogilvie. But gogball was not all that gentle either, and there are references to 'broken ears and nose; two broken legs which were successfully set' and the like.

Regional competitions

The club scene in Cape Town and the Cape country areas was firmly established by the early 1880s. With the same happening in other areas – notably Kimberley and surrounding areas – the first regional and provincial

Newlands' first international match, 1891.

competitions were mere seasons away. It was the growth era of the new game. In 1884, rugby was established along the coast of the former Cape Colony and by then inland and intertown matches between Kimberley, Cape Town (in 1884) and Grahamstown and Port Elizabeth (1885) were already being played. By 1886, the game had grown popular enough in the diamond fields for the Griqualand West Rugby Union to be formed. It moved to Western Transvaal and then to Johannesburg and

Pretoria, with the first intertown matches between the latter two played in 1888. The Transvaal Rugby Football Union was formed in 1889. By the next year, the code had also taken over as the leading sport from Association Football in Pietermaritzburg – the headquarters of the British Army – as well as in Durban. It was this rapid expansion that led to the formation of the South African Rugby Football Board (SARFB) in 1889.

According to the available records, the first intertown match was between Kimberley and Bloemfontein on 22 July 1881 when the players from the diamond fields travelled the 100 miles to Bloemfontein. This was, however, not the first 'tour' by a rugby side – that ground-breaking honour belongs to Natal (or rather, Pietermaritzburg) which visited Kimberley in 1876.

Kimberley's match against Bloemfontein was played on the grounds of the Bloemfontein Cricket Club and was won by Kimberley, who scored five tries and kicked a drop goal over without reply from Bloemfontein. The match, as was the custom in those years, was played with a mixture of the so-called (and Cape Town-adapted)

Kimberley Rugby Club's first touring side, 1884.

Villagers, 1884.

Winchester rules and the Rugby rules which had by then become the preferred game in Cape Town. Club games in Kimberley, as in the early days in Cape Town, were between teams like Home Born and Colonials (the main match of the year!), Kimberley and Government officials, Married and Unmarried, Town and Country, and the like.

The Kimberley rugby side kept themselves in shape with irregular matches against Beaconsfield. The first recorded 'organised' match in Kimberley was played on 4 October 1873 between a side from West End and a group of Grahamstown players who worked in Kimberley – quite probably prospectors. These infrequent matches, well attended by spectators and popular with the players, led to Kimberley being invited to Cape Town for a tour of seven matches in 1884. Grahamstown did not accept the invitation. Kimberley reaffirmed the title they later achieved as the touring trendsetters in South Africa when they accepted the invitation from the Western Province

Rugby Football Union which had been established the year before.

They duly left with a team of 24 players who travelled by mule-wagon to De Aar, where they arrived 60 hours later. From there, they proceeded to Cape Town by train completing a journey that lasted more than five days! The diamond fielders won three matches, lost three and drew one. It was obvious that the new rugby region had what it takes. Their last match was against Union, a team selected from 11 clubs and the best Western Province could offer. This was the highlight of the tour. Kimberley had to use reinforcements because of injuries sustained in their previous matches, and in the end, gave a good account of themselves before narrowly losing what was the first (very unofficial!) provincial match in South Africa. It is interesting to note that the famous Loftus Robert Versfeld, who played a huge part in the establishment of rugby clubs and unions throughout South Africa and after whom the famous Loftus Versfeld Stadium in Pretoria is named, was a member of the Union side. The Griquas players, before their arduous journey back home, took part in an athletics meeting and won seven of the 11 events!

This successful tour, that created much interest in Cape Town and its surrounding areas, had set the scene for the future – and it was a mere year later that the first inter-district tournament with more than three sides took place in Grahamstown during the Grahamstown Show (which, incidentally, is still held annually.) With Grahamstown and Port Elizabeth joining in the fun against trendsetters Cape Town and Kimberley, the four-team tournament was a huge success. Cape Town were the winners of that 1885 tournament; Grahamstown were second and Kimberley took the third place on the log. Port Elizabeth didn't win a single match. But a serious problem persisted. The lack of conformity with different laws applied in virtually every match and even appeals against results of matches played remained a frustration. The establishment of a national controlling body became necessity. It is amazing that it took another four years for this to come about.

GWRFU formed

Griquas became the second rugby union in South Africa in 1886 when the Griqualand West Rugby Football Union was formed on 6 February. Six clubs attended the meeting held in the Central Hotel in Kimberley, i.e. Pirates, Kimberley, Newton, West End, Dutoitspan (better known as Die Pan, which changed its name to Beaconsfield) and De Beers. The decision was taken that a Grand Challenge Trophy would be played for annually and also that representatives of the six founding clubs would in future pick representative sides to represent the new union. The first official cup match (not for the Grand Challenge Trophy but for the Union Cup) followed on 15 May 1886. The venue was a piece of land in front of the Pavilion at Gardens. There were about 2 000 spectators present

Loftus Versfeld.

and the opposing teams were Pirates and Beaconsfield (Dutoitspan). The latter won by a goal against two tries, 6–2. The Grand Challenge Trophy arrived in Kimberley a fortnight after the final of the formal league that followed later in the season and which ended tragically when Alfred Schlemmer was seriously injured in a second-half tackle. He died in hospital a week later – the first known rugby death in South Africa.

The Kimberley club side visited Cape Town for the second time in 1886. And two years later, during their third visit, the first step was taken towards the establishment of the national body when Percy Ross Frames of Kimberley, only 24 years old, and the 21-year-old Bill Bisset of Cape Town, agreed that something had to be done to obtain uniformity in rule interpretations and applications – very much as is the case today, some would say! The SARFB was established the following year and their first meeting took place in the Craven Hotel in Kimberley. Perhaps the name of the hotel was an omen for Dr Danie Craven, who was to become South

For the love of the game

While Kimberley, with their early visits to Bloemfontein, Cape Town, Port Elizabeth and Natal, set the trend as a touring side, the hardships individual players had to go through are not as well recorded.

That the individuals loved their football is very clear. Paul Roos, who in 1906 was to become the first man to captain a South African rugby side overseas, was a teacher in Rustenburg in 1903.

Week after week he cycled from Rustenburg to Pretoria to represent Pretoria Rugby Club's first team – and then, after a cold drink following the final whistle, he undertook the return trip of 130 km to Rustenburg on a gravel road! There wasn't time for mixing with his team-mates because the future Member of Parliament was a very religious man and had to be back home before midnight in order not to be on the road on the Sunday!

Another man to do so was Gerald Pilditch of Harlequins who in the 1920s and 1930s was involved in the decade-long negotiations to obtain autonomy for Northern Transvaal, then still a sub-union of the Transvaal Rugby Football Union. What's more, Pilditch's trip wasn't even for the glory of playing for Quins' first XV.

But the sacrifices these two men made almost pale into insignificance if the travels of Willie Collins, later a cabinet minister, are considered. He travelled 100 km by bicycle from Ermelo to Standerton, where he caught a train to Pretoria to play rugby before undertaking the return trip. And these three players are only the ones we know about …

Many of the players in those early days had to make special arrangements at their places of work in order to fit in a training session before returning home on horseback in the cold Pretoria winters. This was certainly also the norm at other centres, although the chill in the air would have differed from area to area.

But while these were the travel hardships of individual players in Pretoria, consider the problems that teams encountered.

In the 1880s, before the gold rush, matches in Johannesburg were not possible, and to make a trip to Potchefstroom would take six days out of a player's week! Later, when league matches against Johannesburg club sides had become an organised activity, Pretoria sides often arrived in Johannesburg three or four players short as they couldn't get off work in the years when Saturdays were still working days.

Before that, Pretoria players travelled by horse-drawn cart to take part in matches in Johannesburg – and the effects of the journey, it is recorded, could be seen in virtually every match as the trip took its toll on the players in the second half of their matches.

But although Pretoria rugby clubs dominated matters against their Johannesburg counterparts in the early years of the 20th century and beyond, the club fixtures remained in the City of Gold for years to come.

The travelling hardships were of course not limited to the past. Even today club sides in the vast area of Griqualand West travel 400–600 km one way for their Supersport league matches. Kuruman, Sishen, Upington and Kimberley are some of the clubs affected. In addition, some of the players have many, many kilometres to travel to get to training sessions and home matches!

And of course, tales like those of legendary Springbok wing Jannie Engelbrecht and former Transvaal captain Toy Dannhauser when playing for Natal in the 1970s are not uncommon. Both of them had to travel more than 650 km return for a training session – in the case of Engelbrecht from Koekenaap on the West Coast to Stellenbosch or Cape Town, depending on whether it was a club or provincial game. Dannhauser did the trip from Vryheid to Durban for training twice a week – and three times in a week when Natal played, either to King's Park for a home match or to the airport if they had to fly out for an away match.

In Limpopo, the club sides playing in the Limpopo Blue Bulls league also still have hours of travel to play their club games.

Kimberley Pirates, 1884.

Africa's most influential rugby icon – but the owners of the hotel were in fact not related to Doc Craven, who was born 21 years later.

The game grows down the coast

Kimberley, jolly tourists that they were, visited Cape Town again in 1890 when they formed a combined team with Pirates, their great adversaries from the mining town. Pirates and Kimberley were the top sides in the town. In those days, draws were frequent – and in 1887, the two sides met six times before the winner of the Grand Challenge competition was decided! On their tour the combined Pirates and Kimberley side played three matches in Cape Town, winning one, losing one and drawing one, scoring 16 points and conceding 16 – and what's more, they played at the famous Newlands for the first time. But they were still not done with travelling. In

1891, they visited Natal, formally a year old but not nearly as advanced in their rugby structures or game as the Griquas clubs or those in and around Cape Town. Natal followed the popularity of the game that was gradually introduced down the coast by students from the Cape; by fortune hunters who didn't come good in Kimberley; and by the soldiers of the regiments established by the British along the coast and into the Natal Midlands.

In Port Elizabeth, much the same development as in Cape Town took place with only two clubs initially playing. Olympic Football Club was established in 1880, and Crusaders came into being early in 1887. Union from Uitenhage followed and the three clubs took part in triangular competitions. Uitenhage Swifts, over the years one of the leading and most famous clubs in the union, came about in 1890 and was formed by the St Katherine's Church Choir team! Swifts, like many others, were regarded as a 'junior' team and when all of them succumbed,

Sir Donald Currie.

Swifts was the only team to continue with the Arabs of Port Elizabeth providing a fifth team for competition. The first unofficial competitions eventually led to the introduction of the EP Grand Challenge Cup in 1888. Again the Cape blueprint was copied with the country sides slowly taking up the game, albeit some years after the developments in Cape Town. Grahamstown Club (later Albany), Cradock Rovers, Somerset East and Bedford joined the fray with Humansdorp, Graaff-Reinet and Middelburg following suit.

Port Elizabeth played in the early regional competition of 1885, the side being nothing else than a combined team from the Crusaders and Olympic clubs. And they weren't too successful! Crusaders, it must be noted, hold a special place in South African rugby history. They have always had their ground in St George's Park where the Port Elizabeth Cricket Club was situated. It is this ground that hosted the first test played by South Africa against the 1891 British touring side of Bill Maclagan.

St George's is also famous for cricket and bowls. It was

here that the first cricket test was played; the first women's cricket test; the last test before South Africa's expulsion from world cricket; the first-ever test series win against Australia was clinched; the first so-called rebel test in the 1980s took place; as well as where the first test with the resumption of 'normal' cricket was played.

St George's Park is also home to the oldest bowling club in the country. The Port Elizabeth Bowls Club was founded on 14 August 1882 and has not changed home since.

A mere 120 miles north-east of Port Elizabeth, the Border clubs had also started playing rugby as early as the late 1870s, with no or little information available about the really early days. What is known is that Alberts of King William's Town was the first established club, founded in 1878. Buffaloes, today still a force in Border rugby, came two years later. Then Queenstown Swifts and Stars of East London, as well as Uitenhage Swifts (1882) and Pirates (1889) were established by the time the union was formed in 1891. There was also a Pirates club in King William's Town. There was only a single trophy, the Border Cup, for which these sides competed, with Civil Service and Stars also among the early clubs and competitors. Swifts and Alberts contested the 1892 Border Cup final which was decided as a knock-out competition. Swifts won by two goals to nil. By 1893 a league system was introduced with Pirates emerging as the winners. Alberts won the following year and dominated the competition by winning it for three consecutive years between 1897 and 1899.

The first matches in Natal were played under a mixture of Winchester and Rugby rules and commenced around 1873. That was a year after the formation of Bishops College, the forerunner of Michaelhouse that produced their first Springbok 137 years later when Patrick Lambie made his test debut against Ireland in 2010. By 1876 a match between a team of Natalians and the 'Old Colony' was played in Kimberley for the Moor Cup that together with the Murray Cup were to become Natal's major trophies. The famous Maritzburg College came about in 1877 when it was established as a high school and it played both codes of football. Matches between Downtown and Uptown were very popular and Past versus Present at the schools also accounted for much of the interest generated by the game. The first reported intertown between Pietermaritzburg and Durban took place in 1880 – and for years this was a match played with the passion and aggression that has marked rugby in South Africa. It was certainly not a match for the faint-hearted!

Although Natal were late starters, they were nevertheless prepared to tour – no easy matter in those days before railway lines were developed between all towns. As was the case throughout the coastal unions, the regiments that were settled in Durban and Pietermaritzburg, with the schools, played a major role in the growth of first the Winchester/Cape mixture and then the Rugby rules. In Newcastle, a mere three months after the battle of Majuba, the first match was played between the Field Force and Newcastle. Barberton in the South Eastern Transvaal and Komati followed as rugby towns as the

Kimberley's first international, 1891.

Barberton Gold Fields drew prospectors and general fortune hunters to that area.

It is interesting to note that, because of the hold Association Football had on the rugby-playing communities (they owned most of the playing fields), many of the players played two matches on a Saturday – one in an Association match and the other, the strange Winchester and Rugby mixture.

Western Province – winners of the SARFB Trophy, 1889.

Sir TK Murray, first president of the Natal Rugby Football Union.

One can understand why (later Canon) Ogilvie of Bishops was so loathe to allow his pupils to switch to Rugby rules in the late 1880s. There is also the delightful press report of a match played in Natal in 1889: 'Rugby Union was described as being rough in the extreme and Lieut. Sparks had his knee so badly injured that he had to be carried home.'

The report goes on to say that the international between England and Scotland 'fell through' – and that the breach between the two unions was 'unlikely to be healed'. Rough play, it is inferred, was the reason for the 'breach'. The report continues: 'At the Oval (in Pietermaritzburg) on Saturday the game proved to be what was expected – rough in the extreme; and when a player loses so much self-control over his actions as to become pugilistic, the game, whatever it may be, is bound to fill the spectators with a certain amount of disgust.'

An interesting aside to the early years of Natal rugby is that Walter Webb Ellis, son of William Webb Ellis, the man regarded in rugby lore as starting the game, became headmaster of Hilton College just outside Pietermaritzburg, and is credited with starting rugby at this famous school.

The late 1880s and early 1890s were the years for new unions to spring up – and one of the new unions, without the growth history of Kimberley and Cape Town, was that of Transvaal which became one of the giants of the provincial game. It was not only down the coast that the game had developed after the early days in Cape Town. The Free State and Basutoland Rugby Union was formed in 1895. By 1893 Bloemfontein had four teams, and rugby was also being played at Kroonstad. Naauwpoort, just across the Cape Colony border on the route to De Aar and some 300 km from Bloemfontein, was also visited. The clubs drew their players from students returning from abroad and in the Cape and also from those who were disillusioned about the riches in Kimberley that did not come their way and had settled in the Orange Free State. It is of note that Grey College, provider of so many Springboks over the years, was one of the founding clubs. In true pioneering spirit, the Free State attended the 1894 Currie Cup tournament before they were a union affiliated to the SARFB! The fact that the tournament was being held in Cape Town at Newlands – by then already famous – probably made it more enticing!

Transvaal become a force

But well before the Free State took the bold step to become a union, the Transvaal Rugby Football Union was formed in 1889. Contrary to popular belief, it was not the discovery of gold as much as returning students that gave Transvaal the impetus to become a power in the early days – something they have kept up ever since with the normal downturns that all the top unions experience over time. It was during the early 1880s that the game was brought to the Transvaal, with the

Hilton School and Old Boys, 1889.

returning students introducing and fostering the game in Johannesburg. There were, of course, also the British forces in the Transvaal between 1877 and 1881 that initially played among themselves and then against other scratch sides as the game and its popularity developed. After the discovery of gold, people flocked to the area in their quest for riches, bringing diggers from Britain, New Zealand and Australia to Johannesburg. With them came greater support for rugby and they brought new developments in the game with them. The Kimberley migration also brought more players to Johannesburg.

The forerunner of the derby matches between Transvaal and Northern Transvaal (later the Lions and Blue Bulls) started as early as 1888 when Johannesburg and Pretoria met on the rugby field at least once a year. Transvaal were geographically enormous, with its borders and responsibility encompassing the whole of the

former Transvaal province – stretching up to the border with Rhodesia and down to Volksrust on the Natal border, and down to the Vaal River. The present union Blue Bulls and their sub-union, Limpopo; the Valke; the Pumas and sub-union Lowveld; and the Leopards were all part of the Transvaal Rugby Football Union established in 1889. One can only wonder how difficult it must have been, first, to pick the best players in the union and second, to get them together for a match or a tour.

The breakaway of the unions mentioned above was therefore quite normal – and to a large extent also the result of the autocratic way in which the Transvaal administrators dealt with the country districts. Seldom was a club fixture played outside Johannesburg, so the clubs had to travel to the City of Gold to play their matches. This continued until the 1920s, and when the system of the Currie Cup competition was eventually changed

How they scored over the years

In 1884, one of the laws governing the game stated: 'The match is won by either side obtaining two goals. All matches are drawn after five days' play, or after three days if no goal has been kicked by either side.' It sounds far-fetched, but many were the occasions that a match could not be completed and had to be abandoned as a draw after five days of play (not continuous!). From the above, it is clear that the laws of the days were confusing, vague and utterly silly if one compares them with today's intricate laws of the game. But it is the ever-changing and intricate scoring system of those days that bears looking at.

The table below sets out the way in which points could be scored in the 1800s – but there is more to it. For example: a defending side could score for the opposition by making the ball dead behind their own line, called a 'minor' or 'rouge' – a sort of 'own goal'. Today one would call it 'making the ball dead' or 'carrying the ball over'. In those days, it took law changes and years before the concept of kicking for touch instead of scoring for the opposition came about. It was therefore not unheard of to refer to a match as victory by two rouges to nil. Tries were not regarded as paramount and counted only one point until 1889 when the International Rugby Board set the value of a try at two points. It became three points in 1891 and remained so until 1971 when it changed to four points and increased to five points in 1990.

The ever-changing scoring system in the 1880s makes it difficult to work out what the score in a particular match was. One has to look up the system of the day to calculate it! The scores in articles and later in books are given as, for example, 'winning by one goal against three tries' or 'by a try and two touches in self-defence to nil'.

As Stellenbosch have been doing since the days of Doc Craven, Kimberley did in 1889 pertaining to the scoring system. They were asked to experiment with a new points system and the Rugby Football Union (England's ruling body) requested the first president of the SA Rugby Football Board, Percy Ross Frames, to report back on the tests. England was not a member of the IRB at the time where no points were awarded for a penalty goal. England only joined the IRB fray in 1891.

The double whammy, as in baseball, also applied in rugby. When scoring a try, a follow-up of the conversion could result in a second try and another conversion kick at goal!

Changing scoring systems

Year	Goal	Try	Conversion	Penalty	Drop	Goal from mark
1886	3	1	2	–	3	3
1889	3	1	2	2	3	3 (RFU)
	4	2	2	–	3	3 (IRB)
1891	3	1	2	3	3	3
1894	5	3	2	3	4	4
1905	5	3	2	3	4	3
1948	5	3	2	3	3	3
1971	6	4	2	3	3	3
1977	6	4	2	3	3	–
1990	7	5	2	3	3	–

from a localised tournament to home-and-away matches in 1922, Johannesburg hogged the home matches despite the fact that the bulk of the players were from Pretoria! In fact, it was only on the third tour of a British side to South Africa in 1903 that Pretoria was granted a tour match. No matches were allocated to the capital in 1910, and in 1924, they were awarded a solitary match by which time the five touring sides had played 16 matches in Johannesburg.

Three of the first five Transvaal clubs are still running today. Wanderers and Pirates from Johannesburg, and Pretoria, still exist. Pretoria became the first champions when they beat Pirates 1–0 at the Wanderers grounds at Kruger Park in 1889 and then Pirates won the next three competitions. They returned the trophy which had become theirs by virtue of their hat-trick – and the

The Rev Adrian Roberts' team in Pretoria, 1879. It is not known who their opposition was.

competition then became the Pirates Grand Challenge Competition. The first Transvaal side, not at full strength because of the unavailability of players for the hastily put together trip to Kimberley, played in the 1889 tournament for the Board trophy. They lost two matches but beat eventual tournament winners Western Province.

As was the case everywhere else where the game was played, the lack of funds and decent training grounds and facilities hampered the growth of the game. The fields were hard, grassless, covered with red dust and bright sunlight, and the glare irritated both players and spectators. As one sportswriter wrote: 'During the scrum a lot of dust was kicked up and once or twice it obscured the players, and it was difficult to discern what was going on.'

Other unions established early on were South Western Districts Rugby Football Union, (1899) and North Eastern Districts Rugby Football Union (1893). Rhodesia sent teams to take part in the Currie Cup tournaments of

1898, 1899, 1906, 1908 and 1914. Although their Freddie Brooks was invited to play for South Africa in 1906, it was found that he was short of the necessary residential qualification period of five years. A number of famous rugby Springboks from Rhodesia were selected later on to play for South Africa, and Rhodesia also provided a Springbok captain in Des van Jaarsveldt in 1960 against Scotland. Players with Rhodesian/Zimbabwean ties captained South Africa in later years. They included Bobby Skinstad, Salty du Rand, Gary Teichmann and Piet Greyling – and Corné Krige was from Zambia or Northern Rhodesia before its independence.

Those were the early days, and the unions that paved the way. Over the years, the number of unions grew and, at one stage, numbered 22, many of which never played Currie Cup rugby and were destined to spend their years in the Sport Pienaar competition. But more about that later.

3

Turmoil at the top
The woes and fortunes of
13 rugby presidents

South African rugby's administration, stable and without much excitement over its first 70 years, in the 1960s suddenly found itself under increasing international pressure because of the country's apartheid policies. Politicians and controlling rugby bodies alike were propagating for mixed teams picked on merit – and Dr Danie Craven, who was then president of the South African Rugby Football Union, also had internal pressure from the government who wouldn't accede to his on-going requests to allow a change in sports policy and mixed rugby teams.

After the unification of South Africa's various rugby bodies in 1992 these problems and pressures changed in nature – and in many respects, the change led to a more hostile period in South African rugby. The game's administration has since been marked by political wrangling, turbulence, acrimony and court cases. Much of the idealism that rugby as a game stood for in the preceding days was negated. Gone were the days when the game was fortunate in the outstanding men who governed it because of their love for rugby rather than for personal or political agendas.

Percy Ross Frames sets the standards

The initial high standard of administration was set by Percy Ross Frames, the first president of the SA Rugby Football Board which was established in 1889. But, despite the foundation that the Kimberley man laid in the early years of a fledgling national union, his role in history will never be remembered with the same reverence, and indeed awe, as that of Dr Daniël Hartman Craven, who reigned from 1956 to 1993 and is arguably the

Management of the first Springboks, 1906: captain Paul Roos, manager Daddy Carden and vice-captain Paddy Carolin.

Percy Ross Frames.

outstanding rugby personality in world rugby during the amateur rugby years. He will not be remembered with the same respect as Dr Louis Luyt, who was the man in charge when South Africa hosted – and won – the 1995 World Cup or Ebrahim Patel, who was the first man of colour to hold the office or WV Simkins of Border, who was the president in the difficult years spanning the South African (Anglo-Boer) War of 1899–1902 and, save for occasional absences, was at the helm three months short of 20 years – the third longest reign of South Africa's rugby presidents.

Frames had much in common with Craven. Like him, the 25-year-old Frames had the presidency thrust upon him; he too did not have finances to implement a policy; he had no staff; and Frames, like Craven, left a legacy that saw South Africa climb steadily to the top of the rugby world.

Frames' elevation to president came after a discussion with WM (Bill) Bisset of Cape Town in 1888. Both Frames – later a test referee – and Bisset were involved in matches between the touring Kimberley team and club sides in Cape Town. The reason for their post-match talk on this Kimberley tour was the unhappiness that stemmed from the varying rules and interpretations that manifested in matches between the various district teams – and indeed also in domestic club matches of the respective unions. The distribution of profits was another cause for unhappiness.

These matters came to a head when Kimberley paid their second visit to Cape Town in 1888. With Bisset as an ally, Frames decided that a national body had become a necessity to govern and control the game wherever it was played in South Africa. Between them and other influential Kimberley rugby tourists in that team, it was agreed that once a national body was formed, the hosts of the next inter-district tournament would appoint the president, according to one view of the lead-up to the establishment of the SARFB. Kimberley, which then had a direct rail line from Cape Town, was to host the 1889 tournament, and Frames became president.

Another story was that the SARFB was formed in Kimberley in 1889 before the tournament specifically to establish the rules according to which the competition would be decided. It was the first provincial tournament, with the previous tournaments in Cape Town (1884) and Grahamstown (1885) regarded as inter-district competitions. Anyway, Frames was the man in the chair after the meeting held in the Craven Hotel in Main Road. He was re-elected president until 1893, when he stood down because of work commitments and the onerous duties of the position he had performed with such distinction.

During his office, the first international tour took place when WE (Bill) Maclagan's British side visited South Africa for a 23-match tour that included three test matches. All the touring players were from either England or Scotland. Only eight players had experience of test match rugby and the team included 14 students in the playing group of 24 plus a manager and assistant manager.

Frames was also president when the first Currie Cup

tournament was held in 1892. There are no records of the SARFB's board meetings in the first three years, but in 1892, the first official Currie Cup tournament took place – again in Kimberley. (Incidentally, the SARFB trophy which was first played for in 1889, was also presented to the winners at the 1892 tournament, which meant that Western Province not only won the first Currie Cup but retained the SARFB trophy they had won in 1889!)

It is not generally known that South Africa, and in particular Frames, were responsible for the introduction of the penalty in rugby. With RL Cousins he experimented with the introduction of the penalty kick and they reported it to the Rugby Football Union (RFU), which was (and still is) England's controlling body. The proposals were considered and then implemented in the rules of rugby – the first of many from Kimberley to the RFU and also the IRB. Frames played rugby, refereed in the second international of South Africa in 1891 when they played the British tourists in Kimberley – the first test to be staged there – and of course also administered the game in Kimberley where he was honorary secretary of Griqualand West and later became president, positions he held for 11 consecutive years.

While Frames was the first president of the SARFB, Bisset's role in the administration of South African rugby should not be forgotten. He was only 21 years old on that fateful day when he and Frames discussed the need for a controlling body. He missed what would have been his debut test in Kimberley in 1891 because he was involved in a court case, but played in the third test in Cape Town. It was to be his only international cap – his future father-in-law gave him an ultimatum when he asked for his daughter Henrietta's hand: you may marry her, but only if you give up playing rugby! Though he did give up playing rugby, he was the South African manager of Johnny Hammond's team in 1896 and handled three of the 21 tour matches as referee, including the third test. He hereby became one of only six South African internationals who also officiated as referees in a test match. Bisset is regarded as South Africa's first real

loose forward – on the small side, tough and exceptionally fast. He later became the president of the SA Law Association and a mining magnate.

The first known record of SARFB meetings was that of the 1892 meeting, when Frames reported a balance of £24 19s 0d. All previous records were lost during the amalgamation of the Central Mining Company – where the records were kept – and De Beers. At this meeting in 1892 it was also resolved that the rules of England's controlling body, the Rugby Football Union (RFU), would be adopted. At that time, there were two schools of thought on which rules should apply: the RFU and the International Rugby Board. Frames worked incredibly hard – he was also the honorary secretary of Griqualand West and later the union's president. It was only after Frames became unavailable to continue as SARFB president, that HG Cadwallader was appointed honorary secretary to look after matters such as the minutes and the finances. This became a permanent position and in 1893, it was agreed that the SARFB would consist of a president and secretary with two representatives 'from each state, colony or province affiliated to the Board, five to form a quorum'. It is unclear whether the 'five' referred to were voters of unions, as only four unions were recognised as districts or centres for affiliation! They were Western Province, Griqualand West, Transvaal and Orange Free State.

It was only in 1894, during an SARFB meeting in May, that a letter was read in which Mr Donald Currie – later to become Sir Donald – said he wanted the trophy donated to Griqualand West by the touring British team of 1891 to be a floating annual trophy. By then it had been donated to the SARFB by Griqualand West and had indeed been played for in 1892 when Western Province became the first Currie Cup winners. Whether it was called that in 1892 is, however, not certain.

The Currie Cup tournaments took place infrequently and not on an annual basis as desired by Currie. During tournaments, which in those days were held at central venues where all the sides played all the other teams on a round-robin basis, the hosts would appoint a committee. The official board at headquarters – moved about according to the domicile of the president – however retained the right to override any decisions taken by the local and temporary one!

Transvaal hosted the 1895 tournament – and Simkins reported a net profit of £1059 8s 8d. It was a period of development at administrative level, and the decision early on to establish a constitution for the SARFB paid dividends with an established controlling body that that had overcome their cash-flow problems. This prompted a repeat of the invitation for a second British team to visit South Africa. That was also the year that provincial teams registered their colours for the first time, and it is noteworthy that Western Province's famous blue and white striped jersey remains. Border, who had decided on a chocolate brown jersey, stuck to their traditional colours until the 1990s. Although their original colours were retained, the jersey has changed considerably. Orange Free State registered a maroon jersey with an orange collar; Griquas had a navy blue jersey and Transvaal's colours were a dark blue-and-white jersey and stockings, with dark blue shorts. Eastern Province opted for dark blue shorts and a white jersey.

WV Simkins in when the Springbok and green jersey are chosen

Simkins was president when South Africa wore green jerseys for the first time. That was in 1896 when Barry (nicknamed Fairy) Heatlie had the right as national captain to decide on the colours of his team. He picked the colours of the defunct Old Diocesan RFC jersey. It is fitting that this test was played at Newlands, the field that since the early days has been regarded as the seat of South African rugby although Cape Town was not always the SARF headquarters. That the first match in a green jersey was won could perhaps, in retrospect, be regarded as an omen of things to come! Newlands was also the field where the first South African test win was achieved

in 1896. Simkins' term was further highlighted by the first South African side overseas tour with Paul Roos as captain and the popular Daddy Carden as manager.

Carden it is who, in a letter to ID Difford dispels many theories of where the Springbok name came from. The letter reads as follows:

The fact is that the Springbok as a badge existed when my team left South Africa, and here is proof positive. We landed at Southampton on the evening of September 19th 1906, and from the Daily Mail *of September 20th I culled this paragraph: 'The team's colours would be myrtle green jerseys with gold collar. They would wear dark blue shorts and dark blue stockings, and the jersey would have embroidered in mouse-coloured silk on the left breast a Springbok, a small African antelope which is as typical of Africa as the Kangaroo is of Australia.'*

Now as to the adoption of the name. No uniforms or blazers had been provided and we were a motley turn-out at practice at Richmond. That evening, I spoke to Roos (the captain) and Carolin (vice-captain) and pointed out that the witty London Press would invent some funny name for us, if we did not invent one ourselves. We thereupon agreed to call ourselves Springboks, and to tell Pressmen that we desired to be so named. I remember this distinctly, for Paul (Roos) reminded us that Springbokken was the correct plural. However, the Daily Mail *after our first practice called us the Springboks, and the name stuck. I at once ordered the dark green gold-edged blazers and still have the first Springbok pocket badge that was made.*

The popular theory is that, at the first press conference, Roos said his team should be called 'Springboks' in reference to the green playing jerseys and the fact that this was the antelope that roamed the green fields of South Africa. However, the Springbok as emblem was used as far back as 1894 when a South African athletic and cycling team competed in the English Championships. One of the athletes, PJ Blignaut, who later smashed a number of world records in America, wore a green vest for competition and the team of 1898, of which he was also a member, wore the Springbok badge as an emblem during meetings in England.

Simkins, therefore, resigned in 1913 with a number of firsts on his list of achievements – although many of them were not of his own making or approval (he was against the selection of the Springbok as an emblem in 1906). However, he was an extraordinary president who gave unstintingly and with enthusiasm and fair mindedness to the game he loved. With the honorary secretary Jack Heyneman (who became president in 1915) doing a sterling job, South African rugby remained in good hands – although no other rugby contact had been made with countries other than the Home Unions and France against which an unofficial test was played in 1906 (won 55–6 by Paul Roos's side). Heyneman followed Bill Schreiner, a former prime minister of the Cape Colony, who was president of the SARFB for only a matter of months before he left for London as South African High Commissioner at the outbreak of the First World War.

John (Jack) Heyneman establishes new Currie Cup format

John Heyneman, known as Jack, became president with many years of administration to see him through an arduous job. First he had the Great War (1914–1918) to contend with during which he had to keep the game in South Africa alive. There wasn't much to be done, however. Currie Cup rugby was shelved for six years from 1914 to 1920, when a tournament was held for the last time. Thereafter, the competition was played on a home-and-away basis until 1939. The new Currie Cup format resulted in greater profits.

Heyneman was the man at the helm when the first contact on a rather official basis was made between New Zealand and South African rugby. That was in 1919

when a ship carrying the New Zealand 'Imperial Services' team brought decommissioned soldiers to South Africa en route to their home country. Their visit was in no uncertain terms the result of negotiations of former SARFB president Bill Schreiner who was then in London as High Commissioner and who acted as a co-ordinator between the visitors and the SARFB. The Kiwi soldiers played 14 matches – plus an unofficial late match against Natal to increase profits – on a tour that showed their class and skill. It was obvious that South Africa could and should no longer postpone international contact with what was to become their greatest rugby rival.

Heyneman was, like other SARFB, SARB, SARFU and SARU presidents before and after him, an autocrat – but it was at a time when this leadership style was necessary. The success of the Springbok sides in his term of office from 1917–1927 speaks volumes for a sound administration. It was under Heyneman that the Springboks – at last! – undertook the first tour to New Zealand for the initial contact at international level between the two leading rugby countries. That was in 1921. There was an obvious uncertainty about the strength of the two sides which had not played international opposition since the advent of the Great War, but solid planning by South Africa following the New Zealand invitation in 1920 to send a Bok side to their shores ensured a dream start to the competition between these two great rugby nations.

After a drawn series with one win apiece and a scoreless last test, Heyneman insisted that the even greater status of the Springboks after drawing a series with the so-called Invincibles in New Zealand should be exploited with more international contact. That happened in 1924 when Ronald Cove-Smith's British team visited South Africa. Heyneman resigned in 1927. He was succeeded by AJ 'Sport' Pienaar.

AJ 'Sport' Pienaar – autocrat supreme

Whereas Heyneman was described as 'benevolently autocratic' by his peers and authors of his time, Pienaar

Theo Pienaar's 1921 Springbok side that toured New Zealand – the first international contact between the two great rugby nations.

was the true article: a dictator! Although Doc Craven never publicly or in any of his 30 books directly attacked Pienaar, it was obvious that Craven – who later took over the mantle from Pienaar as the longest-serving president – was never close to him. Pienaar served until 1954 and died in office after a period in which the Springboks became the undisputed top side in the world by beating the All Blacks in New Zealand in 1937 after another drawn series in South Africa (1928); won the Grand Slam twice (1931/32 and 1951/52); beat the touring British Lions as they were by then known in 1938; beat Australia (1933 and 1953); and the All Blacks (1949) on tours to South Africa. Only seven losses from 34 matches against the best rugby-playing countries in the world gave the Boks a 79% winning ratio, which put the performances of the last few years into perspective.

The outstanding record was achieved during the term of a man who got his nickname from his love of and involvement in many sports. In fact, he was president of the SA Cricket Board and the SARFB at the same time! South Africa's achievements in international rugby over the span of years that Pienaar was president must also be seen against the background of the Second World War. Not only did Pienaar and the rugby administrators who remained in South Africa during the war have to keep the game going at a decent level, they also had to act as diplomats to ensure fairness between the pro-tour and anti-tour groups in South Africa – roughly divided between the English-speaking and Afrikaans-speaking players.

The essence of the dispute was whether funds from charity matches should be allocated to soldiers via the

Governor General's War Fund. Matches were cancelled (notably a revenge match between Western Province and Boland after the latter, a new union, was not prepared to have any funds dispersed for other reasons than rugby). Three unions, Western Province, Griquas and Eastern Province, however, would not abide by the ruling to refrain from matches with the object of collecting money for the war funds and that resulted in splits in these unions.

As a result, Stellenbosch Rugby Club withdrew from the WPRFU competitions – and clubs under the jurisdiction of the WP Rugby Football Union were warned not to play against the Maties. For two seasons Stellenbosch and also Gardens, Paarl and Maitland, and the junior clubs Tiervlei and Bellville, broke away to form part of a new rugby union which was not under the auspices of the WPRFU. The breakaway Western Cape Rugby Union also received a boost with a number of UCT students joining as Groote Schuur Club. That reduced the Western Province clubs to Hamiltons, Villagers, UCT, Somerset West and the new club Union. Two sides consisting of soldiers, Fortress Green and Fortress White, were also accorded senior club status.

The Maties did, however, play many matches in the country districts. They also played what were later the Pukke and the Paarl Teachers' Training College in Paarl. They even played Tukkies in a full-scale match between the two sides that, in the 1970s, were regarded as the top sides in the country with 50 000 spectators attending their clashes! This Tukkies-Maties clash upset Western Province particularly because the Northern Transvaal Rugby Union had not put a stop to the 'illegal' Maties playing Tukkies – and it led to the cancellation of two Western Province friendlies against Northern Transvaal in 1943. The Boland matches, because of Boland's willingness to allow their clubs to play against the Maties and other sides from the breakaway unions from Western Province and Eastern Province, also greatly upset the Western Province powers that were.

An SARFB enquiry was eventually lodged into teams playing across border against sides from other unions, but amid all the problems and the lack of numbers to make decent club competitions a reality, the game went on – in many cases, through the contributions of schools and the military units stationed in some of the unions. There were also tours undertaken by the military, notably a representative military side coached by Doc Craven that brought an upsurge of interest from spectators who were dwindling because of the poor standard of rugby being played.

However, Pienaar's dictatorial management style kept things together under very difficult circumstances. Even so, the war led to the cancellation or postponement of the planned – but not confirmed – 1940 tour by the All Blacks to South Africa; the second round of the 1939 Currie Cup competition; the celebration of the SARFB's first 50 years; and an international rugby conference.

Pienaar was the man who eventually secured the first post-war tour that led to the only series whitewash the All Blacks have suffered – they were beaten 4–0 in the 1949 series against the Springboks in South Africa. The 1951/52 touring side that returned from the UK and Ireland after a Grand Slam under the astute coaching of Craven was another feather in his cap.

This tour, and especially the appointment of Craven as assistant manager and therefore the automatic coach of the team, is the perfect example of Pienaar's autocratic management style. He did not want Craven as assistant tour manager. Pienaar backed and in fact canvassed votes for Bert Kipling. Craven, then a representative of Eastern Transvaal who had agreed to vote for Kipling, showed his vote to JD de Villiers and George van Reenen as proof that he had obeyed the wishes of Eastern Transvaal and did not vote for himself. Three times the votes between Kipling and Craven were tied. Then, in the third round, someone changed his vote and Craven made it! But Pienaar, at a subsequent luncheon for the departing team, ordered that Craven 'under no circumstances' coach the Springboks.

Craven in a biography admits that he was bitterly disappointed. He was so looking forward to continuing to coach the Boks after having done so in the 4–0 white-wash of New Zealand in 1949. But once Pienaar had or-dered something, it was done. This was confirmed when Craven told Pienaar that he would not have made himself available if he had known about the coaching ban. What would his duties on the tour now be, Craven enquired. To which Pienaar merely replied that manager Frank Mellish (the tour manager) would tell him what his duties on tour were.

But the president of the SARFB did not count on Basil Kenyon, the tour captain, who cruelly didn't play a sin-gle test on tour – or ever again – after an early injury. 'Well, Doc, when are you starting,' Kenyon asked Craven three days after they had set sail for the UK. Craven was taken aback, and replied that he wasn't allowed to coach the team. But Kenyon was adamant. 'I know what Sport Pienaar said, Doc, but I don't agree with it and I want you to coach the side. So let's go and see Frank Mellish and I'll tell him what I want.' Kenyon stuck to his guns and Craven coached. They won all four tests against the Home Unions and also beat France – losing only one of their 31 matches and scoring 562 points against 167.

In those days, the SARFB had to hold their meetings wherever they could find an empty room as they didn't have their own offices. Delegates in or near Cape Town would represent the unions from the Orange Free State and Transvaal. Most of the time the Argus newspaper office was the venue, but the delegates had to leave when the building caretaker decided it was time to go. That's when Pienaar would say: 'Don't worry about what's left (on the agenda). I know how you all feel. I'll finish this agenda myself at home.'

Craven won his first ten test matches in charge, then lost one and won the next two for a record of one loss from 13 outings. It became 14 wins from 17 matches after the 1955 British Lions gave the Springboks a close run for their money, drawing the four-match series 2–all. In 1956, the Wallabies were beaten 2–0 in Australia but the All Blacks – and their referees, it must be said – won the series against the Springboks in New Zealand 3–1. This

Basil Kenyon didn't play in any of the 1951/52 Grand Slam tests.

left Craven with a still enviable record of 17 test wins from 23 matches for a 74% winning ratio. (A comparative analysis is that of the Springboks in 2009 and 2010 when they played 26 matches, winning 16 for a 61% record.)

As Springbok coach, Craven is bettered only by Kitch Christie's full house of wins in 14 tests, and by Izak van Heerden who had a 75% record in the 1962 series against the British Lions.

It is interesting that Craven, after being convinced to make himself available as president in 1956, was asked to remain as manager and coach for the Springbok tour to Australasia. That was a near untenable situation as he found out on the tour. As manager, he didn't have the usual freedom to discuss matters the tourists were un-happy with – like the appalling refereeing – because of his vested interest in every result! It didn't make matters easier that he was also the president of the SARFB, which meant that every complaint was effectively official!

Doc Craven – player, manager, coach and president
Dr Daniël Hartman Craven, known to all as Danie or Doc Craven took over the chair early in 1956. Edgar Tudhope,

who was Pienaar's deputy at the time, agreed to serve from February 1954 to April 1956 after Pienaar's death in office in 1953, but felt that a younger man should take over as soon as possible. Craven was that younger man, and his term began in April 1956. It was to become the longest term in office for any of South Africa's presidents and ended with his death in January 1993, after 36-and-a-half years. The great man had been involved with the Springboks for nearly 62 years of South African rugby's first 104 years – as a 21-year-old scrumhalf and player in 1931/32 until 1938, and thereafter as selector, coach, administrator and president of the SARFB. What's more, Craven had by far the most difficult, challenging tenure of any of the 13 presidents to date.

Luyt later may have had the more aggressive, back-stabbing opposition from the African National Congress (ANC) government's sports officials and affiliates in his five years, but what Craven had to go though at the hands of the National Party government and the Broederbond lasted for the duration of his term. In addition to the continual pressure from the apartheid government and instructions to toe the line regarding players of colour even against teams like the Maoris, he had to contend with international pressure and boycotts.

Craven's personal goal to bring rugby to players of all races was met with resistance at every turn. He also needed diplomacy and a thick skin to combat international rugby's growing impatience and unhappiness with the South African situation. And he did not need the backhand he received from Prime Minister Hendrik Verwoerd in 1965 with what became known as the Loskop Dam speech (more on this later).

Of course, the fact that Craven was, like Luyt, not a supporter of the National Party merely increased the pressure, with vitriolic attacks from prime ministers and cabinet ministers becoming part of his life.

But this is not the place to try and dissect the full political struggle of South African sport since the National Party came to power in 1948, or to examine the reasons for the action of the ANC sports leaders against rugby, particularly over the last two decades. That people of colour weren't part of the national sport long before the formal establishment of apartheid as an ideology is also not a subject for discussion here. Suffice it to say that rugby and cricket had their own controlling bodies for coloureds and blacks as far back as the late 1800s. That indicates that colour has long been an issue in South African sport.

This is emphasised with the action of Maori players after a rough, even dirty, match against the touring Springboks who won 9–8 in 1921. The home side blamed the incidents on the perceived South African feeling against non-whites. Maurice Brownlie's 1928 All Blacks to South Africa did not officially include any Maori, but there were some lighter-skinned players from this indigenous New Zealand race in the side. Even in 1937, before the National Party came to power, the Maori match against the Springboks in New Zealand was scrapped from the tour programme because of the New Zealanders' view that the Springboks would view them as inferior.

Craven, as vice-captain, was instrumental in overcoming that antagonism, and by the end of the 1937 tour, the Boks were invited to the Maori concert at Rotorua – a tremendous honour.

Craven's nightmare started in 1955 when the National Party's first sports guidelines were drawn up, but his greatest humiliation, an act he called 'despicable' in one of his biographies, came in 1965. That was firstly when, en route to visiting New Zealand where the Springboks were touring, Verwoerd made his speech at Loskop Dam, just north of Middelburg in the Transvaal. He said that Maori players would never be welcome in South Africa. Without knowing about the speech, Craven got off the plane at Christchurch to face hordes of journalists. And then, flying on to Rotorua where the Boks were to play, he was met at the home of the Maori by a South African diplomat. He told Craven of the letter received from Verwoerd instructing him to tell the Springboks that it had come to his notice that there had been 'much fraternisation' with the Maori after their match; and, in

Hannes Marais, captain of the 1971 unbeaten Springboks to Australia.

Craven's words, 'Verwoerd conveyed he wanted to draw the attention of the tourists to the fact that they were South Africans and that they "should not indulge in social contact in New Zealand with people they would never associate with socially in their own country". The diplomat, in short, told me that the South African government wanted the Springboks to ease off their friendly associations with the Maori people.'

The Maori knew Craven and trusted and understood him after regular contact since 1937. That night, they fetched him from the hotel he had decided he wouldn't budge from, so ashamed was he for what had been done to his hosts. They convinced him to change his mind. It turned out to be one of the outstanding nights for the tourists who were there and became a fond memory of friendship for Craven.

The Verwoerd speech was not condemned outright by Springbok captain Dawie de Villiers, who years later became a cabinet minister. He did concede, however, that it was a tremendous embarrassment to play against and socialise with what he called 'great people' and to look them in the eye and say: you're not welcome in our country. 'It put us in a precarious position, both with the opposing players and the public that we didn't look for and didn't deserve,' admitted De Villiers.

And so it went on. Not many may remember the Olympic Games in Montreal in 1976 that followed the New Zealand rugby tour of South Africa. Because of the tour, much of the rest of Africa asked the IOC to ban New Zealand from the Olympic Games or they threatened to boycott the Games. However, the IOC had no control over rugby, and despite the its efforts to convince the African nations not to use the Olympics as retaliation, 26 African countries boycotted.

There were also the demonstration tours to the UK in 1969/70; Australia in 1971; and New Zealand in 1981. There was the decree by New Zealand Prime Minister Dave Lange that the SARB president wouldn't again be welcome in New Zealand; Craven's many, many confrontations with Prime Minister and later State President John Vorster; State President PW Botha, as well as sports minister Piet Koornhof and future State President FW de Klerk, then minister of education.

There were the many discussions with Cuthbert Loristen's breakaway coloured body, the SA Rugby Football Federation that had thrown its lot in with the SARB in 1977 (leading to a name change from the SARFB to SARB); with Abdullah Abass's SA Rugby Union (SARU) who were affiliated to the more militant SACOS (South African Council of Sport) body; and even with the ANC.

At the IRB, where he had a stint as president in 1959, only Craven's standing and friendships kept the apparent criticism from becoming open hostility. Craven battled through this, and also a fair share of disgust from the right wingers in South Africa, to eventually have Vorster agree after a near stand-up argument that a team with a few players of colour could oppose the 1975 France tourists. Mixed trials were, however, not possible, Vorster warned him.

Craven feels the way in which he and Abass and their delegation to Koornhof in the 1970s were treated brought a great divide not only in sports relations but especially racial relations in those years – and until Abass's death in 1983, Abass and Craven, who had become good friends, sought a way to integrate the various rugby bodies.

Such was their relationship that, when in 1977 mixed trials were a possibility, Abass would not pursue it. At the time, he confided in Craven that there was not a single player of colour good enough to warrant it.

It was only in February 1991 that the SARU (to which SARF had affiliated in 1979) and the SARB agreed to form one controlling body with the basis of their agreement that there would be one non-racial controlling body for rugby in the country; that all clubs would be open; and that all players would be allowed to play where they wanted. This agreement, of course, came in the aftermath of the lifting of the ANC ban and the release of Nelson Mandela from prison exactly a year before, with Verwoerd, Vorster and Botha mere bad memories for the rugby fraternity.

Craven was the first to institute the so-called rugby clinics – and soon made them multiracial. He also toured the country with players and officials of colour to help in presenting those clinics. He experimented with laws at Stellenbosch that became international laws. At times it brought him into conflict with the IRB, but it was his canvassing and insistence that made the non-kicking rule from outside the 22-metre line a reality; as well as the 10-metre off-side line at line-outs, among many others.

But before all the political pressure and in-fighting, there were the mundane tasks that a president had to take care of – like ensuring sufficient funds for the SARFB; obtaining offices to work from; and hiring staff. By 1957 the SARFB, after 68 years, had its own administrative headquarters. A year later Kockie de Kock became its first full-time secretary and Craven had started what he called a distribution fund with contributions from all the unions. That would enable the SARFB to make decisions with financial implications, rather than borrow money from the two big unions, Western Province and Transvaal and repay them from future tours or tournaments.

In 1971, the SARFB moved closer to rugby action into offices at Newlands – and today they're metres away in the Sports Institute building adjoining the famous rugby ground.

Political interference results in five new presidents

Political interference made governance of South African rugby near-impossible after unification. The National Sports Council worked openly and ceaselessly towards its goal of taking over control of the game and were wholeheartedly supported by the government itself – and the immediate integration propagated at all playing levels, including internationals, conveniently ignored the neglect under apartheid of the game among all races other than white.

The years between 1992 and 2006 led to international derision of South African rugby and especially its administration. It also brought more rugby scandals to the office of president than in the preceding century as a whole. This was the result of political figureheads at the helm who had political party agendas rather than rugby ones; by a lack of experience in rugby governance at national and international level; and because six presidents in that time – Danie Craven, Fritz Eloff, Ebrahim Patel, Louis Luyt, Silas Nkanunu and Brian van Rooyen meant a disintegrated approach to administration. These were arguably the darkest 16 years in South Africa's international rugby history, superseding even the period when the Springboks were ousted from international competition because of apartheid.

The new political dispensation in South Africa and the resultant programmes/agendas to ensure more people of colour in teams at all levels are only part of the reason. The fact that Dr Danie Craven, who had ruled supreme and was arguably the greatest administrator amateur rugby internationally had known, was an ill man by 1992 and little more than a figurehead when tough leadership was needed, exacerbated the leadership problem. His steady hand and resilience under political pressure from

Crisis as Luyt refuses to resign

The refusal of SARFU president Louis Luyt in May 1998 to resign following a vote of no confidence from SARFU led to an ultimatum and threats by the National Sports Council (NSC) that made waves throughout the rugby world. NSC's threat to cancel tours and South Africa's participation in the Super 12 competition would have had repercussions of millions of rand.

An article posted on 8 May 1998 by the influential (London) *Sunday Independent* on their website www.independent.co.uk/ under the heading 'South African rugby plunged into crisis as Luyt refuses to quit' follows:

The future of South African rugby was in crisis last night after the country's white rugby supremo Louis Luyt refused to resign despite a demand by more than half his executive that he go to avert an international boycott.

In an ominous split along racial lines, the four black members of the executive of the South African Rugby Football Union (SARFU) resigned after the notoriously stubborn Big Louis, SARFU president, refused to follow the majority decision.

As a National Sports Council deadline for the resignation of Luyt and his executive expired, the rugby president also refused to support a decision of his executive to apologise to President Nelson Mandela for what they called his 'humiliating' appearance in court last month after a judge insisted he appear in person to defend his decision to order an inquiry into allegations of racism and graft in the game.

Luyt refused to allow a government inquiry. Although SARFU won its court battle with the government it was widely predicted that it would lose the wider war.

Last night Muleki George, the president of the Sports Council, said that the council's threat to invoke an international boycott still stood, after Luyt refused to quit.

A boycott would jeopardise millions of pounds of promised sponsorship in South Africa, Australia and New Zealand, and throw international competition into disarray.

Mr Luyt started the day in typical swaggering style, telling a breakfast meeting organised by a business publication that he would not resign and that the row between him and President Mandela's government was to do with race rather than sport.

With international isolation again looming for a sport which in the apartheid era earned a reputation for attracting racist and right-wing supporters, Luyt said little to take the racial sting out of the confrontation.

'Are we going to remain a lawless society? Because that's what we are, you know,' he said to the loud applause of the audience of white, middle-aged men.

Luyt said that the bitter row with government was not about SARFU but about Louis Luyt. 'This was about someone being in the way, and, let me tell you, I intend to be in the way for a long time to come,' he said. He added that he would bow before no man – presumably not even President Mandela – only to God.

But last night, at the end of the SARFU executive meeting, the usually bullish Luyt looked uncharacteristically shellshocked. It is unlikely that he expected that eight of the 14 affiliated provincial rugby unions would turn against him.

The fear now is that the row over rugby's apparent failure to reach out to the black majority will spill over into an even more overtly racial conflict.

Mr George has warned that protesters will block any tours planned in South Africa by Ireland, England and Wales which begin later this month; though it is doubtful that they would attempt to ignore a boycott urged by President Mandela.

For big sponsors like Rupert Murdoch, who are funding the multi-million pound Tri-Nations competition between South Africa, New Zealand and Australia, a fortune is at risk.

Silas Nkanunu, SARFU senior vice president and one of the four executive members to resign, said last night that the prospect for rugby was now 'gloom' and that the blame rested squarely with Mr Luyt.

the former National Party government as well as the to-be rulers of the ANC would have done much to phase in the new era effectively.

Instead, there was the figurehead Ebrahim Patel. He was co-president with Craven until the latter's death in January 1993 and thereafter with Fritz Eloff for a total of a year. This was in terms of the unification agreement, which then determined Patel's elevation to executive president for a further year. Ineffective and with a few minor embarrassments coming about in his tenure, Patel was not available for re-election and was succeeded in 1994 by the brilliant and often effective, but rarely diplomatic, Dr Louis Luyt. His tenure was marked by controversies and embarrassments and ended in his ignominious resignation in 1998. Luyt was followed by Silas Nkanunu, a non-rugby man from the ANC elite who didn't convince as a leader, mainly because of his lack of rugby background.

He did little wrong, but also little to be remembered by in furthering the rugby cause. After two terms, Nkanunu made way for Brian van Rooyen whose management style and disregard for business principles ended up in a court case; and that brought in Oregan Hoskins, who made his mistakes but brought relative stability from the commencement of his first term of office in 2006. The ship seemed to be back on course. Because it had been out in the international cold for so long, South African rugby was less prepared for the advent of professionalism in rugby than the other major rugby countries, which also didn't help the transition phase.

The unification that came about was not a spur-of-the-moment occurrence. Craven had worked ceaselessly over many years to better the plight of players of colour by providing developmental aid to them and to achieve a single controlling body. Craven was hamstrung by a lack of funds; an apartheid government that remained unyielding in its approach to 'mixed' rugby, and he had to endure years of humiliation by prime ministers and sports ministers as he pursued his quest to improve the

Brian van Rooyen.

game for all. Even before 1977 he started negotiations with the former coloured rugby body SARU. He followed it up with negotiations with the ANC in the 1980s, where he initially left it to Luyt to make the contact through the assistance of former Springbok captain Tommy Bedford. The (expected) unpleasantness that followed from the government, a number of the SA Rugby Board's affiliated unions and the Afrikaans press did not deter Craven. Backstabbing, two-faced promises and the loss of friends were part of what he endured, but he did have the satisfaction and pleasure of experiencing unification in 1992.

Those were only part of Craven's tribulations due to politics. His contribution, discussed elsewhere with those of his predecessors, laid the foundation for the success until 1992. Then, old and frail, he let go. Craven died on 4 January 1993.

Prof Fritz Eloff, deputy president of the SARB before unification, was interim executive (caretaker) president for the two months following Craven's death. Patel assumed office in March 1993, when he became the first person of colour to hold this position.

'Afrikaans arrogance sours Springboks' taste of victory'

That was the heading of the article by Mick Cleary and Lawrence Donegan on the website www.guardian.co.uk on the 26 June 1995 following remarks by SARFU president Louis Luyt at the post-match dinner after South Africa won the 1995 World Cup in Johannesburg. The article reads as follows:

The rugby world was most definitely not in union yesterday after remarks by South Africa's rugby president, Louis Luyt, reduced a banquet to mark the end of the World Cup tournament to acrimonious farce.

In a speech which resonated with the old Afrikaans arrogance, Mr Luyt proclaimed the victorious Springboks as the first 'true' world champions.

'There were no true world champions in the 1987 and 1991 World Cups because South Africa were not there. We have proved our point,' he said.

This prompted New Zealand's defeated captain, Sean Fitzpatrick, to lead his side out of the dinner – but not before some players had approached the top table to take issue with Mr Luyt.

The All Blacks were quickly followed by the French and English. 'It's disgusting. I cannot believe what he has said,' Mr Fitzpatrick said afterwards.

The South African Rugby Football Union president's remarks spoiled what should have been a day of celebration for 43 million South Africans. Morné du Plessis, manager of the new world champions, led the apologies.

'Tired and emotional are the words that come to mind, though I am not sure that I followed the theme at that part of Mr Luyt's speech,' he said.

'The difference between being winners and being a sorrowful lot is fragile. We were not there in '87 or '91, and I have my personal doubts about us being able to do anything in terms of winning the World Cup in those years.'

Mr Luyt, who is to diplomacy what Jonah Lomu is to English wingers, compounded his country's embarrassment by inexplicably singling out the Welsh referee Derek Bevan – who officiated at the Springboks' crucial semi-final against France – for special praise. The match, which South Africa won 19–15, was marked by controversy after Mr Bevan denied the French a last-minute try because of an infringement.

To the astonishment of the 1,000 diners – and to the Welshman's obvious embarrassment – Mr Luyt presented him with a £1,000 gold watch, calling him 'the most wonderful referee in the world'.

'If everyone does not think that, I certainly do. I would ask him to step up and receive this gift as the outstanding referee in the World Cup,' the SARFU president said.

In the spirit of a rapidly disintegrating social event, the mortified Welshman joined his fellow officials as they staged their own walkout in protest at Mr Luyt's behaviour.

'It was something I could have done without,' Mr Bevan said. 'It came out of the blue: I have no idea why he singled me out. It could be misconstrued, and if that is the case, it leaves a bitter taste.'

Louis Luyt – the highs and lows

Luyt's roller-coaster term was highlighted by some outstanding achievements and a number of political controversies; court cases; the advent of professionalism; and a disgraceful (and controversial) departure from the position after a motion of no-confidence was carried by SARFU.

Luyt, twice as Craven's delegate, attended all three meetings with the ANC – two in Europe and one in Harare. This eventually led to the unification of rugby in the country and initially Luyt found an ally in Steve Tshwete, then minister of sport. But it was not a friendship that lasted, as can be seen from the minister's statement when Luyt was forced to resign on 10 May 1998:

Louis Luyt's departure from the centre-stage of South African rugby has ushered in a breath of fresh air for many rugby-loving people here at home and abroad. His autocratic behaviour and outright arrogance as he presided over the fortunes of one of the country's most treasured assets was a painful embarrassment for rugby in particular and sport in general.

He shall be remembered more by the consistent manner in which he resisted all efforts to take rugby across the threshold into the new era and the way in which he alienated this sport from the majority of our people. Under his autocratic leadership, rugby deteriorated to a point where it had become a divisive instrument in the hands of a man who 'will not bow to any man'.

There is a great deal of work for the new administration. The pieces are scattered all over the place. They must be put together speedily in order to restore lost confidences and loyalties, including the morale of the players at all levels.

Development must not just be talked about. It must be seen to be done in a visible way that marks a break with the past autocratic one-man-show.

Once again, the courage of the executive members and the unions that terminated one of the saddest chapters in the history of rugby must be commended.

Luyt was an enigma. A brilliant businessman, a strong, autocratic character who drove targets with little regard for convention or people, he was also at times infantile in his lack of diplomacy. This included the use of his (competent) children and son-in-law in his projects and undertakings while at the helm of both Transvaal (later the Golden Lions) and SARFU. Included in his plus list are the way in which he orchestrated the hosting of the 1995 World Cup in South Africa; the way he handled the (threatening) breakaway faction of players after the game became professional with the announcement just after the World Cup; his negotiations with the ANC and local (coloured and black) rugby bodies not under the auspices of the controlling body that was at that time the SARB; his ensuring two international rugby tours for South Africa – by the 1986 New Zealand Cavaliers and the combined South Sea team thereafter – without

the knowledge of the SARB; his pre-emption of professionalism when he bought a team of stars, mostly from Northern Transvaal, to satisfy his ambition for the Lions to win the Currie Cup in 1993 and 1994; his dictatorial firing of Ian McIntosh as national coach in 1994 and the Natalian's replacement by Kitch Christie which brought South Africa the spoils in the 1995 World Cup.

Luyt was a self-made man in the true sense of the word. He worked his way to a fortune, played provincial rugby for the Orange Free State over a number of years, including against the touring 1960 All Blacks, and represented Northern Transvaal once. With South Africa in the prime of their forward play, he never made the cut for the national side or the Junior Springboks. Like later presidents Van Rooyen and Hoskins, he was a lock.

Outstanding among his many diplomatic mistakes were two acts at the dinner after the 1995 World Cup final, won 15–12 by South Africa in extra time at Ellis Park in Johannesburg. In a speech described by the New Zealand media as 'boorish', Luyt declared that if they had played, South Africa would have won the previous two Rugby World Cups including the 1987 tournament won by the All Blacks. In response, the All Blacks walked out of the dinner – some of them only after remonstrating with Luyt. The losing semi-finalists, England and France, followed the All Blacks out – and much of the good done by the victory and the national unity achieved was undone. In a second major gaffe, Luyt presented the referee in the Springboks' semi-final against France, Derek Bevan, with an expensive watch for 'being the best referee at the tournament'. This rankled. He was obviously not the best in the eyes of the referee adjudicators. Also, France had lost the semi-final to South Africa in a controversial manner in the dying minutes when Bevan had disallowed a try that would have brought them victory. It severely embarrassed Bevan, as he later admitted. The attending referees and international refereeing administrators also left the dinner.

However, these were diplomatic mistakes – and though it was a major failure in Luyt's business career

Dr DH Craven (1909–1993)

SARFB, SARB and SARFU president 1956–1993   Springbok player 1931–1938, 16 tests
Springbok coach 1949–1956, 23 tests, 17 wins (74%)

Dr Daniël Hartman Craven was undoubtedly the most influential man in the 150-year history of South African rugby. This is underlined by the fact that until his death he was either a player, selector, coach or president of South African rugby for nearly 62 of the 104 years since the establishment of the SARFB, and by the many achievements on his lifelong rugby road.

If it is taken into consideration that for seven years during the Second World War, he was not involved with rugby at national level – despite a huge contribution to the game in Griqualand West where he was based – his dedication to South African rugby is clear.

As a player, he made his test debut as a 21-year-old when he was a member of Bennie Osler's Grand Slam Springboks to the British Isles and Ireland in 1931/32. In all, he played in 16 tests, captaining the Springboks in four of them. He was also the first Springbok to play test match rugby in four positions: as a scrumhalf, flyhalf, centre and No 8 in days when specialisation was paramount and replacements not considered as they are today, when utility players come on as replacements in different positions.

Not the most popular of men in Western Province, where Craven considered the Maties more important than the provincial cause, he was also disliked in the North where he received all the blame for the Springbok selection of Province players to the exclusion of those from the North! This was even more so in the later years when Northern Transvaal dominated the Currie Cup competition.

Craven was the longest-serving president of the SARFB, which later changed its name to the SARB, and in 1992 became the SA Rugby Football Union (SARFU). He served in this capacity from 1956 to 1993 – a period of 37 years.

As national coach, Craven won his first ten matches including four against the All Blacks in 1949; a Grand Slam plus a win against France on the 1951/52 tour; a share of

the spoils against the 1955 British Lions in a four-match series; and three of the tests on the Australasian tour of 1956 against the Wallabies and All Blacks. Of those defeats, three came in the 3–1 series loss to the Kiwis.

He was an outstanding academic and completed three doctorates. He was also awarded an honorary doctorate by the University of Stellenbosch. He often stood up to state presidents, prime ministers, cabinet ministers and the Broederbond and worked for the unification of the SA Rugby Board and the SA Rugby Union, South Africa's two strongest rugby bodies.

Like most leaders, he had a dictatorial streak. He also had a dry sense of humour and an ability to understand people, especially his players. He was not liked by many, but respected by most – even his adversaries.

Craven viewed the Currie Cup as the lifeblood of rugby and the benchmark against which a player was measured. In 1931–32, at the age of 21, Craven became one of the first players to be selected for a Springbok side without having played Currie Cup rugby. To his last days, that was something he treasured! He was a member of the Western Province team that shared the Currie Cup twice with Border in 1932 and 1934. He played Currie Cup rugby for Western Province and captained both these provinces. He also captained Northern Transvaal in 1938, when there was no Currie Cup competition.

Craven excelled as an officer during the Second World War, when he became head of the Physical Training Battalion. His influence on Griquas rugby was especially in developing some of their best players.

His aim in rugby, from an early age, was to 'devote the rest of my life to improving the relationship between the races in whatever way I can. I think that sport will always be the catalyst for true permanent change …'

Danie Craven's famous dive pass in the 1937 series against New Zealand.

where he rode rough-shod over many who dared to oppose him, it was typical of his forceful personality. It is ironic that his downfall as SARFU boss would come through the lies of others – including Tshwete and his director-general, Mthobi Tyamzashe – in a court case in February and March 1998. In a later detailed judgment, Justice De Villiers questioned the credibility of the evidence given by President Mandela.

The case followed accusations made by later president of SARFU, Van Rooyen, after he had been beaten 55–3 by Luyt when he opposed him for the Gauteng Lions Rugby Union's presidency in 1997. On the grounds of these charges, a commission was appointed to investigate SARFU – and it was with a vote of 18–4 that SARFU decided to challenge the validity of the commission. Two of the four votes were from Mluleki George of Border and Silas Nkanunu of Eastern Province – both staunch elites, as Luyt called them, of the ANC.

Mandela's subpoena came from the presiding judge Justice Willem de Villiers and not Luyt, who was blamed by an acrimonious press and the government and its institutions such as the National Sports Council (NSC).

The application by SARFU was successful and set aside Mandela's decision to appoint a commission of enquiry.

George, who had failed miserably to oust Luyt as SARFU president at the 1997 AGM, had since become president of the NSC and made it obvious that the control of rugby in the country by his body was of paramount importance to him. The NSC signalled its intent to prevent future test matches, the Super 12 competition and the scheduled visits of Ireland, Wales and England unless the executive of SARFU fired Luyt.

According to Luyt, the late Bill Jardine, Gauteng president of the NSC, vowed to continue the war against rugby. He gave SARFU until 7 May to decide to rid itself of Luyt and fall into step with the NSC and the government's demands, writes Luyt in his autobiography, or face a boycott of international tours and the scrapping of the Springbok emblem.

On 7 May, a crisis meeting of SARFU at Ellis Park passed a motion of no confidence (22 votes to 15) in Luyt who declined to resign. He first had to go through the appeal by the ANC against Justice de Villiers' verdict, he said. Four black members of SARFU left the room in protest.

Silas Nkanunu – first black president of SARFU

But Luyt, reconsidering, sent his letter of resignation on 10 May and Silas Nkanunu became the first black president of SARFU at the AGM at the end of the year. Politics had taken its toll, and as Nkanunu had earlier predicted to Luyt, the law of the jungle applied henceforth. No white administrator has since made himself available for the position of president of SARFU. Only André Markgraaff, who lost his position as national coach because of racist remarks, filled the position under Van Rooyen as deputy president, but he resigned before the end of his term.

Nkanunu and Luyt had their run-ins, but the lawyer and later advocate of the Eastern Cape generally had a calm tenure at the top. He was elected unopposed in 1998 and again for the next two-year term in August 2001, but withdrew from the election race at the end of 2003 at the last moment – and deserves respect for the reasons of his late unavailability. 'I'm happy that I'm walking out of that door with my head held high,' he said in his last address.

Before he announced his decision to withdraw from the election race at the SARFU AGM in 2003, Nkanunu delivered SARFU's annual report and took partial responsibility for the recent crisis in South African rugby. 'Leadership needs to take responsibility when things go wrong,' he said, 'and I accept responsibility, not for causing the problems, but that it happened during my tenure.'

Van Rooyen succeeded Nkanunu on 5 December 2003. Nkanunu, rightly or wrongly, was blamed for the fiasco in 2003 when the Springboks were ousted in the quarterfinal of the World Cup in Australia – and was the last of the many leading members from his administration to fall from grace in the aftermath of the *Kamp Staaldraad* scandal. Nkanunu's withdrawal came a day after the resignation of Springbok coach Rudolf Straeuli and managing director Rian Oberholzer because of the *Kamp Staaldraad* episode.

Nkanunu and Oberholzer departed in acrimonious circumstances but left a healthy balance sheet as legacy. SARFU recorded a net profit of R4,9 million for the financial year to 30 September 2003 which increased the union's accumulated reserves to R47,7 million.

How much of a non-rugby figurehead Nkanunu was can be gathered from the following incidents. He publicly confused Springbok flank André Venter and captain André Vos. When Corné Krige was caught up in traffic in France in 2002, the president called on Bob Skinstad to do the after-match speech in the captain's absence – Skinstad was in South Africa, recovering from injury! His most serious clanger, however, was not in public, but in an address to the Springboks after they had defeated reigning World Cup champions Australia in 2003. The outstanding win came just before the 2003 World Cup and in one of South Africa's darkest years. Nkanunu, who was in the Boks' change room, climbed into them for their 'inept performance' – and did much damage to the confidence of a team that was at a low.

The outgoing president warned his successor that '2004 is going to be a difficult year. The Springboks will always be the yardstick. I must admit we failed here. We (also) failed to deliver on our promise of transformation. It is a responsibility I accept with a heavy heart,' said Nkanunu.

Brian van Rooyen – a rugby man through and through

Brian van Rooyen could be – and was – accused of many things, including maladministration, but unlike his predecessor Nkanunu, the jovial Van Rooyen was a rugby man through and through. A former player and official of Eldoronians Club of the former Transvaal Independent Rugby Football Union (TIRFU,) Van Rooyen was a heart-and-soul club rugby man, but like his predecessors Nkanunu and Patel, he was also not geared for the post that awaited him.

Van Rooyen had a controversial two-year reign as South Africa rugby's president. There were allegations

Oregan Hoskins.

Peter de Villiers.

of financial mismanagement, poor corporate governance and favouritism directed at him. The feeling was that Van Rooyen was more concerned with his position than protecting the interests of the players – and this came back to haunt him. The new professionalism, still in its first decade, had given the players new powers. The players' association indicated their disenchantment with Van Rooyen as president by a 67,1% vote in favour of Hoskins.

Van Rooyen also offered political favours to gather support, such as awarding Rustenburg an All Blacks test when unions that opposed him, the KZN and Free State Rugby Unions, were left with scraps or no tests at all. And like too many rugby managers and leaders of late he often contradicted himself, complaining that South Africa's rugby players were playing too many games and then arranging additional test matches and even committing the touring Springboks to play a match against a World XV in England.

The fact that Van Rooyen had been asked to step down at the end of 2004 indicated that he would have little hope of warding off the challenge from Oregan Hoskins at the AGM in February 2006. SA Rugby's major sponsors – Vodacom, Sasol, Canterbury and Absa – even

threatened to withdraw their sponsorship should Van Rooyen be re-elected in 2006.

He remained defiant, however, and went into the election against Hoskins who predictably became the new president. Van Rooyen was adamant that his mistakes, as highlighted by two reports on bad corporate governance, were honest ones and that there was never any intention to defraud SA Rugby. Nor were there financial losses because of that.

Oregan Hoskins brings stability

Like his predecessors, Oregan Hoskins has made his mistakes – mistakes of judgement as well as diplomacy. But that the lawyer – or rather, former lawyer as he now concentrates full-time on his job as president – has brought a stability to SARU is not to be denied.

Hoskins succeeded Brian van Rooyen in 2006. The latter had the support of deputy president Mike Stofile who worked hard to see Van Rooyen retain his position. The ensuing two-year stint at the top between two adversaries was therefore not a happy one, but Hoskins persevered. Then, in his re-election in 2008, Hoskins fought off the ambition of Stofile who, it must be said, was obviously there for politics rather than rugby. His brother, the Rev Makhenkesi Stofile, was after all the sports minister with little sympathy for rugby's cause.

It was a bitter tussle. It is said that Stofile was assisted in his campaign by current president of the EP Rugby Union, Cheeky Watson, the controversial – and very competent – administrator who now heads the Southern Kings' cause and fought them into a guaranteed spot in the Super Rugby competition. Their promised participation will come into being in 2013. Van Rooyen also worked behind the scenes to get Stofile elected. But it was to no avail, and Hoskins carried the day by a single vote. That prompted Stofile's statement that there is no place for a black man in South African rugby.

Hoskins came into power helped by the vote of the five Super Rugby franchises: the Bulls, Stormers, Sharks, Lions and Cheetahs (the latter two were then still a combined side, the Cats). His support by the franchises was based on the express mandate to keep the Eastern Cape franchise, the Southern Spears, out of the Super 14. (The franchise changed its name to the Southern Kings in 2009). Van Rooyen had promised the Spears a place in the Super Rugby competition during his term (hence the support of Watson to see Van Rooyen back in power).

The existing franchises' proviso for supporting Hoskins was based on the fact that the Spears would have to replace one of the current five sides in the Super Rugby competition. Hoskins did his best, but after his election, SA Rugby lost multiple High Court applications. Judge Dennis Davis, in a final blow to SA Rugby, ruled in favour of the Southern Spears, declaring that SA Rugby had behaved unethically and unlawfully and that the Spears had a legal and binding agreement to play Super Rugby. Spears will join the Super Rugby competition as the Southern Kings in 2013.

One of Hoskins' other miscalculations was admitting at the announcement of Peter de Villiers as coach that the new national coach had not been picked for rugby reasons alone. With no track record of note except a

horrendous run with the Valke, and languishing in lower league coaching in the Western Cape, it came as a surprise that De Villiers was appointed over a man like Heyneke Meyer who had the record, credentials and respect worthy of the position. De Villiers has proved to be a great embarrassment to SARU with some strange utterances to the media.

Hoskins was also outspoken in that he believed there to be an anti-South African bias in the IRB, and – many would say rightly! – accused Australian and New Zealand referees in particular, saying 'Australia and New Zealand need to look at their referees when it comes to games involving South Africa'. This view probably counted in De Villiers' favour when he intimated that with two of his infamous quotes:

Speaking to IRB referee's boss Paddy O'Brien is a complete waste of time ... People don't want to see other teams being successful. That is my biggest problem at the moment. We can't go public about certain things because we don't have all the evidence, but the body language of certain officials when things went against us in that game made us worry ... The officials were so happy when decisions went against us on the day.

And having taken back-to-back drubbings by the All Blacks, De Villiers implied on Australian TV that leniency was deliberately shown towards the All Blacks by the referee:

I've got my own observations about the last two Tests, and maybe I can't say it in public, but we do have a World Cup in New Zealand next year and maybe it was the right thing for them to win the games so they can attract more people to the games next year.

He had to face a SANZAR disciplinary for the latter on a charge of misconduct but was found not guilty.

Other more humorous quotes include the following:

I'm a God-given talent, I'm the best I can ever be. So what you think doesn't bother me. I know what I am and I don't give a damn;

and

What I learnt in South Africa is, if you take your car to a garage and the owner is black or a black man, and they mess it up, you never go back to that garage. If the owner is white, you say ag, sorry, they made a mistake and you go back again. This is how some people live their lives in this country.

Quotas – the enforced inclusion of a number of players of colour in teams – have officially been abolished at all levels of rugby in South Africa under Hoskins. The racial policies upset not only the white players who had been excluded for weaker players of colour, but also the latter who were aware that they had not reached the required level yet and felt slighted by their inclusion. Hoskins has, however, encouraged the South African Super 14 teams, and the national team, to involve a higher number of black players and under the policy of transformation the youth weeks still require a minimum number of players of colour.

It is ironic – and perhaps indicative of the rift between coloureds and blacks in rugby administration – that the hostile Mike Stofile was outspoken about the retention of quotas in August 2009 while Hoskins, who was in charge of the abolishment in his term, reportedly wanted them reinstated.

'We would be crazy to bring back a quota system,' Stofile said. 'It is definitely not the solution. If it comes back on SA Rugby's agenda, I will be the first to reject it.' Stofile said he believed it 'unfair towards black players' to expose them to such measures.

SARU's conflict with the government continued and at one stage the interference of the government included the insistence of the Parliamentary Portfolio Committee for Sport that Hoskins and his executive resign. There was also the continued feud between the 2007 World Cup winning coach Jake White and SARU after White was told to apply to retain his position – despite White's arguing that his contract made provision that he need not reapply.

The feud followed White's autobiography in which he openly attacked SARU, so the stand-off didn't come as a surprise. Then there was the matter of Luke Watson's inclusion in the Springbok squad without White's knowledge. Watson, controversial in many ways and also disliked by many whites for the perceived sins of his father, Cheeky, who was always outspoken against apartheid and played for the black controlling body, the SA African Rugby Association, was viewed as too small and not good enough by White. There is no doubt that he was of international standard but perhaps not the best in his position.

Strange actions and statements could therefore be held against Hoskins, but the good that flowed from his tenure came at the right time. He was re-elected for a third term which has been extended from two years to four. Mark Alexander, an astute businessman from Johannesburg and a rugby man of many years standing, was also re-elected as deputy president and has had much to do with the new-found stability. It's ironic that the two colleagues from the previous term were due to challenge for the same position, but in the interests of South African rugby, Alexander withdrew his nomination.

4

Segregation, frustration and infighting

The history of multiracial rugby in South Africa

More than 50 years before apartheid became official policy under the National Party government, 'black' and 'coloured' players played their rugby in segregation and weren't considered for white sides at any level.

It should be made clear at this point that the need for the use of the terms 'black' and 'coloured' to differentiate between black players for the period before unification in 1992 is unavoidable. References to coloured, black and white players and organisations, as well as to Africans, 'Bantu' and 'Native' are not made in the political context; it is done to differentiate between the various groups that formed different controlling bodies for divergent reasons, and reflects the names that were used at the time to identify them. The name of the white SARFB had a gradual transition until it was generally called the SARB with no fixed date to mark this change although SARB became official in 1979. Likewise, the other controlling bodies over time changed their names which until the 1970s and 1980s included 'Coloured' and 'African' for purposes of identification. In 1992 all the controlling rugby bodies were finally united in the SA Rugby Football Union.

Complete records of the game as played under the various black and coloured controlling bodies were either not kept or have been lost over the years. A detailed account of the development of the game is therefore not possible, and the reported facts that follow have been obtained from accessible records as well as from individuals. What is clear, however, is that justice cannot be done to the rich history of coloured and black rugby in a single chapter of a book.

The Transvaal Bantu Rugby Football Union team – winners of the NRC Cup and Partons Knock-out Cup at the 1944 tournament in Cape Town.

We do know that the coloureds were obliged to form their own controlling bodies to

Dan Qeqe – more than just talk

The Eastern Cape set the tone for black rugby in South Africa – and it was in no small way thanks to the efforts of Dan Qeqe and his love of the game.

His involvement was not limited to rugby. In the 1970s, he was also active in trying to establish non-racial sport generally in the Eastern Cape, particularly cricket.

And Qeqe wasn't all talk. When the Bantu Administration Board denied him access to sports grounds for black teams, he rallied the community to build his own stadium where both rugby and cricket were played. Qeqe designed the grandstand himself, copying the stand at Healdtown, and with the stadium caretaker, Nyawuza, and local labour he helped to build the structure that became the stadium where cricket and rugby thrived. (Healdtown, which had a name change to Healdtown Comprehensive School in the 1990s, is a Methodist school near Fort Beaufort in the Eastern Cape where rugby and other sports were played.)

A substantial financial donation for the building of the stadium, on land which had been secured from a Port Elizabeth motor company, was received from US civil rights activist, Reverend Jesse Jackson.

Qeqe also campaigned for better living conditions and was regarded as a political activist who was detained by the Security Branch of the South African Police. As a deacon of the Edward Memorial Congregational Church, Qeqe also helped to build two churches in Motherwell and kwaMagxaki townships.

Qeqe, a very good hooker, first started playing rugby for Spring Rose in the early 1950s. He climbed through various ranks, from player to coach and then administrator – and was an astute businessman. He led the movement to establish non-racial sports through the development of unrecognised black youth talent in the townships of New Brighton, kwaZakhele, Fort Beaufort and Uitenhage – and was the leading reason for rugby being elevated into a near-cult sport. Qeqe remained Spring Rose's club treasurer up to his death.

Known as the King of Rugby in the Eastern Cape, the word legend aptly describes this man who died in 2005, aged 76.

keep the game going under the British rule of the 1880s and 1890s in the Cape Colony. And just how serious they were about rugby is reflected by the establishment of the Western Province Union (WPU) as early as 1886 – just three years after the Western Province Rugby Football Union and before any other union in South Africa. Blacks also played rugby in segregation in the Eastern Cape.

Kimberley's historic place in South African rugby was given further impetus when the official controlling body of coloured rugby was formed there in 1896 – just as SARFU was seven years before. Kimberley also became the headquarters for the SA Coloured Rugby Football Board (SACRFB).

The Kimberley factor in South African rugby was taken a step further when, in 1898, SACRFB's first provincial tournament was held there. This tournament had the same provinces taking part that contested the SARFB competition in Kimberley in 1889, namely Griquas, Western Province, Transvaal and Eastern Province – and the logical conclusion is that not all the participants in that tournament were coloureds. Eastern Province and to a lesser extent Transvaal's 'non-white' rugby was then dominated by black players of whom a few would probably have been included in the respective sides.

Rugby was also played by blacks in the Eastern Cape in the late 1880s where it was introduced to the Xhosa people by the British settlers and regiments stationed in the area to 'protect' the settlers from the indigenous people. Club rugby among the Xhosas was very popular and some of the oldest clubs in South African rugby were founded in the Eastern Cape – many of them the so-called 'Bantu' or 'black' clubs of that era.

The first provincial controlling body of black rugby was the Eastern Province Native Rugby Board (EPNRB), established in 1905. The SA Bantu Rugby Board only came about in 1935 – but intercity matches, local provincial club leagues and even provincial competitions took place as far back as the 1880s.

The first official black provincial tournament was held in 1936 – and where else but in Kimberley! Three of the four provinces that played in the first SARFB tournament in 1889, and also the SACRFB in 1898, were present at this first black tournament with North Eastern Cape joining Griquas, Transvaal and Eastern Province. The latter two sides played in the final which ended in a scoreless draw.

Both the coloured and the black controlling bodies at various stages had visions of touring abroad as their players had no chance of doing so with the national side, the Springboks. As far as can be ascertained, little was done to try and incorporate the black and coloured bodies into the SARFB, which was the officially recognised controlling body affiliated to the IRB. Aspirations of non-white players to play at the top level, however, remained a dream in the two British colonies of Natal and the Cape, and the two republics of ZAR (Transvaal) and the Orange Free State. Efforts to tour continued after the end of the South African War, under the continued British rule – and well after the Union of South Africa came about in 1910.

The colonial authorities did not entertain the idea of including black or coloured players in any SARFB team. The behind-the-scenes politicking for the formation of

Eastern Cape – a history of disruption

The Eastern Cape, where rugby was almost a religion has an unfortunate history of disruption and squabbles. Fraud; misappropriation of funds; arguments about money; faction disagreements and breakaways; election procedures; disciplinary action ending in court cases; and spectator uprising that led to deaths all helped to make rugby in this area an unstable sport. Some tournaments ended in chaos, with teams or players not arriving; players leaving the pitch because of disagreements with the referees' decisions; and officials being expelled.

In 1969, under the auspices of the SA African Rugby Board, a chaotic tournament was held in Umtata. As a result, prominent people expelled included influential Norris Singapi, Alfred Dwesi and Curnick Mdyesha. In 1970, the Supreme Court set aside these expulsions and the disruptions were partly halted.

In 1982, the cricket icon Eric Majola passed away. Spring Rose Rugby Club, whose chairman was the famous Dan Qeqe, requested that a match be postponed so that those who wished to could attend Majola's funeral. When the Port Elizabeth African Rugby Board then proceeded to take action against those who had attended the funeral, ten of the 12 clubs in the first division broke away and

formed the kwaZakhele Rugby Union (KWARU) that then joined with the coloured body, the SA Rugby Union (SARU) under Abass.

The latter was a non-racial body that challenged the existing rugby order and was also one of the founding members of the SA Council of Sport (SACOS). This defection by KWARU to the coloured bodies (cricket followed suit) gave rise to further divisions in black sport. However, SACOS and the SA Cricket Board of Control (SACBOC), wouldn't accept the purely black clubs that wanted to join as an entity, as they viewed this as a continuation of racial policy – and slowly coloureds joined black clubs and vice versa.

Mono Badela was the chairman of the newly formed KWARU. Six years later, in 1977, he was replaced on the grounds of misappropriation of funds by Dumile Kondile, who in turn made way for Silas Nkanunu. (He became the first black person to be elected as president of the SA Rugby Football Union after Louis Luyt was ousted.) Nkanunu, in turn, was opposed as chairman of KWARU by Amon Nyondo. This led to another split – and was the reason why four teams played on the same field at the same time. (See Two matches on one field! on page 74)

Errol Tobias becomes the first non-white Bok

Errol Tobias sealed his place in South African rugby history by becoming the first black player to start a test match for the Springboks, when he faced Ireland at Newlands on 30 May 1981.

He was 31 when he made his debut – and had the misfortune of playing for South Africa at a time when the Springboks arguably had their best back line in history, with flyhalf Naas Botha and inside centre Willie du Plessis the two players who denied him more than his six caps.

Ironically, it was Du Plessis' injury in 1981 that gave the man from Caledon his – and coloured rugby's – big break; and Botha's departure for Dallas to try out for the Dallas Cowboys gave him his last two caps.

Just as ironic was the fact that a large portion of the country's coloured people was opposed to him playing for the Springboks. Tobias was seen as a sell-out and was accused of collaborating with the whites and failing to make a stand against apartheid. And in a no-win situation, Tobias's selection also didn't please the die-hard rightist elements! They simply did not want a player of colour anywhere near the international team.

Tobias, without any doubt, was not a token selection.

He was a strong-running flyhalf with an eye for the gap and the rare ability to off-load with his hands through the gap, well ahead of him. Tobias helped the Boks' gifted back line (which included players like Danie Gerber and Carel du Plessis) to 12 tries in his six tests. He played in only three test series, however, mainly due to the presence of Botha.

In 1971, Tobias toured England with the so-called Pro-teas, the 'national' side of the breakaway coloured body, the SA Rugby Football Federation. He toured the UK in 1979 with the SA Barbarians. In 1981, he toured New Zealand on the infamous demonstration-ridden tour but failed to make the test side. Tobias retired in 1984 at the age of 34, having played 15 times for the Springboks, including six test matches. He scored 22 points in those tests, from one try, four penalties and three conversions.

Speaking about his years at the top some 20 years later, Tobias said that all he knew about at that stage was to play rugby. 'We had no say in politics. We didn't even have a vote, so all I knew at that stage was to play rugby. My goal was to show the country and the rest of the world that we had black players who were as good, if not better, than the whites, and that if you are good enough you should play.'

the Union of South Africa on 31 May 1910 continued the policies of segregation of the 1800s under British rule and played a major role in allowing the foundations of apartheid to be laid. In the new Union of South Africa each of the four new provinces (Cape Province, Natal, the Orange Free State and Transvaal) kept its existing franchise qualifications – and the Cape was the only one that permitted voting by (property-owning) non-whites.

A delegation of white and black liberals travelled to London, under the leadership of the former Cape Prime Minister William Schreiner (who was also the president of SARFB from 1913–1915), to protest against the colour bar which was enshrined in the new 1910 constitution. But it interested the British government little; they were more concerned with creating a unified country within

the British Empire that could support and defend itself.

The blacks and coloureds remained marginalised. And it was to become worse in the next few years. The Natives' Land Act of 1913 was the first major piece of segregation legislation passed by the Union Parliament, and created a system of land tenure that deprived the majority of South Africa's inhabitants of the right to own land outside of reserves which had major socio-economic repercussions. This impacted on rugby where sports fields were no longer available and societies were removed from their homes and resettled elsewhere.

Laws end hopes for rugby co-operation
The abovementioned Natives' Land Act of 1913 was an

extension of the segregationist legislation of the 1880s and particularly the Franchise and Ballot Act (1892): the Natal Legislative Assembly Bill (1894), which deprived Indians of the right to vote; the General Pass Regulations Bill (1905), which denied blacks the vote and limited them to fixed areas and inaugurating the infamous Pass System; the Asiatic Law Amendment Act (1907) that required all Indians to register and carry passes; the South Africa Act (1910) that enfranchised whites, giving them complete political control over all other race groups. It was followed by the Natives in Urban Areas Bill (1918), which was designed to move blacks living in 'white' South Africa into specific 'locations' as a precautionary security measure; the Native (Urban Areas Act) (1923), which formally introduced residential segregation in South Africa; and the Representation of Natives Act (1936), which removed blacks altogether from the Cape voters' roll.

The legislation in 1923 that formally introduced residential segregation was a death knell to any hopes of people of colour to be incorporated into the official (IRB-recognised) rugby system in South Africa under the SARFB.

The ensuing days until 1992, when rugby unity came about and the various bodies amalgamated as the SA Rugby Union, were marked by continued segregation, bitterness, acrimony, boycotts and infighting. The continual breakaways and dissent, however, were not between the bodies of the various race groups, but rather the result of differing views and power struggles. And it was only after 1992 that all players who weren't white or Asian were referred to as 'black'.

The first coloured Springbok

However, 11 years before unity in 1992, flyhalf/centre Errol Tobias became the first player of colour to be selected for the Springboks. He made his debut in 1981. Ironically, he had to wait for his debut in the revered green jersey of the Springboks as his first test match was against Ireland

in Cape Town. In those days, the visiting side had the honour of playing in their traditional colours while the home side had to adapt – and Ireland played in green!

Tobias was 31 – and he was selected on merit. Three years later, wing Avril Williams followed when he played against South America – but it would be another 12 years after Tobias's debut before the third coloured player would be capped.

That was when Chester Williams made his debut in the second test against Argentina during South Africa's first test series against the Pumas in 1993. Thinus Linee, a strong-running centre, also received his Bok colours for touring to Argentina but didn't play in a test.

Owen Nkumane, now a well-known rugby commentator, became the first black Springbok after unification when he toured the British Isles and Ireland with the Boks in 1998, but he didn't play in any test matches.

These selections were the breakthrough. There was, however, a South African legacy of a hundred years

Chester Williams.

SA Barbarians* – mixing it up on tour

In October 1979, just less than two years after the SARFB, the SA Rugby Federation and the SA Rugby Association merged to become the SA Rugby Board, Springbok Rob Louw took the SA Barbarians rugby team on its first tour overseas, to the UK. This was the first sanctioned multiracial tour by a South African side.

The tour squad had eight white players from the former SARFB, eight coloured players from the former SARFF and eight black players from what was formally SARA.

Seven fixtures were played, the Baa-Baas won four, lost one against Hawick, and drew one against the Scottish Border Club that included ten full Scottish internationals. Results were as follows: Devon (Exeter), won 27–18 Cornwall (Camborne), won 23–7 Scottish Border Club (Galashiels), drew 20–20 Co-Optimists (Hawick), lost 4–24 Coventry, won 41–24 Llanelli, won 15–6 Newport, lost 15–21.

The strength of the touring side and the value from a playing point of view can be gauged by the fact that seven of the touring side became Springboks in the next two years. Orange Free State prop Martiens le Roux, Northern Transvaal hooker Ewoud Malan, Rob Louw and Divan Serfontein (both Western Province) all played in the tests against Bill Beaumont's 1980 British Lions. The touring SA Barbarians side included Errol Tobias who became South Africa's first non-white Springbok 1981. Western Province locks Hennie

Bekker and De Villiers Visser played on the 'demonstration tour' to New Zealand in 1981.

In 1980, 17 of the 24 Baa-Baas in the side to the UK played against the touring Lions. This included a match between the Lions and the SA Baa-Baas. Five of the 1979 tour as well as the Argentine flyhalf Hugo Porta and former Australian loose forward Mark Loane opposed the British Lions.

Two coloured players, Errol Tobias and Charles Williams who were on the 1979 Barbarians tour to the UK, were selected for the Junior Springboks to play against the visiting British Barbarians in 1980. They were the first two players of colour to represent a national South African side since the establishment of the SARFB 91 years before.

The 1979 Barbarians' eight black players were Morgan Cushe, Timothy Nkonki, Lillee Jonas, Sydney Ncate, Bridgman Sonto, Welcome Mtyongwe, Solomon Mhlaba and Arthur Poro. The SAARB also provided the assistant manager, Alfred Dwesi. The coloured players from the SARFF were Hennie and Turkey Shields, Nicky Davids, Charles Williams, Louis Paulse, Hanne Meyer, Errol Tobias and Pompies Williams. The team was coached by the Federation's Dougie Dyers.

This first multiracial tour did not, however, satisfy the world. In South Africa these players, as members of two bodies that had amalgamated with the SARFB, were seen as sell-outs by the SA Rugby Union members who stuck to their slogan of 'no normal

sport in an abnormal society' that was in line with the stance taken by other anti-apartheid sports bodies, such as SACOS and SACBOC. This reverberated throughout the world and the SA Barbarians side under Rob Louw had more than their fair share of demonstrations to contend both on and off the field. British and European reporters were continually seeking information on the social aspects of the tour, and went to the lengths of climbing up drain pipes to see whether the tourists were mixing in their hotel rooms!

This tour by the SA Barbarians was in many ways a breakthrough, stimulating multiracial rugby at all but international (test) levels. The role of the SA Barbarians in expediting multiracial rugby was important. Five years later, the SA Barbarians undertook their second overseas tour, this time to West Germany. The squad of 25 players included 12 white and 13 coloured and black players on a tour where the opposition was poor. In four matches, the Barbarians scored 314 points and conceded only 27. In 1988, a multiracial side undertook a six-match visit to Chile and Paraguay in another series of one-sided games.

*The South African Barbarians were formed in 1960. They first played as a combined All Black and Springbok team under the Bok captain Avril Malan in a fixture versus Natal during the All Blacks' tour to South Africa in 1960. Their highlight was probably in 1969, when they beat the famous British Barbarians in Port Elizabeth.

which was the foundation for these coloured and black pioneers to eventually make their mark in international rugby.

Black rugby in South Africa started in the Eastern Cape. After the settlers had brought the roots of the game to South Africa in various formats such as the Winchester Rules game, the major influence on rugby in the Eastern Cape came from the missionaries and the schools – and in many instances, these two institutions were one and the same, such as St Philip's Mission School whose past scholars went on to play for the Winter Rose Rugby Club in Grahamstown. Schools where the game was played were at Healdtown, Fort Hare and St Matthews, to name just three.

Grahamstown, as a town of education – as it still is today – was therefore one of the major seats of rugby in the region. Black people played informally in the 1880s. The first black team was Winter Rose Rugby Club which was established in 1887 but only officially formed in 1891.

Lily White Rugby Club is the second oldest club in Grahamstown and was established by Rev White in 1894. The club was formed by black students at St Andrew's College. Even though they attended the same school, they were not allowed to play in the same team as their fellow white pupils.

However, these clubs and others in Grahamstown followed in the footsteps of the oldest black club – Union in Port Elizabeth. Union was established in 1887. Their home ground was in kwaMpundu, and a breakaway from Union saw the establishment of Frontiers. However, this breakaway came only after the second club, Orientals, was formed in 1894.

Initially Union played against coloured clubs in Port Elizabeth, but the advent of Orientals brought about a continual battle for black club supremacy that stretched over many years.

Tigers, established in 1895, was a club from Somerset East – and because their only other (black) competition was many miles away, they had frequent matches against the white team from that town. However, from time to time, they also played at Cookhouse, 40 km away – and they covered this distance by foot until 1926, when they first had the use of a lorry! (To put this into perspective: a standard marathon is 42 km!)

Fort Hare v Transvaal universities

One of the highlights in later years was the match between a combined team from Fort Hare and Lovedale that played a combined Transvaal universities side (probably Tuks and Wits) in 1935. The match was played at Alice, the headquarters of Fort Hare. In 1901, a tradition was started when the first of the Easter tournaments was held in Grahamstown. The first tournament only had four participating teams, namely Grahamstown, East London, Midlands and Port Elizabeth, but it slowly grew in stature and size. The popularity of the game, and its expansion, made it necessary to better formalise rugby in the Eastern Cape – and the Eastern Province Native Rugby Board (EPNRB), established in 1905, was the result of these early tournaments.

Easter tournaments

The Easter tournament concept continued on and off in various centres over the ensuing years – but in the last few years it has been resurrected on a more formal basis with the intervention of SARU. The tournaments in Langa, Soweto, Kimberley, Peddie, Mangaung and elsewhere have now re-established themselves as an annual highlight of township teams. 'Tournaments such as the one in Langa are part of a rich culture in township rugby,' said Xhanti Lamani, SA Rugby's manager for club rugby in 2008. 'They are part of our mission to broaden the base of rugby at community level, and revive the old spirit of Easter rugby festivities in the townships.' Over Easter 2011 the Universal Club of Kimberley celebrated their 125th anniversary with a well-attended tournament.

The names of the many controlling bodies

SARFB – South African Rugby Football Board, established in 1889 and the recognised body affiliated to the International Rugby Board (IRB). The name gradually changed in general use by the public and press, but only became official in November 1977 at the amalgamation with the SACRFF and SARU (see below).

SACRFB – South African Coloured Rugby Football Board. This was the original controlling body for coloured rugby, formed in 1896. In 1977, under then president Dullah Abass, the SACRFB wouldn't amalgamate with the other coloured (SARFF), black (SAARB) and the IRB-recognised white body SARFB who selected their teams along colour lines. The SACRFB over time changed its name to SACRB and then to SARU (SA Rugby Union).

SACRFF – South African Coloured Rugby Football Federation. This was the body formed in 1959 after an acrimonious breakaway from the SACRFB. The name was changed to SARFF (SA Rugby Football Federation). The president was Cuthbert Loristen and he and the rest of the Federation were seen as sell-outs by the SACRB/SARU because they were prepared to join under the unification of the SARB in 1977 whose teams still selected along colour lines.

SABRB – SA Bantu Rugby Board, the original national controlling body, established in 1935. Only in 1982 did SARA (SA Rugby Association) start selecting players who were not Xhosas for their test side. Earlier, because of ethnicity, the SABRB first became the SAARB (SA African Rugby Board) and then the SARA, the latter probably in 1978.

EPNRB – Eastern Province Native Rugby Board, it was established in 1905. It was the first controlling body for black rugby in the Eastern Cape.

SARFU – SA Rugby Football Union. The body after unification in 1992. The name was changed to SARU (SA Rugby Union) in 2005.

SABRB's interprovincial tournaments

Gradually intertown tournaments followed the early interdistrict competitions, and in 1936 the first provincial tournament under the auspices of the newly formed SA Bantu Rugby Board was held. The SABRB was established in Kimberley the previous year, like its predecessors SARFB and the SACRFB nearly 40 years before. JM Dippa was the first chairman and the secretary was Halley Plaatje.

The migrant black workers to the mines in the Transvaal and also to the employment market in the Western Cape carried the gospel of rugby to those areas – and also played themselves. The result was that Transvaal fielded a very good side in the first provincial tournament in which they held favourites Eastern Province to a scoreless draw in the first provincial final to share the Native Recruitment Cup (NRC), presented by the Chamber of Mines.

In the following two years, the NRC Cup, as it was called, was won by Eastern Province but relative newcomers to the provincial scene, North Eastern Districts surprised everyone when they won the title in 1939.

In later years, the NRC Cup was only presented to the winner of the league phase, with the overall winner receiving the Graham Remedies Trophy after the final. This trophy was later renamed the Partons Cup for unknown reasons.

The NRC Cup, donated by the Chamber of Mines, was abolished as a provincial trophy in the 1950s because of the exploitation of black labour by the mines.

The cost of hosting the tournaments saw the provincial tournament take place less and less frequently. In 1973, after a number of years without a tournament, the competition was done away with. A total of 28 tournaments in 38 years tells the story of inter-provincial rugby between black sides.

Of the 28 tournaments, Eastern Province won 11 – and to underline the status of the Eastern Cape as the stronghold of black rugby, Border won the title five times and shared it with Transvaal in 1949. Griquas and North Eastern Districts (once each), Transvaal (three times, one shared with Border) and Western Province (four times) were the other winners, with no titles awarded in 1956 and

1969 – the latter because of chaotic organisation.

In 1975, the provincial tournament for black players was replaced by the Bols Brandy Competition on a home-and-away basis, along the lines of the Currie Cup. The first final in the new (decentralised) round-robin competition in 1975 saw Eastern Province underline their supremacy by winning the final against what had been the second best side through the years – Border – 12–7.

However, well before that, the first test between players of the SACRFB and the SABRB took place. It was played at the Port Elizabeth Showgrounds in 1950, and according to available records more than 15 000 spectators attended the test between the sides that both called themselves the Springboks. The Bantu Springboks came out of this first clash with a 14–3 win because of a sharper back line that more than made up for the hammering their forwards took at the hands of the bigger coloured Springbok forwards.

It is interesting to note that the Bantu side's captain was one Grant Khomo. A versatile sportsman – he was also a black soccer and tennis Springbok – he later became president of the SA Rugby Association and held the position from 1970 to 1975.

The SA Rugby Association (SARA) was the new name for the SA Bantu Rugby Board, which was later changed to the SA African Rugby Board (SAARB). The now famous provincial schools week for Under-16 rugby players is named after this stalwart of black rugby and is known as the Grant Khomo Week.

'Mini' merger

Curnick Mdyesha succeeded Khomo as president, and was at the helm from 1975–1985. During this period SARA amalgamated with the SARFB under Dr Danie Craven, and Cuthbert Loristen's SA Rugby Football Federation (SARFF), which was a breakaway from the SACRFB that controlled coloured rugby in South Africa. This 'mini' merger in November 1977 saw the bodies controlling players of colour accepted into the mainstream

Cuthbert Loristen.

competitions under the new name of the SA Rugby Board (SARB).

Under their strong president, Dullah Abass, the decision of the SA Rugby Union (which had been renamed from the SA Coloured Rugby Football Board) not to be part of the unification process was foreseeable when the then minister of sport, Piet Koornhof, declared that mixed rugby at all levels would never be allowed. SARU's stance in keeping to their slogan remained: 'No normal sport in an abnormal society'. It meant that their players were still not allowed to play for composite black and coloured sides, and sides mixed with white players against touring international teams, as had been allowed by the South African government since England's visit for their one-test tour in 1972.

In the 1970s, the SAARB and the SARFB had moved closer to one another – and the continual pressure by Craven on the government to relent resulted in that match against the visiting England side at the Wolfson Stadium in Port Elizabeth. England won comfortably, 36–6, and in the match against the touring Italy side the following year, the black 'test' side, the Leopards lost 24–4, also at the Wolfson Stadium. The Leopards

Two matches on one field!

In 1982 in Port Elizabeth when later SARFU president Silas Nkanunu was ousted as president of the kwaZakhele Rugby Union (KWARU) by Amon Nyondo, the union's 20 clubs split into two camps. This led to what is probably a unique situation in South Africa's rugby history.

Dan Qeqe was ousted with Nkanunu. He was an influential man in Zwide in the Eastern Cape and had a rugby field named after him. It was on this field in March 1982 that four teams ran onto the same field where two matches between the two split factions took place at the same time, with 60 players, two referees and four linesmen taking part or controlling the two matches which were played simultaneously.

For the record: Easterns beat Spring Rose 30–4 in the one match, while St Cyprian were too good for African Bombers beating them 9–4. When the latter match ended, the Wallabies and Orientals took to the field for their clash, which meant that 90 players and three sets of officials overlapped on the single pitch during the time that it took to complete one of the games!

The feeling between the two split factions of KWARU had a tragic sequel when the Wallabies' supporters, believing they had been robbed of the title, clashed with supporters of the opposing faction. Axes and even motor cars were used as 'weapons', leading to the death of six people.

---

furthered their international experience when they toured Italy in 1974. A match against the great unbeaten British Lions side of Willie John McBride was also included on the tourists' itinerary – and despite the score of 56–10 against, the Leopards showed that they had the determination to succeed as they tackled, and tackled and tackled again against a side that is still regarded as one of the best to have visited South Africa.

These matches against the tourists – and also Italy on the 1974 tour – were regarded as tests by the Leopards, as were the matches they had played against the two coloured sides under the SARFF and the SACRFB from 1950. In 1970 the latter, then called SARU to move away from having the word 'coloured' in their name, stopped their sequence of test matches. They were no longer prepared to play against a side that was selected on a purely ethnic basis – and they were strongly opposed to the (coloured) federation which continued to do so. This stance culminated in their decision not to join the amalgamation of the other three bodies in 1977.

In all, excluding matches against international touring sides and their tour to Italy in 1974, the SAARB/SARA's record was:

versus SARFF – played 25: won 13, lost 11, drew 1*
versus SACRFB/SARU – played 12: won 3, lost 6 and drew 3.

*The records of the controlling bodies don't correspond. There are instances where matches were regarded as tests by the one but not by the opposing controlling body.

Touring overseas

A number of players from SARA, the name chosen by the SAARB in order not to be accused of ethnicity, were now frequently invited to play in invitational sides and were included in invitations to tour overseas. In 1977 for the first time, players of colour were invited to take part in the Springbok trials for selection of a team to play against a World XV at the inauguration of the new Loftus Versfeld stands.

Timothy Nkonki and co-centre Hennie Shields then accompanied Northern Transvaal captain Thys Lourens to Argentina where they played for an invitational side as part of the club CASI's anniversary celebrations, and Nkonki and Bok captain Morné du Plessis played in a festival match in France.

SARU clash – Boland against Tygerberg in the 1980s.

Owen Nkumane – the first black Bok.

'Mixed' trials were now the order of the day – but still only players from the white SARB were included in the national team. The breakthrough seemed certain to happen in 1978, but international pressure forced the French Rugby Federation to cancel the Springbok tour of their country. Before the bad news from France, however, Nkonki, Andrew Msuki and Solomon Mhlaba took part in the national trials – and the French withdrawal of their invitation probably cost Nkonki the honour of becoming the first black player to play for the South African national team.

It was nevertheless a season during which a further step towards normalisation was taken with teams from SARA (West and East) and the SA Rugby Football Federation taking part in the Sport Pienaar competition. It was a rude awakening for the newcomers to South African rugby's lowest league at provincial level as their strength was not up to standard and led to the two SARA sides combining for the following year.

The 1981 tour by Ireland brought normalisation closer when the tourists played against mixed sides in every match – including the tests where Errol Tobias became the first player of colour to be awarded Springbok colours when he ran out in the first test at Newlands.

Less than four years after the amalgamation of three of South Africa's four controlling bodies, a number of black players had made a huge impression on South African rugby – and Michael Mboto, Morgan Cushe, Timothy Nkonki, Dolly Ntaka, Aubrey Gidane, Sydney Ncate, to name only a few, had become household names in a rugby-mad country that was becoming increasingly isolated at international level.

Four black players were invited for the Springbok trials in 1985 with an All Blacks side due to visit. However, the tour was cancelled. It came as no surprise after the upheaval that the 1981 Springbok tour to New Zealand had caused.

Bandise Maku.

Tonderai Chavhanga.

Odwa Ndungane.

Akona Ndungane.

Ntaka – unofficial Springbok

Dolly Ntaka became the first black player to wear the Springbok jersey when he was selected for the internal Springbok tour that replaced the cancelled New Zealand visit. However, the Springboks didn't receive colours for the matches they played against the South African Barbarians (Baa-Baas) – a side that varied from one match to the next as the host provincial union where the match was to be played dominated the player corps of the invitation Baa-Baas. Michael Mboto confirmed that he was an above-average player by his selection for two matches against the Springboks on the tour, playing for the Central and the SA Barbarians.

Black rugby had to wait until 1998 when Owen Nkumane got the nod for the Springbok tour to the UK and Ireland – and it is a sad indictment of the provincial unions that players who were regarded as good enough for international honours often couldn't make it into the provincial – and even club – sides.

Since then, however, a number of black players have played international rugby for South Africa – and like Nkumane three of them were hookers: Hanyani Shimange, Chiliboy Ralepelle and Bandise Maku (the latter two both from Pretoria Boys' High). With Lawrence

Sephaka they were the strong men from the front row. There was also flank Solly Tyibilika; the 1999 World Cup centre Kaya Malotana; flank Thando Manana; Gcobani Bobo, a strong centre; and Northern Transvaal flank Tim Dlulane, probably the most promising of all until a neck injury ended his career. At the end of 2010, Lwazi Mvovo made his test debut – and he is destined to go places with his pace, skill and strength.

Also at the back, sevens Springboks Tonderai Chavhanga and Jongi Nokwe impressed with their speed but never became regulars in the national side. The first twins to play for South Africa are the wings Akona and Odwa Ndungane, both reliable and solid players who have made their mark in Super Rugby and on the test stage. Prop Brian Mujati is playing good rugby overseas. There is, of course, also prop 'Beast' Tendai Mtawarira, but he didn't come through the South African structures as his rugby background is Zimbabwean like that of Mujati.

While black players today have an immeasurably better deal than they did 30 to 40 years ago and are now fully part of the rugby system, the accusation remains that not enough is being done for the development of players from the townships. There is merit in these arguments, but those pointing fingers are not always aware of the cost of development by rugby bodies; the fact that very few of the top franchises in South Africa are much more than solvent; and the many tribulations the individual development departments have to go through.

The reality is that politics still plays a major role in South African rugby. Much of the criticism directed at the slow development process is based on the misplaced political agenda of outsiders who pursue transformation in a sport where those individuals who are pushed too fast are the losers.

But it remains a reality that there is work to be done.

Of course, this also goes for what was in the past called the coloured rugby players. Better competition has seen to it that these players have come through in greater numbers at provincial and international level, and there are also more clubs playing in the first divisions of the various unions. Tygerberg Rugby Club in Western Province has made it to the final of the national club championships; and teams like Raiders, SK Walmer and Spring Rose have been more than a handful in their respective rugby unions. Raiders have really embraced the new 'rainbow' rugby, and for years have been making use of players from all population groups.

The first coloured clubs

The breakaways that marked black rugby throughout the years were also evident among the coloured bodies. They were, however, not as many and not as frequently based on petty differences – although these did exist! Most notable was the personality clash between the two leading administrators, Dullah Abass (SACRFB/SARU) and Cuthbert Loristen, who later formed the SA Rugby Football Federation (SARFF).

As in the case of the white clubs that made up the Western Province Rugby Football Union, the coloured clubs developed along the lines of domicile. In fact, there are many instances where groups of people from a street would form a club – and it would be difficult for an outsider to be accepted into that club!

From the available records, it would appear that Roslyn was the first club in Cape Town. Whether this is true is debatable. That was the same year that the Western Province Coloured Rugby Union was formed – and it seems unlikely that a single club would have had the standing or indeed the need to form a union!

Other early clubs for coloured players were Brooklyn, Violets, Caledonian Roses, Olympics, Good Hopes, Meidevlei and Vygieskraal.

The result was that clubs sprang up all over Cape Town and its environs. And from these clubs emerged the various controlling bodies. By 1930, the Western Province area had more than 200 clubs – and controlling bodies followed, with the Western Province League taking over in 1936 as the most influential. The WP Union and the WP Board had largely controlled matters until then. There were, among others, also a Suburban Independent Union and a Kensington Union!

Rugby spread to the Eastern Cape and the Transvaal. The PE Rugby Union was formed in 1893, with Swans and St Mark's the oldest known clubs. There is a case to be made that the Transvaal Coloured Rugby Union came about in 1897, but proof of this – as in so many other instances – is not available; nor is there evidence that the controlling bodies in Transvaal, Griquas and Eastern Province were all established in 1896.

Whatever the real facts about those unions, it is known that the SA Coloured Rugby Football Board did come about in 1898 and that this body was formed in Kimberley, where the first provincial tournament was held that same year.

The role of Cecil John Rhodes in promoting rugby must not be underestimated. Not only was he instrumental in bringing the 1891 British touring side of Bill Maclagan to South Africa by underwriting the tour, he also played a part in the development of coloured rugby by presenting them with the Rhodes Cup, the coveted prize for winning the provincial Rhodes tournament. Western Province and Griquas – as in the Currie Cup in 1892 – were the top sides, and Western Province also won the first provincial competition of the SACRFB when they beat the home side 5–3 with a last-minute try by H Kennie, converted by Seldon.

It wasn't a provincial competition in the true sense for long though. The various controlling bodies all had a claim to take part in the competition, and many of them did. This diluted the provinces' strength as their players split into two or more sides at tournaments.

Unlike the black clubs – essentially because the coloured players lived closer to the white areas than the blacks did – the coloureds were great followers of provincial rugby played under the auspices of the SARFB and also supported the national side, the Springboks – up to the Second World War. Then the reality of the conditions under which they lived and the laws under which they had to play their sport, exacerbated by the new National Party government, brought a new resistance against the system. This included the rugby status quo.

In the 1930s, the legendary Gamat (full names Gasant Ederoos Behardien) was the baggage master for Western Province – and when they played in Cape Town, also for the Springboks. Even in those days, as it had been for years, the coloureds were allocated their own standing room in front of the southern stand, now known as the Danie Craven Stand. But the disenchantment took a new, more aggressive turn – and whereas the idea of an overseas tour in 1938 was to give their players exposure to some form of international competition, politics decreed that this idea should be shelved. Touring would equate to surrendering the principle that had by then taken hold, namely that rugby should not be played along lines of ethnicity. An internal tour was nevertheless arranged and a team of 25 players was selected after the 1938 Rhodes tournament in Cape Town.

Black Springboks against coloured Springboks
The players were awarded colours for the tour in those days when both the black and the coloured players still called their teams Springboks. Selected players each received a Springbok tie, a green blazer and a badge with a leaping Springbok. The team was captained by flyhalf Johnny Niels.

The touring side played nine matches against provincial sides and unions, winning seven of them. The national side lost to Worcester and the WP Board towards the end of the tour when injuries took their toll after nine matches in four weeks on hard fields.

A similar tour was planned for what was called the Federation in 1953. The Federation was an attempt to promote multiracial sport. But the tour fell through.

In 1959, the SA Rugby Football Federation was formed by delegates in Paarl. It should not be confused with the 1953 Federation mentioned above and it wasn't because of politics. The new body followed a breakaway by a group of disenchanted clubs and people of which Cuthbert Loristen became the president. Unhappiness with the SACRFB stemmed from funds not being properly distributed to all the unions after tournaments; the fact that the controlling body was perceived as a closed clique; and that decisions were implemented regardless of meeting resolutions. The upshot was that the WP League withdrew its more than 10 000 players from the SACRFB. They were followed in quick succession by a number of other unions.

This led to the 1959 Paarl meeting and Loristen took the Federation through the amalgamation process in 1977. His election was also instrumental in the first multiracial rugby at international and provincial level being played, with the WP League accepted into the SARB's competition structures in 1978.

The SACRFB, however, were not part of the deal. Their president, Dullah Abass, was a principled man. There would be no sport as long as teams were to be selected along ethnic lines. And while he and Craven moved closer to an understanding at a personal level, sports minister Koornhof put paid to that in 1977.

The new WP League and especially the new federation fuelled the dissent between the two coloured bodies, and led to the eventual withdrawal of the SACRFB from the test matches against the SAARB in 1963. The Federation then slotted into the test schedule in their place – and this was an important reason in their joining forces with SARA when amalgamation came about in 1977. They knew and trusted one another.

Playing in SARB competitions

It was in the 1970s that Western Province's huge reservoir of talented coloured players started playing in the SARB competitions. In 1978, two teams from the SA Rugby Football Federation took part in the Sport Pienaar Cup competition, as did two teams in the SA Rugby Association.

The Western Province League team fared well, but the other three sides – SWD League, SARA West and SARA East struggled against teams of average strength. These three teams decided not to take part in 1979 playing instead in the Golden Cup competition in which white teams of semi-provincial strength played. Western Province League ended joint fourth in Section 1 of the Sport Pienaar competition after winning four of their seven matches. They joined the WPRFU on a trial basis in 1981 and became a permanent member in 1984.

Against the Western Province Currie Cup side, however, it was obvious that, despite some outstanding individual talent, the depth was not there yet and the Western Province side from the Federation lost 51–0.

Eight Federation players were included in the SA Barbarians side for the 1980 tour to the UK. They included Errol Tobias, whose road to the Springbok team had been through the Federation team and later via Boland, whom he represented in the 1980 Currie Cup competition. Avril Williams and Wilfred Cupido made it to the Western Province provincial side in 1982 and more were to follow with regularity. Williams played for the Springboks in the series against the 1984 England tourists and Cupido played for the national Under-23 side, the Gazelles.

In 1985, the Western Province League team, as they were now called, missed out on possible promotion to the

Western Province Rugby Union playing Western Province Rugby Board at Gugulethu Stadium in 1981.

Currie Cup when they were beaten in the Sport Pienaar final by Vaal Triangle who went on to win the promotion matches against Boland.

There have been five coloured Players of the Year, four of them wings: Chester Williams (1994); Breyton Paulse (2000); Ashwin Willemse (2003); Bryan Habana (2005 and 2007); and Gurthrö Steenkamp.

Others who were selected for the Springboks are full-backs Conrad Jantjes, Bevin Fortuin and Zane Kirchner; flyhalf/fullback Earl Rose; wings McNeil Hendricks, JP Pietersen and Gavin Passens; centre/wing Deon Kayser; centres Waylon Murray, Adi Jacobs, Juan de Jongh and Wayne Julies; flyhalf Elton Jantjies; scrumhalves Bolla Conradie, Norman Jordaan, Heini Adams and Ricky Januarie; props Eddie Andrews and Etienne Fynn; hooker Dale Santon; lock Quinton Davids; and loose forwards Hilton Lobberts, Ashley Johnson, Davon Raubenheimer and Kabamba Floors.

5

A competition of two phases
The Currie Cup: SA rugby's Holy Grail

The Currie Cup is often called the Holy Grail of South African rugby. With the first tournament held in 1892, it is the oldest provincial competition in the world, and most probably also the toughest – and is the major reason South African rugby survived its political isolation relatively well.

The provincial passion with which it is supported – with the crowds at the matches by far the best of any non-test competition worldwide – makes it stand out above all comparable competitions worldwide.

Over the 120-odd years since the Currie Cup arrived in South Africa, the competition has been dominated by two sides. Between them, Western Province (31) and Northern Transvaal/Blue Bulls (23) have won or shared 54 of the 71 Currie Cup titles contested. (They twice shared with one another.) The dominance of these two sides can be further divided into two clear phases. The first was the initial years when the Currie Cup was decided by league format, either at tournaments (until 1920) and thereafter on a home-and-away basis (until 1936) and again on three occasions in the 1950s and 1960s.

First, Province dominated the tournaments, with 17 wins and two shares, i.e. 19 titles in the 22 competitions played. (In fact, their record is even more remarkable as they didn't play in the 1899 tournament because of the impending South African War, making it 19 titles from 21 competitions.)

Then Northern Transvaal (only established in 1938) took over the role as dominant team. Since 1968, the Currie Cup has been decided annually and every time by a final. Of the 50 finals contested, Northern Transvaal or the Blue Bulls have won 23 of which

The first clash in a final between the two Currie Cup giants, Northern Transvaal and Western Province, was won 11–9 by the Light Blues.

The Griquas team of 1891. They were awarded what was later known as the Currie Cup for their performance against the 1891 British side.

four were shared; Western Province have won ten with two shared (12); and four other provinces also had a look-in.

The Currie Cup competition though, in its 120 years, has been marked by close – and as far as supporters are concerned, even bitter! – rivalry. First Western Province and Griquas fought it out for the right to be called the country's best; then followed a period when Transvaal became Province's biggest threat, and then, from 1968 onwards, Northern Transvaal became the side that laid down the marker.

Province remained the bitter foe. It was a North-South thing, with the country's politics over the years reflected in the rugby approach of the two sides: Province expansive and liberal in their approach, the Light Blues conservative, rather dour and clinging to the basics of the past! Natal since the 1990s, and the Free State in the 1970s and

later as the Free State Cheetahs in the new millennium, brought a new dynamic to the competition. Over the past ten years or so the Bloemfontein side have arguably been the Blue Bulls' most dangerous opponents.

Transvaal have threatened with only relative success over the years, notably with outstanding sides in the 1920s and 1990s; and Griquas, initially with their clubs spread over a vast area and since the advent of professionalism without the necessary financial power, have been competitive but managed only a single title in 1970 to add to their titles in 1899 and 1911.

It all started in 1892, a year after the first tour by an overseas side. WE (Bill) Maclagan captained the tourists that have since been officially renamed the British Isles, although the team consisted mostly of Scottish and English students. There were also a few international players from these two countries for the first

Barry Heatlie shines for Province and South Africa

Barry Heatlie was a special man and indeed a special rugby player. He first played for Western Province in 1890 as an 18-year-old in only his second season of rugby, and then played test rugby the following year against the British touring side. What's more, he was a member of the Western Province committee – before the establishment of the union – when they invited the 1891 British side to tour South Africa. He was only 19 at the time. Over the next decade, he made a huge contribution to rugby in Western Province and South Africa, both on and off the field.

To this day, he holds the record for being at the helm of a provincial side for the longest period and captained Western Province from 1891 to 1904 with the exception of 1895, when Alf Richards was captain. Heatlie's 28 Currie Cup matches of course fell within the unbeaten 45-match run – in other words, he was never in a losing team in his years with Western Province! In all, he represented Western Province in 34 matches, including five matches against three British touring sides: in 1891, 1896 (twice as captain) and 1903 (twice as captain).

Heatlie also captained South Africa twice – once against the British touring side of 1896 and once against Mark Morrison's tourists of 1903, when he led South Africa to its first test win after the first two tests in the series had been drawn 8–all and nil–all. This was, therefore, also South Africa's first series win.

Brought up on a farm in the Worcester district, Heatlie was a big man for those days. He weighed 208 lbs (95 kg) and stood 6 ft 3 in tall (1,91 m). To put his size into perspective, he was taller and heavier than any player in the first Springbok side – Paul Roos's – that toured the United Kingdom and France in 1906.

However Heatlie, then 34, wasn't in the first Springbok side to tour Britain. When Paul Roos's team left, Heatlie had already left for Argentina. He resided there for 20 years after fleeing South Africa to evade his creditors. The story goes that he was rowed out under cover of darkness by friends to a boat outside Cape Town harbour.

That Heatlie was a great forward is not to be disputed. The legendary Stellenbosch player and coach and later national selector, Oubaas Markötter, said of him: 'I played with him and against him. Heatlie is the greatest all-round forward South Africa has produced. I am inclined to put him down as the best captain ever to lead a Springbok side.' Markötter's statement was made in the early years and by the time he died in 1957, many more South African greats had come and gone. It does, however, emphasise that Heatlie was something special.

Heatlie is also the man who gave the green jersey to South Africa's national teams. As was usual in those days, the South African team played in either white jerseys or jerseys in the colours of the union/club hosting the test match, often with the badge of the local club on their jerseys. That changed in the third test of the 1896 series. 'At the time, I had on hand a supply of dark green jerseys, the colours of the (by then defunct) Old Diocesan's Club. It was decided to wear those jerseys at Newlands, and ever since South African fifteens have been clad in green,' Heatlie is quoted as saying in various chronicles. The South African team for the fourth test of 1896 is pictured wearing these jerseys. Heatlie, as captain, is the only player with the Diocesan badge on his jersey. The caption to the photo in Dr Danie Craven's Rugby Annals 1891–1964 written for the SA Rugby Board reads: 'The first South African side to wear a green jersey in an international match'.

Heatlie's flight in 1905 brought about the first 'high-level' contact between South African and Argentinean rugby. The big man played for the Lomas Rugby Club and then became captain and coach of Gimnasia y Esgrima, leading them to the national title in 1911 and 1912. By then he had been playing top-level rugby for more than 20 years! He represented Argentina in two 'test' matches against an unofficial British touring side.

Heatlie was 43 when he retired in 1915 as a result of broken ribs. He died in South Africa at the age of 79.

international tour of 20 matches. With the side came a magnificent cup of pure gold, valued at £45 at the time. It was donated by Mr (later Sir) Donald Currie, shipping magnate and owner of the shipping line Castle Packet Company that in 1900 merged with the Union Shipping Company to form the huge Castle Union Line. Currie had visited South Africa in 1889 and was enchanted by the country. His instructions were to present the trophy to the first side to beat the tourists. It didn't happen, and Griquas donated the trophy to the SARFB. (Interestingly, Sir Donald also donated trophies for cricket – even before rugby! – soccer, yachting and water polo. These trophies were also known as the Currie Cup for the respective sports. However, they fell into disuse after the first democratic elections in South Africa as these sports decided to award new trophies to their champion sides.)

The forerunner of the Currie Cup competition had its beginnings in 1884 when an intertown competition was inaugurated, and in 1889 the tournament was upgraded to an intercentre tournament. Western Province won the first rugby Currie Cup in 1892 to add to their title as first provincial winners in 1889 when four sides – Griquas, Western Province, Transvaal and Eastern Province – played for the Board trophy, a silver cup donated by the SARFB. Western Province didn't win that SARFB trophy outright. They tied with Griqualand West after a surprise 5–2 defeat against Transvaal, regarded as little more than a scratch team. Transvaal's only win forced WP to rely on a count-out – and as they had beaten Griqualand West in their encounter, Western Province were the winners according to the tournament rules. Both tournaments were played in Kimberley and in the first Currie Cup tournament of 1892 only five sides contested the title: Western Province, Transvaal, Border, Griqualand West and Natal.

Western Province dominate

Those wins by Province in the 1892 tournament were the first in a sequence that saw them remain unbeaten for 45 matches – a record that, in these days of professional-ism, is unlikely to be improved upon. The five consecutive titles in those early days is another record. This ties the record for the most consecutive Currie Cup titles, albeit not in successive years because of the break between competition tournaments. Western Province won in 1892, 1894, 1895, 1897 and 1898. The consecutive five-win title run was repeated by Western Province in the period 1982 to 1986. By then the Currie Cup was decided after finals. Five of Western Province's ten outright wins in finals came in this winning sequence, with their other five wins and two shared titles scattered in the remainder of the period 1939 to 2010.

The supremacy of Western Province in those early years is underlined by the fact that they went through the 1898 tournament without a single point being scored against them in their four matches and notched up 62 points themselves in days when points were scarce; and only 24 points in their first 22 Currie Cup matches were scored against them in the first five tournaments from 1892-1898.

Ironically, the unbeaten Province were dethroned as champions during that early unbeaten run of 45 Currie Cup wins between 1892 and 1911. That was because Western Province opted not to take part in the 1899 tournament because of the imminent South African War. Transvaal also didn't take part and only Griquas, Eastern Province, Rhodesia and Border competed for the title. Griquas won the first of their three titles in that 1899 tournament in Kimberley and followed it up with their second win when they halted Province's unbeaten 45-match run with a 12–0 win in the 1911 tournament in Cape Town. It would be 59 years before Griquas would again be the champions, despite their series of near-wins in those early years. (Of course, by virtue of their performance against Maclagan's side, Griquas were the unofficial first holders – if not winners – of the Currie Cup and added their plaque to the trophy in 1891 to entrench the fact that they were the best side to play the tourists.)

The early dominance by Western Province was to be expected. Through the settlers, especially after the arrival of permanent British control in 1806, the cultural and

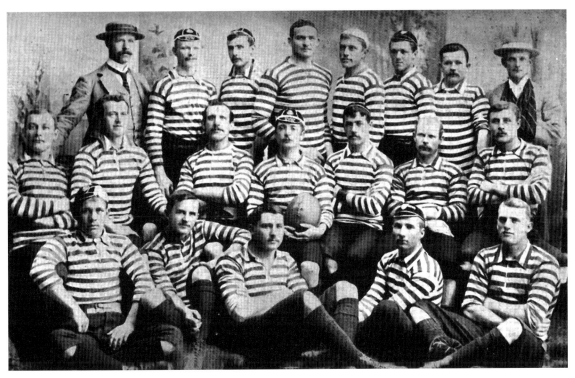

The first winners of the Currie Cup were Western Province in 1892.

political power of the British extended its influence into the region. Part of the cultural legacy was the football and cricket brought to South Africa, and Cape Town was the seat of British control. It is therefore to Cape Town that the settlers and the soldiers flocked and where they settled – at a near-unbelievable rate of 15 000 per year between 1875 and 1890.

The immigrants and soldiers were sports teachers – and through them the first established clubs, the first competitions, the first official structure with the formation of the Western Province Rugby Football Union in 1883 came into being. These numbers and factors gave Western Province a decided advantage when intercity rugby was first played. The early clubs, following on the available number, brought greater competition and input from the settlers from abroad – and the Province advantage was increased by the large number of top-class players developed under these conditions.

In every era, of course, there is a legendary player or players. The first of those was Barry Heatlie. He played in 28 of those early unbeaten Currie Cup matches for Western Province that included the five Currie Cup titles between 1892 and 1898. A full description of his contribution to the game – for Province, South Africa and later Argentina (see box entitled 'Barry Heatlie shines for Province and South Africa.')

Even after Heatlie's departure for South America in 1905, Province remained the yardstick and Griquas their main adversaries. Western Province bagged the first three titles after the South African War in 1904, 1906 and 1908, with Griquas winning in 1911. Their 1908 win, in particular, was impressive. Bob Loubser, Western Province and South Africa's wing, had blistering pace. In fact, he was considered for the Olympic team as a sprinter – and he was a devastating finisher. Inside him, for the Maties, Western Province and the Springboks, was Japie

Japie Krige, brilliant Maties centre.

Boy Morkel, captain in the 1921 tests against New Zealand.

Krige and the modest Loubser gave all the credit for his heroics over the years to his great friend, a co-member of the 'Thin Red Line', as Paul Roos's backs in the UK were called in 1906/07 because of the maroon-clad Maties' influence in the back line.

Loubser showed his class in the great Western Province Currie Cup side of 1908. Krige had by then retired – and Loubser was the hero of the 5–0 win over Transvaal, who played with only seven forwards to try and curb the attacking danger of the Western Province backs. Sommie Morkel and Dougie Morkel were the two men who alternated to assist their backs on the defence. In their own quarter, Transvaal used both Morkels at the back with a six-man scrum.

Transvaal had a very effective pack and Western Province an outstanding back line. Their own pack's form had prompted Transvaal's decision to play with only seven – or sometimes six – forwards. Minutes before the final whistle, Loubser received the ball from a back line movement. His pace took him between the two Morkels to beat fullback Billy Stoll. Even Loubser's former team-mate, Anton Stegmann, was left in his wake. He scored, and that was that – Province had another title.

The highlight of 1908 was followed by Western Province's first defeat in a Currie Cup match and competition in 1911. Although it was Griquas' second title, it was the first time that Western Province had lost in a tournament – and what's more, it was on their home ground, Newlands!

Griquas beat a very good Western Province team away by a comprehensive 12–0 with a good pack and some outstanding defence laying the platform for an unpleasant surprise in Cape Town. But Province were not to be denied, and at the next tournament in 1914, they bounced back. They not only took revenge in no uncertain manner by outplaying defending champions Griquas by a whopping 16–0, but also scored 193 points to 6 in their nine matches. Transvaal, who were second in the tournament in Durban, were also well beaten, 10–0.

In this tournament, Province brought a new approach to the South African game by using the orthodox half-back positions of a scrumhalf and a flyhalf as we know them today. Until then, Western Province had played with a scrumhalf and two inside backs. The 1914 Western Province side, to this day, is regarded as probably their finest of their era.

First World War interrupts the Cup

Once again a war brought a hiatus in Currie Cup proceedings. This time it was the First World War, and no Currie Cup rugby – and indeed very little provincial rugby – was played in the period 1914 to 1920, when the next Currie Cup competition took place. It was held in Kimberley and it so very nearly produced a shock winner. Ironically for Transvaal, it was one of their sub-unions Western

---

Billy Millar – wounded but not beaten

Springbok captain 1910–1913, 6 tests, 37 matches   International referee

One of Western Province and South Africa's greatest players and leaders was Billy Millar. Wounded for two years, his resolute determination saw him return first as a provincial and national rugby player, and again as an international referee. In-between he became a provincial selector and a coach.

Millar made his test debut for South Africa's first overseas tour against England in 1906, his only test on that tour. In 1910, he played in the second and third tests against the touring British Lions side of Tommy Smyth and was then appointed captain of the 1912/13 side to the British Isles, Ireland and France. He captained South Africa in five of his six tests, losing only a single match as test captain. That was his first in charge, which was the second test against the 1910 British tourists. He missed the first test due to work commitments. In all, Millar played in 37 matches for the Springboks.

What made his feats extraordinary was that Millar was seriously wounded during the South African War. He was then only 16 years old – but the doctor's orders that he should do plenty of walking and mountaineering and advice that he take up boxing, paid dividends. He boxed for Western Province, took part in the walking event at the SA Athletics Championships and also made it into the all-conquering Western Province side of 1904. By 1906, he was a certain choice for Roos's team.

Millar was an unqualified success as captain for WP. A fiery character, he was not the national selectors' choice as captain of the 1912/13 Springbok tourists; however, they were overruled by the SARFB. He captained the Springboks in three of their five tests, against Ireland,

Wales and France, with Dougie Morkel and Uncle Dobbin leading the Boks against England and Scotland respectively. The match against England at Twickenham, won 9–3 by South Africa, clinched South Africa's first Grand Slam – something they were to achieve on four consecutive tours. Twickenham was first used for Test rugby in 1910 – and the first team to beat England there was Billy Millar's Springboks. The Springboks played 27 matches on their tour of just over three months, winning 24 and losing to Newport, London Counties and Swansea.

The tour was the last international contact by the Springboks before the First World War. Millar again went into battle, and again was wounded. He told the story of how, after being wounded and lying among wounded Allies, he was recognised by a wounded French soldier who had seen the Boks play in France on the 1912/13 tour. And a wounded English corporal, a spectator at the match between the Springboks and England on the 1912/13 tour, told of another strange coincidence. The corporal related how he was forced to take shelter behind a rudimentary gravestone during a German attack. It was the gravestone of Ronnie Poulton-Palmer, the man who scored the try against the Springboks at Twickenham. The Springbok who scored a try in that match, Jacky Morkel, was also killed in the war – the only two from that match to pay the highest toll.

On his return after the war, Millar took up coaching and refereeing. He became one of only six South African internationals to also referee test matches. This he did against the 1924 British side of Cove-Smith when he controlled the third and fourth test matches.

The great Oubaas Mark

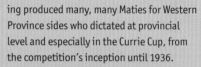

'I could feel that I was in the presence of a man who would influence my very life.' That is how the great Danie Craven remembers his first glimpse of the man who would have a major influence on his life as a player, coach and administrator.

The man was August Frederick Markötter, better known by his school name Oubaas Mark throughout the country and as Mr Mark to his players. The occasion was Craven's first practice at Coetzenburg where he had arrived that week as a 19-year-old from Lindley in the eastern Orange Free State. After only three hours of trials under the eyes of Markötter, the famous Maties coach said: 'You are looking at the Springbok scrumhalf to Britain in two years' time.'

And that in a nutshell describes the great man, arguably the greatest coach in South African rugby history despite the fact that he was not a Currie Cup hero or even renowned for his coaching of Currie Cup teams and never coached the Springboks.

He was the man who took Stellenbosch University from a very good competitive side to four Western Province Grand Challenge titles in the five years between 1903 and 1907. That was the early impetus of a club that over the years became world famous for its rugby and undoubtedly the leading club in South Africa. During this period he also he captained the Western Province Country team that beat Mark Morrison's Lions 13–7 at Newlands – the first non-test side to beat a Lions team in South Africa. Markötter captained the Maties in 1903 and played for the clubs Paarl, Villagers and Wellington.

It was, however, as a coach – and particularly a coach with an eye for spotting and developing young talent – that Markötter will be remembered. Virtually until his death in 1957, Oubaas Mark's identification of players and his coach-ing produced many, many Maties for Western Province sides who dictated at provincial level and especially in the Currie Cup, from the competition's inception until 1936.

It was under Markötter that the Maties developed into the foremost talent factory in the country. Paul Roos's 1906 Springbok squad to Britain included 11 players who had developed under Markötter at Stellenbosch, and had played their part in Western Province's Currie Cup successes in the first decade of the 20th century.

His coaching methods were uncompromising, but built on basics; and his often dour disposition hid a fine sense of humour that made him a popular and much-respected figure that was not to be trifled with.

Like so many of rugby's great men he was also dictatorial, as the following story told of Markötter clearly illustrates when he 'elected' members of the Stellenbosch Rugby Club's committee at an AGM. As chairman of the meeting, he announced: 'I propose Kockie de Kock as secretary and Herman Steytler as his assistant. There are no further proposals.' When Springbok loose forward Andre McDonald was proposed as club captain at the same meeting, Markötter said: 'Andre McDonald has been proposed. Who dares propose against him?' De Kock, Steytler and McDonald were duly elected, the story goes.

Markötter graduated in 1898, and established his legal firm, Kriege & Markötter, in 1900. But by then, it had already become clear that the man who only started playing rugby at the age of 16 in 1893 would spend more time on the rugby field than in his chambers. In a letter to a friend he wrote: 'I definitely decided to dedicate the rest of my life to rugby football.' And so it was until his death in 1957, with his first love, the Maties, benefiting as much from his brilliance as Western Province and South Africa did at higher levels.

Transvaal that denied them a first Currie Cup title. That year, Western Transvaal broke away from Transvaal to form their own union and the fledgling union held their former parent union to a draw. This cost Transvaal a share of the Currie Cup, and Western Province ruled again!

It was Transvaal's second successive tournament as second-placed bridesmaid, and it changed with the next competition. The 1920 tournament was the last to be held

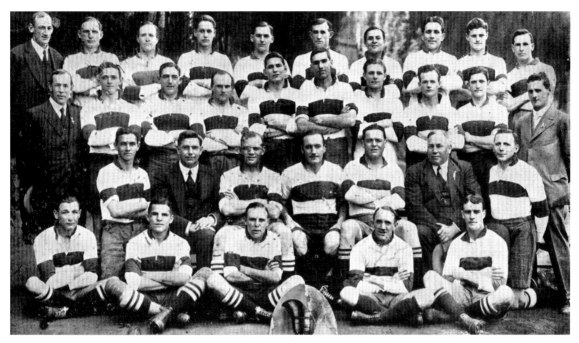

The Transvaal team won the first Currie Cup competition that was played on a home-and-away basis in 1922.

at a centralised venue. According to the records of the time, financial and leave considerations were the reasons for switching to a tournament on a home-and-away basis.

Transvaal had given notice before the Great War that they were going to be a handful. The 1914 performance and the near miss in 1920 were warnings that they would not be denied for too long. Because they also had six players in the first Springbok side to Australasia in 1921, they had a core of experience and confidence when the next tournament came around in 1922.

A new format

They called it the first home-and-away competition for the Currie Cup, but the fixtures were drawn up with a view to make the travel arrangements for each side as easy as possible. The result was that there was little parity in the number of matches each side played at home and away. In fact, in 1927, Transvaal had six home matches and only played away from home on three occasions! And in 1929,

Western Province accepted the strangest of fixtures. The fixtures committee had problems fitting in all Province's matches and to solve the problem the Cape side agreed to play two Currie Cup matches on a single day! They had the depth to do so, and although their first-choice team lost to Transvaal in Johannesburg (11–9), the Western Province 'B-side' did well enough to beat Border at Newlands (24–3). This double-header fixture contributed to Western Province using 48 players in the season – unheard of in those days. And they won the Currie Cup!

In 1922, Transvaal were helped by Griquas, who beat Western Province 9–6 in an earlier league match – and all Transvaal had to do to clinch the title was to draw with Western Province. This they did in a cliff-hanger with the scores at 3–all when the final whistle went. And suddenly the invincibility of Province was being questioned in what many described as 'a good thing for rugby'. But there is no denying class, and Province bounced back in the next three competitions in 1925, 1927 and 1929. Even in the next two competitions in 1932 and 1934 when they were given a huge scare by sharing the Currie Cup titles with Border, Western Province added two more titles to their tally.

Border's two shares were something special. They were achieved in years when Province had all-time greats like Bennie Osler, Danie Craven, Pierre de Villiers, Boy and Fanie Louw, Andre McDonald, JC van der Westhuizen, Mauritz van den Berg, Alfie van der Merwe, George van Rooyen, Frankie Waring, Dai Williams, Morris Zimerman and Koffie Hofmeyr in their squad – all of them Springboks of South Africa's outstanding international era between 1931/32 and 1938, and most of them members of the great 1937 side to New Zealand.

The 1932 title share by Border came after their 8–3 win over Province on a very wet Newlands, with their pack outstanding and playing to the basics by dribbling with handling curbed to the minimum. They out-thought and outplayed a star-studded Province and were full value for the win.

By the end of the 1932 competition, Western Province had won 101 of their 110 Currie Cup matches – well ahead of Transvaal who had 73 wins from their 109 matches and Griquas who had a 63 from 112 record. Border, who again shared the Currie Cup with Western Province in 1934, were only seventh on the rankings after 1932 with a mere 35 wins from 100 matches and a winning record of less than 40%.

Border's next shared title came in East London. Again it was a surprise result, despite the fact that the teams were both unbeaten when they kicked off. A look at Province's 1934 record of 136 points for and only 23 against compared to Border's 34 and 24 against tells the story of the uphill battle that faced the home side, but they were fully deserving of their 11–8 win. When Western Province also lost to Transvaal, Border were favourites to win the Currie Cup outright. It was not to be, however, as Border surprisingly lost 8–6 to Natal in Durban to share the Currie Cup with Western Province for the second consecutive time.

Western Province duly won their 16th title, of which the most recent two were shared, in 1936. Their dominance

Brothers Fanie and Boy Louw – Bok team-mates in 1938; referee and captain in the first Currie Cup final a year later.

of the competition is further underlined by the fact that their record had been achieved in only 19 Currie Cup competitions until then of which they had played in 18!

But it was soon to change – and change dramatically, with the first of the 50 Currie Cup finals (to the end of 2010) played in 1939 in a new format that for some reason simply didn't and doesn't suit Western Province. To date, they've played in 22 finals out of the 50 contested, and won only the said ten matches and drawn two. Northern Transvaal/Blue Bulls have played in 31, and won 19 and drawn four for their 23 titles. Free State/Free State Cheetahs have played in 13 finals with three wins and one draw, while Natal/Sharks have likewise played in 13 finals, with six titles going their way. Transvaal/Lions have been involved in 18 finals and have seven wins and one draw to their credit. Eastern Transvaal and Boland have each played and lost one final, and Griqualand West won their only final.

The Western Province finals nightmare started in the

first final – incidentally a Currie Cup competition cut short by the Second World War that started in 1939. The envisaged double round was curtailed to a single round, and Western Province hosted Transvaal at Newlands.

After their 1922 win, it took Transvaal 17 years to win the trophy again. And what a team Transvaal fielded at Newlands that day, 30 September 1939! Springbok prop Fanie Louw captained a side that included all-time greats such as Otto van Niekerk, Floris Duvenhage, Tony Harris and Jan Lotz. They won 17–6 against a team led by Freddie Turner, who had played for Transvaal the previous season. Five tries against one tell the story of total dominance. Duvenhage scored a try within the first five minutes and Van Niekerk added two more before half-time to just about shut out the home side. It was 14–6 at the break and another try, by Fatty Pretorius, sealed matters. Turner scored a penalty goal for WP and Piet de Wet contributed a try. GJ Roos goaled a penalty and a conversion for Transvaal.

The referee that day was Boy Louw. Only the previous season he had still propped the Springbok scrum against the 1938 British Lions with his brother and Transvaal captain in the final, Fanie. Talk about fast-tracking of referees!

Rugby during the Second World War

There were no further Currie Cup matches and only a hugely disrupted provincial programme until 1945. But during the war some excellent rugby was nevertheless played by a number of Springboks and supplemented by some of the other top players from the land of the Springboks in the north, where interdivisional matches – various 'internationals' between players from different countries within a division – were played when it was possible. The scores are not officially part of matches under the auspices of the then SARFB, and rightly so, but it kept these men occupied as they fought up north.

South Africa's soldiers not only played rugby in their own units, but also played as composite sides against similar teams from other countries in the same regions.

Springbok captain Hennie Muller introduces the Duke of Edinburgh to future Bok captain Stephen Fry before a 1951/52 test.

In the lesser games, the soldiers often played without rugby jerseys/shirts, and barefoot. But in the more important matches, jerseys were 'made' and army boots worn if rugby boots were not obtainable.

Players were later referred to as Springboks, and are, as far as can be ascertained, fully deserving of the title. Included in the various South African sides in the respective regions were players of the calibre of Louis Babrow, Jimmy White, Ebbo Bastard and Pat Lyster, all of them Springboks. Trials were held with selectors travelling between units to ensure that they had the best possible sides to face teams like the very strong Wales and New Zealand. At Helwan in Egypt, a four-nations series with these two sides and England had to contend with such a South African side carefully selected to take on the best. Their captain was former Transvaal flyhalf Charlie Newham, and the convener of selectors was former Bok Attie van Heerden. There were 18 000 spectators in December 1944 when the 'Springboks' beat the British Artillery School 14–0 in a 'friendly' at El Alamein. This was the perfect preparation for the series that started with a match against England, won 21–8 by the South Africans.

Two years before these matches, on 21 October 1942, the South African side were instructed by the Allied

The Currie Cup format: a regular surprise

Since 1939, when the Currie Cup was contested in a final for the first time, only three competitions have been played under the old league system with the team at the top of the log being declared the Currie Cup champion. But even with finals becoming an annual institution in 1968 for deciding the winner, until recently the competing sides were in the dark every year about which format would be used for the competition. Nothing was certain from year to year, as the unions' self-serving interests dominated decisions for the format to be followed in a particular year.

Stability only came in 2004 when it was decided that the top eight sides would play in the Premier Division in a strength-versus-strength system, with a Premier Division of eight teams and a First Division of six teams. A double-round of matches has since been played, with play-offs then determining the winner.

The initial format of a centralised (tournament) league format was relinquished in 1922. In the early days, however, money and transport constraints were a major factor in the decision to centralise competitions. The Currie Cup winners were decided after a round-robin format over a period of a week to ten days, with the log winners awarded the trophy. Only five teams participated in the inaugural Currie Cup tournament in 1892, which was won by Western Province from second-placed Griquas.

In 1899, with the impending South African War, only four sides competed. The venues used in the tournaments before 1920 also rotated. In those early years, the competition was not played annually. International tours took preference and there were disruptions during wartime – and in the 1950s there was a five-year break because of unhappiness with the system and the full international programme.

The early league tournament structure remained in place until 1920, with a varying number of teams participating. In 1904 seven sides competed, with Border involved, and in the following tournament of 1906, Rhodesia took part. North Easterns joined in 1908, and by 1911 there were ten teams when South Westerns were present.

In 1920, the tournament took place at two venues, Bloemfontein and Kimberley, to determine the winner over the same period – a logistical nightmare. Thereafter a league system on what they called a 'home-and-away' basis replaced the centralised tournaments. Western Province, who had dominated by winning ten of the first 13 Currie Cup competitions, again exerted their dominance and won four of the next six competitions by notching up four outright wins (1925, 1927, 1929 and 1936), and shared the trophy twice with Border in 1932 and 1934 in the other two competitions. In 1936 the league format was used for the last time except on three occasions in 1957–59 (a single competition), 1964 and 1966.

By 1939, the tournament had grown to 12 teams, split into north and south regions. The winners of the sections played one another in the first Currie Cup final – but it was after only a single round as the double round had to be scrapped because of the impending Second World War. It was the jubilee year of SARFB and the provincial competition that started with the Board Trophy in 1889 with the first Currie Cup tournament only played in 1892. Transvaal beat Western Province 17–6 at Newlands in the first final in 1939 in the new format that was to become a nightmare for Province.

In 1954, the Currie Cup structure was changed. Fifteen teams were divided into three sections, and semi-finals were played for the first time. Northern Transvaal and the Orange Free State met in what was called a semi-final. The winner of that match was Northern Transvaal. They were pitted against Western Province, who won the Currie Cup with an 11–8 win at Newlands.

Northern Transvaal were victorious in 1956. They beat

Eight Army to 'play' a match behind the railway station at El Alamein. That was two days before the Battle of Alamein and the objective was to bluff the Germans into believing nothing of importance was imminent. Two days later, four of the players who took part in the 'bluff game' were killed and 11 wounded in the battle that finally broke the back of Rommel's Africa Corps.

South African sides' rugby jerseys were green, where

Natal 9–8 at Kingsmead Cricket Ground in Natal's first appearance in a final. This time Natal had to take the long route via the so-called semi-final for the honour of meeting Northern Transvaal. The Light Blues were given the right to advance to the final without a play-off.

The next Currie Cup was decided on a league basis over two seasons, 1957 and 1959. There were no Currie Cup matches because of the visiting French side in 1958. By the end of 1959, Western Province had gathered one more league point than Northern Transvaal, and the trophy returned to Newlands. No final was played. Unhappiness over this system and a full international programme led to the Currie Cup being cancelled for five years, until 1964.

Then, and also in 1966, in an attempt to give every side affiliated to the SA Rugby Board a chance to win the Currie Cup, the competition was divided into five sections of three teams each. The five section winners went through to a further league competition without a final. Western Province finished top of the standings and were crowned winners, as in 1966 when the same system was used. Again a French tour halted Currie Cup proceedings, and no competition was played in 1967.

In 1968, it was back to finals – and this has been the case since, with the competition also taking place annually since then. In 1968, the number of teams in the competition had increased to 16 and they were divided into two pools. Northern Transvaal won their third title after beating Transvaal in the final.

In four instances the finals were drawn and the trophy shared: in 1971 between Transvaal and Northern Transvaal at Ellis Park (14–all); in 1979 (15–all) and 1989 (16–all) in two Newlands finals between Western Province and Northern Transvaal; and in 2006 when the Free State Cheetahs and the Blue Bulls drew 28–all in Bloemfontein. It was after this final that it was decided that the Currie Cup would not be shared again and that a winner had to be determined if sides were still tied after extra time.

Since 1968 a number of formats have been used to determine the finalists. In the 1970s, the top 15 – and later 16 – sides played for the Currie Cup, while the Paul Roos competition was introduced for the other unions and also Natal Country Districts and Transvaal Sub-Union. Divisions of all the Currie Cup sides into sections – and on occasions even one big league – were used.

In the early 1980s, in an effort to keep the sides of the B-Section interested in the competition to its end, the two top sides in the B-Section played the two top sides in the A-Section in semi-finals – and so it was that Natal played in the 1984 final against Western Province at Newlands, after beating the A-Section's second-placed side Free State in such a semi-final!

Later in the 1980s, there was the decision to give the top sides' log-leaders the right to go into the final without a play-off, with the second and third-placed sides having to fight it out in the 'semi-final' to play the log leaders in the final.

In 1999, all 14 teams played in a round-robin competition over a single round. The Lions and Sharks, tied at 52 log points each, played in the final. By 2001, the 14 teams were divided into two sections, with the top four of each going through to the Currie Cup proper for an eight-team competition while the bottom three of each section played in the six-side Bankfin Cup competition. Both competitions then had semi-finals. The same format was used in 2002.

It gave all the sides the opportunity for glory, but ultimately the argument was that there were too many easy matches with big scores, making a mockery of the competition.

Since 2003, the top eight sides have played in the Premier Division and the other six sides in the First Division. There were no semi-finals in 2003, but that was resumed in 2004. Two promotion/relegation matches at the end of each season gave the latter the opportunity to advance into the top league the following year.

possible. The colouring came from Russian soldiers' webbing soaked in hot water. The golden collars were in one instance made from the ground next to a prisoner-of-war camp!

The members of South Africa's Sixth Division rugby side went on a four-month tour after the end of the war but before they were demobbed. They played matches in Italy, Germany, England and France, and the team

A captain of many talents

Jan Pickard: WP president and captain   Springbok forward 1951/52–1956

An underachiever, some would say about Jan Pickard, Western Province captain in the 1950s. And to some extent, that would be true – but it would also be unkind. He was an outstanding lock – and a No 8 at test level – and someone the opposition was wary of. He was a hard, abrasive player and would have been called an enforcer in today's rugby jargon.

Dr Danie Craven described Pickard as a 'great footballer'. For Craven, that was the highest honour he could bestow on a player. 'He played some outstanding games, but he probably did not reach the heights he should have. He had so much potential,' wrote Craven. 'What I can say without hesitation is that he was an outstanding captain. Not only would his teams do well, but Pickard always set an example for his team-mates.

'I think his success in business points to him being firstly an individual. Perhaps that was our mistake, as coaches and selectors, that we did not give him enough freedom. I am convinced with more responsibilities he would have reached greater heights.'

Pickard was involved in many an incident – on and off the field. It was said that he could keep a whole opposing pack and a referee busy during a game, allowing his seven forwards to concentrate on the indignant opposition that would be looking for his blood!

One of his favourite tricks was to pick an opponent who was on top of his game in a particular match and to put the referee onto him, as he did in a match between Western Province and Natal. On that particular day Junior Springbok lock Lappies Labuschagne was a great irritant to Province. And when a flare-up broke out, Pickard instructed his little scrumhalf, Aubrey Luck, to drop to the ground. As he did so,

Pickard called to the referee: 'Mr Ref, look what Labuschagne has done to our scrumhalf!' After that Labuschagne was closely watched by the referee and couldn't play the aggressive game he was known for!

In 1956, when Salty du Rand had already been selected as captain of the Springbok side to tour Australia and New Zealand, Pickard was involved in an altercation with his former Maties and Western Province team-mate. It cost Du Rand the tour captaincy, although both of them toured with the Boks. Du Rand captained the Springboks in the first test against New Zealand when tour captain Basie Vivier was not selected for the test team.

Pickard played in only four test matches in three series. He was not always as fit as he should have been. His image as an enforcer, which today probably would have seen him off the field as much as on it, and his penchant for standing in the

included future Springbok captain Stephen Fry (against the 1955 British Lions) as well as wing Cecil Moss who played for South Africa in 1949 and later coached the Springboks. That touring side was coached by the former Springbok prop and vice-captain Boy Louw. Basil

Kenyon, captain of the side that won the Grand Slam in 1951/52 captained the Sixth Division side that were wartime champions of the Middle-East! (Kenyon didn't play in a single test on that tour of the British Isles, Ireland and France because of an eye injury. Hennie back line, were 'weaknesses' held against him by many a selector. But that was no surprise: he was after all noted as a Maties third team flyhalf by Oubaas Mark who moved him to the forwards. Within two seasons he became a Springbok lock!

Pickard, 29, was an established businessman even before he went on the 1956 tour to Australasia. Those first years as a businessman saw him grow his own business to eventually control 13 listed companies on the JSE. Pickard's liquor companies were the foundation of his empire; Sportsman's Warehouse comes from his stable; and Comair, Rennies and KIC were others in which he had a noticeable influence.

As president of the Western Province Rugby Union from 1981, he turned around the average performances since 1936 when he led his executive and the provincial team to a record five consecutive Currie Cup final wins from 1982–1986. When he became president, Western Province had won only two titles finals from six finals since 1936.

Pickard first captained Western Province in 1953 against Boland. He then took over the captaincy and led the side to the Currie Cup title in 1954 and for the 1957–59 competition. This was a rare feat, as no other captain in Currie Cup history had won the Currie Cup in competitions under the league format as well as in a final. He is also the only player who held the Currie Cup aloft as captain and later president of a union.

Pickard's business acumen was also largely responsible for the resurrection of the ageing Newlands into a modern stadium. He surely would have captained Province many more times, but had a Springbok captain in Hennie Muller and a future Bok captain in Stephen Fry ahead of him in the captaincy stakes.

His grandson Francois Louw, flank for the Stormers, Western Province and Maties, was capped for the Springboks in 2010.

Muller led the side in all five of the tests against the four Home Unions and France and continued the job against the 1953 Wallabies for a total of nine test captaincies of which eight were won.)

Northern Transvaal's first title

With the soldiers were back, club and provincial rugby regained a semblance of normality. In 1946, the Currie Cup competition was resumed. The two sides that would between them win or draw 35 of the 50 finals over the next 64 years, Western Province and Northern Transvaal, qualified to battle it out for the honours in that return to Currie Cup hostilities. The match was played at Loftus, the first of 17 finals to be played there until 2010. Northern Transvaal and later the Blue Bulls won 14 of those matches at Loftus and lost only three. Six of the finals at Loftus Versfeld were against Western Province, of which Northern Transvaal lost only one. That was in 1983, the second of Province's five-match winning sequences between 1982–1986.

Hansie Brewis – outstanding kicker and elusive runner.

That 1946 final is referred to by many as Con de Kock's match – and not for the right reasons. Northern Transvaal's future Springbok flyhalf Hansie Brewis had earlier kept Northerns in contention with two drop kicks, one with each foot. With the drop kick still worth four points in those days, Province led 9–8 with less than a minute's play remaining. Northern Transvaal then won a line-out deep in their own territory; Brewis kicked diagonally and wing Johnny Lourens gave chase. The ball rolled and rolled and rolled. Lourens chased it for all of 75 yards with Western Province players in pursuit.

With the ball close to the try line, young Western Province fullback Con de Kock tapped it over the side-line which was just a foot or two away. But it was winter on the Highveld, and the grass was hard and the ground dry. He slipped when nudging it to the touchline and the ball bubbled over his foot; Lourens picked it up; and Northern Transvaal had their first title, winning 11–9. And Western Province had lost their second consecutive final, albeit with seven years between the two matches.

That match at Loftus set the pattern for the many close, tense games in future finals. In Cape Town there was huge criticism about the way Northerns had played the game, with the ball not once reaching their wings. But it was a winning pattern and a game plan that to this day brings success more often than not, with the 1946 win built on the boot of Brewis and the grinding play of the Light Blues' forwards.

It was Western Province's third successive final when they faced Transvaal at Newlands in 1947. Province turned the tables against Transvaal who had beaten them in the pre-War final eight years before. The score was 16–12 in favour of Province, with the home side's backs particularly outstanding on their home turf at Newlands and offsetting the very good pack of the visitors. The best team had won, and a surprise drop kick from centre Dirkie de Villiers after half-time when the teams were tied at 9–all probably swung the close encounter the way of the home side. It was a topsy-turvy season for Province, who surprisingly lost to Rhodesia

and also struggled to overcome Eastern Province 6–5 to ensure a final. Ironically Northern Transvaal, who had won the previous final in 1946, faltered in 1947 when it counted and would have a ten-year wait before winning the Currie Cup again. They seemed on their way to the final, but Transvaal beat them in the league match to top their section and set up the Newlands final. This 19-year gap between Currie Cup titles was the worst Northerns have encountered.

As became the trend in the next two decades, no Currie Cup competition was played during an international season with the All Blacks visiting South Africa in 1949. In 1950 Western Province were back in the final – and again Transvaal were their opponents. This was the first time that Western Province played in four consecutive finals and they bettered it in the period when they played in five between 1982 and 1986.

In 1950, Hennie Muller was captain of Transvaal. Two years later he captained Western Province before returning to Johannesburg. Muller was a new full-time captain for Transvaal after the retirement of Jan Lotz the previous year. In 1949, Lotz had still captained Transvaal against the 1949 All Blacks – and the Transvaal great was then 39 years old! The West Rand hooker for years thereafter coached at his former club and played a major role as administrator, selector and coach in the Transvaal.

In 1950, Transvaal – as they had done in 1947 – eliminated Northern Transvaal from the final with a comprehensive 17–9 win and were at home against Western Province. Again it would be a battle between the Transvaal pack and the Province backs – and this time the grunting, grinding men clinched it for Transvaal to leave Province with only one win in four finals. Western Province had backs of the calibre of the classy Dennis Fry at flyhalf and another Springbok as halfback partner in Ballie Wahl, Chum Oschse and Roy Dryburgh.

This time, there were no slip-ups from Transvaal. They won 22–11 with a side containing big names throughout – and even their backs weren't remotely as average as the Cape press made them out to be. But it was up

Chris Koch, Boland's Springbok prop.

Natie Rens broke the Boland hearts.

front that they did the damage with a pack consisting of Okey Geffin, Barry Schmidt, Franz van der Ryst, Basie van Wyk, Gert Dannhauser, Gert Kruger, Piet Malan and Hennie Muller. Eight of the Transvaal players in that final were included in the Springbok side to tour the UK, Ireland and France little more than a year later and Hennie Muller was the tour vice-captain. After the injury to team captain Basil Kenyon, Muller led the side in all five tests against the four Home Unions and France.

Western Province had the early lead through a Jan Visser try converted by Richard Boyes, but Johnny Buchler hit back with a 45-metre drop goal before Western Province regained the lead through Osche's first (unconverted) try. Two penalties by Geffin gave Transvaal a 9–8 half-time lead. Captain Muller scored another Transvaal try (12–8). Osche scored his second, but then future Springbok Des Sinclair with an own try and one he made for Fancy van Staden, both converted by Geffin, put it beyond doubt at 22–11.

Heartbreak for Boland

There was no Currie Cup in 1951, and Western Province missed their first final during the next Currie Cup campaign in 1952 when Transvaal, with a new-look side and new captain Basie van Wyk, travelled to Wellington to play Boland. In 1952, Western Province trounced Boland 20–3 in the league phase. With these two teams then squared up following Province's two surprise away draws (both 6–all) against Border and Eastern Province, Boland and Western Province had to play out to reach the final. Boland won what was effectively a semi-final 5–0.

It was probably the strongest side ever fielded by Boland, and included five players who were or would become Springboks: Buks Marais at centre, Steve Hoffman on the wing, Bertus van der Merwe at hooker and the Koch cousins, Chris and Bubbles. Willem, brother of Chris, was also in the outstanding pack that Jan Burger led. Willem played for the Junior Springboks and narrowly missed selection for the Boks. The Transvaal team also included four future Springboks: Natie Rens, Hansie Oelofse, Franz van der Ryst and Basie van Wyk, as well as Junior Bok Pa Pelser.

Boland could have won that day. They missed two reasonably easy penalties and a conversion, and they had a try disallowed. Transvaal were 8–6 ahead at half-time following a try by Pelser and penalty and conversion by Rens against the two drop goals from Boland's Marais. A fine try by Steve Hoffman put Boland ahead until close on the final whistle, when Rens dropped a beauty to deny Boland 9–8. Pelser became one of Transvaal's greats, despite never being capped for the Springboks. As captain and coach he became a legend.

Transvaal, on a Currie Cup roll despite having to play with a young side against Boland, had to wait another 19 years for their next title, which they shared with Northern Transvaal in 1971 – and then repeated it the next year. A further 20 years on, they did the double again, with six of their nine titles therefore coming in braces!

With the Wallabies visiting South Africa in 1953, the next Currie Cup competition was played in 1956, before the strangest Currie Cup competition yet played followed the Kingsmead final.

The league system returns – and Province prosper
In 1954, Springbok lock Jan (Bull) Pickard took over the reins as captain at Western Province. Jan Bull as he was called throughout South Africa was tough, uncompromising, and full of tricks as many a referee could have attested. He was a little on the lazy side, but according to Dr Danie Craven who moulded him at Stellenbosch, Pickard was an outstanding captain who led by example. In the pre-tour pen sketches of the players for the 1956 Springbok tour to Australia and New Zealand he was described as a 'bullocking player with amazing strength' – and he took Province to their next Currie Cup title, their first since 1947. This time, by 11–8, Western Province turned the tables on Northern Transvaal who

had beaten them 11–9 at Loftus in 1946. The 1954 final was played at Newlands.

The victory was built on good planning by Pickard who instructed the quick flank Dawie Ackermann and No 8 Ivor Dorrington to cut Hansie Brewis off from his backs. Province drove from set pieces to give their backs less pressure from the Northerns loose forwards, and when leading 8–0 against the wind by half-time, the match seemed secure. It became 11–0 before Francois (Lucky) Roux scored and Brewis added his customary drop goal. A second try by Roux was (controversially) disallowed by referee Ralph Burmeister, but the title went to the best side on the day.

That loss left Northern Transvaal on a solitary title (in 1946) from the six Currie Cup competitions played, having appeared in only two finals. Province, with two titles from five finals were clearly ahead in the race against what became their greatest rival. But Northerns changed matters in 1956 when they beat Natal in Durban. The Light Blues played without their touring Springboks to Australasia with the league format for all teams completed without the international players who were then on tour.

It was a last-minute try (how often have Northern Transvaal and the Blue Bulls done that?) that clinched matters for Northerns. Scored by Schalk van Dyk, it gave

Roy Dryburgh – the only 1956 Springbok in the final.

them a close 9–8 win – but it could have been so different on that gloomy, drizzly day at the Kingsmead cricket ground. While Northerns had opted to play without their internationals, Natal selected Roy Dryburgh, and despite a sterling performance in the semi-final against Province – his old side – and also in the final, the experienced test player missed a very kickable goal deep into the second half that would have put Natal out of sight. Natal's next final appearance was a full 28 years later, in 1984 against Western Province after a strange semi-final that brought much glee in Durban!

The Currie Cup was important enough that the SARFB wouldn't allow international tours to steal the competition's glamour! And true to form, with the British Lions visiting in 1955, there was no Currie Cup in that year. It is somewhat of a deviation from the normal pattern that the competition did take place in 1956.

But then came 1957 – and the first part of the Currie Cup that was to be decided over two seasons. That was weird in itself but the fact that the second season would only take place in 1959 with no Currie Cup matches in 1958 made it a strange and incomprehensible competition. (In 1958, France visited South Africa for the first time.)

Good wins in 1957 against weaker sides that were stronger in 1959 – or vice versa – obviously had a huge influence on the end result. Western Province were nevertheless in a class of their own over both seasons and thoroughly deserved to add their title to the SA Board Trophy. They had to draw or beat Transvaal in their final fixture at Newlands to win the Currie Cup, and did enough with the scores tied at 11–all, with three tries by the Currie Cup winners against two by Transvaal.

Then followed the longest Currie Cup break outside of the two world wars, with the next competition only played in 1964. The general unhappiness about the 1957–59 tournament as well as a full international programme caused the Currie Cup to be put on ice for five years. In between, there was the 1959 Junior Springboks' tour of Argentina; a visit by Scotland in 1960 and, of course, the major event, the 1960 series against the All Blacks; the 1960/61 Grand Slam tour; the 1962 visit by the British Lions and the Wallabies who came to South Africa in 1963; as well as the Wales visit to South Africa for a one-off test in Durban in 1964.

Once again the 1964 competition was decided by league format – for the last time! The second most ridiculous competition format used in the Currie Cup competition applied in this competition. In an attempt to give every side affiliated to the SA Rugby Board a chance to win the Currie Cup, the competition was divided into five sections of three teams each. The five section winners went through to a further league competition. Western Province finished top of the standings and were crowned winners, as in 1966 when the same system was used.

Again a French tour halted Currie Cups proceedings, and no competition was played in 1967.

6

The struggle for the golden cup
A new Currie Cup giant emerges

Exactly 20 years after winning the Currie Cup for the first time, the Sharks repeated the feat in 2010 – this time in Durban – for their sixth title. And while their first win in 1990 over Northern Transvaal at Loftus was deserved, Natal (as they were then known) were arguably not the best side throughout the season. But then, the decision to settle the Currie Cup from 1968 onwards by a final has brought a number of surprise results. In 1990, Natal out-planned and surprised an arrogant Northern Transvaal – only the second defeat in a final for Northern Transvaal at their stronghold that even then was called Fortress Loftus.

The Sharks' win in 2010 came on the back of an impressive series of wins in the league phases of the competition that consisted of a double round of matches among the top eight sides in South Africa. It was an outstanding performance. As in 1990, it was against the odds, and in the end was a rather one-sided final with the scoreline of 30–10 the fourth biggest in the history of the 50 finals. Flyhalf 20-year-old Patrick Lambie was the star of the show with his 25 points – the second most in a final after Derick Hougaard's 26 against the Lions at Ellis Park in 2002. Lambie's impressive tally included two tries.

Lambie, after an outstanding season, was awarded his Springbok colours for the 2010 end-of-year tour and played in all four tests as well as the match against the British Barbarians. He is the first Michaelhouse old boy to be awarded national colours in rugby. The Sharks' performances through the season saw six of their young players awarded Bok colours for the first time, namely Lambie, Lwazi Mvovo, Charl McLeod, Willem Alberts, Andries Strauss and Keegan Daniel. With Odwa Ndungane, Adi Jacobs, Alistair Hargreaves, Tendai 'Beast' Mtawarira, Ryan Kankowski and brothers Bismarck and Jannie du Plessis, the Sharks had 13 players in the tour group to go to the UK.

But it wasn't all Lambie. The Sharks' 2010 pack was superb, and the team's defence,

Coach John Plumtree celebrates the Sharks' 30–10 Currie Cup final win over Western Province in 2010.

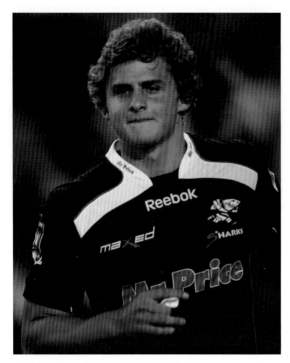
Patrick Lambie – 25 points in the 2010 final.

when Province tried to climb the mountain back into the game, even better. But most impressive, probably, was the way in which they repelled defending champions Blue Bulls a fortnight prior to the final when they completely dominated the first half and then grimly hung on at the end for a narrow but deserved 16–12 semi-final win in Durban. It should not be forgotten that the win in the final was their second over the finalists of the 2010 Super 14 competition, the Stormers and Bulls playing under different names but with mostly the same personnel. The passion that goes with the Currie Cup saw 52 000 spectators crammed into King's Park for a day of above-average rugby fare – the kind of crowd for rugby lower than test level other countries only dream of.

It was just about all over after 26 minutes when the score stood at 23–3, and despite a good fight back by Schalk Burger's men from then on, the 23–10 half-time score was added to only by Lambie with a late try he converted himself. The Province skipper afterwards conceded that his team had been comprehensively out-played. Elated Sharks coach John Plumtree, former Springbok Sevens player and member of the first Natal side to lift the Currie Cup in 1990, said of the win: 'The way we played as a team was amazing. But the big thing here is that it doesn't matter which individuals you have, this was a team effort. Nobody gave us a chance in the build up to this game. The experts were writing us off, and that motivated us. Then the crowd got behind us and really helped us get the win.'

Plumtree is a New Zealander by birth. He played 40 matches for Taranaki, and after his 80 matches for Natal/Sharks during which time he won two Currie Cup medals (in 1990 and 1996), he returned to New Zealand for a few years where he represented Hawkes Bay. He was an All Blacks trialist.

It was the Sharks' second title in two years – but as a sobering interjection: it was also only their second since 1996 when they beat the Golden Lions 33–15 at Ellis Park. For their win in 2008 they beat the Blue Bulls 9–3 at King's Park. It was no mean achievement against a side that had dominated the era from 2002 with seven finals appearances in eight years.

Just as Western Province dominated the Currie Cup in the era until finals were first played, so Northern Transvaal and later the Blue Bulls, as they were called from 1998, were the outstanding side in the 43 seasons from 1968 when the Currie Cup was contested every year. There were also seven finals played between 1939 and 1968 when it was decided that every Currie Cup winner would in future be crowned by way of a final. It was a refreshing change and has proved to be hugely successful. The public interest in the competition soared and, with it, the publicity and the revenue. What's more, all the sides currently involved as franchises in Super Rugby – the Bulls, Stormers, Sharks, Cheetahs (the Free State Cheetahs and Griquas combined) and the Lions have had their taste of Currie Cup success in a final.

Northern Transvaal/Blue Bulls have the proud distinction of having won 19 and shared four of the 50

Deaths in Currie Cup rugby

Although two players have died in hospital following Currie Cup matches, only one death was the result of injuries sustained in a match. The only player to be fatally injured in a Currie Cup match was Western Province fullback Chris Burger in August 1980. His death in the Universitas hospital on the Sunday morning followed a neck injury sustained in a ruck in the Currie Cup match against the Free State. Burger was a versatile and very skilful back and also represented Western Province at flyhalf and centre.

Ironically Burger had considered retiring at the end of that season – and 90 minutes before the incident that cost him his life, he was part of a guard of honour for Rampie Stander, the Free State and Springbok prop who had collapsed on the Thursday while preparing for the match that claimed Burger's life. The former Maties strongman had suffered a stroke.

Ockert Brits, Transvaal's young No 8, died of a heart attack after the match against Northern Free State in Welkom in 1984. His death was, however, not related to injury sustained in the match. Brits collapsed at half-time and died on his way to the Welkom hospital.

In 1991 Jan Lock, strongman of the Northern Transvaal scrum, who had been out with injury, was making a return to the game in a curtain-raiser to the Currie Cup final against Transvaal at Loftus. The searing October heat was apparently too much for the big man. He died in the change room after the match.

Burger's death led to the founding of the Chris Burger Fund by the Western Province captain in that Bloemfontein match Morné du Plessis and his team-mates. In 1989, Petro Jackson, a young player from Kylemore in Stellenbosch died during a rugby match. The coloured rugby controlling body at that time, SARU, then founded the Petro Jackson Fund. Unity in 1992 resulted in the two funds amalgamating to become The Chris Burger/Petro Jackson Players' Fund. In August 2010 the Fund celebrated its 30th anniversary – and Du Plessis, now in his early sixties, still heads up the cause.

The Fund has two primary objectives: to assist the victims of catastrophic or serious rugby injuries in SA; and to develop and implement initiatives that aim to educate, inform and create awareness around rugby injuries.

In 1987, the Fund purchased the leasehold rights to a specially designed suite in the Danie Craven Pavilion at Newlands Rugby Stadium exclusively for the use of disabled rugby players in wheelchairs.

The Fund runs the 'Power of Prevention' programme through which it has established the 'SpineLine', a 24-hour emergency response service for rugby injuries; the 'Rugby Medic Club', which trains hundreds of club and secondary school medics annually; and the 'Coaches Logbook', a practical aid for coaches with advice on conditioning, safety, techniques and more.

The Fund hosts an annual banquet and golf day through which it raises much needed funding for its activities. As SARU's official Social Responsibility partner, the Fund receives a generous annual grant from the governing body.

The game of rugby is of necessity one of risk because of the physical contact involved, and annually there are a disturbingly large number of spinal and other serious injuries resulting from the game, as well as deaths. Changes in the rules, better training facilities, reassurance that there are always first-aid and reaction units available and a continual awareness campaign have all combined to curb these tragic results of the game.

Going back in time
The first recorded death in South African rugby was in 1884 when Alfred Schlemmer of West End was tackled on his way to the try line in the first final of the Grand Challenge competition in Kimberley against Beaconsfield. He died in hospital a week after the match.

In a freak accident in 1907, Walter Wright died as a result of an injury during a rugby match. Described as a talented Pirates three-quarter, he apparently crashed into one of the bulky flagpoles that were used those days on the B field of the old Wanderers club.

Western Province's Hennie Bekker and Divan Serfontein with the Ross Frames Cup and Currie Cup in 1982.

final in every instance, winning at Loftus in 1968 and 1969. They impressively dispatched Transvaal (16–3) and Western Province (28–13) in those finals.

A disturbing trend was noticeable though. In the six matches under coach Buurman van Zyl that they played away from Loftus, Northern Transvaal won only three – all in Bloemfontein against the Free State in the 1970s. Worse was to come. First they faltered in Kimberley in a huge upset, losing 11–9 to Griquas in 1970. Then it was Transvaal – albeit through a strange refereeing decision and an uncontrolled crowd – that held them to a 14–all draw in 1971. In the away losses against Griquas and Transvaal and the draw against Province at Newlands in 1979 Northern Transvaal showed vulnerability. It was further highlighted as they lost their next two away finals – no longer under Van Zyl's coaching – that were played at Newlands in 1982 and 1985. A win against Transvaal at Ellis Park in 1987 was an exception, and Northern Transvaal again drew at Newlands two years later. By 1989 their away record in finals since 1968 read: played nine – won three, lost three, drew three.

When rugby officially became professional in 1996, Northern Transvaal were not ready for it. A perfect example of this financial impact in the initial stages was the contrasting performances in the 1990s by Northern Transvaal (renamed the Blue Bulls in 1998) and what was then the Gauteng Lions. Whereas the Light Blues struggled, the Lions under Louis Luyt had one of the best eras in their history – and they dominated the years 1990–1999 with the Sharks, winning three times and also reaching three other finals.

Northern Transvaal regained the Currie Cup in 1991 after their surprise loss to Natal the previous year. Then followed the worst spell in their history where they went without a Currie Cup title for six competitions until 1998. What made it even worse for the Loftus faithful was that their team didn't even make it to a final in that time and nearly lost their A-Section Currie Cup status! However, the decade from 2000 brought a new dominance by the Blue Bulls in their second golden era. They reached seven

finals played. They also featured as losing finalists in a further eight finals for an involvement in 31 of the 50 finals. Their first golden era was in the years 1968–1980 under Buurman van Zyl (13 seasons) and Salty du Rand (one season) when they played in 12 finals, won nine times and shared the trophy twice. Northerns lost only the 1970 final against Griquas. Twice they missed the final – in 1972 when Van Zyl was ill and again in 1976.

Northern Transvaal only became an independent union in 1938 and didn't start their quest for Currie Cup fame very well. Of the first six Currie Cup competitions they took part in they won only two (in 1946 and 1956) and lost one of their two finals. They thus missed out on the other three Currie Cup play-offs. Then Western Province won the next three Currie Cup titles when they were again played as league competitions (1957–59, 1964 and 1966).

Northern Transvaal however showed their mettle after the Currie Cup was played every year and decided by a

Currie Cup's greatest match-winner

In a competition that has seen more than 20 000 players playing Currie Cup rugby over 120 years, the name of Naas Botha stands supreme as the biggest match-winner in the competition's history. It is no coincidence that in Botha's era Northern Transvaal dominated the Currie Cup scene.

Of course, there has been a series of absolutely magnificent performances from many players over the years. Some outstanding tries, some monstrous penalty kicks, some special individual performances in matches and finals all contributed to making the Currie Cup arguably the most famous and undoubtedly the best supported first-class competition in world rugby. But Botha's feats over a period of 16 Currie Cup seasons (1977–1992) consistently won matches for Northern Transvaal – and it is no coincidence that their dominance in the Currie Cup was curbed in the two years when Botha was overseas, trying out for the Dallas Cowboys in gridiron.

His rugby career wasn't confined to those 16 seasons though, as he continued until 1995, playing a little club rugby for Adelaar in Pretoria and also an invitation first-class match. Here it was hoped that he could show his skills in an invitation XV. The reason was that Springbok coach Kitch Christie harboured ideas of including Botha in his World Cup squad. But time had caught up with the great player at 37, and Christie had to shelve his plan.

Two statements from Dr Danie Craven sum up Naas Botha's brilliance. 'Give me Naas Botha and I'll conquer the world,' and then, after what was only Botha's second test, in 1980 against South America in Durban, Craven said, 'He will be our greatest ever'. Three drop goals, a penalty and the conversion of captain Morné du Plessis's try in that test saw Botha accumulate 26 of the Boks' 44 points in the two-test series.

It is a fact: Botha was a brilliant kicker – whether from the hand or at the posts. But even better was his tactical acumen and vision, and despite criticism that Botha could do little but kick, South Africa's back line was feared throughout the rugby world. One of the best back lines the Springboks have fielded, it included players like Divan Serfontein, Danie Gerber, Willie du Plessis, Gerrie Germishuys, Ray Mordt, Michael du Plessis and Carel du Plessis. Add fullbacks of the ilk of Johan Heunis and Gysie Pienaar, and the point is made that Botha could indeed play with a back line and was not limited to the kicking game.

For the sceptics, there was also Botha's brilliant display of running rugby for a World XV at Twickenham in 1986, during the International Rugby Board's Centenary celebrations. This was the Naas Botha that those who had watched club rugby in Pretoria over the years had come to know.

Botha's critics were especially scathing about his defence, but conveniently overlooked the great try-saving tackle in the north-east corner of the Free State Stadium against the British Lions in 1980. It was his first year of test rugby – and there were many more counting tackles in his career. Northern Transvaal coach Buurman van Zyl ordered Botha to stay on his feet: 'You don't help us by being on the ground or in a maul.' Van Zyl maintained that others could do the defensive work and even devised a special defensive strategy to enable match-winner Botha to remain on his feet to kick his team to tactical wins or with his deadly drop goals.

He was a skinny, long-haired 19-year-old University of Pretoria player when he was drawn from the Tukkies Under-20 side by Van Zyl. His senior debut was for Northern Transvaal against South Eastern Transvaal. His captain was Thys Lourens, 15 years older than Botha. Lourens, Botha and coach Van Zyl would form the near-unbeatable Northern Transvaal triumvirate.

Botha played in only 28 test matches for South Africa, but still set a long list of records at international and provincial level: most points, most drops, most Currie Cup titles and most Currie Cup finals played (shared with Northern Transvaal team-mate, Burger Geldenhuys). He was also captain of Northern Transvaal a record 128 times and scored a record 2 511 first-class points including the record 1 699 points in the Currie Cup.

Botha won many, many matches for Northern Transvaal and South Africa, but there were two outstanding performances which were arguably his best: the 1985 Lion Cup against Western Province at Newlands, and the Currie Cup final against Transvaal at Ellis Park in 1987.

The 1985 Lion Cup mud bath

The match at Newlands was a Lion Cup knock-out match. Everything favoured the home side which had won the Currie Cup for the three preceding years and then continued their run in 1985 and 1986 for a five-title Currie Cup record. The field was wet and the mud was thick. Northern Transvaal were not accustomed to playing in wet conditions, let alone mud that made constructive rugby almost impossible.

Barely recognisable in the mud that was Newlands, Botha covered, and even tackled; but above all, he turned Western Province around endlessly with his great tactical kicking, and the only try in the 12–3 win came from his cousin Hendrik Kruger.

But was that mud show his best performance? 'No,' Botha says, 'the win in 1987 against Transvaal must take pride of place. Don't forget, that was a Currie Cup final.'

The 1987 final

The 1987 Currie Cup final win was particularly satisfying. The Transvaal press had made it clear that this would be their team's big year. They looked unstoppable in the early part of the competition after losing the 1986 final to Western Province at Newlands, but looked to be the genuine article in 1987. Botha, however, warned that 'the Currie Cup isn't won in May' — and he had the last laugh. He kicked four penalties and four drop goals in the 1987 final at the cold, rainy Ellis Park, where hail also pelted down during the match. The 24–18 win was one of Botha's favourite wins and the match, he feels, was his best provincial performance.

Overseas and back

Botha was a half-year professional with Rovigo in Italy before professionalism was really accepted and played in Italy from 1987 to 1993, winning two national championships with them. From Rovigo he returned to help the Bulls in their Currie Cup campaigns after the end of the northern season. Botha's efforts for the Italian club saw the title of honorary citizen bestowed upon him by Rovigo.

When Botha returned from his Dallas stint, Northern Transvaal regained the Currie Cup after Province's five-year run. Northerns won the Currie Cup in 1987 and again in 1988 when they beat Western Province. They shared it with Province at Newlands in 1989. They then lost it to Natal in 1990 but regained it in 1991, with Transvaal the losers once more. Botha's last Currie Cup season in 1992 saw Transvaal and Natal fight it out for the coveted Currie Cup, with Transvaal again denied.

Botha bowed out of the Currie Cup in 1992. He continued with Rovigo and played for Adelaar before being coaxed back by Kitch Christie in 1995.

Outstanding career summary
Provincial and Currie Cup:

❏ In 1977, when he was only 19 years old, Botha made his debut for Northern Transvaal.

❏ He captained Northern Transvaal in 1980 when he was 22.

❏ He became the youngest captain to win the Currie Cup at 22 years and 217 days.

❏ Botha holds the Currie Cup record of 1 699 points. He kicked five drop goals against Natal in 1992 and a total of 20 drop goals in the Currie Cup in 1985.

❏ His total of 179 matches – 128 as captain – for Northern Transvaal included 123 Currie Cup matches.

❏ Botha played in 11 Currie Cup finals, sharing the record with Springbok flanker Burger Geldenhuys, who also captained Northern Transvaal.

❏ With Thys Lourens and coach Buurman van Zyl, Botha formed the triumvirate that was the nucleus of the Light Blues' success in the 1970s and 1980s. Botha and Lourens hold two contrasting records: Botha was the youngest Currie Cup winning captain at 22 years and 217 days, and Lourens the oldest at 35 years and 138 days.

❏ Botha's SA record of 138 points in Currie Cup finals is well ahead of the second-placed 62 by Willem de Waal of the Free State Cheetahs and Western Province.

❏ In 1979, 1981, 1985 and 1987 Botha was voted South Africa's Player of the Year – a record. Only two other players have won the award more than once: Gerald Bosch and Uli

Schmidt both won it twice.

- ❏ Botha scored a total of 210 drop goals for Northern Transvaal and South Africa, including 20 in a single Currie Cup season (1985). In 1992 he kicked five drop goals in his last Currie Cup season against Natal.

International rugby:
- ❏ Botha made his test debut against the South American Jaguars in 1980 and also played against the British Lions.

- ❏ He secured a win in the third test against the Lions in Port Elizabeth in 1980 when he converted a try from touch in near gale-force wind and driving rain, and was dubbed the 'Nasty Booter' by the British press.
- ❏ In 1981 he scored 20 of the Springboks' 24 points in the second test against the All Blacks in Wellington.
- ❏ Botha captained South Africa to a series win over the New Zealand Cavaliers in 1980. He was captain

when South Africa were re-admitted to international rugby in 1992. In all, he played in 28 tests and was captain in nine.
- ❏ In 2006 he was also admitted to the IRB's Hall of Fame to underline his standing in international rugby.
- ❏ Botha scored 312 points – then a South African record – in internationals. That included 18 drop goals.
- ❏ He received the State President's Award in 1992.

finals and won five titles (one shared) between 2002 and 2009. The Free State Cheetahs were also a force to be reckoned with between 2004 and 2009, playing in five finals of which they won two and shared one with the Blue Bulls.

Western Province, after their record five-in-a-row titles in 1982–1986, had a six-year finals drought between their 1989 draw and 1995. Then followed a mini-resurrection as they played in five finals between 1995 and 2001, of which they won three and lost two before another Currie Cup hiatus. With their only final appearance since being the 2010 loss against the Sharks, they have now been without the trophy for nine years. But the Lions are worse off. Their last trophy came in 1999, and their two finals since against the Bulls in 2002 (31–7) and the Free State Cheetahs in 2007 (20–18) were lost, the latter cruelly in the last three minutes.

Griquas, although they beat all the top sides and franchise holders, simply lacked the depth to advance to the semi-finals and beyond.

The undisputed greatest feat by a South African side playing in competitions below the international teams was achieved in 2009 when the Blue Bulls won the Currie Cup as well as the Super 14. Both were won convincingly against the Chiefs (61–17) and the Free State Cheetahs (36–24).

2009 – 'A dagger removed'
The 36–24 win against the Free State was revenge for their loss against the Bloemfontein side at Loftus in 2005. It looked to be one-sided in 2009 as the Blue Bulls ran up a 24–0 lead in only 25 minutes against a side that had done well to make the Currie Cup final after a disastrous Super 14 tour down under. The big lead was due mainly to one man: Fourie du Preez. The scrumhalf genius set up all three of the early tries through two outstanding place kicks that were converted into the easiest of tries by Francois Hougaard and Bryan Habana. He also timed his pass to Habana perfectly for the wing's second try. But Free State Cheetahs fought back magnificently

and at 30–21, they were very much back in the match before two penalties by Morné Steyn put another thriller beyond doubt.

Anybody who doubted the importance of a Currie Cup win, even in a season of Super 14 glory, should have heard the Blue Bulls' hard man Bakkies Botha that night. It was like a dagger removed, the big lock said, and added that the loss in 2005 against the Free State Cheetahs 'really hurt'. Of course this was in some measure also compensation for the previous year when Northerns had slipped up against the Sharks in Durban (14–9).

The 2009 final was the ninth between the Blue Bulls and the Free State Cheetahs. Seven wins, one draw and that single loss in 2005 tell the story of Northerns/Blue Bulls' dominance in finals against the Free State/Free State Cheetahs.

Finals – and Northern Transvaal dominate
Northern Transvaal, after an unhappy start to the Currie Cup competition with only two wins from seven finals in the ten competitions they contested, suddenly took off in 1968. To this day there are many – some of them players under his coaching – who say that Buurman van Zyl wasn't a great coach. That he had the fittest and best motivated team around, and that he knew how to work with his charges was, however, indisputable – and his record speaks for itself. Under Van Zyl, the team suddenly had more frequent training sessions and a fixed game plan.

Van Zyl's appointment as the first official Northern Transvaal coach was at the suggestion of Daan Swiegers, later a convenor of the national selection panel. Until 1967 Northern Transvaal's selectors had taken turns to coach the provincial team during a season.

The first team to realise that matters in Pretoria had changed were Transvaal in the 1968 final. They were beaten 16–3 in Pretoria in a season when Western Province's lack of class tight forwards eliminated them from the trophy race. Once again Transvaal's forwards impressed throughout the season, and the general prediction was that Northerns would not be able to contain their pack. But what nobody bargained on was that Northern Transvaal would play superlative rugby – and it was their forwards in particular, and discarded former Transvaal flyhalf Alan Menter, who did the damage.

It was Northern Transvaal's first home final since their first win in 1946. And they entertained their supporters with a near-perfect performance by the pack and some clinical tactical kicking by Menter. Northerns were 10–0 up at the break after two converted tries by big winger Koos Meiring and his fellow wing Willem Stapelberg. It became 13–0 shortly afterwards with a Meiring drop kick from a mark. Transvaal's only points came after 55 minutes through a Jannie van Deventer penalty, and with a 16–3 win, the scene had been set for future forward dominance by the Light Blues.

1969 – Frik's final

In 1969 Western Province were convincingly beaten, 28–13, in another Loftus final. Province had outplayed Boland under Springbok captain Dawie de Villiers in the dying seconds in the semi-final (11–9) after a better Western Province season than in 1968, but remained unconvincing in their forward play. However, Northern Transvaal were not as good as in the previous year's final and were marginally ahead at 11–8 at half-time. Then they suddenly trailed 13–11 two minutes after the break as Province's steamroller Gert Muller – who was also a provincial sprinter – scored his second try with a touch-line conversion from HO de Villiers.

Then followed probably the most outstanding individual performance in the history of the Currie Cup. It came from Frik du Preez, only six weeks away from his 34th birthday. Within nine minutes he turned the match on its head by scoring two penalties and a try when his team were only 16–13 ahead ten minutes into the second half. Perhaps the big man – not tall for a lock even in those days – who could out-jump any forward in the world and did so on numerous occasions, could have done a little

Frik du Preez – 'gedrop, geplace en gescore.'

more work in the tight/loose during his career. Perhaps he could have been a little fitter. But he was one of the very best produced by Northern Transvaal and South Africa in any position.

It was tight and far from a match won, despite the 16–13 lead. Then Northern Transvaal captain Piet Uys threw Du Preez the ball after a Province scrum transgression. It was 60 metres out. Frik let fly with a drop kick that went true and straight, and easily over the cross bar. Amid the wild scenes that followed on the stands, the national selectors had to bear the brunt of their folly to drop the great man from the last two tests as they were heckled by the jubilant Northern Transvaal supporters.

Then came his try, and his great friend Mof Myburgh

The man who changed Northern Transvaal's fortunes

Buurman van Zyl: coached 13: won 9, drew 2, lost 1, missed 1 final

Buurman van Zyl of Northern Transvaal was easily the most successful coach in the history of the Currie Cup competition.

In his 13 years at the helm of the most successful team over a period, he coached Northern Transvaal to nine titles plus two that were shared. His only loss in a final was in 1970 when Griquas surprised Northern Transvaal 11–9 in Kimberley. In 1976 Northern Transvaal didn't qualify for the final. (Van Zyl didn't coach the side in 1972 because of illness.)

In addition to these finals, Buurman van Zyl's Northern Transvaal played in 116 Currie Cup matches between 1968 and 1981, winning 99, drawing four and losing only 13.

Although there are critics – and even players – who said that his success was built on discipline rather than good coaching, it remains a travesty of justice that he was never invited to coach the Springboks. (He had been earmarked to coach South Africa in 1982 but died in January of that year.)

Brigadier Jacobus Gerhardus Marthinus van Zyl played 79 matches for Eastern Province over a provincial career spanning 15 years, from 1937 to 1951, while he was a policeman in Port Elizabeth. This included the match against the 1949 All Blacks. He also represented Eastern Province as a javelin thrower and took part in South Africa's 1936 Olympic trials.

Buurman van Zyl, Thys Lourens and the Currie Cup.

'Oom' Buurman, as he was called, became Northern Transvaal's coach in 1968. Prior to that, he was a coach with the very strong Pretoria Police club. Van Zyl put a high premium on fitness and discipline and his strongest trait was probably getting the best out of his charges. It must also be said that he had an exceptional reservoir of talent to work with, and in his time 35 players coached by Van Zyl became Springboks – some because of their individual talent, and no doubt quite a few because of his influence on their careers. Of course, it also helped to be a member of an outstanding side.

Buurman, Thys Lourens and Naas Botha were the pillars on which the success of that first golden era of Northern Transvaal was built. Under Van Zyl, Northern Transvaal continued with the simple, basic pattern that won them their first Currie Cup in 1946, leading to much

disenchantment in the Cape because of the dour game plan followed. It was and is effective, however, and to this day the Blue Bulls stick to a structure that is difficult to break or subdue. His BDF principle (for Basics, Discipline and Fitness), as well as the way in which he worked with his players and cajoled those who needed it at the right time, were the basis for his success.

Buurman van Zyl's record in Currie Cup finals is as follows:
1968: beat Transvaal (Loftus) 16–3
1969: beat WP (Loftus) 28–13
　　　1970: lost to Griquas (Kimberley) 9–11
1971: drew with Transvaal (Ellis Park) 14–14
1972: Van Zyl ill; team coached by Salty du Rand
1973: beat Free State (Loftus) 30–22
1974: beat Transvaal (Loftus) 17–15
1975: beat Free State (Bloemfontein) 12–6
1976: N Tvl didn't make the final*
1977: beat Free State (Bloemfontein) 27–12
1978: beat Free State (Bloemfontein) 13–9
1979: drew with WP (Newlands) 15–15
1980: beat WP (Loftus) 39–9
1981: beat Free State (Loftus) 23–6

*In 1976 the Free State and Western Province contested the final in Bloemfontein, with Free State winning 33–16.

was the man who set it up. Myburgh broke through a line-out. Not the most mobile of men or known for his handling skills, he off-loaded perfectly as Du Preez came thundering through on his shoulder. On his run of more than 30 metres, Du Preez left two defenders in his wake because they couldn't keep up in a near replay of the run that brought him that famous try against the 1968 British Lions (also at Loftus). This time the last man he simply ignored was Western Province fullback HO de Villiers as Frik Du Preez ran over him to score.

The game had been won – but Big Frik still had one more arrow to fire at the selectors who had left him out of the test team. Northern Transvaal were given a penalty inside their own half, and with the crowd demanding it, captain Uys again passed the ball to Du Preez. It seemed impossible, but this time he took his time as he meticulously placed the ball. Straight and true it went.

Frik du Preez had won the Currie Cup for Northern Transvaal in those nine golden minutes when, as Mof Myburgh summed it up afterwards: 'Ou Frik het godrop, geplace en gescore!'

The final score was 28–13 to Northern Transvaal – and Western Province had again been denied in a final, their fourth loss in six.

Two years later, when he scored three tries and kicked a penalty drop over at Newlands to help his side to a 21–9 over Western Province at Newlands, Frik du Preez was cheered for minutes afterwards by the Newlands crowd – usually hostile to anything in a light blue jersey! – and carried off the field in the days when spectators were still allowed to run onto the field. It was his last match at South Africa's Home of Rugby.

1970 – Kirkpatrick's triumph

In 1970 one of the biggest upsets in the history of the Currie Cup occurred. Western Province were beaten away by Griquas (22–18) and Transvaal (16–9) – and the signs were there that Griquas could be there or thereabouts at the run-in. They had the nucleus of a team that coach Ian

Kirkpatrick had been building for seven years with the objective of winning the Currie Cup – and they did just that.

A record Currie Cup final win was predicted for that big day in Griquas' Currie Cup history on 26 September 1970. Kirkpatrick, one of South Africa's greatest coaches, was the man behind the selection of his former Springbok team-mate Mannetjies Roux for the side. And Kirkpatrick's role can't be underestimated. He saw the team for only 10–12 training sessions in a season, when many of them would travel hundreds of miles to play their Currie Cup matches. They did their training on Friday nights, the only session since the match before!

The 1970 win followed a building process of eight years, after the former Griquas Springbok who had played his final international rugby the year before, returned from Bloemfontein to Kimberley. A year after retiring as player, he started the road to glory. The 1964 competition started off without a number of players, who had either moved to other centres or had retired. Griquas lost their captain and other stalwarts to injury, and had to be content with the Sport Pienaar trophy played for by the second-placed teams in the five Currie Cup sections. In 1966, Griquas drew with eventual Currie Cup champions Western Province but did little more in the competition, and in 1968 – the first year of what would become an annual competition for the Currie Cup – Griquas won the Sport Pienaar trophy again. By then, Piet Visagie, who had become a Springbok against the French in 1967, was a difficult customer – both with his general play and as an exceptional kicker. In 1969, in another strange competition structure, Griquas were beaten by Boland (13–0) to be eliminated from a semi-final play-off against Western Province. Griquas were not yet one of South Africa's top sides. They threatened and they won, but not with the consistency needed to make them a feared side. Opponents, however, were wary of them; of that there was little doubt.

Some lucky wins helped Griquas through the year in 1970. They narrowly beat Natal at King's Park in Durban and Border in East London. North Western Cape and North Eastern Cape brought easy wins. They were on track for the Currie Cup and their win against Western Province in Kimberley made the critics really sit up and take notice. The score was 22–18, and a 43–16 win against Eastern Transvaal showed that they really meant business. They were also helped by other sides. Natal held Transvaal to a draw when a Transvaal win would have meant a play-off match for the Kimberley side who were now in the final.

To retain their sharpness and work on teamwork, Griquas played Free State in a friendly where Mannetjies Roux was injured – and he was the heartbeat of the side. Roux, in a race against time, was declared fit shortly before the final. It was his 44th match for the union in which he had grown up but only got to represent late in his rugby life. It was also his 25th match as captain of the side.

Afterwards, the Light Blues admitted that they were perhaps a little overconfident. And also that the best team had won. They were uncomplaining about the 53-yarder that Griquas' No 8, Peet Smith, lofted through the uprights, four minutes before full time. Griquas ref Ben Calitz was the man in the middle in the days when the home side still provided three referees from whom the visitors could pick their man, but there were no complaints from Northerns on the issue of the referee.

Before the match, Frik du Preez had said to his old friend and room-mate Mof Myburgh: 'This is not how one feels before a Cup final'. There was looseness, a lack of focus, noticeable among the Northerns players.

Griquas led for most of the match. But the 16 000 or so spectators who had packed the De Beers Stadium felt that the might of Northern Transvaal would deny them.

Two great breaks by the home side's centre Koos Waldeck and scrumhalf Joggie Viljoen – who became a Springbok the next year – put Buddy Schwartz through for two unconverted tries, in only his second match for Griquas. After the first 30 minutes, Griquas were 8–0 to the good. Waldeck's gap was taken on the halfway line and went to his captain Roux, who sent Schwartz over. Up front, the home side were under tremendous pressure

Mannetjies Roux captained Griquas to a surprise title.

throughout, although the efforts of their lighter pack in their quest to keep the Light Blues at bay played a huge part in the victory. Springbok Piet Visagie turned the visitors around with smart tactical play and pin-point kicks, but the crowd remained disbelieving as half-time arrived with Griquas 8–3 ahead.

Then Northern Transvaal used their proven tactic of driving up-field, and Griquas were in trouble against the wind. Northern Transvaal wing Chris Luther kicked his second penalty, and Du Preez made the nightmares come true for the home crowd with a bullocking try. Griquas were suddenly 9–8 behind, and the Light Blues were in command. Four minutes from time Roux called up his veteran No 8, Peet Smith, for a crucial penalty. It was against the wind. The kick was struck beautifully, and flew as straight as an arrow. 'I just hoped; prayed that it would have the length,' Smith said afterwards – and added he was confident of success as he had kicked longer penalties in his time.

There were tears in the eyes of Griquas captain Roux, and tears streamed from the Griquas players' cheeks in the change room as what they had achieved sank in. Long after the final whistle, Griquas supporters were still milling about in front of the main stand, and their chants of 'We want Mannetjies, we want Mannetjies' were eventually answered when the famous Springbok came to the balcony clad only in his shorts.

1971 – One for the crowd!

The final in 1971 between Transvaal and Northern Transvaal at Ellis Park was yet another gripping one. Transvaal had to beat Free State and Griquas in play-off matches because of a tie on the log after the round-robin phase. Then followed a semi-final against Natal, won 21–10. There was great glee in Pretoria with the realisation that the three tough matches would lead to a fatigued Transvaal side in the final.

But Transvaal president, Jannie le Roux, had the semi-final and the final moved out at the SARFB meeting, and it was the Light Blues who had to pay the penalty of too little rugby while their neighbours sharpened theirs in play-offs. A hastily arranged friendly against Rhodesia was the only match preparation Northern Transvaal had in five weeks of kicking their heels.

The final ended in controversy with a last-minute try by Transvaal to draw the match 14–all. A try by Northerns lock Piet du Plessis, converted by Chris Luther, followed by a try by Tobias du Toit for the home team, took Northerns into a 5–3 half-time lead. A penalty and a drop goal by fullback Jannie van Deventer then gave Transvaal a 9–5 lead before Northern Transvaal flyhalf Dudley Gradwell slotted in two drop goals and Luther kicked a might penalty on full time. It seemed all over at 14–9 to Northern Transvaal and their supporters

ran onto the field in joy to carry off their heroes. But referee Gert Bezuidenhout had other ideas and with spectators still on the field, Transvaal kicked off and regained possession. Captain Piet Greyling and fellow flank Simon Norwood launched an attack. When they were stopped close to the line, Springbok prop Theo (Sakkie) Sauermann was there to barge over. Van Deventer kicked the all-important conversion and it ended 14–all. The president of the Golden Lions Rugby Union, Kevin de Klerk, played in that match. He partnered Jannie van Aswegen at lock for Transvaal. Van Aswegen was one of Griquas' outstanding players the previous year when they beat Northern Transvaal.

1972 – Bosch wins the day

In 1972, Transvaal first eliminated Free State in a play-off before beating Eastern Transvaal 25–19 in the only Currie Cup final ever played at Springs. It was flyhalf Gerald Bosch's day – and the match seemed over at half-time, when Transvaal led 18–3 after a couple of early Bosch drop goals had put the homeside on their heels. But Eastern Transvaal came back after the break and gave Transvaal a very hard time in the second half. In the end, both sides scored two tries, with Bosch's boot making the difference in the scoreline. His 17 points included a record at that stage of three drop goals in a final.

Tommy Symons and Johan Esterhuizen scored tries for Transvaal, and Bosch kicked three drop goals over, two penalties and a conversion. For Eastern Transvaal, Koos Mulder and Ben Stander scored a try each, Boesman Wilkinson added two penalty goals and a conversion, and Bennie Dercksen contributed a penalty.

1973 – Free State's emergence

In 1973, the Currie Cup was divided into four sections, and each side played only four matches. Transvaal lost to Western Province (18–7) and that eliminated them from the competition that year. But Northern Transvaal were back. They beat a tough Rhodesia at Loftus in the one semi-final while the Free State defied all logic by beating Western Province on a wet Newlands that should have suited the home side. It was a brilliant final. Playing without a number of injured players, Northerns took control with their impressive pack. That was to be expected. Free State, on the other hand, ran with the lesser possession. Five minutes before the break, the score stood at 10–all. Then Moffie de Klerk scored a try, and Dirk de Vos kicked his second drop kick over – and it was time for Northern Transvaal to use their backs. In the end, the 30 points by Northerns in their 30–22 win was the highest scored in a Currie Cup final at that stage.

1974 – Transvaal denied again

With the strange three-section Currie Cup competition employed again in 1974, Transvaal were back in business, narrowly losing 17–15 in the final to Northern Transvaal. Transvaal beat all sides except Eastern Province in their cross-section league matches, but then trounced the coastal side in the semi-final (30–6). That set up the final against Northern Transvaal at Loftus.

If possible, this final was harder than the one in 1971, and was described as the hardest Currie Cup final yet. In 1973, Transvaal hooker Dave Frederickson landed up in hospital with internal injuries after a legitimate tackle by Moaner van Heerden; tough man Van Heerden himself struggled to get up after a tackle at the kick-off, and Thys Lourens had teeth broken in what was an uncompromising battle.

Steve Strydom, unlucky to miss out as a fullback on the 1965 Springbok tour to Australia and New Zealand, was never a favourite referee in Pretoria. His popularity took a further knock that day when Northerns were not given a single penalty close enough to have a shot at the posts.

The bounce of the ball denied Transvaal on two occasions, in the home side's in-goal area. And then, with four minutes to go, Transvaal's flyhalf Gerald Bosch was ready to drop the winner with the score at 17–15 to Northerns. It was Transvaal's scrum put-in in the days when scrumhalves still had to feed the ball in straight at the scrums. Willie Kahts however struck a tighthead with the considerable assistance of big Hans Weber on his tighthead side, and Northern Transvaal had won another thriller.

1975 – Spies's heartbreak try

The 1975 final was won 12–6 by Northern Transvaal, after probably the most famous try in Currie Cup history. It was scored by the late Pierre Spies, father of the current Springbok No 8. He was a winger who could really convert his chances with blistering speed and a high knee action – he was a Springbok hurdler after all.

The win came on a wet, muddy field, and the scores were tied when the last movement and kick forward by Christo Wagenaar set up the try for Spies. The wing had dominated Northern Transvaal's scoring in the seasons that he played for them in the 1970s, when he scored most of his tries towards the end of matches after Northern Transvaal had softened the opposition pack. Outside the borders of the Northern Transvaal Rugby Union it was regarded as unimaginative rugby – but that is how Northerns won then and it remains the basis of their successful game plan.

Northern Transvaal's jumpers took 14 Free State throw-ins in the line-out. Springboks John Williams and Louis Moolman, two of the best that South Africa have fielded, were the Northern Transvaal locks. In the final analysis, their work in the line-out where the Free State locks were not allowed the illegal latitude of the previous encounter between the two sides pulled Northerns through to their first hat-trick of Currie Cup wins.

Behind them, flyhalf Len Gerber dictated territorial play in conditions that suited Northern Transvaal more than Free State, who wanted to run. Northerns kicked and drove, kicked and mauled – and took Free State's line-outs even if the Light Blues' kicks went out and Free State had the put-in. No tries had been scored until two minutes from time when Free State centre Pikkie du Toit

Pierre Spies eludes the Free State defence, 1975.

broke through and scored under the posts. De Wet Ras's conversion was good and the scores were 6–all.

It was not the end of the plot, however. Gerber kicked off. The ball was mauled up; taken to the blindside; forward again. Then big Louis Moolman plucked it out and passed to scrumhalf Tommy du Plessis who fed Gerber who in turn passed to Christo Wagenaar. There was a man from an off-side position when Wagenaar received the ball, and he had no option. Wagenaar kicked it to the right, high and into no-man's land. It bounced high, very high considering the very wet field, and the bounce seemed to elude Pierre Spies.

But, reaching up at full pace Spies got his fingertips to the ball, tapped it and caught it, without losing a stride. Free State No 8 Kleintjie Grobler and Spies's opposite wing Gerrie Germishuys could do little as he went over in the corner. Keith Thorreson's conversion mattered none, but

he slotted it in for a wonderful 12–6 win – deserved, but also lucky.

1976 – Free State's first

In 1976 there was a rare absence of a Northern Transvaal side in a final – for the first and only time with coach Buurman van Zyl at the helm. Free State won their first title when they outplayed Western Province at the Free State Stadium, 33–16. It was only the third time that Free State had beaten Western Province, and what made it more of a feat is that they had lost the two round-robin matches to Province that year. Thanks to Natal's 7–6 win over Transvaal and the latter's defeat against Northern Transvaal, Free State made it to the final despite these two Province defeats.

It was a team effort of the highest order by Wouter

Hugo's team that secured the Free State win. At last their backs fired, and they ran Province ragged. Free State were also on top in the tight phases. The Western Province pack was marched back metres near the end of the match. Doc Craven said afterwards that the 1976 final was one of the best, if not the very best, of the 16 finals played to that date.

1977 – Easy for Northerns

In 1977, Northern Transvaal were back as champions as they beat defending champions Free State 27–12 at Loftus. It was a one-sided match; probably sealed in the first two scrums, when Northern Transvaal simply went on the run with the Free State pack.

Three tries again underlined the worth of the under-rated Northerns backs, with the star back line of the Free State this time unconvincing. Naas Botha, then only 19, contributed 15 points in his first final, including his first drop goal in a final.

1978 – Close for the Light Blues

In 1978, Northerns again faced Free State, this time in Bloemfontein. Northern Transvaal won only 13–9, although the scoreboard flattered the home side. Once again, two tries by Northern Transvaal's backs and none by Free State showed that Northerns could indeed score with their backs. Naas Botha had matured into a match winner of the very highest order. It was Thys Lourens's eighth and last final. It was the fourth time he held the Currie Cup aloft as captain and it is interesting that he was never on the losing side in those eight matches.

1979 – The two Du Plessis' final

It was the two Du Plessis' last final in 1979. Morné captained Western Province, and Daan was appointed in place of the injured Thys Lourens. It was a disappointing match, and the 15–all draw was a fair reflection of a

Morné and Daan du Plessis after Western Province and Northern Transvaal drew the Currie Cup final 15–all in 1979.

match neither side deserved to win.

Naas Botha took the decision to drop at the end when a try was a vague possibility. The drop goal was successful and tied the scores. Botha scored all 15 of Northerns' points, which included two drops. That drop denied Morné du Plessis, one of South Africa's greatest captains of all time, the pleasure of holding the Currie Cup aloft as a winner instead of a captain who only once shared in the spoils.

1980 – The record hiding

In 1980, there was humiliation for Western Province, who four years before against the Free State had suffered the biggest defeat yet in the Currie Cup. They were just a shadow of one of the country's best sides in the 1980s. With their captain Morné du Plessis a late withdrawal in 1980, the team captained by Hennie Bekker went down 39–9 to Northern Transvaal at Loftus. That remains the largest defeat in a Currie Cup final.

It was a strange season for Western Province. They switched between brilliant and mediocre during a season that will be remembered for the death of their fullback Chris Burger after a serious neck injury. They beat Transvaal 37–0 in one of the highs; but Northern Transvaal won all three of the two sides' clashes, with the drubbing in the final the lowest point of the playing season.

It was a near walk-over in the 1980 final as Northern Transvaal ran in five tries to nil and had a further three seemingly good tries denied by the referee. The scores came from Edrich Krantz (two), Thys Burger, Willie Kahts and Moaner van Heerden, and Naas Botha added a further two drop goals and 19 points to his Currie Cup tally.

1981 – The Springbok debate

The argument whether to use returning Springboks who didn't help their team to a final first reared its head in 1956. Then Northern Transvaal opted not to use their Springboks for the final against Natal who, on the other hand, used their only Bok Roy Dryburgh. When 1981 came around, however, Northern Transvaal caused a stir when they decided to field eight of their ten Springboks to New Zealand. Theuns Stofberg and Willie Kahts were injured.

Northern Transvaal were odds-on favourites, although long not the most popular side in the country despite – or because of! – their success as they were seen as a side with a dour approach to the game. Free State had opted to leave their Springbok stars out of the side for the final. Northern Transvaal's 23–6 win, built around their Springboks, was as easy as the score suggests and included three tries to nil as well as another drop goal in a final by Naas Botha.

But that was the end of an era. Buurman van Zyl, who ten years previously couldn't coach due to ill health, died in February 1982. His death, coupled with the rise of Western Province and the two-year absence of Botha when he went to the United States to try out for the gridiron side Dallas Cowboys, saw Northern Transvaal enter five years without a title.

1982 – Western Province start their surge

In those five years Western Province set the record of five finals wins in five years, equalling their five titles between 1892 and 1898 and again from 1925–1934 (although those were not in successive years). Northern Transvaal also won five consecutive titles between 1977 and 1981 but had to share the 1979 Currie Cup with Province.

Because of his versatility, the brilliant former Maties, Western Province and Springbok utility back Dawie Snyman arguably didn't reach the heights expected of him. He simply wasn't allowed to specialise. But he compensated to some extent when in 1982 he became the youngest coach to win a Currie Cup final. The season saw another record as three brothers, Springboks Willie, Carel and Michael du Plessis played in the final.

It was Western Province's first outright win since the introduction of finals in 1968. But the 1982 win at Newlands was as impressive as they come. Northern Transvaal's old discipline was gone and mistakes abounded. And Province at last had a good and hard-working tight five, something they had so often lacked in the past.

There was also a new atmosphere in Western Province rugby that permeated the playing ranks. Their president Jan Pickard attended virtually every practice and flew to be present at all Province's away matches. They had two Maties, Divan Serfontein and Hennie Bekker, as captain and vice-captain respectively, which ensured continuity in planning and approach.

Northerns were beaten 24–13 early in the 1982 season, and that provided hope in the Cape that the time had at last come for a title, with a title share in 1979, the last year of celebration.

Naas Botha didn't play. His left leg was in plaster after a tackle from Jannie Els in a Northerns match against Eastern Transvaal. But such was the dominance of the Western Province forwards that even the great Naas wouldn't have salvaged victory for his team. Province were 14–3 up after ten minutes and one of the special tries from the outstanding left wing Carel du Plessis took it to 18–3 just 18 minutes into the game.

Province, impressive and the best team over the season, were undeniably also the best on the day. Their discipline – only two penalties were conceded in the second half of the final – played a major part in their success.

1983 – Another impressive win

Retaining the Currie Cup title in 1983 was almost as impressive. Log-leaders Western Province first had to play Natal, who finished second in the inferior B-section, in the semi-final. Then they encountered Northern Transvaal in the final, this time at Loftus winning 9–3. Nearly as special as the Currie Cup title was the fact that it was the first Western Province win in any match at Loftus since 1964. It was also the first time the Light Blues had lost a final at home.

Western Province coach Dawie Snyman pointed out that defending a trophy was probably more difficult than winning it. That made the 1983 title even more deserving.

Wynand Claassen.

1984 – WP rampant!

In 1984, Province scored 53 Currie Cup tries and conceded only seven, amassing 361 points and conceding 124 in the competition. They won the Currie Cup against Natal at Newlands after the B-Section side had caused a major upset by beating second-placed A-Section side Free State in Durban. It was another of those strange systems where the B-Section sides were appeased by giving them an opportunity to win the Currie Cup.

Natal were skippered by former Springbok captain Wynand Claassen and gave Western Province an unexpectedly difficult match. Ironically that year Natal couldn't win promotion to the A-Section as they had faltered at the promotion play-off stage.

Western Province were made to work hard for their 19–9 win after an early defeat to Free State and two close wins against Northern Transvaal. But it wasn't a good final and Province played one of their poorer matches of the season. Divan Serfontein, who had won three Currie Cup finals as captain, called it a day after the 19–9 win. He first became captain in 1981 and his positive influence, together with that of Snyman, had contributed enormously to a golden era for Western Province.

1985 – Overcoming injuries

But it wasn't over yet. In 1985, coach Dawie Snyman had his most difficult season in charge, with injuries playing a major role in a successful year that didn't produce the top rugby of the foregoing seasons. Yet Province retained the Currie Cup for the fourth consecutive season.

Losing four league matches in 1985 meant Western Province ended second on the A-Section log to Northern Transvaal. They met in a tough final at Newlands and Western Province were again too good for the perennial winners of the previous decade as they won 22–15. Although the losers had the better of the line-out battle, Western Province were deserved winners with their forwards grinding Northern Transvaal down. Province scored two tries through lock Hennie Bekker and wing Neil Burger while Northerns again had to rely on Naas Botha who scored all 15 of their points through two drops and three penalties.

1986 – A record five!

Western Province's most impressive and sustained golden era ended in 1986 with a 22–9 win over Transvaal at Newlands.

It was a victory for running rugby over the conservative pattern employed by Transvaal. It was also the first loss in a final by Transvaal's captain Jannie Breedt. With yet another system used in the competition Transvaal had to play Natal in the Durban semi-final, a match they won 18-4, while Western Province advanced to the final by virtue of heading the log.

There was more to the Province win than simply running with every ball. Again their forwards did enough to keep the visitors at bay in the final before their backs took over. In fact, shortly before the end, Transvaal were still ahead, 9-8. Then Province centre Goggie van Heerden scored two tries in quick succession. The well-known radio presenter John Robbie played for Transvaal in the final and during the season also succeeded with four of his trade-mark drop kicks from scrumhalf.

Captain Naas Botha and his team celebrate their 1988 triumph.

1987 – Botha brilliance
The 1987 final produced one of the best individual performances by a player in a final. Northern Transvaal played Transvaal, in rain and hail, at Ellis Park. It was the Naas Botha game – as he scored all 24 of the points in the 24–18 win (read the details in the box entitled 'Currie Cup's greatest match-winner' on page 105.) Botha kicked four drop goals and four penalties and kept his forwards going forward with an immaculate tactical display. They responded magnificently to deny Transvaal their second Currie Cup in two years.

1988 – Naas again!
Western Province were not quite finished, though. In 1988 they lost the final by a single point at Loftus, 19–18.

Western Province had to play B-Section winners Northern Free State in the semi-final, and after an impressive league phase and a 26-8 semi-final win over the Free State side in Welkom went into the final as favourites – especially as Northern Transvaal had had a break of four weeks between their last league match and the final. Three penalties and two drop kicks and an immaculate tactical kicking display by Northerns' Naas Botha put paid to another Province title.

1989 – Province snatch a draw
In 1989 Northern Transvaal were in command and minutes away from another Currie Cup title and it seemed certain Western Province were to suffer their second defeat in a final at Newlands as they trailed the Light Blues 15–11. But then Carel du Plessis, arguably the best left wing South Africa has produced, rounded off sustained Western Province pressure at the end when his brother Michael switched play from a ruck. Carel cut through and scored in the corner. At the least, they would share the Currie Cup. It was up to inexperienced Western Province flyhalf Riaan Gous to bring the Currie Cup back to Newlands. His conversion seemed good but swerved at the last moment to pass the upright – and the two great adversaries shared the Cup for the second time, both times at Newlands.

That was the end of the decade between 1980 and 1989 when the two top sides in the competition dominated by winning all ten titles on offer: five to Western Province and four to Northern Transvaal, with one drawn.

7

Two teams dominate the nineties

Natal and the Lions break the Currie Cup drought

If the 1980s belonged to Western Province and Northern Transvaal, Transvaal and Natal dominated the decade of the nineties. Seven of the ten Currie Cup titles on offer between 1990 and 1999 went to those two teams – which had been shut out from glory for some time. In 1993 Transvaal – by now the Lions – won their first title in 21 years. Their 1972 win against Eastern Transvaal had been their last previous success. And Natal had not won a Currie Cup since their establishment in 1890.

The nineties did, however, also see the previous decade's dominant sides Northern Transvaal (1991), later the Blue Bulls (1998) and Western Province (1997) interrupt the two top sides' title wins.

It was also a period of disruption and adaptation. Professionalism only came in 1996, although it had been hovering for years. No single rugby country – perhaps with the exception of Argentina – had completely adhered to the IRB's strict laws on professionalism which it had jealously guarded over the years. In South Africa, Transvaal had taken the lead in compensating players. And they did so unabashedly. From the late eighties, after Louis Luyt had come into office as president of the TRFU in 1984, they openly procured players from other provinces.

Northern Transvaal were the main suppliers of these quality players and provided Transvaal with their outstanding captain, Jannie Breedt. Like another Springbok captain, Morné du Plessis of Western Province, Breedt never had the honour of winning the Currie Cup as a captain in his 102 matches as Transvaal skipper over a period of seven years. He was captain in four losing finals, and it would be fair to say that if it hadn't been for Naas Botha's brilliance in two of those finals, Transvaal probably would have

Transvaal captain Jannie Breedt laid the foundation for the Lions' three Currie Cup wins in the 1990s.

had two more Currie Cup titles – they also lost by a single point (14–13) to Natal at Ellis Park in 1992.

Breedt undoubtedly set the platform for the Transvaal side that in the following two years, as the Gauteng Lions, won just about every trophy on offer – including the Super 10, the M-Net night series and the Lion Cup.

Natal, on the other hand, had not come close to a title

The nine battlefields

By 2011, 50 Currie Cup finals had been played at nine venues. Seventeen of those finals were decided at Loftus Versfeld while Newlands hosted the second most, 11. Ellis Park (now Coca-Cola Park) was the venue for six of the finals while Free State's six finals were played at the Free State Stadium/Vodacom Park, which hosted five, and Springbok Park, one.

Durban's first final in 1956 was played at the Kingsmead cricket ground, and since their next final in 1990, six more finals have been hosted at King's Park/ Absa Stadium.

There have only been three finals outside the cities of Cape Town, Johannesburg, Pretoria, Durban and Bloemfontein. In two of those finals, last-minute heroics won the Currie Cup. The 1952 final was played at Boland Park with its lovely setting in Wellington with Transvaal flyhalf Natie Rens sinking Boland hopes with a last-minute drop goal (11–9); in 1970 De Beers Stadium in Kimberley saw Griquas surprise Northern Transvaal 11–9 after Peet Smith's long penalty against the wind three minutes from time; and two years later Transvaal beat Eastern Transvaal 25–19 at the PAM Brink Stadium in Springs.

The two fields in Kimberley and Springs have also hosted international matches. South Africa won only one of those matches. The Springboks lost to Britain in 1891 and 1896 and drew in 1903; in 1964 they were beaten 8–6 by France in a disastrous one-off test at PAM Brink – a warning of what was to come the next year when they lost seven from eight matches; and they beat Argentina 49–29 in 2002.

since the sixties when the last two Currie Cup titles were decided by league format (in 1964 and 1966). These competitions and the 1957–59 competition were the only three digressions from the seven finals between 1939 and 1956 and the resumption thereof in 1968.

What's more, in 1984 Natal's final against Western Province at Newlands was not based on a season of excellence. It came after a single outstanding performance, courtesy of one of the many strangely contrived competition structures.

Natal had won the 1984 B-Section and then surprised Free State 26–15 in the Durban semi-final. They then faced Western Province in the final after the Cape side had beaten Eastern Transvaal 53–0 in the other A- versus B-Section semi-final. (In 2010 terms, Natal's feat would have meant Eastern Province, winners of the First Division, beating Western Province, who were second in the Premier Division, for a place in the final.)

Natal languished in the B-Section for five seasons, 1982–1986. In this period there was only the near-win in the 1983 Currie Cup semi-final, when Natal lost 7–3 to Western Province at King's Park, and the Newlands final in 1984 when they lost 19–9. Ironically, in both those years Natal won the B-Section but couldn't win their promotion play-offs against Northern Free State who were at the bottom of the A-Section. On both occasions Natal then had to regroup for the semi-final to try and make it to the Currie Cup final!

Only one final (lost) in 1956 emphasised that Natal were seldom a real force in the Currie Cup with the exception of the period 1956–1966 when only three titles were decided. In 1966 they lost a crucial match in the league against Western Province where a win could've won them the Currie Cup. The Natal side under Izak van Heerden, one of South Africa's finest coaches, arguably would have been Currie Cup champions in the sixties had there been more than just the two competitions in 1964 and 1966.

That was to change – and dramatically so from that first win in 1990. When Currie Cup glory eventually came for

Natal, it was a breakthrough and the first of six titles of which four came in the nineties. The 1990 win set them up as a powerhouse in South African and world rugby. It was a victory built on years of planning that included the five years in the B-Section.

1990

The side of 1990 under the captaincy of Craig Jamieson brought glory in their centenary year. The road to the title was, however, not smooth. Natal, somewhat fortuitously, won their opening Currie Cup match 18–9. Free State fullback André Joubert's five missed goal attempts contributed in no small way to Natal's win and the winning margin flattered them. Transvaal was a tough match, but Natal won 25–19 before a fight-back draw of 18–all against Western Province at Newlands where Natal came back from 12 points down to scrape a draw in the last ten minutes.

A big win against their nemesis in Welkom followed when they beat Northern Free State; then there was a 24–9 victory against a 14-man Northern Transvaal at King's Park; a close win against Western Transvaal in Potchefstroom; and a narrow one-point win against Eastern Province in Port Elizabeth.

The scrum was Natal's Achilles heel, as it had been in so many previous campaigns. Scotland – and later Springbok – hooker John Allen returned from overseas for six matches, but had to leave because of club and international commitments overseas. Big Tom Lawton, the Wallaby hooker regarded as the world's best, was then lured to Durban to help Jamieson's side through the final phases in 1990, playing in eight matches for the Sharks. His bulk and expertise did the trick. With former Transvaal Springbok, the big, abrasive Wahl Bartmann – then in his first season with Natal – plus new acquisition Guy Kebble from Western Province at loosehead, Natal cleaned up Western Province 21–12 at Kingsmead in the return match.

Natal were on target – but then the Welkom bogey so nearly struck again. It took a Joel Stransky drop goal to

Breakthrough! Captain Craig Jamieson holds the Currie Cup aloft after Natal's first win in 1990.

save them in the return match against Northern Free State before they were hammered by Northern Transvaal in Pretoria (28–6). Transvaal then came close (27–25) to winning at King's Park. Natal looked shaky. But, with three defeats and a draw, Natal finished second on the Currie Cup log and were to meet Northern Transvaal at Loftus Versfeld, on 6 October 1990.

After the final, outspoken Northern Transvaal captain Naas Botha made a remark that caused him to be rather unpopular. He said it had taken Natal 100 years to win the Currie Cup and that it would be another 100 years before they achieved that again. The Northerns captain was wrong. That was evident when Natal thrashed Northerns 54–15 at King's Park the following season.

The 1990 final is also a match remembered for the shrewd move of the Natal selectors under convenor Piet

Ian McIntosh coached Natal to their first Currie Cup victory.

Tony Watson – a significant try.

Strydom in naming a 'false' side with a changed pack from the one announced running onto the field; Natal coach Ian McIntosh's clever implementation of the replacement rule to Natal's advantage; and one of the legendary Currie Cup tries of all time by Natal's right wing, Tony Watson.

It was a great try. Watson later described it as somewhat lucky, but it was nevertheless a beauty. Perhaps it wasn't as spectacular as that of Pierre Spies 15 years before when Northerns outplayed Free State but it was significant in many ways.

The try set up the Natal win in 1990 – and with official professionalism just around the corner, it also resulted in a welcome financial boost that put R1,5 million in the NRU's coffers. It might not sound like much now, but it was about R20 million in today's terms. And that excludes the substantial spin-offs that go with a champion side, even in the days of ostensible amateurism.

The day of that important final hadn't started well for Northern Transvaal. Their centre Pieter Nel slipped in the tunnel as the sides ran on and couldn't play. Future Springbok fullback Theo van Rensburg was moved to centre and Gerbrand Grobler was brought in as fullback.

But Northerns appeared to be gaining the upper hand when Watson's try came.

A desperate Van Rensburg, on cover-defence from the centre, was caught off balance as Watson raced down the line. Watson afterwards said it was a try that needed extra speed. He was the man who could provide it. The dropping of his shoulder to eliminate Van Rensburg was also a class act.

The winning try was followed by a Stransky penalty from the halfway line after a late tackle by the Light Blues' centre Jannie Claassen in the Northerns' in-goal area after the try.

The score was 12–9 to the home side when Watson brought a hush to Loftus, and the double score made it 18–12 to Natal on the day they came of age, as coach McIntosh described it afterwards.

1991

In 1991 Transvaal let the chance slip for revenge for 1987 when Naas Botha and his forwards had won the battle of Ellis Park 24–18 in wind and rain. Northern Transvaal won back the Currie Cup for the last time under the captaincy of Botha, who retired from top-class rugby in South Africa after the 1992 season.

From 1987–1991 Northern Transvaal played in the Currie Cup final five years in a row, winning two, losing two and drawing one. If that was average for Northerns, worse was to follow. Their next final – and title – was only seven years later, in 1998, before another drought without a final until 2002.

The 1991 season was indeed a strange one for Northern Transvaal, who had to work hard to get back to the top after the unlikely defeat by Natal in the 1990 Currie Cup final. Two big hidings – 54–15 against the self-same Natal in Durban and 24–9 against Transvaal – led to a jittery and unconvincing start to this season of revenge. After Botha's return from Rovigo, the Lion Cup title followed. They then beat Transvaal 35–12 and Western Province 28–9 in the Currie Cup.

Yes, Northern Transvaal were on the march and nearly back to their best.

However, it was too little, too late – or so it seemed. To have any chance, Northern Transvaal had to rely on Free State to beat Western Province. They did so. A spectator ran onto the field and tackled him as Western Province's Springbok FC Smit surged towards the try line. Well inside Free State's 22 m area a try was not a certainty but a definite possibility. It would've sealed the match for Province. With Izak Beneke scoring a surprise Free State try right at the end it became a three-way tie in second place, with Transvaal sitting pretty at the top of the log.

Northerns were spending the weekend at Sun City as a thank-you gesture to the players, their wives and girlfriends. Now they had to rush back to prepare for the play-off match against Province on the Wednesday at Loftus where they won 34–21, and then went to Bloemfontein where they beat Free State, 27–23.

A week later Northern Transvaal beat log-leaders Transvaal convincingly 27–15, after tying 6–all at half-time. Four tries to nil tell the story of their domination. In the end Transvaal's three-week break while waiting for the play-offs to take place and their gamble to field players just back from injury helped to make this an unlikely Currie Cup year for Northerns. They won the final at Loftus with better possession from the first phase and because Botha played the territorial game so well.

1992

Transvaal and the Gauteng Lions played in five of the six finals between 1991 and 1996 – but again there was heartbreak for Breedt in 1992.

In the 1991 Currie Cup, Natal won only 11 of their 21 matches and were a shadow of the 1990 champion side. However, in 1992, the inconsistency of the previous year was gone. A record 31 points against Western Province in Natal's 31–19 win at King's Park was an indicator of things to come, but Naas Botha then scored all 27 points at Loftus as Northern Transvaal beat Natal 27–24. That was the last loss of the year for Natal in the Currie Cup. There followed a 19–11 win over Western Province at Newlands – the first since the semi-final in 1956, and only the second time that Natal had won at South Africa's 'Seat of Rugby'.

Natal also, for the first time, finished top of the log in the Currie Cup.

Natal had to travel to Ellis Park for the final. In those days there was a ruling that two sides would change venue from their last play-off clash against one another – and that was the 1986 semi-final in Durban. It mattered little, and Natal led 8–3 at half-time in the 1992 final through an early try by Gary Teichmann following a break by Pieter

Controlling the Currie Cup

In 2010 Craig Joubert became the 25th referee to officiate in a Currie Cup final when he was in charge of the match between the Natal Sharks and Western Province in Durban.

Because of the initial infrequency of Currie Cup finals – the first seven were played between 1939 and 1968 – only 25 referees have officiated in the highlight of the South African season.

André Watson's seven finals still lead the list, with Free State's Steve Strydom on six and Freek Burger and Jonathan Kaplan each on five. Watson handled six consecutive finals between 1996 and 2001 and was also in charge of two World Cup finals in 1999 and 2003.

With referees in South Africa now contracted to the SA Rugby Union, the principle of 'neutral' appointments is outdated. This has been taken even further at Super 14 level where, since 2009, referees have been in charge of matches where teams of their own country are involved against overseas opposition.

Although six international players have also officiated in test matches, former Springbok prop Boy Louw was the only ex-Springbok to handle a Currie Cup final. He did so in the first Currie Cup final – just a year after his retirement in 1938 when he still played against the British Lions. His brother Fanie, also a Springbok prop, was captain of one of the finalists, Transvaal, who beat Western Province at Newlands in that first final in 1939.

The following is the list of referees for Currie Cup Finals, with home teams listed first (referees since 1998 are no longer members of a union but of SARU and reference to their unions is an indication of where they lived in the year of their Currie Cup appointment):

1939: Western Province v Transvaal: Boy Louw (Western Province)
1946: Northern Transvaal v Western Province: Carl Basson (Northern Transvaal)
1947: Western Province v Transvaal: Albie Henkes (Western Province)
1950: Transvaal v Western Province: Eddie Hofmeyr (Transvaal)

1952: Boland v Transvaal: Chris Ackermann (Boland)
1954: Western Province v Northern Transvaal: Ralph Burmeister (Western Province)
1956: Natal v Northern Transvaal: Bowden Coombe (Natal)
1968: Northern Transvaal v Transvaal: Bertie Strasheim (Northern Transvaal)
1969: Northern Transvaal v Western Province: Fonnie van der Vyver (Northern Transvaal)
1970: Griqualand West v Northern Transvaal: Ben Calitz (Griqualand West)
1971: Transvaal v Northern Transvaal: Gert Bezuidenhout (Transvaal)
1972: Eastern Transvaal v Transvaal: Piet Robbertse (Eastern Transvaal)
1973: Northern Transvaal v Transvaal: Piet Robbertse (Eastern Transvaal)
1974: Northern Transvaal v Transvaal: Steve Strydom (Orange Free State)
1975: Orange Free State v Northern Transvaal: Justus Moolman (Eastern Province)
1976: Orange Free State v Western Province: Gert Bezuidenhout (Transvaal)
1977: Northern Transvaal v Orange Free State: Jimmy Smith-Belton (Eastern Province)
1978: Orange Free State v Northern Transvaal: Gert Bezuidenhout (Transvaal)
1979: Western Province v Northern Transvaal: Steve Strydom (Orange Free State)
1980: Northern Transvaal v Western Province: Steve Strydom (Orange Free State)
1981: Northern Transvaal v Orange Free State: Johan Gouws (Eastern Transvaal)
1982: Western Province v Northern Transvaal: Steve Strydom (Orange Free State)
1983: Northern Transvaal v Western Province: Johan Gouws (Eastern Transvaal)
1984: Western Province v Natal: Cassie Carstens (Northern Transvaal)
1985: Western Province v Northern Transvaal: Steve Strydom (Orange Free State)

1986: Western Province v Transvaal: Steve Strydom (Orange Free State)

1987: Transvaal v Northern Transvaal: Freek Burger (Western Province)

1988: Northern Transvaal v Western Province: Jimmy Smith-Belton (Eastern Province)

1989: Western Province v Northern Transvaal: Jimmy Smith-Belton (Eastern Province)

1990: Northern Transvaal v Natal: Freek Burger (Western Province)

1991: Northern Transvaal v Transvaal: Freek Burger (Western Province)

1992: Transvaal v Natal: Freek Burger (Western Province)

1993: Natal v Transvaal: Freek Burger (Western Province)

1994: Orange Free State v Transvaal: Stef Neethling (Boland)

1995: Natal v Western Province: Tappe Henning (Northern Transvaal)

1996: Transvaal v Natal: André Watson (Eastern Transvaal)

1997: Western Province v Free State: André Watson (Gauteng Falcons)

1998: Blue Bulls v Western Province: André Watson (Gauteng Falcons)

1999: Natal v Lions: André Watson (Gauteng Falcons)

2000: Natal v Western Province: André Watson (Falcons)

2001: Western Province v Natal: André Watson (Falcons)

2002: Lions v Blue Bulls: Jonathan Kaplan (Boland)

2003: Blue Bulls v Sharks: Shaun Veldsman (Boland)

2004: Blue Bulls v Cheetahs: André Watson (Falcons)

2005: Blue Bulls v Cheetahs: Jonathan Kaplan (Boland)

2006: Blue Bulls v Cheetahs: Jonathan Kaplan (Boland)

2007: Cheetahs v Lions: Mark Lawrence (Mpumalanga)

2008: Sharks v Blue Bulls: Jonathan Kaplan (Western Province)

2009: Blue Bulls v Free State: Jonathan Kaplan (Western Province)

2010: Natal Sharks v Western Province: Craig Joubert (KZN)

Note name changes:
- Northern Transvaal became the Blue Bulls.
- Transvaal became the Gauteng Lions, later the Golden Lions, then the Lions and then again the Golden Lions.
- Eastern Transvaal became the Gauteng Falcons, then Falcons/Valke, now Valke.
- Orange Free State became Free State.
- Mpumalanga was formerly South-Eastern Transvaal and then South-Eastern Transvaal and Lowveld.

Jonathan Kaplan had refereed 143 Currie Cup matches by end 2010.

Number of finals refereed (50):

7 André Watson

6 Steve Strydom

5 Freek Burger, Jonathan Kaplan

3 Gert Bezuidenhout, Jimmy Smith-Belton

2 Piet Robbertse, Johan Gouws

1 Boy Louw, Carl Basson, Albie Henkes, Eddie Hofmeyr, Chris Ackermann, Ralph Burmeister, Bertie Strasheim, Bowden Coombe, Fonnie van der Vyver, Ben Calitz, Justus Moolman, Cassie Carstens, Stef Neethling, Tappe Henning, Shaun Veldsman, Mark Lawrence, Craig Joubert

(**Statistics:** www.rugby365.com and Gabriel Pappas, GLRU)

Celebrating after the 1993 Lions break the 21-year Currie Cup drought: Pieter Hendriks, Ian Macdonald, Louis Luyt, Hannes Strydom and Kobus Wiese.

Müller. What had become known as 'McIntosh's direct rugby' was used for the first hour with new Natal captain Bartmann again the scourge of his former side, getting Natal across the advantage line with his powerful drives.

Natal had the edge on the scoreboard throughout, and in the end, it was a missed penalty that let Natal in for the title. But the better side had won and their record throughout the year also made this a deserved victory.

For the fourth time as captain of Transvaal, Jannie Breedt was on the losing side in a final – but he had put his side in the frame since his first lost final as captain in 1986. The next year Francois Pienaar captained the side that became the Gauteng Lions Rugby Union that year (later the Golden Lions) and immediately struck pay dirt on the solid foundation laid by Breedt.

1993

The 1993 Currie Cup success came despite the impatience of Luyt that resulted in a host of coaches being used

between his coming to power in 1984 and 1998 when he was succeeded by the late Jomo King. Luyt even took over the team's coaching himself for a match or two!

Pa Pelser, Apies du Toit, Derek Minnie, Ray Mordt, Kitch Christie, New Zealanders Alex Wyllie and Laurie Mains, Dawie Snyman, Koos Ehlers, Hugo van As and Harry Viljoen plus assistants were among those tried as mentors. None overstayed his welcome – and in fact, most were fired by Luyt. Even coach Kitch Christie, who won the 1995 World Cup for South Africa despite having a very limited period to select and prepare the Springboks, was not accepted back into the Transvaal fold.

An influx of players from Northern Transvaal – mostly Springboks – joined Transvaal. From across the Jukskei came coaches Christie and Ray Mordt. That was enough to make Luyt's Currie Cup dream come true. The 1993 final was their third in three years and this time, playing away in Durban, they won 21–15.

It was a match Natal probably should have won. Even in the first half, when they played against a strong wind, they dominated territory. But outstanding planning by Christie and Mordt neutralised the scrum advantage Natal had as well as the driving play of Bartmann. Ultimately it was the Lions' greater fitness that clinched it with Natal contributing to their own downfall with two mistakes that led to the only tries in the match. Firstly Gavin Johnson picked up a loose ball, shrugged off a tackle from Müller and went over with assistance from Rudolf Straeuli. Then former Northern Transvaal hooker Uli Schmidt, playing in his seventh Currie Cup final, scored his first try in a final after a handling error from Natal wing Cabous van der Westhuizen. The Lions' other points came from three penalties and a conversion by Johnson.

1994

The Lions' fourth successive Currie Cup final in 1994 was played at Springbok Park in Bloemfontein as the Free State Stadium was being rebuilt. They routed Free State 56–33 and scored seven tries, one of which was a penalty try. The Lions were 31–16 ahead at half-time and added a further 25 points in the second half. The score set a host of records: the winning score of 56 points; the aggregate 89 points by the two teams; the seven tries by the winners; the total of ten tries in the match.

It sounds scintillating, but the tackling was very average on both sides – and it is a sobering thought that Free State's 33 points had previously been bettered on only two occasions by a winning team in a Currie Cup final!

This 1994 win was achieved with Mordt as coach. Christie had taken over the reins as Springbok coach, less than a year before the World Cup, after Ian McIntosh's sacking by Luyt who was by then also president of SARFU.

1995

In this see-saw decade, it was again Natal's turn. In 1995, they won their first title at home after the defeats in 1956 against Northern Transvaal and 1993 against the Lions.

Ray Mordt – Lions' winning coach in 1994.

In 1995, Natal became the Natal Sharks. It was also the year in which Ian McIntosh returned as coach. Mac, as he was – and is – known to all had a stormy return. Not all the players wanted him back and some senior players' heads rolled after a management decision confirmed he would remain in charge.

The Sharks were ready for professionalism, and two of France's finalists in the 1995 World Cup semi-final were secured for the province following a secret car-park meeting between NRU president Keith Parkinson, lock Olivier Roumat and flyhalf Thierry Lacroix.

They had also acquired the services of flyhalf Luke Smith, who had arrived from Northern Transvaal. He scored 158 Currie Cup points. On a number of occasions his kicking made the difference between winning and losing.

The Natal Sharks went into the final against Western Province with only two losses from ten matches – against Western Province and the Lions – and won back the Currie Cup.

The 1995 season was also noteworthy for the appointment of Gary Teichmann as Sharks captain. Bartmann, who had commuted by plane between Johannesburg and Durban to train and play, had called it a day because of injury and business commitments.

Van der Westhuizen, who dropped the ball the previous year to let Uli Schmidt in for the winner, this time got the favourable bounce from a kick by the French Lacroix – and the long-haired winger made amends for his error in 1993 by stretching the Natal Sharks lead to 10–3 after a conversion by Lacroix.

With Lacroix and Western Province's Joel Stransky trading penalties, the score stood at 16–12 when Province's Tiaan Strauss scored a try to see his side into the lead, 17–16. Stransky missed the conversion and two late Sharks penalties gave the home side a 25–17 win.

1996

The Lions bounced back in 1996 for their fifth final in six years, and again faced the Natal Sharks. This time the final was at Ellis Park. There was an added sting to the match when World Cup hero and Transvaal captain Francois Pienaar was dropped from the national team by new Bok coach André Markgraaff. The Natal Sharks captain Gary Teichmann had taken over the Bok reins that year.

In yet another Currie Cup format, the 22 sides were split into two sections. The strength versus strength concept was abolished, and big scores were the order of the day. The Sharks won the quarterfinal against Griquas 51–3 and the semi-final against Free State 35–20.

Snyman snatches the record for Western Province

Titles as coach: five (1982–1986)   Playing career: 10 tests (22 matches for Springboks)

In 1982 Dawie Snyman became the youngest coach in Currie Cup history to win a Currie Cup, and his record as coach is bettered only by the legendary former Northern Transvaal coach Buurman van Zyl. In fact, Snyman went one better than Van Zyl when he won a record five finals in five successive years between 1982 and 1986. Van Zyl's best was five titles between 1977 and 1981, but one of those was shared with Province in 1979.

Snyman was only 32 years 89 days old when Province beat Northern Transvaal in 1982, and the record stood for 23 years until Rassie Erasmus became the youngest successful finals coach at 31 years 351 days when Free State beat the Blue Bulls at Loftus in 2005.

Snyman, a former Grey College learner, was selected for Hannes Marais' 'Invincibles' who toured Australia in 1971. He made his debut for the Maties first team as a 19-year-old. Snyman is one of the few players who was selected for South Africa before playing provincial rugby. He played his first test in 1972 against England, which South Africa lost 18–9.

Snyman was forced into early retirement because of injuries. However, he was so good a player that his mentor Doc Craven said of him: 'He is so gifted that he didn't know how much effort to put into his play.'

Craven had such a high regard for the Matie who came to him as an Under-19 player from Defence in Pretoria where he was injured that the Maties supremo earmarked him to be his successor as coach at Stellenbosch. And Craven thereby proved he could pick future coaches as well as he did players!

Snyman also had a stint as coach of the Lions after Louis Luyt's initial success in buying players to win the Currie Cup petered out with no succession plan. He coached the Lions in 1997 and 1998 – and when he didn't bring home the goods, he followed a large number of other unsuccessful coaches of the Luyt era.

Snyman played in ten test matches and 12 tour matches for the Springboks. His older brother Jackie was also a Springbok and played in three tests.

Dawie Snyman's brilliance as a rugby player was probably suppressed by the versatility that saw him play at flyhalf and fullback for South Africa.

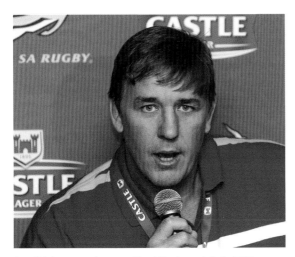
Gary Teichmann took over as Natal Sharks captain in 1995.

Sharks centre Jeremy Thomson opened the scoring in the final from a ruck, and the boot of Gavin Lawless – son of Springbok Mike who played in the late fifties and sixties – kept the home side in the picture as they trailed only 10–9 at half-time. Lawless won the lead back for Transvaal with his fourth penalty (12–10), only for Sharks flyhalf Henry Honiball to slot one in. With Lawless responding, the score stood at 15–13 to the Lions when, with only 15 minutes to go, André Joubert cut in to receive on the inside from Thomson. The gap was there and his acceleration carried him through.

Five minutes later it was Joubert who chipped ahead and got the favourable bounce when a simple off-load would have sufficed. But all's well that ends well, and the Natal Sharks had, at last with a whopping 33–15 scoreline, made it back-to-back Currie Cup titles to clinch their fourth title in the nineties.

For the next two years, the two top sides of the nineties had to take a back seat as Western Province (twice), Free State Cheetahs and the Blue Bulls made it to the next two finals in 1997 and 1998. In both years André Watson, who would later control two World Cup finals as referee, had to make close calls that meant the difference between winning and losing.

In both instances later replays showed that he was

André Joubert – two tries in 1996.

right in his judgement – and it underlined that a referee keeping up with play simply has an edge over those who do not!

1997

In 1997 the title went to Western Province when they beat the Bloemfontein side 14–12 at Newlands. A pass from Free State centre Helgard Müller to speedster Jan-Harm van Wyk on the wing was – rightly – adjudged forward by Watson who was in a perfect position to make the call right at the end of the match. Van Wyk was the season's top scorer with 16 Currie Cup tries. In a career of 77 matches, he scored 63 tries as one of the country's most lethal attackers. He was never selected for the Springboks but did represent the Boks' Sevens team the next year.

Müller played in 245 matches for Free State – a South African record – and captained the side 89 times. At one stage in his career, he played in 65 consecutive matches, all of them as captain. His younger brother Pieter played 33 tests for the Springboks.

With their Springboks overseas, the Natal Sharks continued from where they had left off in 1996 and clocked up a record 29 successive wins before they went down 33–28 to Northern Transvaal in their last league match. They then lost 40–22 in the semi-final against Free State who thereby qualified for the final they lost so cruelly with the try disallowed.

1998

The Blue Bulls and Western Province, as if to remind the other sides that they were the traditional Currie Cup giants, contested the 1998 final at Loftus. Northern Transvaal, now the Blue Bulls, shouldn't have been there. They were down 17–3 in the semi-final against the Natal Sharks and seemed out of it. Then Joost van der Westhuizen, in a brilliant display and captaining them in the absence of Ruben Kruger, took control with a sniping break that sent his side on their way. The Blue Bulls won the semi-final 41–17.

In the final, Watson had to make the call – contentious at the time but proven correct – as he denied Western Province victory. At half-time the Blue Bulls led 14–6. Then converted tries by Chester Williams and Charl Marais reduced the deficit. With the game almost over and the score at 24–20 to the Blue Bulls, Springbok centre Robbie Fleck sent Williams over for his second try on the corner flag. But Watson was again on the spot

Joost van der Westhuizen led the Blue Bulls to the 1998 title.

and ruled the pass forward. The Blue Bulls had scraped another title against their greatest rivals.

1999

Just as the Blue Bulls and Western Province showed some muscle to prove they were the Currie Cup competition's pace-setters, the Lions and the Natal Sharks in 1999 contested the final as if to say: this is our decade.

This time the Natalians had to bid farewell to some of the biggest names over their 109 years as a union: André Joubert, Gary Teichmann and Henry Honiball – who was injured and didn't play – and coach Ian McIntosh had decided to call it a day.

The Lions were coached by losing All Blacks 1995 World Cup coach Laurie Mains. He was replaced as New Zealand's national coach after the Springboks had beaten his team in the 1995 World Cup final. Mains was the latest in Luyt's long line of coaches and another import for the Lions. He made a huge impact, and the new discipline eventually became too much for Springbok World Cup hero James Small who retired midway through the season.

This time it was the Lions, impressive throughout the season with a scintillating new style, who dished it out after the heavy 33–15 beating they had taken at Ellis Park in 1996. They ran in tries by AJ Venter, Thinus Delport (2), Chester Williams and Leon Boshoff. Kobus Engelbrecht converted twice and also kicked a penalty. The scoreline of 32-9 equalled the second biggest win yet in a Currie Cup final.

Although the Natal Sharks made it to the final, all was not well that season. They did trounce Free State Cheetahs 45–8 in the semi-final but earlier in the season suffered defeats against Griquas (29–23), SWD Eagles (28–14) and Eastern Province (22–16). Most impressive of their performances was the 65–29 win over Western Province – the biggest Currie Cup defeat ever suffered by the Cape side. But generally the Sharks were in too much of a stop start season.

What was interesting after this fourth final between Transvaal/Lions and Natal/Sharks was that the away side had won on every occasion!

The Natal Sharks played in the next two finals of 2000 and 2001 (both against Western Province) and lost both, in Durban and Cape Town respectively, where the scores were 25–15 and 29–24. Three defeats in three consecutive Currie Cup finals between 1999 and 2001 pointed to a decline following their great run between 1990 and 1999 that had produced four titles in six finals.

Similarly, the two titles in the new decade also pointed to a resurgence of Western Province after their last title in 1997.

Ironically, however, Province have not won the Currie Cup since that 2001 title and have lost their only final since in 2010. Natal Sharks, on the other hand, have since beaten the Blue Bulls (14–9 in 2008) and the self-same Province (in 2010, with a trouncing of 30–10).

Thinus Delport – two tries in the 1999 final.

2000

Rudolf Straeuli had taken over the coaching after the retirement of Ian McIntosh the previous year. He also had a new-look side after the retirement of Teichmann, Honiball and Joubert – especially as other stalwarts like Steve Atherton, Shaun Payne and Adrian Garvey were no longer part of the system. Experience was indeed at a premium.

It was a young, promising side but the Natal Sharks were not yet ready for the big time as their Super 12 campaign underlined when they ended last.

In the 2000 Currie Cup final Western Province exploited the Sharks' inexperience and ran in a 25–15 win in Durban.

2001

The 2001 Currie Cup was again a competition where all 14 of the unions contested the Currie Cup in two sections, with the top four from each advancing to the elite Top 8 competition. Province topped the Top 8 section and beat Free State in the semi-final, 40–18, while the Sharks beat the Lions in Durban, 16–9.

In 2001, Western Province won back-to-back titles for the first time since their golden era in the 1980s. It was unquestionably flyhalf Braam van Straaten's game. He equalled Naas Botha's record of 24 points in a final with a try, two conversions and five penalties.

Although Western Province had by then already qualified for the final, the Sharks beat them in Durban in their league match, 36–13. This was the cause for much optimism in Durban, but Van Straaten had other ideas. The visitors were in control throughout and thoroughly deserved the win.

The Blue Bulls, who lost by small margins against the two finalists shortly before the play-offs, had given clear notice of things to come in the not-too-distant future.

The Western Province drought in the Currie Cup since 2001 has given rise to concern that the outstanding young talent of the region, which boasts probably most of the country's top rugby schools, does not manifest at junior national level; and especially that the continual flow of talent through to the provincial side has not been as strong as in years gone by.

Rassie Erasmus, who had moved to Cape Town as Director of Rugby after his successes with the Free State, slowly put this aspect right towards the end of the first decade of the new millennium. The wins by both the Western Province Under-19s and Under-21s in 2010's national junior competitions gave promise of a bright future.

2002

Under coach Heyneke Meyer the Bulls lost all 11 of their Super 12 matches and conceded 500 points and 76 tries

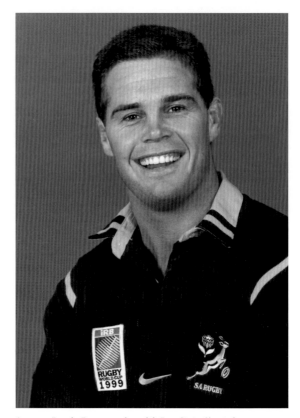

A young Rassie Erasmus wins with Free State Cheetahs.

in the 2002 competition. Meyer was fired as Super 12 coach, though he continued to coach them in the Currie Cup.

The Blue Bulls' Currie Cup win in 2002, the first since 1998 and only the second since 1991, therefore came as something of a surprise. The pressure was squarely on Meyer as it had been decided that only six teams would compete for the Currie Cup the following year. These six teams would be decided on grounds of their records in the 2000, 2001 and 2002 seasons – and the Blue Bulls were in trouble after their poor performances in the preceding two years. (They finished tenth in 2000 and seventh in 2001. This meant that in 2002 they had to at least qualify for the semi-finals – and that was the minimum target set for Meyer in his contract.)

The Blue Bulls finished fourth on the 2002 log. They

Blue Bulls back at the top

When rugby officially became professional in 1996, Northern Transvaal were not ready for it. A perfect example of this financial impact in the early stages of professionalism was the contrasting performance in the nineties by Northern Transvaal (renamed the Blue Bulls in 1998) and the Gauteng Lions.

The advent of professionalism included Northern Transvaal's worst spell in their history where they were without a Currie Cup title for seven years until 1998. What made it even worse for the Loftus faithful was that their team didn't even make it to a final in that time and nearly lost their status as an A-Section Currie Cup side.

It was not only the pay-for-play concept that stumped Northerns/Blue Bulls. They had lost the core of their team to Luyt's Transvaal and Lions since 1986; Naas Botha had retired; their long-standing president Prof Fritz Eloff called it a day in 1995 after a term that started in 1965; and importantly, they simply didn't have the depth the union had become renowned for in past years. They would regain this depth and a new Blue Bulls dominance in the new millennium, however.

The Blue Bulls' second golden era began in 2002. They reached seven finals and won four titles in the eight years between 2002 and 2009. The Free State Cheetahs were also a force between 2004 and 2009, playing in five finals of which they won two and shared one with the Blue Bulls. Four of those finals were against the Blue Bulls.

Western Province, after their record five-in-a-row titles in 1982–1986, had a six-year finals drought between their 1989 draw and 1995. Then came a mini-resurrection as they played in five finals between 1995 and 2001, of which they won three and lost two before another Currie Cup hiatus. With their only final appearance since the loss against the Sharks in 2010, Western Province have now been without the Currie Cup for nine years.

But the Lions are worse off. Their last title was in 1999. Among other factors contributing to their success from 1986, was Lions president Louis Luyt's luring what was the bulk of the Springbok side that won the 1995 World Cup. These loan players had helped Transvaal/Lions into six finals though success only came in 1993 and 1994. However, the acquisition of the mercenaries came back to bite them in later years.

No planning for the future had been done and the Lions had a poor time of it as they were outplayed in their next two finals, losing 33–15 to Natal in 1996 and 31–7 to the Blue Bulls in 2002 – then the second biggest defeat in a final.

Only in January 2011 did the Lions obtain the services of former Blue Bulls junior and Vodacom Cup coach, Nico Serfontein. The coach, who played a major role in establishing the famous Blue Bulls structures and a succession plan for their senior team that had seen the Pretoria outfit rise to the top, was instructed by the GLRU to do so in Johannesburg. He had more than 20 years of neglect to tackle.

Griquas, although they beat all the top sides including the franchise holders, simply lacked the depth to advance to the semi-finals. Financial constraints that have led to the loss of players and a lack of top feeder schools are among the main reasons for their up-and-down performances.

faced log-leaders Natal Sharks in Durban in the semi-finals – and that match and the final against the Lions put Derick Hougaard, then only 19, in the limelight. Hougaard's kicking, and his drop-kicking in particular, surprised the Sharks.

As he did in the semi-final, Hougaard dictated the final against the Lions at Ellis Park.

Two dropped goals, five penalties and a try as the cherry on top saw the youngster set a new Currie Cup points record of 26 in a final. The score against the Lions was 31–7.

2003

The 2003 Currie Cup final showed how the Blue Bulls had matured in the previous two seasons since Meyer had proposed new structures for success. They lost 15–19 to Griquas at Loftus, and were routed by Western Province at Newlands, 63–26. Then the Blue Bulls won their next seven matches in a row and scored 50 points in three of those encounters – and were back in the final. (No semi-finals were played in 2003.)

In the final, the Blue Bulls, for the second time in their 26 finals, scored 40 points when they thrashed Natal 40–19, scoring five tries. Richard Bands, Danie Coetzee, Victor Matfield, Bakkies Botha, Joost van der Westhuizen, Derick Hougaard and Jaco van der Westhuyzen were with the World Cup team in Australia in 2003 and didn't play in the final, making the achievement even more impressive.

The 2003 season was undoubtedly the Blue Bulls' most successful season up to that point. The union played in every possible final of a national competition.

2004

In the 2004 final the Blue Bulls and the Cheetahs met in the first of their five finals over the next six years. The match was marked by one of the finest tries scored in a final when Northern Transvaal centre Ettienne Botha dummied and sidestepped to score under the posts. He became the first player to twice score two tries in a Currie Cup final, having achieved that the previous year.

Botha's scintillating form gave him the award of Currie Cup Player of the Year, but the man, who at times captained the Blue Bulls, never became a Springbok. He died in a car accident in 2005.

The Blue Bulls were undoubtedly the top side of the season. They were at the top of the log from start to finish and lost only one match, 33–36, to the Lions. The final was a tough match, as all their finals in this decade against Free State Cheetahs were, but the Blue Bulls were deserved winners and in control for most of the match in their 42–33 win.

2005

In 2005 Free State Cheetahs utility back Meyer Bosman, who became a Springbok in that year, scored the winning try against the Blue Bulls at Loftus Versfeld. The 20-year-old clinched the Currie Cup for his side six minutes before the end. The score was 29–25, and it was the only time that Free State had beaten the Blue Bulls in their nine Currie Cup final encounters.

Once again the competition was one of runaway wins in a season where all 14 sides played in a first round that was split into two sections. The top four sides of each section went through to the Premier Division, and each section's bottom three played in the First Division.

Free State finished second to Western Province in their section, but the latter lost to Free State Cheetahs for the second time in two seasons when they went down 16–11 in the Newlands semi-final after the Top 8 league phase. Free State's Newlands bogey had clearly been overcome, and was good value for the win after a 10–3 half-time lead. The Blue Bulls were the top side in the competition, and went through the Premier Division's eight matches unbeaten. They beat the Lions at Loftus (31–23) to set up a home final.

In 16 matches in the competition the Free State had conceded only 28 tries, including one each in the semi-final at Newlands and the final at Loftus. It was this outstanding defence and the unerring kicking of flyhalf Willem de Waal, who scored 195 Currie Cup points that year, that won the season for Free State. Bevin Fortuin and Meyer Bosman rounded off a great season for Free State with second-half tries to see their side home after trailing 12–9 at half-time.

It was the Blue Bulls' third loss in their 16 finals at Loftus.

2006

The competition in 2006 was decided between the top eight sides that played a double round, with the top

Meyer Bosman's boot secured one title and brought a share of another for the Free State Cheetahs.

Kabamba Floors' try and Willem de Waal's penalty shortly thereafter seemed to have sealed the match for Free State. But Blue Bulls centre JP Nel then broke the line to score after a sustained Bulls attack. Morné Steyn, replacement for Derick Hougaard, converted from wide out with three minutes remaining to tie the scores at 25–all. In extra time Steyn kicked a penalty, and Bosman's penalty hit the cross bar. The Blue Bulls were still ahead, 28–25. But just six minutes from time, in a repeat of the previous year's final, Bosman struck a long, angled kick to make it 28–all.

It was not over yet. The Blue Bulls were awarded a penalty near the halfway line. But Bulls captain Gary Botha, fearing that Free State could run from their own line and perhaps take the spoils if the kick missed, ordered that the ball be kicked into touch. That decision by Botha was instrumental in bringing about the change in the Currie Cup regulations that would ensure that no Currie Cup final would again end in a draw.

Free State Cheetahs' sudden rise to the top over the last two seasons was attributed to young coach Rassie Erasmus. The former Springbok flank, who also captained his country once, opted for less running rugby and a game plan where mistakes were minimised – and in 2004 he became the youngest coach to win a Currie Cup final at the age of 32 years 351 days – about three months younger than Dawie Snyman was in 1982 when Western Province won the first of their five successive titles.

four then battling it out in the semi-finals. In the tough, outstanding final in Bloemfontein, Free State simply wouldn't give in – and it was the Blue Bulls that twice had to come from behind when they seemed beaten.

Both the semi-finals were won convincingly. Free State Cheetahs beat the Natal Sharks 30–14 in Bloemfontein while the Blue Bulls set up a repeat final of 2005 when they beat Western Province 45–30 at Loftus Versfeld.

The lead in the final changed hands four times in ten minutes in the second half. With time running out,

2007

In 2007 the Lions lost a very close final in Bloemfontein 20–18 to Free State Cheetahs. The Lions were ahead 15–6 through tries by Willie Wepener following some brilliance from flyhalf Earl Rose and by scrumhalf Jano Vermaak. A Rose penalty took it to 18–6 after 65 minutes and they seemed on course for a title.

But Free State Cheetahs replacement flank Heinrich Brüssow scored a try converted by kicking machine

Willem de Waal – a points machine for the Free State Cheetahs and Western Province.

Heinrich Brüssow – more than just a fetcher for the Free State Cheetahs.

Willem de Waal. Tewis de Bruyn, the Cheetahs reserve scrumhalf, wriggled his way over near the corner to tie the scores with three minutes left – and De Waal, who for the fourth consecutive season was the top scorer in the Currie Cup, kicked the conversion from the touchline for a 20–18 win.

It was the home side's third title – one of which was shared – in three years, and their fourth title overall.

In the run-up to the final it was interesting to note what over-confidence in rugby can do: the Lions got to the final following a 19–12 semi-final over a seemingly cocksure Sharks side in Durban after being routed by them 19–3 just weeks before!

2008

The Sharks won 12 of their 14 matches to top the 2008 Currie Cup log. They then beat the Golden Lions 29–14 in the semi-final in Durban to set up the final against the Blue Bulls who were second on the log. The Blue Bulls

qualified for the final after their 31–19 semi-final win against Free State Cheetahs at Loftus.

In the final the Sharks accounted for the Blue Bulls, 14–9. What was more, they put paid to their poor home run in finals. Their last two in Durban were lost and they had only a single win from their last five finals. It was also their first Currie Cup final win since 1996 when they beat the Lions in Johannesburg. That win was followed by four consecutive losses in finals.

Two tries by Frans Steyn and Ruan Pienaar – converted by French international Frédéric Michalak and Pienaar respectively – to none by the Blue Bulls tell the story of the Sharks' dominance in their 14–9 win. It gave the Sharks their fifth Currie Cup win and also broke the home side's run of four Currie Cup final losses and a 12-year drought since their last Currie Cup title in 1996.

John Plumtree, coach of the Natal Sharks, aptly summed up the importance of the win: ' ... this Sharks team needed to come to the realisation that they could win a final; that a final was not something that was going to always prove a bridge too far for them.'

Two years later, in 2010, in what will be remembered as Patrick Lambie's final, the Sharks proved that they had indeed learnt to win. They cleaned up favourites Western Province with the third biggest win in a Currie Cup final at what was again called King's Park.

2009

The crowning achievement by a provincial side in the 120 years since the first Board competition in Kimberley in 1889 was recorded in 2009 when the Blue Bulls won the Currie Cup as well as the Super 14. Both were played at Loftus and both were won rather convincingly against the Chiefs (61–17) and Free State Cheetahs (36–24) respectively.

The win against Free State was revenge for their loss against the Bloemfontein side at Loftus in 2005. It looked to be one-sided in 2009 as the Blue Bulls ran up a 24–0 lead in only 25 minutes against a side that had done well to make the Currie Cup final after a disastrous Super 14 tour down under.

Of course the 2009 win was to some measure also compensation for the previous year when Blue Bulls had slipped up against the Sharks in Durban (14–9).

2010

2010 was the Natal Sharks and Patrick Lambie's great Currie Cup year, discussed earlier. It was also a good year for Province, despite their huge defeat in the Currie Cup final.

Fourie du Preez set up the Blue Bulls' first three tries that set them on the road to victory.

8

The pillars of South African rugby

Craven Week, Vodacom Cup and so much more

In its first century South Africa's rugby was built on the natural strength of its players; the raw talent; and near-fanatical following of the game from an early age, especially from the country districts.

It worked, and it worked well. South Africa's test record in 1991, exactly a century after its first test, was the best in the world and it was with great anticipation that the country's rugby followers welcomed South Africa's re-admittance to international rugby in 1992.

The Currie Cup, they felt, was the best, strongest and toughest competition in the world. Other provincial competitions such as the Lion Cup, the Paul Roos and Sport Pienaar competitions, the Southern Cross Shield, intervarsities, club rugby (that was perceived to be at a very high level), the schools system and especially Craven Week provided the stars who came through to fill the Springbok squad.

However, all there was to measure their belief against were two narrow wins against an invitation World XV in 1989, and a series win against the unofficial New Zealand Cavaliers in 1986 in an era when professionalism was not yet accepted but practised extensively – in approach and financially – everywhere but in South Africa.

Their re-admittance in 1992 was therefore a rude awakening. A single win from five tests in 1992 and three from seven the next year showed that the world beyond South Africa's borders had moved ahead. Internationally, law interpretations, coaching methods, conditioning, tactics and administration were streets ahead.

There were also few structures in place. Junior provincial sides played on an ad hoc basis; matches between provincial B-sides were few; and uniform coaching methods

Youth weeks are the lifeblood of South African rugby.

Sports physician's concerns about SA schoolboy rugby

While the youth weeks and the many Easter and other tournaments as well as the league and knock-out competitions provide a solid base for future strength at provincial and international level, a number of negatives have manifested over the past decade.

Dr Jon Patricios, president of the South African Sports Medicine Association, is outspoken about what is wrong from a medical point – and that does not include the injury side of it. A former team doctor for the Lions and Golden Lions, he is an avid rugby fan and concerned about the way the game is moving.

One of his greatest worries is the move to performance-enhancing drugs – and he blames that on the competitive nature of rugby at schools level.

Excerpts from formerly published articles obtained from Patricios read as follows:

I am a fan of the game, in particular what I had perceived to be school rugby's ability to accommodate all body types: the nippy halfback, the deft kicker, the lithe three-quarter, the gutsy loosey and the fatty in the front row. But I can detect through the window that my sports medicine practice affords me that the situation has changed quite dramatically. The emphasis is now above all else size, strength and power. In order to achieve target weights ('the coach says that to make the front row I need to be 95 kg'), schoolboys are resorting to extreme measures, using supplements both legal and banned.

The schoolboy rugby environment has become disproportionately competitive over the last 10 years. Scholars and institutions are showcased by means of their rugby achievements. Ranking systems, published in national newspapers and on the internet, have been contrived to rate schools according to how they perform on the sports field. Many schools' status is determined by means of their progress in regional and national knock-out tournaments. Most dangerously, unions are contracting players at Under-18 level and fast-tracking them into professional rugby. Not only does this spell an end to the era of competitive youth club rugby where Under-21 players would have to earn provincial honours in the skill and character building club rugby environment, but failure to be noticed at school level may result in a promising player finding himself in the rugby wilderness. Failure to make the Craven Week may be a death knell for an aspiring rugby career. At least one major union is even contracting Under-15 players from other provinces, relocating and schooling them in their new province!

The upshot of the knock-out competitions, the rankings, the youth contracts and the accompanying

– even within an individual union – were not applied. It would take nearly ten years before the Blue Bulls' Heyneke Meyer introduced this concept with great success for his union.

Those early years after unification SARFU, which became SARU, progressed well in putting the structures in place. SARU have formulated a growth strategy that covers both participants and supporters, and a number of activities are already well on their way to meeting these objectives. This includes the development and implementation of programmes to establish sustainable rugby clubs; education/training programmes to develop and hone the skills of coaches, referees and administrators; and an innovative junior and youth rugby policy to ensure the on-going growth of the game at school level.

In addition to the major professional competitions, the following additional levels of rugby exist:
- ❏ the national sevens team, and an increasing number of sevens competitions and tournaments throughout the country, notably the North Region Sevens series
- ❏ the Vodacom Cup competition, a breeding ground for future stars at provincial level

demands on young players is a highly pressurised sporting environment created by the competition, the coaches, parents and peers. As a result of this 'pressure cooker' state in our youth game, I believe that, should the status quo not be addressed, a number of unfavourable scenarios may play themselves out.

Firstly, we are likely to have fewer boys progressing to senior level. More are likely to have suffered serious injury, some will feel that the 'system' has left them behind and many will be 'burnt out' – greatly relieved that the days of compulsory sports participation are over.

Secondly, those that do participate in further rugby will be limited to players who were identified from the 'talent pool' early on. They, in turn, having been exposed to such high intensity preparation in an attempt to win competitions and make the grade, may suffer from physical and mental fatigue and are thus unable to produce rugby of the quality expected from them over a career that one would expect to last up to 12 years.

Finally, in an effort to be noticed and be included in a system that rewards with bursaries and scholarships to 'rugby' universities, provincial contracts and the possible trappings and sponsorships that accompany this, our youth are resorting to any means to achieve early rugby recognition. This may mean year-round rugby training at the expense of other sports and scholarship, the utilisation of a range of nutritional supplements most of which have little scientific basis, and outright cheating (Tour de France-style) by utilising anabolic supplements

and stimulants to enhance and maintain performance at the required levels.

One often hears the question asked as to why our school, Under-19 and Under-21 teams perform so consistently and yet South Africa fail to produce the same standards at Super 14 and National levels.

The scientist in me suggests that burnout and recurrent injury may be important reasons; the cynical side of me suggests that, with increasing drug vigilance at higher levels, the cheats may not be able to use the ergogenic aides they had been relying on.

In a letter that Dr Patricios wrote for the SuperSchools website, he says:

Over-enthusiastic fathers, paranoid that their sons may lose out on a university bursary, are determined to see their boys through the season despite serious injury; the relief I see on a boy's face when you prescribe a period of rest to recover from injury; the stretch marks, swollen nipples and rampant acne of the anabolic steroid user; the 13-year-old asking what supplements he should be drinking for a rugby physique! All of these scenarios are playing themselves out with alarming frequency.

It is time to address the year-round training, the mental and physical stresses, professional contracting, supplement and drugs abuse that have permeated the South African schoolboy game. Let us create a system that encourages our young men to play to live, not live to play.

- ❏ the Varsity Cup which enhances the intervarsities that over the years provided lots of fun and also top-class, tough competition for many future Springboks
- ❏ the national club championships that are being resurrected
- ❏ amateur provincial leagues
- ❏ sub-union competitions
- ❏ unions' club competitions
- ❏ national youth weeks and many, many Easter and other schools tournaments for various age groups.

These are in addition to provincial competitions for the women's teams and a Springbok women's side that competes internationally.

The Vodacom Cup

The Vodacom Cup is the third-tier competition in rugby union in South Africa, behind Super Rugby and the Currie Cup. It is played at roughly the same time as the Super Rugby competition and serves as an important developmental platform for South African rugby. It was first held in 1998, and was won in its first year by Griqualand West who, like the Golden Lions, had won it four times by the end of 2010.

The competition was initially instituted to fill a void for those professional players who were not included in the Super Rugby franchise teams. As a back-up to the players doing duty in the Super 12 of those years, mere club practices and training would not have been sufficient. Also, the teams without representation in the Super franchises would have been totally out of their depth when those players returned for the Currie Cup tournament later in the season.

The Vodacom Cup therefore creates a platform for talented young players who might otherwise not get a chance to make their mark.

Divided into a North and South section for the league phase, the Vodacom Cup features matches against sides from the same section in one year and cross-section league matches the next. The top four teams from each section play quarterfinals for places in the semi-finals and final. Since 2010 the Namibian Welwitschias and Argentine's Pampas have also played in the competition to gain experience against good sides. (The Welwitschias played in the competition between 1999 and 2001 and then rejoined in 2010. Pampas XV become the first team to win the title without losing a match in 2011.)

The development aspect of the competition was emphasised with a first prize of R1 million put up for the winners of which R500 000 had to be used for development. The Blue Bulls have won two of the three money prizes by securing the titles in 2008 and 2010. Both times the Free State Cheetahs were the losers, and in both instances the loss was of heartbreaking proportions.

The last few years have seen real effort and close matches. It is as if the competition has suddenly become of greater importance to the unions – and while the franchise unions in particular take the competition seriously in order to nurture young talent, teams like Griquas have seized the opportunity to build for the Currie Cup. It is therefore no wonder that Griquas have won the

competition four times and have lost in two more finals. This process is also the reason they have been performing well in the Currie Cup of late. (They last won in it 1970.)

In the first two years, unlike the close finishes in 2008 and 2010 and the real contest in 2009, the finals were near-farcical. Griquas beat the Golden Lions 57–0 in 1998, and in 1999, the roles were reversed when the Golden Lions won by a staggering 73–7.

The next three finals were marginally closer, but still not a reflection of a great competition. These scores were:
❏ 2000: 44–24 (Griquas v Free State Cheetahs)
❏ 2001: 42–24 (Blue Bulls v Boland Cavaliers)
❏ 2002: 54–38 (Blue Bulls v Golden Lions).

Ironically, Bulls and Springbok captain Victor Matfield, who cut his teeth on the Vodacom Cup series, played for Griquas in that drubbing against the Lions. It was also the season of his Currie Cup and Super Rugby debut – for the Cats – after moving to Kimberley from the Blue Bulls' Under-21 side.

Matfield is just one of many Springboks who came through the Vodacom Cup, which has become an important part of the system that has been put in place. His lock partner in the Springbok side, Bakkies Botha, is also one of those Boks. He first played Vodacom Cup for what was then the Falcons (now the Valke) in 2000 and, after moving to Pretoria, became a Blue Bulls Vodacom Cup player in 2001.

From 2001 to 2004, the teams finishing outside the top four in the pool phases played in a secondary competition, the Vodacom Shield.

The three highlights of the competition from an outsider's point of view were the last three competitions. In 2008 the Blue Bulls beat the Cheetahs at Loftus Versfeld when the first woman to officiate as a TMO, test referee Jenny Bentel, had a near-impossible task in making a close, very difficult call in the 84th minute. She decided that the Cheetahs had not scored and the Bulls won 25–21.

Two years later it took a drop kick launched in last-sec-

Francois Brümmer – last minute drop goal.

The Golden Lions' hat-trick between 2002 and 2004 is the best winning sequence to date.

The Vodacom Cup champions are as follows:

2011: Pampas XV
2010: Blue Bulls
2009: Griquas
2008: Blue Bulls
2007: Griquas
2006: Valke
2005: Griquas
2004: Golden Lions
2003: Golden Lions
2002: Golden Lions
2001: Blue Bulls
2000: Free State Cheetahs
1999: Golden Lions
1998: Griqualand West

ond desperation from Blue Bulls flyhalf Francois Brümmer to clinch the match 31–29 at Loftus Versfeld B-field. (Heavy rains over the prior weeks had forced the game to the B-field to spare the Loftus stadium pitch that was used for a Super Rugby match that afternoon.)

The Cheetahs went into the break 16–8 up, before the Blue Bulls came back to lead 28–22. But the visitors seemed to have snatched victory when prop Riaan Vermeulen was driven over for a try, converted by Louis Strydom, to put the Free Staters 29–28 up in the dying minutes. It was then that Brümmer let fly, under pressure and from nearly 50 metres out, well after the hooter. It was a drop kick that was literally worth a million rand!

Sandwiched in between these two finals was a one-man show by Griqualand West's Riaan Viljoen, who scored all 28 of his team's points as they beat the Blue Bulls 28–19 at Loftus. His points came from a try, seven penalties and a conversion. The Blue Bulls' points were also scored by one man and consisted of a try, conversion, drop goal and three penalties from Francois Brümmer.

The Bulls had the longest finals streak in Vodacom Cup finals, playing in the season's highlight four years in a row from 2007 to 2010 but they won only two of them.

The youth weeks

Craven Week was first played in 1964 and is the greatest tournament for schools rugby in the world. That can be said without any fear of contradiction after 48 Craven Week tournaments have been held all over South Africa, and with hundreds of former provincial schools players making it through the Craven Week into the SA Schools side, the provincial junior and senior system and even to international level.

When the idea of a provincial schools week was first mooted in the year that South African rugby celebrated its 75th anniversary, it was not welcomed by everyone. Although provincial schools rugby had been played since the 1920s and became a more organised series of friendlies over the years, there remained a conservative attitude among some who maintained that schoolboys should not be pushed too soon. At many schools – yes, even in the old Transvaal where cup competitions took place – the boys played without numbers on their jerseys to enforce the idea that it was a game for the team and not the individual. Many schools, most of them English

48 tournaments in 29 centres

Since 1964, the 48 Craven Week tournaments have been held in 29 different locations from Cape Town in the south to Windhoek (Namibia) and Harare (Zimbabwe) in the north.

'The Coca-Cola Craven Week is a South African institution and we make a point of ensuring both main centres and smaller towns are able to play host to the different events. This has proven hugely successful in exposing the events and the emerging rugby talent to a very broad portion of the South African community,' says Mervin Green at SARU.

The Craven Week for high schools has taken place at the following venues:

1964: East London
1965: East London
1966: Pretoria
1967: Cape Town
1968: Bloemfontein
1969: Pietermaritzburg
1970: Salisbury – now Harare
1971: Kimberley
1972: Potchefstroom
1973: Stellenbosch
1974: Johannesburg
1975: Pretoria
1976: Wolmaransstad
1977: Oudtshoorn
1978: Middelburg
1979: East London
1980: Stellenbosch
1981: Worcester
1982: Windhoek
1983: Upington
1984: Bloemfontein
1985: Witbank
1986: Graaff-Reinet
1987: Paarl
1988: Port Elizabeth
1989: Johannesburg
1990: Durban
1991: East London
1992: Pretoria
1993: Secunda
1994: Newcastle
1995: Bloemfontein
1996: Stellenbosch
1997: Kimberley
1998: Vanderbijl Park
1999: George
2000: Port Elizabeth
2001: Rustenburg
2002: Pietermaritzburg
2003: Wellington
2004: Nelspruit
2005: Bloemfontein
2006: Johannesburg
2007: Stellenbosch
2008: Pretoria
2009: East London
2010: Welkom
2011: Kimberley

rugby-playing schools, wouldn't allow their boys to be considered for the provincial sides.

There was a view that provincial rugby – and especially in an organised tournament – was against the spirit of the sport and contrary to educational principles. But the idea was accepted and went ahead.

It was rather amateurish – and by saying that no fingers are pointed at the organisation of the tournament by Border Schools, which was outstanding. It was even more admirable if the short period they had to put on the greatest schools show is considered. They had no assistance from the SARFB, as it still was then; there was no umbrella SA Schools body of any sort.

Little more than three months after the idea was first broached by 1949 Springbok Piet Malan, Border proudly hosted the first tournament with 15 schools participating. For many of the unions, picking a provincial schools side was a novelty – and is fair to say that many deserving players missed out on this tournament because of the lack of trial structures and procedures that in all probability would have seen stronger sides selected.

The man at the organising helm of the tournament was Jan Preuyt, an East London schoolmaster for 31 years. The SA Schools committee had its birth at that first Craven Week where Preuyt was elected as chairman, a position he would hold for 25 years. The committee included Trens Erasmus (Western Transvaal), Wouter du Toit (Transvaal), Hennie Lochner (Boland) and Meyer Sauerman (Eastern Province).

In 1974 Preuyt was manager of the first SA Schools

Piet Malan, who suggested the Craven Week.

Unions throughout South Africa cater for very young players.

team to tour Italy and France. Preuyt also managed the national schools side to Wales in 1983. In 1986 he became the first president of the SA Schools Union, SASU, which encompassed all sporting codes.

The teams that took part in the first Craven Week were Boland, Border, Eastern Province, Eastern Transvaal, Griqualand West, Natal, North Eastern Cape, Northern Transvaal, Orange Free State, Rhodesia, South West Africa, South Western Districts, Transvaal, Western Province and Western Transvaal.

However, the number of teams varied from year to year and have only stabilised to some extent in the last 10 years. More and more teams, especially from the country districts, were invited and by 2000, there were 32 teams, including Namibia and Zimbabwe who returned as participants.

Although the number of teams taking part in Craven Week was reduced to 20, the concept was expanded to include an additional Academy Week for players who were unfortunate to miss out on selection for their province's

best XV, and also to include more sides from the country districts. An Under-16 Week acts as a 'feeder' for the Under-18 Craven Week, and is named after Grant Khomo, a leading administrator and former player of what was then the SA African Rugby Football Board. There is also an Under-13 Craven Week; and the LSEN (Learners with Special Educational Needs) have their own Under-18 provincial week. More than 1 500 young rugby players across South Africa are awarded their provincial colours and take part in the four youth weeks each year.

The Academy side was initially seen as the second best XV selected from all the Craven Week players after the week's matches. It often ended in embarrassment for the national schools selectors with the Academy XV beating the SA Schools side in the annual matches! Now, after their own week, the best of the Academy week players are selected to play in an Academy XV that takes part in the Craven Week.

A forerunner of the Academy side came in 1887 when the former SARB launched the Project Tournament which

A boost for club rugby

The decision by SARU early in 2011 to hold the national club championships without the country's university sides was a huge boost for the so-called 'open clubs', and seen as a solid basis from which to start rebuilding club rugby.

Through the years, the open clubs have been at a considerable disadvantage. Even before the advent of official professionalism in 1996, the universities had first pick of the best rugby players in the country as they could offer bursaries and accommodation during their time of study. As the varsities' power increased, so did the school-leavers aspire to gain entry to those institutions where their rugby would be advanced by the best coaches and team-mates in South Africa!

The 2011 SARU decision also promised an enticing final annually, which is proposed between the open club winners and the top varsity team to determine South Africa's top club. This showdown will provide another highlight to the season.

Ironically, the decision which had long been mooted came after open clubs had won the previous two national club championship titles. College Rovers beat Maties, Varsity Cup champions for the last three years, in the 2010 final, while Hamiltons accounted for NWK-Pukke in 2009. Before that Pirates were the last open club to be crowned champions when they beat another open club, Tygerberg, in 2001.

In practical terms, the SARU decision means that open clubs will now have more opportunity to advance in the 16-team competition. With few exceptions, the open clubs were eliminated in the first round in the past, leaving matters to be fought out by the university sides.

To date, Maties have won 12 of the 15 finals in which they have played since 1975 – and they had won all of their finals since 1981 until the 2010 loss. Their only losses were against Tukkies in 1976, fellow Western Province (open) club Villagers in 1980, and College Rovers in 2010.

There was a period in the 1990s when the title was not decided during a tournament but with teams playing on a home-and-away basis but this was abolished in 2001.

Open clubs have won only 11 of the 36 club championships titles to the end of 2010. Durban Crusaders is the only club to have won it two years running and Despatch is the only other open club with two titles. (Pretoria Police should perhaps also be regarded as an open club in the years in which they won it as they were not officially restricted to police members playing for them in 1995 and 1996.) The most consecutive wins are by Maties (three, 1977–1979). The only open clubs that have won the competition are Villagers (1980), Pretoria Harlequins (1983), Despatch (1985 and 1988), Roodepoort (1989), Old Greys (1991), Durban Crusaders (1993 and 1994), Pirates (2001), Hamiltons (2009) and College Rovers (2010).

Club players are also given the opportunity to play at a higher level than their domestic competitions, with the provincial amateur league providing the better players with a chance to play with players from other clubs in a provincial team against similar sides from other unions.

had a quota requirement (regarding the players' skin colour) of 50–50 set for selection. In 2010 this was again the breakdown for the Academy sides, while Craven Week required that at least nine black players should be selected for the provincial squad.

While the cherry on top for Craven Week is undoubtedly being selected for the SA Schools side, SARU have now moved towards selection of a High Performance (HP) group – in the Under-18 as well as Under-16 age groups.

High Performance squads

Nineteen players who were selected to the SA Schools team for 2010 were included in the 32-man South African Under-18 High Performance squad that competed in a series of international friendlies in 2010.

The Under-18 group was selected by the national selectors and involved Springbok Sevens coach Paul Treu and SA Under-20 coach Eric Sauls. Treu's appointment was made in the hope that he would be able to identify potential players to go on and represent the Bok Sevens in future IRB Sevens World Series. That he did, and in 2011 Paul Jordaan, barely out of school, was an instant success in South Africa's sevens team on the IRB circuit. Jordaan is one of five promising schoolboy players contracted in 2010 by Treu. The former Grey College schoolboy was just 19 when he received his Springbok blazer.

'This (High Performance) programme was initiated to prepare potential players who could one day represent the SA Under-20 side in the IRB Junior World Championships or to compete in the IRB Sevens World Series with the Springbok Sevens. This squad was identified by our national selectors who attended the recently held Coca-Cola Youth Weeks while also considering the Under-18 players from tertiary institutions and rugby clubs,' said SARU High Performance Manager, Herman Masimla, after selection of the HP squads in 2010.

'This Under-18 group will also have the added incentive of progressing to the SA Under-19 squad next year (2011). We are already in the process of arranging international friendlies against the French and Argentinean Under-19 teams.

'These structures have been put in place to ultimately ensure that we produce the finest junior rugby players in the world.'

This awarding of national colours to schoolboys didn't have Craven's support. He wanted Craven Week to be a festival, not a competition and certainly not trials. This was the reason why no 'schools test' was played against the 1969 Australian side that visited South Africa. In 1974 the great man had to relent, however, and a national schools side was selected and toured France and Italy. There has been a SA School side selected every year since, though matches against overseas opponents have been infrequent.

Although Craven's idealism was a good basis to work from, there was little chance of a non-competitive tournament taking place. There is no official winner but there is no doubt that the last match on the last day is seen as a final – and the winner of that match is

Harry Viljoen – SA Schools player who became the national coach, and Louis Luyt.

regarded as the Craven Week champions.

What would have aggrieved Doc Craven even more is the fact that the Craven Week tournaments – and even the more junior tournaments, including the Under-13s – are being used by scouts to identify talent. Under-13s are lured to rugby schools and even placed in those schools by unions that (partly) foot the bill; Under-18s are being hunted for the future provincial success of rugby unions.

Despite these negatives, Craven Week – and all the other youth weeks – has played its part in the identification of raw talent. This became even more significant in 1980 when Craven got approval to have the week opened to players of all races. In 1996 the so-called 'quota system' was introduced. This was to ensure that the better players of colour who still didn't have the same opportunities to develop their rugby at schools level, would not be missed.

It is interesting to note that two former SA Schools players, Nick Mallett and Harry Viljoen, became Springbok rugby coaches.

But there is, of course, more to schoolboy rugby than the Craven and other youth weeks. A number of competitions – catering for players as young as Under-9 – take place in some of the unions, although the trend has lately been to move away from knock-outs and trophy rugby. Instead the schools now agree, as they did in the

Grey College: Churning out the Springboks

Grey College, leading provider of Springboks, added four to their tally in 2010. Bulls lock Flip van der Merwe and flank Deon Stegmann made their respective test debuts against the visiting French side in June and against Scotland on the year-end tour. Andries Strauss, cousin of sometimes Free State captain and Springbok hooker Adriaan Strauss, was selected after an outstanding performance in the 2010 Currie Cup final for the Sharks. Like Cheetahs prop Coenie Oosthuizen, he played one match on the tour, against the British Barbarians.

Coenie Oosthuizen

The former Orange Free State, now the Cheetahs, have over the years relied heavily on the rugby production line that is Grey College, the oldest school north of the Orange River opened on 17 January 1859. They first played football against another school in June 1881. The opponents were the Anglican school in Bloemfontein, St Andrew's.

That first game was a version of the Winchester game, as brought to South Africa from England and played by Diocesan College in Cape Town in the 1870s. In the 1890s, Grey College regularly played against men's teams in the Orange Free State. They became the second winners of the OFS Grand Challenge Cup in 1896.

Grey's peak rugby period was in the latter half of the twentieth century; and between 1986 and 1990, they were unbeaten in 80 successive matches.

Grey have produced more players for Craven Week than any other school, and also more players for the national schools side than any other school in the country. They hold the record with six players from Grey College in the 1981 SA Schools side.

Herman van Broekhuisen, who was a Western Province player, represented South Africa in 1896 and was the first Grey College old boy to do so.

The Grey College old boys who have played for South Africa are: Herman van Broekhuisen, Boet McHardy, Sarel Strauss, Henry Martin, Louis Babrow, Piet de Wet, Popeye Strydom, Gert Cilliers, John Wessels, Johan Spies, Morné du Plessis (captain), Dawie Snyman and his brother Jackie, Theuns Stofberg (captain), Robbie Blair, Jaco Reinach, Helgard Müller and his brother Pieter, Andries Truscott, Johan Styger, Heinrich Fuls, Ruben Kruger, Ollie le Roux, Naka Drotské, Werner Swanepoel, Charl Marais, Gerrie Britz, CJ van der Linde, Ruan Pienaar, Jannie and his brother Bismarck du Plessis, Frans Steyn, Heinrich Brüssow, Adriaan Strauss, Wian du Preez, Flip van der Merwe, Deon Stegmann, Andries Strauss and Coenie Oosthuizen.

The school has also produced five test match referees, namely Reg Stanton, Att Horak, Steve Strydom, Justus Moolman and Gerrit Coetzer. (Paul Roos Gimnasium have produced 42 Springboks, 33 of them before the Second World War. Bishops have produced 35, of which 10 are post-war Boks.) Source: www.rugby365.com and SA Rugby

very early days, to arrange their matches against teams of equal strength.

However, a school's prestige still remains largely dependent on its sports – and particularly rugby – performances. Some of the top high schools identify promising players at Under-13 level and offer them bursaries for the next year as the schools start building for a super rugby side in four years' time.

Some of the more pleasurable rugby experiences – for players and spectators – are the various schools weeks, held mostly over the Easter weekend. With schools from all over the country invited to attend tournaments such as those at Kearsney, St Stithians, St John's and the Wildeklawer tournament, the boys get an opportunity to play against opposition they would not meet during a domestic season.

There is a ranking list for schools, the existence of which has been debated over a period. Whatever these merits might be, the names of Grey College, Grey High, Paul Roos, Paarl Gimnasium, Outeniqua, Monument, Waterkloof, Paarl Boys High, Boland Landbou and Afrikaanse Hoër Seunskool have been there for some years and will probably remain near the top, given the professionalism that has crept into schoolboy rugby.

SA junior sides

These top rugby schools, to a large extent, provide the players for South Africa's junior sides that take part in the IRB Under-20 World Championship – an annual tournament since 2008 which replaced the two separate tournaments for Under-21s and Under-19s. South Africa won the Under-21 title in 2002 and 2005, while the Under-19s were champions in 2005. (The Under-19 IRB tournament was held from 1998 to 2007, and the Under-21s played from 1996 to 2006.)

Many of these players went on to represent South Africa at senior international level including team members selected for the 2011 World Cup in New Zealand.

At home, however, South Africa decided to stay with the two age groups. Both the provincial competitions for Under-21s and Under-19s are divided into two sections of seven teams each and in both age groups the A-Section teams play a double round with a final at the end of the season. There is promotion/relegation in both age groups.

Sevens

In a strange disregard for the pecking order, South Africa's Springbok sevens side is denied the playing personnel that could make it the world's best on a continual basis.

Only three national sides are allowed the honour of being called the Springboks: the national side that competes in test matches and the Tri-Nations and World Cup competition; the sevens side that plays on the IRB Sevens World Series circuit; and the national women's side.

But spare a thought for the national sevens coach, Paul Treu. A former Super 12 player for the Stormers and the Bulls and a sevens player who led his country in the IRB Series, this unassuming former teacher from Swellendam who holds a Master's degree in educational psychology also played for the Emerging Springboks. Since taking over as sevens coach from Chester Williams in 2004, Treu has virtually had to build a new team every season. While any coach accepts the role of injuries, he is regularly deprived of his stars who are being pounced on by gleeful Super franchises and Currie Cup unions after showing their class on the international sevens stage.

It is not generally known, but Treu literally has to negotiate the use of every single player with the unions – which means that he does not have free access to the top 400–500 players in the country. He also has no right to the national Under-20 players – and in 2010, he was denied the use of two players who had excelled for him because a union needed them for the national Under-21 competition's play-offs. This lukewarm approach to sevens by South Africa is in contrast to Australia, where the sevens competition is used to groom players for higher honours. The 2010 Wallabies boasted a very good back line – and every one of them had progressed through the national sevens team. The All Blacks also make use of their sevens team when players return after long-time injury.

Sevens is a totally different game from the 15-man version. It takes time, effort and patience to teach and drill in the different structures – on attack as well as defence. And most of Treu's time is taken up by teaching the game to his new selections that provincial coaches don't need for their own campaigns – and that includes the Vodacom Cup. Treu's playing experience in 31 tournaments, during which he scored 70 tries, as well as the 2001 World Cup, has stood him in good stead.

He started coaching the national sevens side before he had officially retired! He took over from Williams in 2004 when Williams – himself a former Bok sevens player – resigned to take up a coaching position with the Super 12 Cats franchise. Treu, who was struggling with a knee

The Springbok sevens side after winning the 2007 IRB title in Dubai.

injury, was offered the job – and the rest is history. Since Treu's appointment, South Africa – despite a poor 2010 brought about by the loss of virtually his entire team – has won numerous tournaments in the IRB Series; the IRB Series in 2008/2009; a bronze medal at the Commonwealth Games in Delhi (2010); and has produced a number of Springboks and Super Rugby players for the South African system.

After starting off with a win in only his fourth tournament in charge, Treu has brought through Springboks including Bryan Habana, Jaco Pretorius, Gio Aplon, Kabamba Floors, Heinrich Brüssow, Ryan Kankowski, Akona Ndungane, Jongi Nokwe, Juan de Jongh, Tonderai Chavhanga and Earl Rose during his tenure.

Two Springbok icons captained the Springboks at sevens: Bobby Skinstad and Chester Williams – who incidentally are two of the four Maties who captained the

Boks sevens. The other Maties captains are the very first Springbok sevens captain Dion O'Cuinneagain (1997) and Kevin Foote (2004). O'Cuinneagain later represented Ireland as a No 8 in test rugby when sevens internationals could still play test rugby for another country.

A dedicated coach who roams the world in search of new techniques and tactics, Treu is regarded as a top tactician by his peers. He has established a permanent base camp in Stellenbosch where the broader sevens squad does its preparations for the international tournaments – and SARU, at the recommendation of Treu, now also contracts sevens players. This gives Treu first option on their services and also ensures a little more continuity in team selections. It also makes the step up easier for players who have to fill in because of injury.

In 2009 Treu started working towards the expected inclusion of sevens in the 2016 Olympics – something

(Blue) Diamonds are forever

A development project that is probably unique in South African rugby is the Blue Diamond Rugby Club, founded with the objective of making sure that youth rugby is played, developed, managed and co-ordinated within the union's area of jurisdiction, on a non-racial, non-political and democratic basis. The Blue Diamond Rugby Club acts as one of the youth clubs in the union and the club works primarily with the schools in the inner city of Pretoria; it provides coaching as well as support based on available resources for participating schools such as Eendragt, Oost Eind and Jopie Fourie.

A mere two years after starting with the project, the Blue Bulls have been rewarded with seven children from the project being selected for provincial teams.

'We are proud of our achievements,' said Danie Lerm, who heads the Blue Diamonds project. 'We have eight teams participating at primary school level, and every year we see a steady increase in the number of participants, which is brilliant because our main aim is to keep the children off the streets. But we were particularly proud this year because seven of our players graduated to provincial teams, more than double the three players selected last

year. Three of them are Under-14 players, two Under-13s and two Under-18s.'

Looking ahead, Lerm said that they were considering extending the project to Under-19 level, which could serve as a doorway for players to filter into the club rugby structures.

'The project currently runs up to Under-18 level, but we found that once the guys reach the age limit, they stop playing completely,' said Lerm. 'So by extending it to Under-19, it will give those guys a chance to play club rugby. And if one considers the interest shown in the Blue Diamonds by some of these children, it should keep the guys off the streets for longer.'

Former Blue Bulls Under-21 and Vodacom Cup Nico Serfontein who is now with the GLRU, was initially involved with the project. 'For years we have been focusing on areas like Soshanguve and Mamelodi, and forgot about the guys right under our noses. This programme also fits in perfectly with the union's strategic plan to develop human capital and increase player numbers. All this makes this project so so rewarding.'

which has since become reality. He is increasingly looking at young talent, even at schools level – and the introduction of the first two teenagers at international level was a revelation. Paul Jordaan and Tshotsho Mbovane both impressed against the more experienced, bigger and stronger players from inter alia Fiji, Samoa and new Zealand. and showed that Treu was indeed on the right track.

There have been some truly great South African sevens players over the years. At the end of 2010 Fabian Juries, who reverted to fifteens in 2009, was third on the all-time try list with 179 tries behind the two leaders, Argentina's Santiago Gomez Cora (230 tries) and England's Ben Gollings (211). This is an outstanding achievement considering his relatively few appearances

(43 tournaments). Juries is also eighth on the all-time list of points scored with 925 points.

Stefan Basson, in only 19 tournaments in four years, is fifteenth on the IRB's point-scorers list with 691 points. Mzwandile Stick, who opted out of sevens to play for the new franchise Southern Kings which he captained, is tenth on the list of point scorers (855 points in 30 tournaments, including 86 tries). Marius Schoeman, who played in 41 tournaments and scored 103 tries, and Renfred Dazel are others who excelled at the game, while big Frankie Horn, not as prolific a try-scorer as the others, is still doing yeomen work for the Boks.

The 2010/2011 IRB season saw the emergence of a new talent who promises to become the greatest sevens player produced by South Africa. Cecil Afrika, in only

Hoërskool Monument's Ivan Botha charging defenders of Hoërskool Outeniqua during the tournament for schools' second teams hosted by Monnas in 2011.

his second IRB season, and despite injury preventing him from playing in two of the eight 2010/2011 tournaments, was top scorer in the IRB series. Other players blooded for the first time in this and the preceding season, like Branco du Preez, Sibusiso Sithole, Chris Dry and Bernardo Botha, show promise for South Africa's onslaught on the 2016 Games.

In recent years, South African sides below the national team have started playing in various competitions, which have also become more plentiful. The Zambian Sevens; the top sevens tournament in Africa, namely the Safari Sevens in Nairobi; the Middelburg Sevens; the Singapore Sevens; the Dubai Sevens' competitions for teams below the invited IRB Series sides; the national provincial championship; the North Region Sevens series; the very popular @lantic Sevens series for schools and the Nelson Mandela Bay Sevens are probably the leading tournaments/competitions. Saheti High School in Johannesburg and Villagers in Cape Town also host

tournaments for schools.

South Africa has an outstanding record at the Melrose Sevens in Scotland where the game was first played, and an annual tournament was held in 1883, according to folklore.

The Maties (twice), Shimlas, University of Johannesburg and Hamiltons teams won five of the seven titles between 2004 and 2010. Hamiltons, with their veterans, were in Scotland once again in 2011 to defend their title.

In 2008, the SA Students side won the World Students title under coach Freddie Grobler. A national student team now regularly plays overseas to prepare in between the student world cups. At Tukkies' Academy a lot of attention is also given to sevens specialists.

The North Region Series started in 2004 and had the same problems that Treu has to deal with. Competing teams were frequently denied the use of even Under-19 players in provincial squads for the national Under-19 competition that started months later. It hampers the quality of a competition that is played throughout the year on the same basis as the IRB Sevens Series, with a tournament in each of the represented unions – Limpopo, Pumas, Lions, Valke, Blue Bulls, Leopards and Lions. As in the IRB series, the points earned in each tournament are added on a log to determine the Series winner after eight tournaments.

The Series has grown in stature, and a representative North Region side is now selected to take part in international tournaments in Kenya and Zambia. They also played in the Bafokeng international tournament in 2010, which the Springboks won.

The frequent provincial competition throughout the year was instrumental in three of the four semi-finalists at the provincial championships emerging from the North Region competition in 2010 – and a substantial number of players have progressed through the North Region system to play Currie Cup and Vodacom Cup rugby.

Academies

Sevens is arguably not being used to the full for the development of players in South Africa, and neither have the rugby academies that have sprung up over the past decade been as successful as hoped. There are, of course, the more professional academies, run by rugby unions and top clubs, but there are also academies run by schools. All of these have one objective: to lure and develop good players for the unions and the clubs/schools.

Many of them combine the rugby academy with tertiary education – classes in the morning, rugby in the afternoons. In the case of the Tukkies/Blue Bulls academy, their players are released to neighbouring unions Pumas and Valke for the national Under-19 and Under-21 competitions; they also play club rugby for clubs other than Tukkies to bolster the club system. Refereeing, coaching, first aid and such asides to the game are part of the academy courses.

There are however a number of these academies that

Tag rugby to learn the game

Tag Rugby became an associate member of SA Rugby in 2009 after starting their activities in 1992.

Tag rugby is a high-paced, contact-free version of rugby, in which tackles are simulated by pulling Velcro strips from belts worn by the players. It can be played on any surface and requires minimal equipment beyond the belts, tags and a ball. It can be played by players as young as five years of age. Boys and girls of all ages can play in the game which has no scrums, line-outs or kicking. The focus is on running and passing, attacking and supporting.

The game is a means to improving handling skills and increasing the numbers of children playing rugby, and can also be used as a training aid for schools and clubs that already play contact rugby. Tag rugby is also being used to introduce teenagers (and adults) of both sexes to the game of rugby in high schools that have not offered rugby as an extramural. That is especially the case as unions try to encourage schoolgirls to take up rugby.

are run purely as enterprises. It is not uncommon to see advertisements inviting participants to a three-week holiday course that costs R20 000.

The selection of High Performance groups by SARU over the past few years is a major step towards getting on par with Australia's academies where most of the Wallabies are developed to international level in a country that has little in the way of rugby structures or playing personnel.

Development

Development, on the other hand, has various forms. In most of the bigger unions in South Africa there are junior leagues and weekly coaching is done at senior clubs. Matches from Under-8 age-group level are played between clubs – and provincial sides selected from junior

The women of the Lions and Blue Bulls do battle in the provincial competition.

Women

Women's rugby has been struggling to get a foothold in South Africa. Their performances at the two World Cups in 2006 and 2010 were not up to standard. However, there is not much in the line of competition to produce quality players, and national coach Denver Wannies' work to take his team to tenth position in the 2010 World Cup is just reward for his effort.

A provincial women's league, with two sections, still does not function well. Teams continue to withdraw from provincial fixtures, and with the best players concentrated in a few unions, the provincial competition is very much a contrived effort with players being loaned across borders to keep the neighbours going. This makes it extremely difficult for players at international level to take the step up and adapt to the greater pace they need to be competitive.

Varsity rugby

University rugby has long been the backbone of South Africa's national team. When Dawie Snyman (South Africa's 453rd Springbok) and Morné du Plessis (455) were elected in 1971, together they became the 100th Bok to come out of Maties (Stellenbosch University). A single university had therefore provided 22% of the Springboks up to that point. Ikeys (University of Cape Town), Tukkies (University of Pretoria), Shimlas (University of the Free State in Bloemfontein) and Pukke (University of Potchefstroom, now called North-West University) have also produced a number of outstanding players for the national side.

This, however, was to change as professionalism saw to it that most promising players went into provincial age-group structures rather than to university. The intervarsities of earlier years were also diluted to some extent and had to be fitted in between the rigours of provincial and international rugby. Teams such as Tukkies, Maties, Shimlas, University of Johannesburg and NWU-Pukke have been weakened because of call-

clubs in the more senior age groups play one another in the latter half of the season. These matches provide the better players who did not make the sides to the formal SARU age-group weeks with an opportunity to play with and against better players.

There are also provincial opportunities for players in the townships. Most of South Africa's rugby unions have a youth league system since many black schools, in particular, do not offer rugby as a sport. Many of these unions also compete at provincial level in the Under-12, Under-13, Under-16 and Under-18 age groups.

ups to the various provincial sides – including the Under-21s and Under-19s.

The universities' game was given a boost in 2008 with the introduction of the FNB Varsity Cup competition. It provided a new interest. At Stellenbosch 9 000 season tickets were sold for the 2011 season – and that's not for the Varsity Cup only! With a Varsity Shield competition added in 2011, the top 12 university teams in South Africa therefore now take part in a competition format Dr Danie Craven mooted in the 1950s.

In the 1970s the universities played the Ted Sceales knock-out competition. (Maties, ironically did not take part despite Craven's earlier wishes!) This competition was dominated by Tukkies who were then at their peak and at one stage were unbeaten for 50 matches. The Ted Sceales also gave the lesser teams the opportunity to play against the country's best teams that in those days included provincial players and Springboks and regularly drew crowds of 40 000.

At a lower level than the elite varsity competitions the backbone of university rugby is played with great fervour among the residences at most universities and in faculty leagues at others.

As is the wont of the game and students in particular, there have been inter-residence matches from the earliest rugby days in South African universities. However, the first formal 'koshuis' competition was only in 1949, when Dagbreek won the Maties title. With more than a thousand players at Maties and Tukkies from the 1950s onwards, the competitions prospered. The top rugby-playing universities now have three or even four leagues to accommodate players of all standards.

'Koshuis' rugby has been recognised and now forms part of a lower-tier competition in the Varsity Cup series, with one team from each of the competing Varsity Cup sides competing. Over the years many hundreds of provincial players and even Springboks have progressed to these higher levels despite only playing 'koshuis' rugby at university.

Golden Oldies

At the lower (or is it older?) end of South Africa's rugby structures is the Golden Oldies tournament. South African sides have been playing national tournaments from the mid-1980s and some teams have attended International Golden Oldies tournaments where the fun and friendship of rugby is revived every second year. In 1998 Cape Town hosted the international event with 196 teams taking part. There are no prizes but the rugby is tough with teams divided into groups of equal strength. Great former internationals, including the British Lions' centre Jeff Butterfield, Springboks Thys Lourens, Tim Cocks, Louis Moolman and brothers Joggie and Eben Jansen, Gerrie Germishuys and many, many provincial players have lengthened their playing careers with this hard but fun-filled form of the game.

9

Test matches
The grip of South African rugby loosens

In 2011, a full 150 years after the first steps in South African rugby were taken with the introduction of the football game according to the Winchester rules, the Springboks were preparing for the defence of their World Cup title in New Zealand in September and October.

That in itself made it a special year. Test schedules were changed, and players followed different training schedules to ensure that they peaked at the right time. Provincial and franchise coaches were requested, to the detriment of their own careers, to use the country's top players sparingly.

It was a season when every Springbok supporter held their breath hoping that top stars such as Victor Matfield, Fourie du Preez and Morné Steyn would not be injured in the Super Rugby or Tri-Nations competitions – especially after the February setback when experienced Cheetahs and Springbok flank Juan Smith injured his Achilles tendon, putting him in a race against time to make the hugely important tournament. And then more injuries to key players followed.

The physical management of the Boks was no easy task. South Africa were contract-bound to select their best team for every match they played in SANZAR's Tri-Nations competition – and they had to walk close to the off-side line during the Tri-Nations after flaunting the competition rules and largely ignoring the agreement in 2007. The same applied to the Super Rugby teams' coaches who, first, had an obligation to win matches for their franchise in an important and very tough competition; and secondly had the contractual SANZAR sword hanging over them should they not pick their strongest side at the behest of the Springbok management.

A day to remember. The Springboks played the All Blacks at FNB Stadium in 2010.

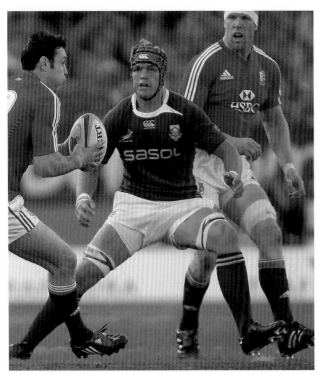

Juan Smith – early season injury.

The coaching staff had a talented national side, many of whom were at the 2007 World Cup. Veteran captain John Smit (33 years old in April), Victor Matfield (34 in May) and Bakkies Botha, who turned 32 in September, came into the year hoping to make it to their third World Cup. While the experience of these old-timers was a definite boost as Bok coach Peter de Villiers continued his planning for the World Cup defence early in 2011, it also put more pressure on the Bok management to ensure these players were not over-played.

Such is the pressure of professionalism that the Super 14 was upgraded to a competition with 15 sides, and 33% more matches were played in 2011. For financial and contractual reasons, the introduction of this new competition simply couldn't wait for another season; and there was no chance of the Tri-Nations teams – South Africa, New Zealand and Australia – selecting their own preferred opposition for World Cup warm-ups instead of bashing one another. The only allowance was a reduced 2011 Tri-Nations, with each side playing the others twice and not three times as in non-World Cup years.

Just months away from what would have been the unofficial 150th anniversary of the first game of rugby in South Africa at Diocesan College, the Springboks secured the country's 250th test win when they beat England 21–11 at Twickenham in their last match of 2010. It was a fitting milestone and also the seventh successive win against England in a sequence that started in November 2006.

These wins against a rugby force from the very early days reinforced the strength of South African rugby. In its first 179 tests until the unification of the country's four controlling bodies in 1992, South Africa were the undisputed kings of rugby. The Springboks had won more matches against all countries than they had lost, even against their biggest foes New Zealand, and they had lost only two test series in the 1900s.

More rugby in less time

In the 100 years since their first test match in 1891, South Africa played 179 tests – and it is a sobering thought that professionalism brought a further 216 matches in the next 20 years up to 2011! A good example of the increase in the number of games is that the Springboks had played only 37 matches against New Zealand by 1992, but since unification a further 44 tests had been added!

The return to the international fold was, however, not altogether pleasant. One win from five matches in 1992 and only three from seven the following year showed that South African rugby had fallen behind. Compare these figures to their previous record of losing only two series in the 1900s – against the 1958 French side and the 1974 British Lions – and the fact that a great rugby country like Wales had still not beaten the Boks by 1992.

Nineteen years on, South Africa have only a 40% winning record against the All Blacks after losing 33 and drawing one of their 44 matches since 1992 for a 23.87% record in this 'new era'; and against Australia,

Maori people slighted

The New Zealand Cavaliers tour followed only 16 years after Maori players were allowed to be included in a visiting All Blacks team for the first time. Although that wasn't the sole reason for the unhappy (demonstration) circumstances under which the Boks toured in 1981, the Maori saga started in 1921.

It followed an insensitive report sent to South Africa by journalist Charles Blackett in which it was said that it 'was bad enough to play a team of officially designated New Zealand natives …' and went on to say that thousands Europeans frantically cheered on a band of coloured men to defeat members of their own race was too much for the Springboks who were frankly disgusted.'

It caused huge insult to the Maori people, more so because in 1919 the South Africans had requested that no players of colour be included in the New Zealand Services team to visit South Africa. Ranji Wilson, a player of class, was notably omitted – and the tour went ahead.

The slight was repeated in 1928, when the great George Nepia had to stay home when Maurice Brownlee's All Blacks visited South Africa. No match against the Maori was played on the 1937 tour to New Zealand. This state of play of visiting New Zealand sides was to continue in 1949 and 1960, with Maori players only welcome to visit in 1970.

The irony is that the Springbok tourists who were on all the tours – even when they didn't meet in 1937 – were made to feel at home by the Maori people in Rotorua and Napier and enjoyed the company of this fervent rugby nation. And on the 1981 tour, marred by demonstrations, a pleasant match ended in a draw after a missed drop kick was wrongfully judged as successful by the referee! It was nevertheless a good day for rugby relationships – and jovial Maori captain Billy Bush said during a pleasant post-match function: 'A draw against the Springboks is a win!'

Lose for the sake of rugby, Maori team told

A player in the 1956 New Zealand Maori rugby team claimed in 2010 that a government minister told them to lose the match against the Springboks to prevent All Blacks sides being barred from South Africa. `

Muru Walters, the fullback in the 1956 team and later an Anglican bishop, said then New Zealand Minister of Maori Affairs, Ernest Corbett, visited the Maori side in their dressing room before the match and told the players they should lose 'for the future of rugby'. Corbett, who died in 1968, purportedly said the All Blacks may otherwise never be invited back to South Africa. The Maori team were beaten 37–0 at Eden Park in Auckland.

Walters said in a radio interview that Corbett's instruction had 'ripped the guts out of the spirits of our team'.

'What he said was: "You must not win this game or we will never be invited to South Africa again,"' Walters said.

'I thought he was joking, but then another official came in and said the same thing … "For the future of rugby, don't beat the South Africans."'

Walters' claims came as New Zealand Maori celebrated the centenary of being given official status in 1910, and after a refusal by the New Zealand Rugby Union to apologise to indigenous Maori for excluding them from All Blacks teams that toured South Africa in 1928, 1949 and 1960. In those years, New Zealand rugby omitted coloured players from national teams to tour South Africa at the request of South Africa's rugby authorities.

the winning ratio since unification is a poor 44.15% compared to 78.57% before readmission.

Despite these somewhat depressing figures for a South African supporter, the average wins since 1992 remained around 63% – and South Africa have two World Cups to show in this period while New Zealand have none!

However, the maintenance of the winning ratio is skewed by the poor opposition that has come into the equation. Samoa (six matches), Romania (one), Canada (two), Italy (ten), Fiji (two), Tonga (two), Spain (one), Uruguay (three), United States (two), Pacific Islands (one) and Namibia (one) have given South Africa 31 easy

Springboks in the blood

The Stegmann, Delport, Olivier connection:
Jan and Anton Stegmann, Willem Delport, Eben Olivier,
Thinus Delport

When Thinus Delport was selected for the Springbok tour of the United Kingdom and Europe in 1997, he became the fourth generation of his family to play Springbok rugby. And although there are many rugby families at various levels, including the Springboks, Delport's case is perhaps something special.

On his mother's side, his great-grandfather Ebbie Stegmann missed selection for the Boks because of injury – but Ebbie's two brothers Anton and Jan both played test rugby. Anton was a member of Paul Roos's 1906 'grand slam' side – the first Springboks to tour overseas. Anton also scored the first-ever try in a Springbok jersey; also the first overseas try, against East Midlands as the 1906 tour kicked off in Northampton.

The next generation to represent the Springboks was on father Gerard's side. Willem Delport was the brother of Thinus's grandfather Gert and toured with Basil Kenyon's 1951/52 great Springbok side to the UK and Ireland.

Willem Delport, in turn, was the uncle of Eben Olivier, who is the son of Willem and Gert's sister. Eben played in 16 tests after being selected as a replacement on the 1965 tour to Australia and New Zealand.

With Eben Olivier and Gerard Delport cousins, the fourth Springbok generation came with Thinus Delport's selection for the Boks. He played in 19 tests, including the 2003 World Cup; represented the Golden Lions, Cats and Sharks; and was just short of 150 premiership matches for Gloucester and Worcester in England.

Thinus then played in Japan for two seasons; also for the Northern Hemisphere against the Southern Hemisphere in the tsunami-memorial fundraiser; six matches for the British Barbarians; and represented a World Invitation XV against a team of former All Blacks.

But the Delports from Kirkwood's rugby pedigree is not limited to their Springboks. The 1951/52 Springbok hooker

Willem's son Kobus, also a hooker, represented Eastern Province in more than 80 matches and also captained them; Eben Olivier's brother Eric represented Eastern Province, as a fullback; and Eric's son – also Eric – played Vodacom Cup for Western Province. Eric Jnr's brother Otto was a flyhalf for Free State Country Districts.

Thinus's father Gerard played for Eastern Province in 1971–1972; and Thinus' uncle Tertius – a former cabinet minister – played scrumhalf for Eastern Province, captaining them on a few occasions. Tertius also represented Maties at scrumhalf ahead of Springboks Dawie de Villiers, Dirk de Vos and Gert Brynard; and played for both the Southern and Central Universities.

Last but not least albeit at a lower level of representative rugby: Thinus's brother Fritz played for the Kwaggas, and youngest brother Gerrie for the Lions' club juniors to expand the list of representative players; and young Johann van Niekerk, a grandson of Tertius Delport, captained the Eastern Province primary schools' Craven Week team that finished the tournament unbeaten!

The Bekker family from Pretoria

There are only three instances where three brothers represented South Africa at rugby. And while this is special in itself, the case of the four Bekker brothers and their sister is unique.

All five of them were Springboks. Jaap, Dolf and Martiens played rugby for South Africa; Daan won a silver medal for boxing at the 1960 Olympics in Rome and a bronze medal in the 1956 Olympics in Melbourne in the heavyweight division and also played flank for Northern Transvaal; and sister Connie Lategan was a Springbok athlete.

Jaap, one of the strongest props produced by South Africa, and wing Dolf played together in the third and fourth tests against the visiting 1953 Wallabies. Martiens was capped in 1960 against Scotland.

Jaap was the best-known of the family of Boks, and played in 15 tests between 1952 and 1962 and also in 39

Springbok tour matches. He represented Northern Transvaal in 56 matches between 1951 and 1956.

Three Du Plessis brothers from Stellenbosch

Three Du Plessis brothers from Somerset-East represented South Africa on the rugby field. All three became Springboks when they were at Maties and all three were special players.

Willie, the eldest, made his debut in 1980 and played in 14 tests and 20 Springbok tour matches. He was an outstanding distributor of the ball and played in the great era where the Springboks probably had their most outstanding backs of all time, including Divan Serfontein, Naas Botha, Danie Gerber, Ray Mordt, Gerrie Germishuys, Johan Heunis, and also his brother Carel du Plessis.

Carel is arguably the best left wing South Africa has produced. Like his brothers his test appearances were limited because of South Africa's isolation due to politics. He played in only 12 tests (22 tour matches), captained Western Province and also coached the Springboks.

The youngest Du Plessis to play for South Africa was Michael. Brilliant as a flyhalf or centre, he was unorthodox and his eight tests also didn't give the world the opportunity

Brothers Michael and Carel du Plessis played together in sevens tests. Carel also played in a test with brother Willie.

to see him at his best at international level.

There was a fourth brother, Jacques, who played for Eastern Province – and he too was a back who excelled as wing at Currie Cup level.

Three Luyts: same tour, same tests

The three Luyt brothers, with the Du Plessis and the Bekker brothers the only set of three brothers to play for South Africa, went one better by being in the same touring side and also playing in three tests together.

All three Luyts were in the Springbok team on the 1912/13 tour to the UK and France with Billy Millar's side. John was a forward, and Dick and Fred played in the back line.

Fred was an outstanding flyhalf and played in all three tests in 1910 against the British Isles team. His brother Dick was in the same back line in the last two tests.

On the 1912/13 tour all three of the brothers played against Scotland, Wales and England. John and Dick also played against France, while Fred and Dick were team-mates against Ireland.

Five of ten Morkels on the same tour – but not blood

And then, of course, there were the Morkels. Although they were not related, ten of them played for South Africa. (This is not the 'record', as over the years, 11 Du Plessis have been selected for South Africa).

On the first three Springbok tours – in 1906/7 and 1913/13 to France and the United Kingdom and in 1921 to Australasia – there were Morkels in the team.

In 1906 there were brothers Dougie and Sommie, as well as Andrew; in 1912 there were four Morkels, Gerhard and Jacky, as well as their cousin Boy, and Dougie who was on his second tour; and again their number in a touring side increased when five Morkels toured Australia and New Zealand in 1921, namely brothers Harry and Royal, and Henry, Gerhard and Boy. In 1928 PK played against the visiting All Blacks.

Dougie (in 1910 and on the 1912/13 tour) captained the Boks in two tests and Boy was captain in all three tests in that first series against the All Blacks in New Zealand in 1922.

Marijke Nel.

Strange family combinations

A unique family combination is that of Springbok women's player Marijke Nel who followed in the footsteps of her grandfather Philip Nel, who captained South Africa on the tour of the great 1937 side to Australia and New Zealand, and also in the home test series against the Wallabies in 1933!

Ten sets of fathers and sons have played rugby for the Springboks. But there is an eleventh set, somewhat different from the others. Thys and Phillip Burger also both have Bok blazers in their cupboards.

Thys played for South Africa in the 1980s. He was a replacement (who scored a try when he came on) in the macabre test against the United States in 1981 with only 45 spectators – the smallest crowd in South Africa's rugby history. Philip, a speedster who in 2011 returned to the Cheetahs Super Rugby team after a spell overseas, played for the Boks' sevens team in 2006.

wins and inflated the Springboks' success record since 1992 which reads: played 221 – won 138, drew 4, lost 79.

If the easy wins against teams which are not regarded as first-tier rugby sides are discarded, South Africa's success rate since 1992 would have been only 57.37%.

Just how poor the opposition from these minnows was is reflected by the following 17 winning results from 31 of the matches played against them: 60–8, 74–10, 62–31, 101–0, 74–3, 39–3, 51–18, 60–14, 60–18, 72–6, 60–10, 134–3, 105–13, 59–7, 64–15, 26–0, 55–11.

The undisputed highlights of Springbok rugby were the two World Cup wins in 1995 and 2007, and the three Tri-Nations wins in 1998, 2004 and 2009, all of which are described elsewhere. There were, however, many other highlights in the 120 years since that first test in 1891– just as there were some disappointing results and very low points, many of them the result of politics.

New Zealand have certainly been the Springboks' main rival, through the years. It took three series before South Africa could enforce their supremacy over them following two drawn series between the countries. The All Blacks' first contact in international matches only came in 1921, 30 years after South Africa's first international match against the 1891 British touring side of Bill Maclagan. That was when the 1921 tour under Springbok captain Theo Pienaar took place. Pienaar didn't play in any test matches, but was a great leader whose influence permeated through to the team that came back magnificently after losing the first test in Dunedin 13–5.

Under the on-field captaincy of Boy Morkel, the team won the second test in Auckland 9–5. And then came a battle of the giants in a nil-all draw in cold, wet and windy Wellington, not always the happiest hunting field for South Africa. It was played, as is often the case in Wellington, on a field that resembled a lake with muddy outcrops only here and there and ice blowing into the players' faces.

It was a successful tour, despite the drawn series that saw the two sides still regarded as 'joint world champions'. But it was also a tour where the problematic

A family of Springbok captains

Morné du Plessis, despite playing in only 22 tests, was one of South Africa's greatest rugby players and captains in a nine-year test career spanning 1971–1980 – and has the distinction of being part of the only father-son combination to captain the Boks.

His father Felix led the Springboks in three of

Morné du Plessis

their four home tests in the whitewash of the All Blacks in 1949 – the first South African series after the Second World War.

Morné, like his father 37 years before, led the Boks to a series win over the All Blacks, when South Africa won the 1976 series 3–1.

Morné made his debut as Springbok No 8 in 1971, in a three-test away series to Australia. It was the first – and only – invincible tour by a Springbok side, led by Hannes Marais, and they won the three tests 18–6, 14–6 and 19–11.

It was another three years before the Boks played their next test series, with the 1972 single test against England splitting the two divergent series. For in 1974 Marais was in charge of a Springbok side that lost the series 3–0, with the last test at Ellis Park drawn.

Morné du Plessis played in the first two tests, with losses of 12–3 and a record loss of 28–9 inflicted on the Springboks. Through the rest of his 22-test career Du Plessis would play in only two more losing matches.

Du Plessis made his debut as captain when France toured South Africa in 1975, and the Springboks won 38–25 in Bloemfontein and 33–18 in Pretoria.

Then came the 1976 All Blacks. The Boks won the first test 16–7, lost the second 15–9, and won the last two tests 15–10 and 15–14. In 1977 the Springboks played a World XV in Pretoria and won 45–24. After that Du Plessis led the side to wins over South America in 1980 and then the British Lions in the same year.

Felix du Plessis

In October 1980 the Springboks toured South America but Du Plessis played in only one of the two tests, leading his team to a 30–16 success against the Jaguars in Santiago. His final test was a November clash against France in Pretoria.

Du Plessis played 22 tests for South Africa and was on the winning side 18 times. He captained the Springboks in 15 matches, winning 13 times and losing only twice. In 1995, he managed the victorious Springbok team in the World Cup held in South Africa.

Du Plessis is a founding member and chairman of the Chris Burger Petro Jackson Players' Fund that provides assistance to rugby players who have sustained serious rugby injuries.

His stature in the world of rugby, and in sport in general, was recognised by the Laureus World Sports Awards. He serves on the World Sports Academy that is a group of 42 world-renowned sportsmen and women who act as the electoral college for the Laureus World Sports Awards and who promote the use of sport for social change throughout the world.

Du Plessis' mother Pat, like her husband and son, also captained South Arica at international level – in hockey. Two of his uncles, Horace and Norman Smethurst played soccer for South Africa – and Horace also captained South Africa!

Du Plessis and Dawie Snyman – also born in 1949 – were recognised as the Maties' 100th Springboks when they were selected on the same night.

Du Plessis mostly played fullback for his school and didn't make the Free State schools side for Craven Week. At Stellenbosch, however, he was immediately put into the Under-19 A-side and eventually captained Western Province over 100 times. He also played Currie Cup cricket for Western Province.

situation around the Maori, due in no way whatsoever to these rugby-loving people, first reared its head. This would in future put a huge strain on relations between the two countries' rugby controlling bodies.

En route to New Zealand the Springboks played four matches in Sydney – three against New South Wales (now the Waratahs) and one against a Metropolitan XV. There were no tests but the matches were hard enough to have the Springboks leave for New Zealand with eight serious injuries. Jack Siedle, who was injured in his first match for the Boks, took no further part in the tour and never played for South Africa again.

Start of a great era

That 1921 tour started one of the great eras in South African rugby – or if the Second World War is a cut-off, two great eras! From 1921 to 1953 the Springboks played in 41 tests. They won 31, drew two and lost only eight for a winning ratio of 78%. In the process they drew two series with the All Blacks, and beat them in two – in 1937 in New Zealand, plus a whitewash in South Africa in 1949. The Wallabies were beaten in South Africa (1933), Australia (1937) and again in the 1953 test series in South Africa. There were two Grand Slam tours in 1931/32 and 1951/52; the British Lions lost three and drew one test in 1924 and lost two tests in 1938; and the test against France in 1952 was won 25–3.

In this period, South Africa set what was then a world test record by beating the Scots 44–0 at Murrayfield on the 1951/52 tour, still regarded as one of the best test performances of all time. In 1937 the Springboks became the first and only side to beat New Zealand at home until the British Lions emulated them in 1974; and the Boks also gave the All Blacks their only whitewash in a series by winning all four tests in 1949, where Okey Geffin's boot made the difference.

Danie Craven was involved in 30 of those 41 tests, either as a player or a coach in a time where winning for your country was more important than giving replacements

Gary Teichmann.

a three-minute run; or resting players for an upcoming World Cup. Yes, things have indeed changed because of professionalism.

It is a happy coincidence that a series against New Zealand on virtually every occasion kick-started a good period in South African rugby. So it was in 1921 when the Boks took over the mantle as the world's best team over the next 16 years; and in 1949 when they had an outstanding run until 1956, winning 14 of their 17 tests; in 1960 from which time they won 15 of their 21 tests; in 1970, when they won seven from ten over two years; and 1976, when they went on to win 21 from 26 matches. That included the lost demonstration-stricken series in New Zealand in 1981 that produced possibly the most bizarre test in history.

In 1965 the Springboks lost the series in New Zealand after a horrendous seven-match losing streak but bounced back to beat France in 1967 and take the series against the British Lions of 1968 quite comfortably (3–0 with one drawn), beat France twice on tour and then the

Wallabies of 1969 in a sequence that produced 11 wins, two losses and two draws after the 1965 disaster.

The 1956 series loss against the All Blacks in New Zealand, however, had few positive spin-offs. The next series after South Africa's first series loss in their history brought their second loss when France beat the Boks by drawing one test and winning the other in 1958.

After unification, the All Blacks really took control. They won their fourth successive home series against the 1994 team of Francois Pienaar quite convincingly, winning two tests and drawing one. Refereeing could be blamed for the loss in the first test, but the Springboks' discipline was shocking. It cost the Boks the first test. Worse was to come. One of the main culprits in the first tests was prop Johan Strauss – and after the next he was cited for the infamous biting of All Blacks captain Sean Fitzpatrick's ear. By then he had already been sent back to South Africa by the Bok management.

It was not a pleasant tour against an All Blacks side that didn't have a good year, apart from the series win against South Africa. SARFU president Louis Luyt and team manager Jannie Engelbrecht's spats were unpleasant in the extreme; on one occasion he asked Luyt to leave a Springbok change room after arriving during the course of the tour. At least the Boks were made to feel welcome in what was to be their last full tour of New Zealand. After that, professionalism put a stop to tours which were replaced by the Tri-Nations competition. This tour was the first time that a Springbok side had returned home without winning a test.

After South Africa won the World Cup against New Zealand at Ellis Park in 1995, Fitzpatrick's All Blacks toured South Africa in 1996. The first of the four tests in Cape Town was a Tri-Nations encounter with the rest making up the last full series played between the two countries. The All Blacks won the Tri-Nations match 29–18. It was to be the last time that World Cup captain Pienaar would lead the team onto the field. He was dropped after accusations from coach André Markgraaff that he was feigning an injury.

Gary Teichmann replaced Pienaar as captain. The Boks lost two of the next three tests: the first in Durban 23–19 and then at Loftus, 33–26. Some pride was restored in Johannesburg when the Springboks won 32–22.

All Blacks series win at sixth attempt

But it was too late to win the series, and the All Blacks had got the monkey of winning a series in South Africa off their back at their sixth attempt (excluding the New Zealand Cavaliers tour in 1986). It didn't get better for the Springboks. The All Blacks' victory march went on after the 1996 series win and the Springboks lost eight matches on the trot against the old foe between 2001 and 2004. In 1999, for the first time since the nil–all draw in Wellington in 1921 and in Dunedin in 1965, the All Blacks held the Springboks scoreless when they won 28–0 in Dunedin, while another Tri-Nations match in 2008 saw them repeat the dose with a 19–0 win in Cape Town.

In this same period, the Wallabies also kept their scoreboard clean when they beat the Springboks 49–0 in Brisbane in 2006. The All Blacks (55–35 in 1997 in Auckland) and England (53–3 at Twickenham in 2002) put 50 points past South Africa.

There are, of course, many memorable matches between South Africa and New Zealand, and some outstanding individual feats.

In the first series in 1921 there was a dour fight for supremacy, and in the end it was a solid performance rather than brilliance by the Springboks that saw them share a close series, with the nil–all draw in Wellington a true reflection of the series. This third test was a day when each side controlled matters when playing with the wind. On tour the Boks conceded only 13 tries in their 19 matches – and as it would be from then on, the greeting after the last test was: 'till we meet again'.

In the days when the IRB still had little say over matters like international tours, the All Blacks were invited by the SARFB to tour South Africa in 1924 – but opted not to, citing the importance of club football as the reason!

In 1926 they accepted a tour to South Africa which took place in 1928 – with no Maori players. The four-test series followed the 1924/25 tour of the All Blacks 'Invincibles' that included three continents and 38 matches. They won the Grand Slam, and also beat France and Canada. The Springboks, on the other hand, had won a test series against Cove-Smith's 1924 British Lions but had no other international contact or preparation.

The 1928 series ended all square with two test wins each – and it is interesting to note the Boks' win in the Durban test, when they beat the All Blacks 17–0, remains their biggest win over New Zealand to date. That was one of the great flyhalf Bennie Osler's best performances in a brilliant career.

It was nine years before the sides met again. The Springboks left their captain Philip Nel out of the first test team and lost 13–7 in Wellington. They bounced back in Christchurch (13–6) and then shocked New Zealand to win 17–6 in the final test in Auckland. It was a victory built on the tactic of opting for scrums instead of line-outs as they were allowed to do by the laws of the day, and on scintillating back play on a field that was slippery but not muddy. Five tries to nil in the win tell the story of total dominance.

It was a breakthrough win, the first time that a team had won a series between what were to become traditional rugby foes.

Much had been made on the tour of the long dive pass from scrumhalf Danie Craven. The Springboks exploited that with Craven motioning flyhalf Tony Harris to stand further and further away from him. All Blacks flyhalf Dave Trevathan followed suit to mark him, and Craven flipped the scrum ball to Freddie Turner who had run into the gap that had been created. The ball went to Flappie Lochner and to Louis Babrow who scored. That was his second try and the Boks' third after Lochner had scored shortly after the start of the match, and the Boks never looked back from there.

With the 1940 New Zealand tour postponed because of the Second World War, hostilities between the teams were

Okey Geffin – lethal boot.

only resumed in 1949. New Zealand's loss was blamed on poor refereeing decisions– and many South Africans conceded that it was a rather fortuitous series win, with the 4–0 score out of proportion when the quality of the sides in the tests is considered.

The All Blacks lost the first test 15–11 after Geffin kicked a record five penalties. Other penalties were missed by Jack van der Schyff, and the All Blacks were rather upset with referee Eddie Hofmeyr. He also handled the third test, a game of poor rugby, and Geffin won it 9–3 with three penalties to an All Blacks try.

From an attacking point of view in a gritty series, the Springboks had Hansie Brewis's try in the second test in Johannesburg to savour. Renowned for his kicking, and especially his drop-kicking, the little genius received the ball from a scrum. He feinted to drop at goal, but opponent Jim Kearney was in his way so Brewis changed direction, running around to the left of the scrum. A grubber looked like his next option, but he spotted the gap and scored a marvellous individualistic try. The Boks won the test 12–6.

Touring was fun – but also arduous. Leaving Johannesburg by train on the Saturday straight after a game against Transvaal that they won 13–3, the 1949 All Blacks reached Bulawayo on Monday morning, left for Victoria Falls and arrived back in Bulawayo on Wednesday morning for the match that same afternoon against Rhodesia! Eight nights on the train and three in hotels saw them back in Pretoria for the match against Northern Transvaal.

All Blacks revenge

After the 1949 series loss, New Zealand swore revenge. In 1956, they won the first test, the Boks the second. The All Blacks won the third at Wellington which can only be described as a war with former professional boxer Kevin Skinner brought in to soften the Boks. Jaap Bekker's bloodied face after that test, won 17–6 by the All Blacks, tells the story of a tour that was seldom pleasant and interspersed with complaints by Craven – team manager and by now also SARFB president – about poor and biased refereeing. It was a reverse of 1949. The fourth test at Auckland was also won by the All Blacks.

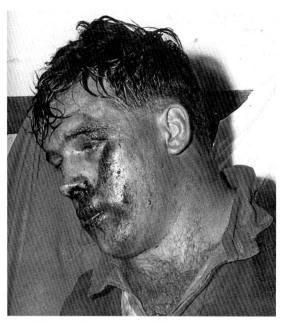

Jaap Bekker bore the brunt of the All Blacks' revenge.

In 1960, the highlight was the brace of tries by left wing Hennie van Zyl in his first test. It was based on a Natal move, with another debutant Keith Oxlee at flyhalf feeding his provincial wing Mike Antelme on the inside. Twice, once in each half, they did just that and twice Antelme broke the line and the ball was moved to Van Zyl who rounded big All Blacks fullback Don Clarke on both occasions. It was a tough series, with Martin Pelser making his mark as an iron man. His clashes with Kevin Briscoe, the Kiwi scrumhalf, are legendary.

In 1965, after seven successive losses against France, Ireland, Scotland, Australia (twice) and New Zealand (twice), the Boks played the third test in a wet, muddy Christchurch. The luckless Boks – for they had been very competitive and somewhat unlucky in the 6–3 first test defeat – were trailing 16–5 at half-time. It was an eighth loss, surely, thought the South African supporters who listened through the crackling of the 1965 radios. But then came three tries where John Gainsford, Mannetjies Roux and Gertjie Brynard did the deeds of wonder, with Brynard scoring twice and Gainsford once. The scores

Joggie Jansen's tackle turned the first test in 1970.

were tied at 16–all when big lock Tiny Naude put over a penalty in the atrocious conditions to clinch the match 19–16 and open up the series again.

It was a relieved Bok side – and a few hours later, a humiliated side when they heard of the Loskop Dam speech by Prime Minister Hendrik Verwoerd. The Boks lost the fourth test in Auckland 20–3, but that one win was a standout performance after a great comeback in what was a black year for South Africa on and off the field.

In 1970 the first All Blacks touring side to South Africa was selected on merit. New Zealand had insisted: no Maori players, no tour. Three Maoris – Sid Going, Buff Milner and Blair Furlong – and Samoan Bryan Williams were included in the touring side that boasted a new record of winning 17 test matches on the trot. They also won their ten provincial matches before the first test – and then Joggie Jansen hit them in the first test with a tackle that was heard and also felt many, many metres away. All Blacks flyhalf, Wayne Cottrell, coming around to the blind side where he felt there was space, was nearly tackled in two. The Boks were 6–0 up at that stage,

but that tackle shook an All Blacks side that was playing well. It shook them enough for the Boks to pull it off 17–6 against all odds.

It was in the All Blacks' 9–8 win in Cape Town that All Blacks fullback Fergie McCormick stiff-armed Syd Nomis who was chasing the ball, loosening his teeth in the tackle. It was also a tour of crowd violence, notably in Kimberley where some louts attacked spectators who carried Bryan Williams off the field, and in Port Elizabeth.

Another noteworthy test against the All Blacks took place in 1998. The Springboks won 13–3 at Wellington in a year in which they beat the All Blacks twice in two outings. Pieter Rossouw, who came in from the left wing to receive from flyhalf Henry Honiball, made the breach and scored the try. That set the Boks up for their first Tri-Nations competition win. The victory in Durban in the next clash against the All Blacks, where the Springboks came back from 23–5 to win 24–23, became one of the most famous wins against New Zealand.

The bizarre 1981 tour

No story of the history of clashes between the All Blacks and South Africa would be complete without relating the 1981 tour. It was a tour of acrimony, demonstrations, violence, family feuds – and it ended with a bitter penalty that smacked of unfairness and bias at Eden Park in Auckland where a light aeroplane continually flew over the stadium and pelted the players with flour bombs. The demonstrators dominated the tour, limiting the Springboks' freedom of movement and often causing them to sleep inside the stadiums where they were to play. In addition, the management didn't want captain Wynand Claassen in the team and also had little understanding of the political issues surrounding what everyone knew would be a politically daunting tour.

The Boks, sans Claassen, lost the first test 14-9. They were rudderless, uncertain and very average. Few had given them a chance of success anyway. Their training sessions were often behind barbed wire with police

A day to remember

The announcement by SA Rugby Union president Oregan Hoskins that the Springboks would play New Zealand at FNB Stadium on 21 August 2010 was greeted with joyous disbelief by the journalists present and extremely well accepted by the public.

'This is an historic day and one in which the whole of South Africa can celebrate,' said Hoskins. 'I am delighted to say that the Lions needed no encouragement from SARU to make the switch,' said Hoskins. 'It has presented logistical and contractual challenges to them but I would like to commend Lions president, Kevin de Klerk, and his team for their determination to make this dream a reality.'

De Klerk said the decision had only been taken after consultations with key stakeholders such as sponsors, suite and season ticket holders and the rugby clubs of the Golden Lions Rugby Union.

The decision to move to the 94 700-seater national stadium which hosted the Fifa World Cup final created significant landmarks:

❏ 5 000 tickets were sold exclusively at Computicket outlets in Soweto for just R100.
❏ More than 9 000 of the available tickets were sold at R350 – the lowest price for a major Springbok Test since 2005.

❏ Free parking was incorporated into the ticket price for every four tickets bought.

The vuvuzela dilemma

The venue announcement excited the public but not so the announcement that vuvuzelas would not be allowed at the test where the Boks were to begin the home leg of their 2010 Tri-Nations campaign.

The statement by the Golden Lions Rugby Union (GLRU) president Kevin de Klerk followed investigation into the use of vuvuzelas at rugby matches.

'We have done our research and have found that vuvuzelas interfere more with rugby than with soccer,' he said. In some quarters this was thought highly unlikely and it was seen as a political decision.

However, after the Super 14 final at Orlando Stadium between the Bulls and the Stormers earlier that year, both the Super 14 captains Victor Matfield and Schalk Burger, who were also playing for the Springboks, agreed that the vuvuzelas had affected communication with team-mates and also the referee. Hoskins pointed out that referee Craig Joubert had to allow added time for the captains to communicate with their players in the Super 14 final. And so the decision was final – no vuvuzelas!

---

looking on; they saw little of the picturesque New Zealand and its lovely cities and towns; they were often split up into a test squad staying at the field before a match, with the rest staying at private homes.

The division went further than this. Coach Nelie Smith and Claassen started the tour with a rift between them that became a chasm. The players were obviously affected by the problems at management level.

The unpleasantness of the tour was, however, not confined to the Springboks. The whole of New Zealand was split between pro-tour supporters and those who objected to the Springboks' presence. Families were divided on the issue – and a tour match in Timaru was

even cancelled to give police a break! Another match, against Waikato in Hamilton, didn't take place as the demonstrators stormed the pitch and couldn't be removed without resorting to violence.

As it was, the Boks played without Claassen in the first lost test, making Dawie de Villiers (1965) the only tour captain to start in a first test in New Zealand on the four tours including 1981. In 1994 Francois Pienaar also missed the first test and Tiaan Strauss stood in for him. Incidentally, all five of the first tests in New Zealand were won by the All Blacks.

The Boks won the second test (24–12) against all expectation, which set up the third as a clincher. It was a bizarre experience where, on match day, the Boks suddenly had to include four players who were billeted out at homes after injury withdrawals by the selected Springboks. They only heard of their selection when they arrived at Eden Park on Saturday morning to join the test team who had slept there.

The Springboks played right into the flight path of the light plane that swooped over the field again and again, dropping flour bombs. They were 16–3 behind at the break. Then the back line, under-strength because of injury but still very potent, struck for South Africa. Ray Mordt finished the match with a hat-trick, the first by the Boks against the All Blacks. His third try tied the scores at 22–all.

Naas Botha missed a difficult conversion on time, and the match was allowed to go on. Welsh referee Clive Norling had three different stories after the match about why the Springboks were penalised with a free kick that was changed to a penalty (in those days) but the story that probably was the closest to but not the whole truth was that it would've been a shame to have such a match end in a draw!

If only Botha had kicked that conversion …

Norling's fourth story, according to former Northern Transvaal president Hentie Serfontein, was that he had made a mistake by awarding the penalty.

It mattered none. The final score was 25–22 to New Zealand in what was a terrific match between the world's best sides – and it is not unfair or biased to say that the best side lost this time, even though the refereeing culprit was a so-called neutral referee.

Wrong day, small crowd

The tour wasn't over yet, and another surreal test took place. The Boks had moved on to the United States where they were due to play their first-ever test against the US Eagles. Politics and court cases marked the friendlies against Wisconsin and Eastern, and the test match – scheduled for the Saturday – was won 38–7 by South

Africa on the Friday afternoon, with even the non-playing Springboks kept in the dark. There were only about 45 spectators present at the polo field, which reeked of horse dung and sloped by about three metres from end to end. The replacement players in the test marked the field and erected the posts – and some of them even took part in the match with Thys Burger scoring a try when he came on!

Demonstrations were nothing new for South African touring sides. They had started on previous tours, and the 1969/70 tour of the four Home Unions was particularly unpleasant. The demonstrations certainly had an effect on the tourists but shouldn't excuse the fact that this was the first Springbok side to return from the UK without a single win. They lost to Scotland and England and drew with Ireland and Wales.

The highlight of the matches against the Home Unions is probably the 3–0 win against Wales in 1960. It pelted down for days; Cardiff Arms Park was drenched, and ice cut into faces on match day as the Boks awaited the singing of the anthems before a packed crowd that didn't mind the weather.

The Boks, as they did throughout the tour of 34 matches in a wet British summer, played with their forwards and on this particular day gave little ball to the backs. It took a penalty – his first of many – by Natal flyhalf Keith Oxlee to give the tourists a first-half lead. They were playing with the wind, but such was the blustery, strong wind that the rather easy kick swirled and wobbled over the cross-bar for a 3–0 half-time lead that didn't change until the final whistle. Wales attacked for virtually the full second half with only a brilliant No 8 Doug Hopwood and scrumhalf Piet Uys – in his debut test – keeping them at bay with their combination behind the scrum.

Just hours after the final whistle, the stadium field was a metre under water as the river Taff flooded the ground and city.

This 1960/61 touring side, captained by Avril Malan, lost only their last match against the British Barbarians

John Smit – captain without peer

John Smit holds just about every South African test and captaincy record. The most auspicious is that of having captained the Springboks 76 times, a world test record. He has been South Africa's first choice captain since he was appointed by World Cup winning coach Jake White in 2004, and has only been absent on rare occasions because of injury.

John William Smit was born in Pietersburg in 1978 and went to Pretoria Boys High School. He was head prefect in 1996 and played in the First XV from 1994 to 1996. Smit then represented the Blue Bulls at Craven Week, played SA Schools and led the South African Under-21 side to the SANZAR/UAR title in 1999 at tighthead prop.

John lives in Durban with his wife Roxane, their daughter Emma-Joan and son Tyron, where he plays his provincial and Super Rugby with the Natal Sharks and the Sharks respectively. Smit's biography, *Captain in the Cauldron – The John Smit Story*, written by Mike Greenaway, appeared in 2009.

He holds Springbok records for most tests as captain (76), which is also a world record; is South Africa's most capped hooker (80) and most capped Springbok forward (102).

Between October 2003 and June 2007, Smit played in a record 46 consecutive test matches for South Africa, though it was only in 2004, when he was made captain by White that he became a regular member of the starting XV.

Smit took South Africa to the 2007 Rugby World Cup and led South Africa to a series victory against the visiting British and Irish Lions for the 2009 Tri-Nations title when South Africa won five of their six matches, including a clean sweep of three wins against New Zealand.

At the end of 2010, Smit was South Africa's fourth most successful captain (after Morné du Plessis, Joost van der Westhuizen and Gary Teichmann), having led the Springboks to victory in 51 of the 76 tests (one drawn) that he captained, a win percentage of 67,1%. He has won more tests as captain than any other Springbok has played as captain.

After the 2007 World Cup, Smit signed a two-year deal with Clermont. After just a year with them he rejoined the Sharks.

Salient facts:

- ❏ Position: Hooker and prop
- ❏ Club: Crusaders RFC
- ❏ Provinces: Sharks and Natal Sharks (since 2000); Clermont-Auvergne, France (2008)
- ❏ Springbok number: 691
- ❏ Test debut: 10 June 2000 versus Canada in East London, aged 22
- ❏ Total tests: 102
- ❏ Tour matches: 1
- ❏ Total Springbok tours: Argentina, Ireland, Wales and England, 2000; France, Italy, England and USA, 2001; RWC in Australia, 2003; British Isles, Ireland and Argentina, 2004; Argentina, Wales and France, 2005; Ireland and England, 2006; Ireland and Scotland, 2007; RWC in France, Wales and Scotland, 2007; Wales, 2007; Wales, Scotland and Ireland, 2008; Wales, Scotland and Ireland, 2009; France, Italy, Ireland and England, 2009
- ❏ Tour captain: Smit was captain of Springbok touring teams to British Isles, Ireland and Argentina, 2004; Argentina, Wales and France, 2005; Ireland and England, 2006; Ireland and Scotland, 2007; RWC in France, Wales and Scotland, 2007; British Isles, 2008; France, Italy, Ireland and England, 2009
- ❏ He was SA Rugby Young Player of the Year nominee in 1999 and voted Players' Player of the Year in 2005.

when they fell into the trap of trying to play Barbarian rugby while the home side, contrary to tradition, decided to play to win at all costs! The tour record was thus: played 34 – won 31, drew 2, lost 1.

For some reason the Home Unions did not have the same attraction for local supporters when they started visiting South Africa for (mostly) one-off matches. Ireland and Scotland first visited in 1960, Wales followed in 1984 and England beat the Boks in their first test in South Africa, 18–9, at Ellis Park in 1972.

The longest tour

In 1960/61, the Springboks played 34 matches in four months, which made it the longest tour – in matches – undertaken by a South African team. The longest tour in months was that of Basil Kenyon's 1951/52 Springboks who played rugby for four months excluding the sea travel to the UK and back in their time away from home!

France were first visited in 1906 by the ground-breaking side of Paul Roos – the first 'Springboks'. They were beaten 55–6 but it was not regarded as an official test – or indeed a tour match, as it was hastily arranged against a side that literally applauded the Boks' good moves in scoring 13 tries! Their first test against the Springboks was in 1912 when the Boks won 38–5 in Bordeaux. Inconsistent, especially in their early years on the international scene when they charmed with their pen play but were fickle in execution and results, France have always been a handful for South African sides. (And for the All Blacks, it must be said. France eliminated them from the 2007 World Cup, a repeat of their shock win in the 1999 World Cup – and they also won a series in New Zealand.)

France have tightened up their play tremendously. After winning 15 of the 18 tests against France between 1974 and 1997 with only two losses and a draw, the Boks have struggled in more recent times, winning only three of the ten encounters and drawing one.

The Wallabies were also always welcome visitors to South Africa because of the open brand of rugby they played. Like the French, they were not taken too seriously until recently.

Australia did surprise in 1933 when they won two of the three tests on their first tour to South Africa. The Wallabies were narrowly beaten in both tests on the 1937 Australasia tour, with the Boks' focus squarely on the New Zealand series ahead. In 1953 the Wallabies won the first of four tests on their second tour and lost both matches to the 1956 Springboks who were en route to New Zealand. Poor team selection and musical chair-like selection of the two Malans, Abe and Avril, as captain, saw the 1963 series squared. Both tests in 1965 were lost by the Springboks during their string of seven successive defeats that year. The Springboks then won seven tests on the trot against the Wallabies in 1969 and 1971, the last three coming during the tour by South Africa's only invincible touring side under Hannes Marais.

All in all, the Wallabies were very competitive but not a real power. But then came 1992 and the resumption of matches against the Wallabies. Of the 43 tests played since then, Australia have won 23 and South Africa 19, with one test drawn. South Africa's second biggest defeat (49–0) came at the hands of the Wallabies in Brisbane in 2006. With very few rugby players in a country dominated by Australian Rules, Rugby League and soccer (all after cricket of course!) their systems, including effective academies, have pulled them through to two World Cup rugby titles. They have won the last four matches against South Africa and eight of the last 14 encounters since 2006.

Bok nemesis

Interestingly, South Africa have lost their last eight encounters in Brisbane, the last win coming under Marais in 1971. Even in 2009, when the Springboks won the Tri-Nations, their only defeat from six in the tournament was in Brisbane. There is no discernible reason for this.

Argentina

Argentina, a top-ranked nation, only started playing against South Africa after unification. After 13 matches, they are still without a win against the Springboks, although they have mostly been stern competition. In the boycott days Craven somehow convinced them to select a South American side with token players from the other rugby-playing nations on their continent and they surprised the Boks by beating them in Bloemfontein in 1982 with the great Hugo Porta the general of their side. The score was 21–12 after they had been thrashed 50–18 at Loftus the week before. In 1984 they again visited South Africa, but then had to play as the Jaguars as their team included a player from Spain. Eight matches and one loss stand as South Africa's record against the Pumas in disguise.

There has been regular contact with Argentina since the 1930s when a Junior Springbok side visited there; and in the 1970s SARFB sent Natal's successful coach Izak van Heerden over to assist the South American side with their rugby. Renowned for their scrummaging, the Pumas have been inconsistent of late as the top Argentina players ply their trade in Europe because their controlling union doesn't have the financial muscle to keep them in the country. With Argentina's imminent admission to the lucrative Tri-Nations competition, this could change in the near future.

Cavaliers

Not included in the series of matches between the All Blacks and South Africa are the New Zealand Cavaliers. They arrived in South Africa in 1986. With South Africa ostracised and shunned by rugby nations throughout the world, this was a desperate attempt to give what was then a very good South African side proper opposition.

It was a rebel tour – and it nearly took place the previous year in place of the official 1985 tour of South Africa that was cancelled by New Zealand Prime Minister John Lange. He did give the go-ahead, however, should the players wish to go on the tour as individuals. As it happened they were stopped from boarding the plane after having checked in for the flight to South Africa via Los Angeles by a telegram pointing out that they would be in contempt of court should they go to South Africa following court proceedings.

A year later, with All Blacks lock Andy Haden the driving force from New Zealand's side and Robert Denton, then managing director of Ellis Park (Pty) Ltd, a near-full All Blacks team arrived in South Africa. (Only scrumhalf and captain Andy Kirk, who was on his way to Oxford, and wing Stuart Wilson, whose father was ill, declined to tour.) At that same time, Danie Craven and Fritz Eloff were in London, attending an IRB meeting. They pleaded ignorance about the tour, as did the NZRFU.

John Smit – record-breaking captain.

It was a tour from hell. The first match was against the Junior Springboks; three days later they played Northern Transvaal, then the Orange Free State and Transvaal with Western Province following a week before the first test at Newlands. Natal, the SA Barbarians, Western Transvaal and three more tests followed. The Cavaliers lost three tests and, in true tradition between the two sides, they were unhappy with Welsh referee Ken Rowlands who handled all four tests.

For the first time in South African history, the tour had a sponsor (Yellow Pages) and in another first, the Boks played with a sponsor's logo on their jerseys (Toyota). It made other companies aware of the possibilities of rugby sponsorship which only really came with the introduction of official professionalism in 1996.

The tour saved South African rugby, Craven admitted afterwards.

10

The SANZAR disillusion
The reality of professionalism in rugby

The effect of professionalism on rugby has not only reverberated through boardrooms. It has also affected the way the game is being played; competitions at all levels, from primary schools to internationals; the futures of players after retirement; and even supporters.

Rugby has become a big game. At management level, the bigger unions in South Africa look at an annual turnover of between R150 and R200 million. This amount excludes the cost of administering the bigger stadiums, where turnover of course also varies with R70 million regarded as a reasonable figure. Depending on the management thereof, the profit could be substantial – as could the loss!

Of the turnover of R150–200 million, at least R50 million of the bigger unions' money goes to players – while a substantial amount, of course, goes to travel and accommodation, especially for the Super Rugby sides, and administration. A further R15 million is spent on amateur rugby such as provincial sevens, schools, women's rugby, club rugby and referees.

The Super Rugby series and Tri-Nations rugby are regarded by SARU as more important than the Currie Cup. These SANZAR competitions have first option when it comes to the selection of and the draw on players. The national players are therefore involved with Tri-Nations tests when the Currie Cup commences. Some of them are also, at the behest of the national coach and his management staff, rested before the end of the year tours to the UK and Europe. Indirectly, therefore, the whims or wishes of the national coach can greatly influence the Currie Cup competition's outcome.

The unfairness of the system is extrapolated. In 2010 there was the incomprehensible

Springbok flank Schalk Burger, who captained the Stormers in the history-making 2010 Super 14 final.

Clash of the young Boks: No 8 Ashley Johnson tackles another young 2009 Springbok, hooker Bandise Maku, in a Super Rugby clash between the Cheetahs and Lions. Ryno Benjamin is the Cheetahs player in support.

situation where all nationally contracted players had to be rested and weren't allowed to play in the Currie Cup's final league rounds – even if they had not played any rugby for an extended period because of injury! These players, in dire need of game time, therefore sat out the last few weeks of the Currie Cup series while other (non-contracted) players who were overplayed and had not missed a match in the season were available for their provincial sides!

This strange ruling on the resting of players and also the understandable preferential selection rights for tests and Super Rugby are obvious drawbacks for the stronger Currie Cup teams. It also dilutes the competition. But it has its advantages. It gives the major provinces the opportunity to blood their young players and future stars. In fact, the absence of Springboks has even made for a more exciting Currie Cup competition as provinces without Springbok stars, like Griquas in particular, were more competitive against the under-strength powerhouse teams without their Boks.

The standard of rugby in the Currie Cup competition also remained very high. In 2006, for example, with 24 contracted players withdrawn from the Currie Cup competition to rest them for the 2007 World Cup, there was the outstanding 28–all final between the Free State Cheetahs and the Blue Bulls in Bloemfontein – and as the SARU communications manager Andy Colquhoun wrote then, the Currie Cup competition 'comfortably survived' the lack of big stars.

There is merit to the argument that the return of the national players towards the business end of the Currie Cup series changes the playing field. The better teams – depending on the national coach – have their best back, thereby obtaining an 'unfair advantage'. The counter argument is of course that these sides, had they not been 'robbed' of their internationals in the early parts of the Currie Cup, would in any case have dominated throughout.

However, overall the system gives young talent a chance to impress in the absence of the established Springboks – to the extent that a number of new young Springboks were blooded by Springbok coach Peter de Villiers on the year-end tours of 2009 and 2010.

But professionalism has its negative effects. Court cases regarding contracts; money ruling over loyalty; acquisition of players by affluent unions instead of building an own reserve strength; and players succumbing to the lure of the pound, euro and yen are just a few of them. There is also too much rugby and not enough rest, according to leading sports scientist Prof Tim Noakes.

Fickleness in selection at both provincial and national level, the inability to look past the influence of the quota system and the exchange rate have also seen South African stars pursue their careers overseas, thereby bolstering the competitiveness of British and European rugby. In 2010 a total of 240 South African players were plying their trade abroad – and an estimated 70 of those South Africans played top-class rugby in France's Top 14 league, an average of five per club!

With the Vodacom Cup series a further professional drain on players' numbers, the demise of club rugby is another disadvantage of professionalism. This is exacerbated by the fact that hundreds of young players lose interest in playing club rugby when they realise they're not in the fast lane of development for a professional future. Making it to the big time out of the club system is well-nigh impossible, and the upshot is that club rugby's numbers and standards are further diluted.

At international level, the negatives abound. With overburdened players being rested or injured, the northern hemisphere sides in particular are guilty of touring with weakened sides. The huge defeats do not do much for the game or for the spectator support for tests on such tours.

The camaraderie in the game – yes, even at international level! – is something that sets rugby apart. Or is that something of the past? Little mixing of players after test matches takes place and many of the South Africans playing overseas only got to know their international adversaries after club matches abroad!

Future after rugby

One of the most serious – and long-term – legacies of professionalism in South Africa is that many, many of the players who either don't make the grade at professional level or those finishing after years in the game at the highest level are not trained for any other profession.

This is to a large extent the result of the expectations created for younger players.

It is not commonly known that some of the leading unions identify talented players as early as Under-12. In many instances young players are contracted by high schools after good performances at the annual Under-13 Craven Week. This is the first step to what the youngsters – and often their parents – see as possible glory and international fame. For a large portion of these young stars there is then the discipline and training in the various high performance systems before they eventually make provincial schools and junior sides (Under-19 and Under-21).

This further strengthens their resolve and confidence to make it at senior level.

The reality is totally different. With some 450 Craven Week players annually coming into the system after school, there are never enough vacancies in the provincial junior sides to take them all. And after all, only the top provincial sides really provide a possible professional future.

But even for those who make it to this elite junior professional level where they train professionally and are paid and coached professionally, the next step to senior provincial level is even more difficult. The truth is that senior provincial sides do not lose nearly as many players annually as they receive from the junior provincial system. However, many of the youngsters persevere with the sport and find themselves on the peripherals of the provincial squads until they realise by age 25 or 26 that they won't break through. Jobless and mostly without a qualification, the job market then becomes a difficult new challenge for which they're not prepared.

Even established provincial players – some earning a relatively modest fee for their services at the smaller unions – face the above problem. Because of a lack of work experience outside of rugby, they continue playing until they realise they are going to have to earn their money elsewhere. And there simply aren't enough opportunities for all retirees to coach professionally.

The future of players after rugby is a major problem, says Piet Heymans of the SA Rugby Players Association (SARPA). In Australia, and to a lesser extent in New Zealand, players are encouraged to pursue academic qualifications to prepare them for the future – and although this, to some extent, is happening in South Africa, few of the top players have qualified academically and many remain unprepared for life after rugby.

Heymans, who was appointed as CEO for SARPA when it was founded in 1998, is a man who understands the game and its players. He captained the South African Under-20s in 1987, with Francois Pienaar and Joel Stransky in the side. Heymans says some of the unions have still not adapted to the present situation after the amateur days, even after 15 years of professionalism, and the legal contracting between unions and players remains a source of great concern and exasperation for SARPA.

Former Springbok winger Pieter Hendriks, who played

Hennie le Roux – a business career.

in the era of 'shamateurism' as well as in the early days of professionalism, believes that while players in the top flight are well paid and will have something to fall back on after their retirement, the problem of poverty-stricken ex-professional players could become a serious problem. 'They are not trained for anything outside of playing rugby and have no experience in the job market. This could become a major social problem for the rugby bosses,' Hendriks says.

Management transition

With passionate amateur rugby men often not well versed in matters of money, the transition phase to efficient management of the new system took time – even at national level. While these and future problems manifested, the poor showing of South Africa's best in the Tri-Nations and Super Rugby competitions since professionalism is an indictment of the inefficient administration at all levels – a legacy from the amateur days when rugby men controlled matters without much knowledge of, or interest in, financial matters.

Some of South Africa's most influential former captains and national selectors, provincial and even national

Kabamba Floors – playing the professional game.

coaches and administrators agree that part of the cause of the poor performances is due to an unacceptable skills level of the players. And for that the coaches, from the lowest to the highest level, must be taken to task.

If one accepts the official stats kept in test matches, the following is a case in point.

One of South Africa's leading players performed as follows in the last four Tri-Nations tests in 2010:

❏ missed 11 from 39 tackles (72% success rate)
❏ conceded 15 turnovers – nearly four per match
❏ carried the ball under the wrong arm for fending off opponents
❏ shot up on defence, again letting in a number of tries through breaking the defence line.

Meyer's vision bears fruit

In 2001, Bulls and Blue Bulls coach Heyneke Meyer started with the nucleus of the Bulls team that won the Super 14 for the third time in 2010. By then this nucleus had won five Currie Cups, two Vodacom Cups and three Super 14 titles.

It underlined a planned approach built on structures – and Meyer's legacy extends far beyond the trophies won by the Pretoria teams. It set a new standard and the realisation that structures are the way forward. And although it took time, this approach of identifying players for junior structures and then taking them through the various levels with a uniform approach to coaching has been taken over by other unions/franchises and is now also being implemented at national level.

After the coming and going of a succession of coaches in the lean years following the last of the Blue Bulls' Currie Cup triumphs in 1991 (winning the cup in 1998 being the only exception), Meyer was once more asked to take over the coaching after the unsuccessful 2001 season. This was something of a surprise, for just two years before, he had failed miserably when his team had ended the season second last in the Super 12, with only one win.

The 2002 season was no better. Meyer's Bulls became the first team in the Super 12 to lose all 11 of its matches, conceding 500 points and a total of 76 tries. Meyer was fired as Super 12 coach, but continued to coach the Blue Bulls in the Currie Cup. Here his vision of two years earlier at last began to bear fruit. In 2003 every Blue Bulls team which took part in the then SARFU competitions reached at least the finals. Meyer's Currie Cup team had also turned the corner and won the competition three years in a row, from 2002 to 2004.

And then he broke through with a first Super 14 win for a South African franchise in 2007 when the Bulls beat the Sharks in that epic final in Durban.

Under Meyer, first the Blue Bulls and thereafter the Bulls, have been the pace-setters at every level of provincial competition, from Under-19 upwards. Meyer's visionary thinking gave the union an advantage over the other major unions – until they started following suit and catching up, as the Sharks and the Stormers have done since 2008 with increasingly more competitive performances at junior level to boost their Super Rugby campaigns.

Meyer had a formula for success in the Super 14:

❏ at least ten players with international experience
❏ a substitute in every position who was as good as the first choice, and could also be used as an impact player
❏ experienced leaders, of whom at least five have captained a team at this level
❏ eight players who have played in at least 50 Super 12/14 and 50 Currie Cup matches
❏ eight players who have played in at least 20 tests
❏ consistency (in 2007 consistency was a vital factor because it was the third consecutive year that practically the same players, under the same coach, had developed into a cohesive unit).

Some might disagree, but the proof is there! And after all, others are now following the recipe ...

There are of course many other reasons or excuses for South Africa's inability to really impose itself on the Tri-Nations and Super Rugby competitions. But this mediocre record is a major worry – as is the rather average showing of South Africa at the Junior World Championships over the years.

Tri-Nations woes

The following stats tell a sad story of Springbok rugby in the first five Tri-Nations series after professionalism came about in 1996. South Africa:

❏ won only one of those competitions (1998)
❏ won only eight from 20 matches
❏ gathered only four bonus points in those 20 matches
❏ scored 414 points against 495

- scored 40 tries with 45 against
- totalled only 40 log points in 20 matches (New Zealand totalled 61, Australia 46).

The initial shock of professionalism can however not be blamed in isolation. In the following ten seasons (2001–2010) the Springboks' Tri-Nations record deteriorated further. In this time they:

- won the Tri-Nations competition only twice (2004 and 2009); were second once; and finished last on the other seven occasions
- accumulated only 93 log points from 48 matches
- gathered only six bonus points for scoring four or more tries in those 48 matches
- scored 91 tries against 120
- only twice scored more tries than they conceded – in 2004 (13 to 10) and 2008 (13 to 11).

Between 1996 and 2010 the Springboks scored more points than they conceded in a series only four times; and in only three competitions did they score more tries than they conceded.

But there are a few positives. The Boks hold the record for the highest score in the competition (61–22 against Australia at Loftus in 1997). They also won 53–8 against the Wallabies in Johannesburg in 2008. On the downside are the most points conceded by a team in a home Tri-Nations test (52) in Pretoria in 2003; and the biggest defeat in the competition (49–0 against Australia in Brisbane in 2006).

1998: Mallett brings the title home

The Springboks' first Tri-Nations series title came out of the blue. The All Blacks had won all eight of their matches in the first two competitions in 1996 and 1997, and South Africa had only two wins to show – one in each of the campaigns – after going into the 1996 season as defending world champions.

They had a new coach in Nick Mallett. He replaced Carel du Plessis who was fired following a poor record as mentor. Du Plessis's last test in charge was ironically after the Boks had recorded the highest Tri-Nations score over the Wallabies in 1997 mentioned above.

The Springboks won all four of their matches in the 1998 competition – the All Blacks, none after their initial successive eight in 1996 and 1997! (It was the first time since 1949 that the All Blacks had lost four successive tests. It became five when they lost a Bledisloe Cup test against the Wallabies in 1998.)

The 1998 season was a continuation of what would become a 17-match unbeaten run under Mallett (in charge for 16 of those tests after Du Plessis' last). It tied the New Zealand record between 1964 and 1969.

Two one-point squeaks (14–13 against Australia in Perth after Matt Burke missed a sitter for the Wallabies) and the All Blacks in Durban (24–23) saw the Boks at the top in 1998. That missed Burke kick in retrospect made the difference on the log. But that is how close things are at test level!

Interestingly, that was the first rugby test to be played in Perth.

The highlight from a South African viewpoint was undoubtedly their come-back in Durban. Behind 23–5 with only 15 minutes remaining, the new-found Springbok confidence coupled with some excellent replacements by Mallett helped them to what seemed an unlikely win.

First scrumhalf Joost van der Westhuizen and replacement loose forward Bob Skinstad scored to bring them within reach of New Zealand. Then, with time running out, Springbok hooker James Dalton was pushed over for an attacking line-out. The try was awarded by referee Peter Marshall, but that was before the days of the TMO. Television replays clearly showed that Dalton had not grounded the ball and he confirmed that after the match. It mattered none! New Zealand were surprisingly beaten when they had seemed home and dry. It was Bok revenge for the previous year when the All Blacks had come back from 23–7 to win 35–32 at Ellis Park.

That come-from-behind win in Durban, important as

The young Cheetahs Springbok prop Coenie Oosthuizen came through the ranks.

it was, was, however, not the clincher. Despite the win over the All Blacks, at least a draw against Australia at Ellis Park was still needed for South Africa to be crowned champions.

The scoreline of 29–15 in South Africa's favour in what was effectively a final pointed to an easy win – and it was. Two converted tries and five penalties for the Boks against five penalties for the Wallabies tell the story of dominance. The Tri-Nations title was also important in a much bigger context: South Africa, for the first time since their World Cup final win in 1995, looked like a champion side. Bok captain Gary Teichmann underlined this: 'Saturday was bigger than the World Cup final. The crown won then can (now) be worn with justification.'

End of Mallett's good days
All was not well, however. Mallett's bubble burst with five defeats from 13 matches in 1999 following the 13–7 defeat by England on the 1998 year-end tour. The loss at Twickenham broke the Springboks' 17-win sequence.

In 1999 two wins against a poor Italy (74–3 and 101–0) were followed by South Africa's first-ever defeat against Wales (29–19 in Cardiff). Then followed a 28–0 Tri-Nations drubbing against New Zealand in Dunedin – the first time in 49 tests since 1921's 0–0 draw that the Springboks were held scoreless by the All Blacks; another crushing defeat (34–6) a week later against Australia in Brisbane; and a 34–18 loss against the

Peter de Villiers – a good 2009 spoiled on the year-end tour.

ments and a poor record. Mallett resigned as national coach in September at the start of a disciplinary hearing into allegations that his comments had brought the game into disrepute.

It would be six years before South Africa would again taste success in the Tri-Nations. The Boks' last position and single win in 1999 would be repeated in the next four years, giving the Springboks five last places and only five matches won in the five series between their titles in 1998 and 2004.

Two more coaches

Two more coaches followed between August 2000 when Mallett resigned and November 2003 when Straeuli was ousted. Harry Viljoen won eight from 15 matches in his year in charge. But Viljoen, disillusioned by the public criticism that accompanies the post, ended his contract almost two years early. It was in keeping with the 42-year-old's coaching career. He had finished his coaching stints with Transvaal, Natal and the Stormers early, citing personal reasons on each occasion.

This time media criticism was the reason for Viljoen's decision. 'You don't know the pressures until you're there yourself and I've struggled to handle them. There's another two years to the World Cup and facing that would have been a problem.' Under Viljoen the Springboks won only five of 11 tests.

Rudolf Straeuli became the eighth Springbok coach in less than ten years – an indictment of the uncertain management at SARFU which is a contributory reason for the poor showing of Springbok sides since 1992.

Straeuli won his first four games, with two victories over Wales, a 20-point win against Argentina and a runaway 60–18 defeat of Samoa. But against the top rugby countries Straeuli's record was poor, and there were record defeats against France (30–10); Scotland (21–6); England (53–3); and New Zealand (52–16). Straeuli as coach also won only two out of the 17 games played against the top six teams in the world.

All Blacks in Pretoria. The defending champions' only win in the 1999 Tri-Nations came in their last match and was a close 10-9 win against the Wallabies at Newlands. The Springboks finished last with a single win.

The trend continued in the unsuccessful World Cup which, as in the Tri-Nations, was marked by strange pronouncements and even stranger selections by Mallett. He dropped his captain Gary Teichmann after their relationship soured, but the coach lasted for another year at the top after the World Cup. Then in 2000 Mallett accused SARFU of 'greed' for selling Tri-Nations championship tickets at what he felt were inflated prices. This further alienated the SARFU executive after earlier pronounce-

No Super 14 trophy, but the Sharks' two Springbok front brothers Jannie and Bismarck du Plessis show their delight at winning the 2010 Currie Cup.

2004: A second Tri-Nations title

After the poor 2003 season – for various reasons one of the lowest points in South African rugby history – when the Springboks had a nightmare year on and off the field, new coach Jake White turned things around. The paltry four Tri-Nations tries scored in four matches in 2003 increased to 13 in 2004. Although they won only two of their four Tri-Nations matches – as did New Zealand and Australia – South Africa clinched the closely fought series by a single log point by virtue of 'losing bonus points' in both their (away) defeats for being within seven points of the winners' score.

Those two bonus points in the Christchurch and Perth

defeats were followed by two very good wins in South Africa in a series where all six wins were achieved by the home sides. As in 1998 the Wallabies were the Springboks' opponents in the last match the Boks had to win. But unlike the relatively easy win in 1998, this effective final in 2004 went right down to the wire, with the Boks winning 23–19. Australia scored three tries by Lote Tuqiri, Stirling Mortlock and George Smith against South Africa's two by Victor Matfield and Joe van Niekerk. Percy Montgomery's three penalties and two conversions to Matt Giteau's two conversions made the difference.

South Africa's only real dominance in this match was in the third quarter after Australia had dominated

Bull's coach Heyneke Meyer's belief in planning, structure and continuity paid off.

three-match year-end tour. De Villiers took along a second side on the tour. There was great excitement and the venture was branded as a tour of the old kind where there were a so-called Wednesday and a Saturday side. It was, however, far from reality. There were two separate touring sides, two sets of management and the test team and the 'dirt-trackers' were rarely together at the same venue!

Two losses to England club sides by the second-tier team that abounded with surprise selections – few of whom came through as test Springboks in 2010 – marred a good 2009, a season with ultimately only a 57% Springbok success rate for De Villiers.

However, South African sides beat what was put before them in 2009 as will be discussed later. The Super 14 competition also went the Bulls' way to add to De Villiers' two outstanding achievements in a golden year for South African rugby. As a result, the Springbok coach was named the IRB Coach of the Year and the Springboks, the Team of the Year.

the first 40 minutes. The Boks were 7–0 behind shortly before half-time, but took a commanding 23–7 lead until Montgomery and Breyton Paulse were concurrently yellow-carded 11 minutes before time. Two tries in the last eight minutes put the match back in the melting pot. When Mortlock scored his try which was converted, there were still eight minutes left with the score at 23–14 to South Africa. Smith's last-ditch effort left the Wallabies with only a minute to get the winning score – which had to be a try. It was too little too late.

2009's wins and woes
South Africa's third Tri-Nations title came under yet another coach. Controversial Peter de Villiers had the satisfaction of coaching the Springboks to the title in 2009, a year in which the Springboks also beat (a committed but rather average) British and Irish Lions side in a three-match series. However, what should have been a great year was spoiled with only one win against lowly Italy on the

Bulls kick off the good times
The Bulls' second Super 14 title had to compete with the vibe of the 2009 British and Irish Lions tour that started on the same day that the Super 14 final was played. Loftus was packed; the Royal Bafokeng Stadium in Phokeng, just outside Rustenburg, was not. A Super 14 final was obviously regarded as more important than a tour opener!

After all, it was a rare final in a competition in which the South African sides had not exactly excelled since it was instituted in 1996. An unfair travelling load where South Africa's franchises (in rotation) had to fly over Australia and the Tasman Sea to play in New Zealand, then return for matches in Australia and go back to New Zealand again; the inability – or reluctance – of South African sides to embrace the franchise system fully; and also the inflated opinion of South Africa's talent reserves and especially the below-par skills levels of too many of the Super Rugby players all contributed to poor results.

Breaking the barrier

When announcing that the Super 14 semi-final and final would be moved to Orlando Stadium, the CEO of the Blue Bulls Company (Pty) Ltd, Barend van Graan, had mobilised one of the most memorable nation-building moments since the 1995 Rugby World Cup. The play-offs were a resounding success with all races embracing the moment and making it a special occasion.

The semi-final was – by far! – the biggest rugby game ever to take place in a township. It also broke all television records. Rugby had made significant inroads and black viewers accounted for almost 30% of the total viewing audience of 2,9 million (over the age of 16). That was more than double the number in 2009 when the Bulls beat the Chiefs in Pretoria.

With the semi-final being hosted in Soweto, the SABC also broadcast the game live, leading to an increase in black viewership which was 127% compared to the 2009 Super 14 final. The total black viewership of more than 840 000 was almost 30% of the total audience. There was also a significant increase in female viewers that showed a 140% rise from 2009. In fact, they accounted for 51% of the viewers!

But it was inside Soweto and the stadium itself that the real hype was noticeable. Spectators arranged for parking in the township yards; visited the shebeens and eating places; mixed freely with the people of Soweto who lined the streets for this big occasion, many of them with Bulls shirts and flags.

Inside the stadium, with hours to go before the semi-final, black, white, coloured and Indian spectators danced to typical 'rugby' music of the Bulls supporters in the beer garden, and sang along. Spectators who trekked to the stadium without tickets found a shebeen and watched the game from there. What's more, they booked a table at the shebeen for the following week's final against the Stormers after the Bulls' win over the Crusaders when the 3 000 remaining tickets for the final were snapped up within minutes!

Super Rugby reality

The general performances of the South African franchises in 15 years of Super Rugby showed that the depth of South African rugby was not as good as many perceived it to be. The following abbreviated results show:

❏ In 1996, both Transvaal and Western Province won only three matches, with Province also drawing one but ending last; Natal lost the final to the Blues 45–21 in Auckland.

❏ In 1997, a relatively good year for South African sides, Northern Transvaal won three and drew three matches; and Natal were eliminated in the semi-final with the Blues thrashing them 56–3.

❏ In 1998 the Cats (combined Lions and Free State Cheetahs) won only two matches and the Bulls three; the Sharks lost their semi-final match against Crusaders 36–32.

❏ In 1999 the Bulls won one match and the Cats four; the Sharks, seventh from 12 teams, were the best of South Africa's teams.

❏ In 2000 the Cats, under new coach Laurie Mains, finished fourth but lost the semi-final to the ACT Brumbies 27–5; the Stormers were fifth; the Sharks won one match and drew one; the Bulls won one and drew two from 11 matches.

❏ In 2001 both the Cats and the Sharks made it to the semi-finals! The Sharks beat the Cats 30–12 in Durban but were then hammered 36–6 by the ACT Brumbies in the Canberra semi-final; the Bulls won only three matches.

❏ 2002: No wins for the Bulls, one for the Cats and four for the Sharks from their 11 matches saw the South African sides fill the last three positions on the log. The Stormers were seventh in a very poor year for South Africa's teams.

❏ 2003: The Cats were last with two wins, the Sharks

second from the bottom with three wins and the Stormers fourth from last with five wins. It emphasised that something was amiss in South Africa's challenge.

❏ 2004: One win for the Cats, a lost semi-final for the Stormers against Crusaders (27–16) and a sixth place for the Bulls.

❏ 2005: The Sharks were last with one win and a draw, the Cats one place above them with two wins and a draw, and the Stormers fourth from the bottom. The third-placed Bulls lost their semi-final against the Waratahs 23–13.

❏ 2006: The Western Force came into the fray, and took last spot. The Cats split up with the Cheetahs becoming the one franchise and the Johannesburg partner continuing as the Cats. (They would only later become the Lions.) The Cats from Johannesburg were second last with two wins and one draw, and the Bulls lost their semi-final to Crusaders 35–15.

❏ 2007: At last! The Sharks topped the log and the Bulls were second. They both won their semi-finals. The Sharks beat the Blues 34–18 in Durban and Crusaders lost their match in Pretoria 27–12 to a rampant Bulls team. The Pretoria franchise went on to win the final in dramatic fashion with a last-gasp try by Bryan Habana to beat the Sharks 20–19 in Durban. But a sobering thought is that the Lions (12th from 14), the Cheetahs (11th) and the Stormers (10th) were outclassed.

❏ 2008: The Bulls could do no better than tenth place. The Lions won twice and drew once and the Cheetahs were second-last with one. The Sharks went into a semi-final by virtue of their third place but lost 28–13 to the Waratahs in Sydney.

❏ 2009: The Bulls won their second title. They finished first on the log, beat Crusaders 36–23 in the Pretoria semi-final, and then thrashed the Chiefs 61–17 in the Loftus final. The Cheetahs were last with two wins from 13 matches and the Lions, third last, won only four matches.

Victor Matfield led the Bulls to three Super Rugby titles.

❏ 2010: The Bulls did it again! This time they played both the semi-final and final at Orlando Stadium in Soweto because Loftus was used for the 2010 Soccer World Cup. The Bulls beat Crusaders for a third successive semi-final. The Stormers beat the Waratahs 25–6 in their semi-final at Newlands before losing 25–17 to the Bulls in the Orlando final. But if the Bulls' third title and Orlando was euphoric, there was also the reality that the Lions had set a new record of the wrong kind in losing all 13 of their matches (plus the last one the previous season!) and conceded nearly six tries per match on average.

Try time! An elated Bulls wing, Francois Hougaard, sprints in for a semi-final try against Crusaders.

2007: The great derby final

In 2007 the Bulls were the first South African side to play five matches on their Australasian tour. After two earlier setbacks at home with defeats to the Sharks in Durban and the Western Force in Pretoria, they became the first SA team to win three matches in Australasia. That set up their season and enabled them to be at least in the running when the last matches of the tournament dawned.

Before their last league match (coach Heyneke Meyer's 91st match with the Bulls) they were only sixth on the congested log. They needed a 'full-house' of five points against the Reds, which would have pitted them against the Sharks in Durban in the semi-finals.

However, there was a possibility of the Bulls ending third and even second on the log. Calculations showed that a win by 45 points or more against the Reds would put the Bulls in third spot for an away semi-final against the Crusaders. But, if they could do the unthinkable and beat the Reds by 72 points or more, the Bulls would host a home semi-final.

On the Friday before the match, Meyer told every player he had 'made them a shareholder in his belief that the team would beat the Reds by at least 72 points', Bulls manager Wynie Strydom said later. And Meyer's charges didn't disappoint him with the biggest win in Super Rugby history as they trounced the Reds 92–3. The Bulls scored 13 tries after trailing 3–0 two minutes into the game! By half-time the score was 38–3 to the Bulls and they added 54 points after the break. The Bulls' 89-point margin was the largest in the competition's history, eclipsing the Crusaders' 77-point (96–19) win over the New South Wales Waratahs in 2002.

The Bulls' long-standing captain Victor Matfield was full of praise for his side after their historic 92–3 win. 'It all began with the basics, the scrums, line-outs and tackling. After that our attacking mindset came into play and we patiently worked our way to the massive points total.

'Since returning from Australasia, we have performed really well to beat the Stormers, Lions and Blues, but nothing comes close to what we achieved tonight. It was awesome, truly awesome.' He conceded, however, that Crusaders would pose a serious threat in the semi-final.

It wasn't the end of the season yet. The redoubtable Crusaders awaited in the semi-final, albeit in Pretoria, while the Sharks had beaten the Stormers 36–10 to end top of the log with 45 points. That ensured a home semi-final for the Sharks against the Blues and, should they win, also a home final.

Just how close matters were on the log is reflected by the three sides tied in second place on 42 points, with only points difference separating the Bulls (plus 165), Crusaders (plus 147) and Blues (plus 120). The Sharks were the first South African team to top the Super standings at the end of a season and it was the first time that

Not the first choice of Springbok coach Peter de Villiers, Morné Steyn (above) and Heinrich Brüssow (right) were the Bok stars of the series win against the 2009 British and Irish Lions.

South Africa had two teams in the tournament semi-finals since 2001 when the Sharks and the Cats clashed.

In the semi-final against Crusaders no tries were scored by either side. Derick Hougaard dominated proceedings behind a Bulls pack that was superior to that of the visitors and his eight penalties and a drop goal were just reward for a side that was better on the day and won 27–12. Dan Carter scored all Crusaders' points.

The Sharks secured their home final with 20 points scored in the last quarter as they beat the Blues from Auckland 34–18 following a 14–6 half-time lead. By 13 minutes after the restart the Blues had fought their way back in a tight contest to lead 18–14. Percy Montgomery

shrank the lead to 18–17 with a 62nd-minute penalty. However, the last 30 minutes belonged to the Sharks. They were rewarded for their dominance, and a penalty by Montgomery and two converted tries by Butch James and Waylon Murray in the last eight minutes put the result beyond the Blues.

In the 2007 final Bryan Habana became the Bulls' hero when he scored a try after the final hooter to steal the Super 14 title from the Sharks, ensuring the Bulls' 20–19 victory in Durban. It was a cruel twist of fate that caused

Bok flankers Schalk Burger (left) and Heinrich Brüssow (right) share the joy of clinching the series against the 2009 British and Irish Lions with fullback Frans Steyn.

the better team on the day to lose when the Sharks allowed the Bulls to run at them in the dying minutes and failed to keep possession. The Sharks seemingly had the game wrapped up at 19–13. Lock Albert van den Berg had scored to deservedly put his team in the lead with two minues left. Frans Steyn failed to kick the easy conversion, which would have forced the Bulls to score twice in two minutes.

To add to his woes, Steyn also missed a line clearance as the Bulls threw everything into the attack and took play into the Sharks' 22. Habana then carved through the tired Sharks' defence from the right wing and slipped through in the middle next to the uprights for an easy conversion by Derick Hougaard that secured the win.

'I knew we had a chance in a million,' Habana said afterwards. 'I saw the game opening up in front of me as the Sharks players charged towards me in a defensive cordon. I saw a gap to slip through for what will be one of my most treasured rugby memories in future years.'

And the next day, a number of the adversaries from both sides, sore bodies and all, assembled for their bus trip to Bloemfontein to join the rest of the national squad at the training camp before the two-match England series.

2008: SA sides empty-handed

The Sharks reached the 2008 semi-final in finishing third

in the Super 14 competition, but were outplayed in their away match against the Waratahs, losing 28–13. But the Bulls were nowhere!

Staying at the top is almost as difficult as getting there, they often say. And so it was for the Bulls in 2008. It was the Bulls' worst year since their resurgence to the top in 2003. They lost the Currie Cup final to the Sharks (14–9) and were especially disappointing in the Super 14 competition where they ended tenth in a poor attempt to defend their title.

Perhaps they can be forgiven for the slump. The bulk of their side had won the World Cup in 2007 to add to the Super 14 crown, and motivation was perhaps not quite at a high. They also had a new coach. Heyneke Meyer had departed for Leicester in the aftermath of the disappointment of not getting the Springbok coaching job that SARU president Oregan Hoskins had admitted went to Peter de Villiers because of politics. With Meyer went protégé and match-winner Derick Hougaard. And inspirational captain Victor Matfield had left for money and a change of scenery and was playing for Toulon in France.

At national level, 2008 was Peter de Villiers' first season as coach. The Boks won two of their six Tri-Nations matches, beat England 42–6 at Twickenham – the sixth successive win over England – and beat Wales three times. Argentina and Italy (at home) and Scotland were also beaten. It was a reasonable year, but they were not winning consistently against the top sides.

2009: Year of the Boks and Bulls

Matfield was back with the Bulls for the 2009 season. He said he had great sympathy for Frans Ludeke's problems, pointing out that Ludeke was only appointed as Meyer's successor in December 2007: 'Starting the job in December meant he was two months in arrears. Things will begin to go much more smoothly once he finds his feet. I'm looking forward to supporting him to the fullest.'

Matfield was right. Ludeke, who was fired as coach by the Lions just two seasons before, helped the Bulls and Blue Bulls to bounce back. In 2009 they won both the Super 14 and the Currie Cup. Meyer was also back but as director of rugby and no longer the Bulls' head coach.

The Bulls have been in three finals and have won all three. Each title was special. Whereas the 2007 win over the Sharks was the first Super Rugby title for a South African side, the win in 2009 stood out for two reasons: it provided the first double with both the Super 14 and Currie Cup titles going to the Pretoria-based side. It was also the biggest win in a final, 61–17, against the Chiefs at Loftus. And in 2010 the Bulls added to their tally by moving both their semi-final and the final match to Orlando Stadium – the first time representative rugby matches of this magnitude had been played in Soweto.

They duly won for the third time in three attempts – and what's more, all three of their title victories were achieved on different grounds! It is interesting to note that the Bulls had to see off the semi-final challenges of the Crusaders before all three of their finals. And just how impressive that is can be gauged by the fact that the Saders had seven titles to their name.

Crusaders' first defeat in nine semi-finals came at Loftus in 2007. They won their next – and the title – in 2008 and then suffered their second loss from 11 semi-final appearances in 2009. Then the Bulls rubbed it in to make it three semi-final losses for Crusaders from 12 in 2010!

As individuals, the Bulls pack did well enough, but as a unit they were not altogether great in the first half of the 2009 semi-final at Loftus and had to come back from 20–7 down after 24 minutes. There were too many errors on defence, on attack and also in the line-outs where the Bulls lost some of their own throws to a competitive Crusaders side.

But the Bulls were a different team after the break and their momentum, coupled with the obviously tiring Crusaders pack, saw the possession and the fortunes change dramatically. Bulls flyhalf Morné Steyn kicked

Springbok prop Beast Mtawarira vaults over a ruck in the test series against the 2009 British and Irish Lions.

a record four drop goals and nine other points to take his side from a deficit to a well-deserved 36–23 win to set up the Chiefs final at Loftus. He was the toast of the blue-clad Loftus and missed only a monstrous fifth drop attempt and one that hit the posts from 10 attempts.

Into the final the Bulls went against a side that they had beaten at Loftus a month before. But then, at 33–27, it was close. This time it was an avalanche and another record for the Bulls on a night that Bulls captain Victor Matfield said was 'the best night of my life'.

It was the first home final for the Bulls – and Matfield thanked their fans for the support. People started queuing for tickets immediately after their semi-final victory. 'Arriving here on Monday morning and seeing everybody

queuing here, we almost couldn't get to training on Monday,' Matfield said.

The skipper, who scored one of eight Bulls tries, said continuity had been the key to their success.

'I think it's just nice that we had the same plans throughout the year. That's one thing that we believe in at the Bulls, we do the same things, we just try and do it better every week and fortunately the ball bounced for us and we're very happy with the result.'

Steyn again had a superb match with the boot, kicking six conversions (missing only two), two penalties and a drop goal for another 20 points on his way to a glorious Super Rugby season. His 191 points consisted of one try, 33 conversions, 29 penalties and a record 11 drop goals.

Steyn sinks the British and Irish Lions

It was to become an even bigger year for the Bulls' fly-half. He received his first cap in 2009 despite Springbok coach Peter de Villiers' not being convinced that Steyn should be the first choice. But Steyn took his opportunities when they were presented at national level; stopped what looked like the winning British and Irish Lions try in the first test in Durban with a brilliant save at the end when he was on as replacement; and in Pretoria in the second test he kicked the series-winning penalty after the hooter from 55 metres, again as a replacement. Then he played his considerable part in the Tri-Nations series triumph and helped the Blue Bulls to their Currie Cup triumph with a stupendous pressure kick in the semi-final against Western Province at Newlands to clinch the match 21–19. Time was up when he slotted the long, angled semi-final penalty to take the Blue Bulls to the final at Loftus against the Free State.

Thank heavens for Steyn. In a 2–1 series win over the 2009 British and Irish Lions he was ultimately the difference. De Villiers' poor bench management; his selection of a near 'second string' Springbok side for the third test; his thoughtless and often tactless remarks after tests and sometimes rudeness in media conferences; and the fact that the Lions arrived without a number of stars who were injured all contrived to make it a very interesting tour.

The Springboks narrowly won the first two tests 26–21 and 28–25. The wins were greatly assisted by three crucial mistakes by the Lions. In the first test, wing Ugo Monye twice ran with the ball under the inside arm which made it difficult to ward off fenders with the try line beckoning. This made Steyn's saving tackle on the big winger in the first test in Durban that much easier.

Then followed the uncharacteristic mistakes by the experienced Ronan O'Gara who firstly didn't kick a ball out and then challenged Jaque Fourie illegally right on the final hooter – and again Steyn was the hero from inside his own half. However, the most important mistake and arguably the series-decider came from the Lions management. They

Fourie du Preez – brilliant on the break and an outstanding tactical player.

selected an under-power tight five and were well beaten in the scrums where they had bargained on dominating what they perceived as a weak point of the Boks.

It is ironic that the two Springbok heroes of the series, Morné Steyn and Cheetahs flank Heinrich Brüssow, were never De Villiers' first choices.

The Lions tour was nevertheless a great experience. It always is. This time there was the added bonus of avenging the Boks' 1997 series defeat when they scored nine tries to three but lost! The roles were reversed this time, with the Lions paying the penalty because of Steyn.

The spectator support on the tour was not as good as expected beforehand. Blame that on too much rugby –

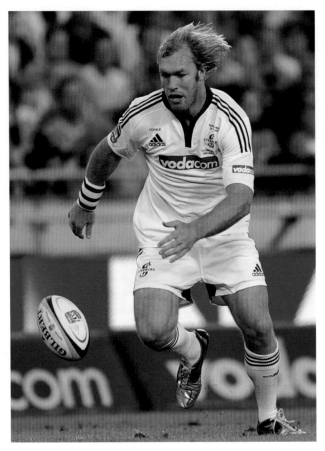

Schalk Burger – critical of referee Craig Joubert after losing the 2010 Super 14 final.

to mix with supporters from both sides. The importance and success of the tour is underlined by the 30 000 tourists that visited South Africa over the duration of the ten matches to support their side.

However, the unfortunate reality is that there will be less place for composite sides from four unions as professionalism grows – and also less chance for success as it becomes increasingly difficult to compete with only a month or less of preparation with players from four rugby cultures, approaches and game plans.

The impressive 2009 Tri-Nations title

The first of South Africa's goals for 2009 had been achieved. 'This series victory ranks alongside our World Cup win,' said Springbok skipper John Smit afterwards. Then he switched to what still had to be achieved, with the 2009 Tri-Nations series first on the list.

The 2009 Super 14 win was only part of a very successful season for the Springboks in the Bulls side. Many of them went on to play a major part in the series win against the Lions – and some of the Blue Bulls youngsters grabbed part of the glory in the successful 2009 Currie Cup campaign when the stars weren't available. There were also a number of Bulls names among the new caps at the end of the year when De Villiers announced the two squads for the tour(s) to the UK, Ireland and Europe.

With Matfield and his Springbok team-mates from the Bulls already boasting two of the greatest wins of the rugby world, the 2009 Tri-Nations series loomed as a final challenge.

It was undoubtedly the most impressive of South Africa's three Tri-Nations titles. They finished eight points ahead of second-placed New Zealand, winning five matches and losing only in the Boks' hoodoo city of Brisbane, 21–6. The scene for the title win was set after the Boks' two home wins over New Zealand in Bloemfontein (28–19) and Durban (31–19). They also beat the Wallabies in Cape Town, 29–17. It was the

and also on the fact that this Lions side had, with the exception of Irish centre Brian O'Driscoll, no real world-class stars. They also had to tour with a squad that differed greatly from the one identified by coach Ian McGeechan because of injuries; and the team was largely under-prepared due to the respective home unions' selfish pursuits, which gave McGeechan little time to gel players from four countries.

What was pleasant, however, was to have a *real* tour – albeit the shortest in the Lions' history – with provincial and composite sides also facing them outside of the tests. And full marks were awarded to the British and Irish Lions' management for allowing their players

Tutu applauds Orlando decision

The Bulls decision to play the 2010 semi-final and final of the Super 14 competition at Orlando Stadium in Soweto proved to be a resounding success – and a nation-builder that carried through on the 2010 World Cup success. It was applauded by far more than the rugby fraternity.

Archbishop Desmond Tutu, anti-apartheid campaigner and Nobel Peace Prize winner, said the Bulls' decision was the 'most important development in the sport since the Springboks won the World Cup in 1995'.

'It is one of those special South African moments that proves we are better off for having one another, and that despite the challenges we face, our society is on the right track,' Tutu said.

Springboks' physical approach that gave them the early advantage. The Boks, already regarded as the world's most abrasive side, more than lived up to this reputation in those two wins.

Steyn scored all 31 points in the Durban 31–19 win over the All Blacks to set a string of records. The match produced only two tries, one to each side. Steyn added a conversion and eight penalties to his try. Victor Matfield was again imperious in the line-outs; and halfbacks Fourie du Preez and Morné Steyn dictated the Durban field-kicking contest on the platform provided by the forwards.

Coach De Villiers and his team were surely allowed a little smirk after they beat the Wallabies 32–25 in Perth in a scintillating running display. There had been much criticism – born from Australasian defeats, no doubt! – that the Springboks were too one-dimensional and fed on their opponents' mistakes. The Boks let up slightly towards the end of the match to provide the Aussies with a slightly more flattering final scoreline than they deserved on the day after leading 32–13 with only 12 minutes to go.

The match that mattered following the four wins and one loss was won in a pulsating clash against the All Blacks at Waikato Park. The irrepressible Boks had run up a commanding 22–6 lead through tries by Du Preez and Jean de Villiers. They then hung on in one of the classics between the two giants of world rugby. To rub it in there was the reality that it was the first time since 1949 that South Africa had won three consecutive tests against the Kiwis.

Yes, 2009 was indeed a great year … and even the disappointing year-end tours to the UK and Europe couldn't diminish that glory. The Boks were duly crowned IRB Team of the Year and Peter de Villiers, IRB Coach of the Year.

And that made the decline in Springbok standards and results in 2010 even more unfathomable and unacceptable.

2010: Bulls' glory and Boks' decline

If 2009 was good for Morné Steyn, 2010 was even better. Steyn wasn't finished at Super 14 level and improved Dan Carter's Super 14 record from 221 points to 263 in 2010. This time there were five tries and only three drop goals, with 38 conversions and 51 penalties making up his record tally. Coach De Villiers had also seen the light – and Steyn became a fixture in the test team.

Former Bulls coach Heyneke Meyer's belief in continuity was never more clearly stated than in the team the Bulls put out for the 2010 final against the Stormers – courtesy of two previous finals in three years. Nine of the Bulls squad joined an elite squad by being involved in their third final. (Only two other teams have won the title more than twice – the seven-time Crusaders, who have a number of players with three or more championships to their credit, and the Blues.)

The Bulls players in the starting XV in Soweto who had appeared in the franchise's two previous winning finals were centre Wynand Olivier, flyhalf Morné Steyn, scrumhalf Fourie du Preez, No 8 Pierre Spies, locks Victor Matfield (the captain in every final) and Danie Rossouw, and prop

Gurthrö Steenkamp. On the bench were utility forward Derick Kuün and loose forward Pedrie Wannenburg who were also involved in the previous Bulls finals.

There were 12 players who had been in the squad in the previous year's thrashing of the Chiefs: fullback Zane Kirchner; centres Jaco Pretorius and Wynand Olivier; fly-half Morné Steyn; scrumhalf Fourie du Preez; loose forwards Pierre Spies, Dewald Potgieter and Deon Stegmann; locks Victor Matfield and Danie Rossouw; and props Werner Kruger and Gurthrö Steenkamp. Derick Kuün and loose forward Pedrie Wannenburg were on the bench in 2010, and Bakkies Botha wasn't available because of a suspension.

Wings Gerhard van den Heever and Francois Hougaard and replacements hooker Bandise Maku, prop Bees Roux, lock Flip van der Merwe and utility back Jacques-Louis Potgieter were the only newcomers to a Super Rugby final change room.

That wasn't the only advantage the Bulls held over the Stormers who had only Bryan Habana with experience in a final (he had played for the Bulls in their preceding two finals!). The Bulls also knew what the effect of the vuvuzelas would be. This new craze that spread abroad after the 2010 World Cup was an interference of serious proportions, Matfield admitted later. It made it difficult to communicate on the field – and not only the players but also the referee were affected.

It was tough, but perhaps easier than the final score-line intimated with the Bulls absolutely dominant in the first 20 minutes when the game was effectively won. So comprehensive was the win that arguably none of the Stormers forwards would have found a place in a combined side if one were selected on their performances that day. The Bulls pack emphasised that the Stormers tight five, for all their improvement, still had a long way to go – and that goes for the scrums in particular, where they simply could not stand up to the Bulls' pressure; and for their penchant to line up among the backs when the hard graft of the Bulls in the rucks and mauls was left to two or three Stormers players to counter.

It was a game in which the Bulls halfbacks Morné Steyn and Fourie du Preez judged their high kicks perfectly and smothered the Stormers' expansive danger with their tactical acumen and territorial dominance.

'Fourie was brilliant with his tactical kicking tonight,' Bulls captain Victor Matfield said afterwards. He was right. The man, who surely is the best scrumhalf this country has produced, played an immense role in the victory in which his vision and tactics used the Bulls' dominance in possession to good effect.

The Bulls became only the third side to win back-to-back Super titles. The Blues achieved it in the first two years of the competition, and Crusaders have done so twice. Matfield, with Reuben Thorne and Richie McCaw of the Crusaders, have now skippered a side to three Super titles. This was the Bulls' third title in four years. It was also their 20th successive win at home, for there can be no doubt that the Orlando Stadium had become home to the Bulls and their fans who embraced the stadium and Soweto over the two weekends.

The way in which referee Craig Joubert was criticised by Stormers captain Schalk Burger and coach Allister Coetzee after the match rankled. It was widely speculated that they might face a formal sanction for their criticism.

'We thought we'd be able to get quick ball, and we knew Craig was the type of referee who penalised defending teams heavily. But like Schalk said, he penalised one team and coached the other,' Coetzee added. It was a serious allegation, but the matter was not referred to SANZAR. However, South Africa's refereeing boss André Watson thought it important enough to issue a statement that there was no coaching at the breakdowns as alleged by Burger and Coetzee.

'... I went through every clip of the match – we have the technology to do so ... There were 167 rucks in the match. The Stormers took the ball in 85 times and the Bulls did so on 82 occasions. Craig (Joubert) spoke 25 times to the Stormers and 28 times to the Bulls at the breakdowns.

'On not a single occasion did he repeat any warning.

He throughout warned both sides only once where it was applicable and then penalised them if they persisted.

'The Bulls were penalised seven times at the breakdowns and the Stormers six times. Every penalty but two, where he penalised immediately, came after warnings to the offending side.'

Matfield, when asked whether the Bulls could repeat the title win in 2011 was adamant that they could. 'It will be harder. The more successful a side becomes, the more is the pressure. But we definitely can do it again,' he said.

Those were brave words in a season where the franchises had to compete in below-strength teams because of players being rested; and where the focus of the top players on the World Cup could have an influence on their play.

There was also the fact that the other South African franchises had caught up with the Bulls in emulating their structures that fed the professional sides. The Bulls had a terrible start to the season and just after the halfway stage had won only four of their nine matches, with only a remote chance of making the play-offs. The Stormers and to a lesser extent the Sharks were setting the tone from a South African perspective – and the hopes were high that the title could remain in South Africa.

The Super 15 decision

The Blue Bulls in 2010 didn't continue their early Currie Cup dominance, but had the satisfaction of winning back-to-back Super 14 titles. Considering that South Africa had not won a Super Rugby title before 2007 when the Bulls beat the Sharks in Durban with Bryan Habana's heartbreak try, the double of 2009 and 2010 was indeed special. With their three Super 14 wins in four years, they also became the permanent holders of the Super 14 trophy with the introduction in 2011 of the Super 15 (marketed as the Super Rugby competition) that had its own (new) prize.

Money was the reason for the decision to embark on a new Super Rugby structure in 2011. The Super 15 was implemented – and despite the obvious shortcomings of the system, the overriding objective of money was pursued. This set up the possibility of South African sides playing seven matches in a season against one another if the Neo Africa Tri-Series in Cape Town is added to the equation: twice each in the Super 15 and the Currie Cup, the possibility of two play-offs in the two competitions and also a match in the Neo Africa series!

Whether South Africa really wanted the new Super 15 format is debatable. The headache that was Brian van Rooyen's legacy as SARU president was his promise of the inclusion of the Southern Kings in the Super Rugby competition. This allowed South Africa's administrators little option but to support the proposal by New Zealand and Australia for an expansion.

SARU hoped that it would allow them an extra team. Instead, they now have the problem of a court decision and a promise to the Kings that the East Coast side would be admitted in 2013 – and unless the competition is expanded to a Super 16 by then, the last-placed South African side in the competition will forfeit their position, regardless of whether they are a stronger unit than the Kings!

Monetary considerations decreed that the Super 15 would not include a South African side. The double round derbies would benefit both the Australasian partners that didn't find the Super 14 as financially rewarding as South Africa with its consistently big crowds. For that, the isolation years can be thanked (to put a positive spin on that dark era in South Africa's rugby history!). South Africa's provincialism and support in derbies developed to a near frenzy in the era when little international rugby was possible – and it has remained so.

While the administrators are undoubtedly smiling about the new financial boost the Super 15 will probably provide, the South African players are not as enchanted. There is no match harder than a South African derby, and this was the players' lot with the 2011 introduction of the Super 15 series. It will in future increasingly tax their bodies as rugby slaves to the national controlling institutions that are their bosses.

Statistics

TEST MATCHES BY DECADE

Decade	Played	Won	Lost	Drawn	Win%	Prog. Win %
1891–1900	7	1	6	0	14.3%	14.3%
1901–1910	10	5	2	3	50.0%	35.3%
1911–1920	5	5	0	0	100.0%	50.0%
1921–1930	11	6	3	2	54.5%	51.5%
1931–1940	17	13	4	0	76.5%	60.0%
1941–1950	4	4	0	0	100.0%	63.0%
1951–1960	28	18	8	2	64.3%	63.4%
1961–1970	46	26	14	6	56.5%	60.9%
1971–1980	28	20	6	2	71.4%	62.8%
1981–1990	18	14	4	0	77.8%	64.4%
1991–2000	94	60	32	2	63.8%	64.2%
2001–2010	127	78	47	2	61.4%	63.3%
	395	250	126	19		

The two Du Plessis's, Morné of Western Province and Daan of Northern Transvaal, with the Currie Cup after the final in 1979.

SOUTH AFRICA'S TEST RESULTS SUMMARY – 1891 TO 2010

Opponents	Played	Won	Lost	Drawn	% Won	Points for	Points against	SOUTH AFRICA Tries	Conversions	Penalties	Drop goals	OPPONENTS Tries	Conversions	Penalties	Drop goals
Argentina	13	13	0	0	100%	544	272	70	52	29	1	26	20	33	1
Australia	71	41	29	1	58%	1347	1239	164	94	148	17	128	81	152	12
British Isles	46	23	17	6	50%	600	516	95	48	52	7	68	30	59	14
Canada	2	2	0	0	100%	71	18	10	6	3	0	2	1	2	0
England	32	19	12	1	59%	661	491	61	44	84	12	34	22	89	7
Fiji	2	2	0	0	100%	80	38	10	6	6	0	4	3	4	0
France	38	21	11	6	55%	764	568	88	59	89	7	50	27	80	19
Georgia	1	1	0	0	100%	46	19	7	4	1	0	1	1	4	0
Ireland	20	15	4	1	75%	401	236	59	31	30	5	24	14	32	3
Italy	10	10	0	0	100%	533	129	74	59	15	0	11	7	19	1
Namibia	1	1	0	0	100%	105	13	15	12	2	0	1	1	2	0
New Zealand	81	33	45	3	41%	1261	1514	124	81	161	27	155	92	195	19
NZ Cavaliers	4	3	1	0	75%	96	62	7	7	15	3	5	3	11	1
Pacific Islands	1	1	0	0	100%	38	24	4	3	4	0	4	2	0	0
Romania	1	1	0	0	100%	21	8	2	1	3	0	1	0	1	0
Scotland	21	16	5	0	76%	518	237	66	44	43	5	24	17	30	3
South America	6	5	1	0	83%	156	86	22	16	6	6	7	5	13	3
S America & Spain	2	2	0	0	100%	54	28	9	3	4	0	3	2	4	0
Spain	1	1	0	0	100%	47	3	7	6	0	0	0	0	1	0
Tonga	2	2	0	0	100%	104	35	16	9	2	0	4	3	3	0
USA	3	3	0	0	100%	145	42	23	16	2	0	4	1	6	1
Uruguay	3	3	0	0	100%	245	12	38	23	3	0	0	0	4	0
Wales	25	23	1	1	92%	698	351	87	56	55	2	31	17	54	2
W Samoa/Samoa	6	6	0	0	100%	316	65	44	30	11	1	9	4	4	0
World Teams	3	3	0	0	100%	87	59	11	5	10	1	9	7	3	0
	395	250	126	19	63.3%	8938	6065	1113	715	778	94	605	360	805	86

SOUTH AFRICA'S SEASONAL TEST RECORD

Year	Played	Won	Drawn	Lost	Points for	Points against	% Won		Total wins	Total matches
							Season	Overall		
1891	3	0	0	3	0	11	0.00	0.00	0	3
1896	4	1	0	3	16	34	25.00	14.29	1	7
1903	3	1	2	0	18	10	33.33	20.00	2	10
1906	4	2	1	1	29	21	50.00	28.57	4	14
1910	3	2	0	1	38	23	66.67	35.29	6	17
1912–13	5	5	0	0	104	8	100.00	50.00	11	22
1921	3	1	1	1	14	18	33.33	48.00	12	25
1924	4	3	1	0	43	15	75.00	51.72	15	29
1928	4	2	0	2	39	26	50.00	51.52	17	33
1931–32	4	4	0	0	29	9	100.00	56.76	21	37
1933	5	3	0	2	50	42	60.00	57.14	24	42
1937	5	4	0	1	72	47	80.00	59.57	28	47
1938	3	2	0	1	61	36	66.67	60.00	30	50
1949	4	4	0	0	47	28	100.00	62.96	34	54
1951–52	5	5	0	0	100	14	100.00	66.10	39	59
1953	4	3	0	1	79	38	75.00	66.67	42	63
1955	4	2	0	2	75	49	50.00	65.67	44	67
1956	6	3	0	3	47	41	50.00	64.38	47	73
1958	2	0	1	1	8	12	0.00	62.67	47	75
1960–61	10	7	2	1	81	43	70.00	63.53	54	85
1961	3	3	0	0	75	22	100.00	64.77	57	88
1962	4	3	1	0	48	20	75.00	65.22	60	92
1963	4	2	0	2	50	29	50.00	64.58	62	96
1964	2	1	0	1	30	11	50.00	64.29	63	98
1965	8	1	0	7	55	102	12.50	60.38	64	106
1967	4	2	1	1	62	31	50.00	60.00	66	110
1968	6	5	1	0	89	60	83.33	61.21	71	116
1969–70	8	4	2	2	101	62	50.00	60.48	75	124
1970	4	3	0	1	59	35	75.00	60.94	78	128
1971	5	4	1	0	81	40	80.00	61.65	82	133
1972	1	0	0	1	9	18	0.00	61.19	82	134
1974	6	2	1	3	57	91	33.33	60.00	84	140
1975	2	2	0	0	71	43	100.00	60.56	86	142
1976	4	3	0	1	55	46	75.00	60.96	89	146
1977	1	1	0	0	45	24	100.00	61.22	90	147
1980	9	8	0	1	208	130	88.89	62.82	98	156
1981	6	4	0	2	128	83	66.67	62.96	102	162
1982	2	1	0	1	62	39	50.00	62.80	103	164
1984	4	4	0	0	122	52	100.00	63.69	107	168
1986	4	3	0	1	96	62	75.00	63.95	110	172
1989	2	2	0	0	42	35	100.00	64.37	112	174
1992	5	1	0	4	79	130	20.00	63.13	113	179
1993	7	3	1	3	169	146	42.86	62.37	116	186
1994	9	5	1	3	225	164	55.56	62.05	121	195
1995	10	10	0	0	308	121	100.00	63.90	131	205
1996	13	8	0	5	352	260	61.54	63.76	139	218
1997	13	8	0	5	535	307	61.54	63.64	147	231
1998	12	11	0	1	361	136	91.67	65.02	158	243
1999	13	8	0	5	447	236	61.54	64.84	166	256
2000	12	6	0	6	301	301	50.00	64.18	172	268
2001	11	5	1	5	271	223	45.45	63.44	177	279
2002	11	5	0	6	284	318	45.45	62.76	182	290
2003	12	7	0	5	338	280	58.33	62.58	189	302
2004	13	9	0	4	408	276	69.23	62.86	198	315
2005	12	8	1	3	416	243	66.67	63.00	206	327
2006	12	5	0	7	258	321	41.67	62.24	211	339
2007	17	14	0	3	658	257	82.35	63.20	225	356
2008	13	9	0	4	360	195	69.23	63.41	234	369
2009	12	8	0	4	276	249	66.67	63.51	242	381
2010	14	8	0	6	397	344	57.14	63.29	250	395
Totals	395	250	19	126	8938	6065				

SOUTH AFRICA'S TEST RESULTS BY OPPONENT

ARGENTINA

Played 13   Won 13   Lost 0   Drawn 0   PF 544   PA 272

Year	Winner	Score	Venue
1993	South Africa	29–26	Buenos Aires
1993	South Africa	52–23	Buenos Aires
1994	South Africa	42–22	Port Elizabeth
1994	South Africa	46–26	Johannesburg
1996	South Africa	46–15	Buenos Aires
1996	South Africa	44–21	Buenos Aires
2000	South Africa	37–33	Buenos Aires
2002	South Africa	49–29	Springs
2003	South Africa	26–25	Port Elizabeth
2004	South Africa	39–7	Buenos Aires
2005	South Africa	34–23	Buenos Aires
2007	South Africa	37–13	Paris
2008	South Africa	63–9	Johannesburg

AUSTRALIA

Played 71   Won 41   Lost 29   Drawn 1   PF 1347   PA 1239

Year	Winner	Score	Venue
1933	South Africa	17–3	Cape Town
1933	Australia	6–21	Durban
1933	South Africa	12–3	Johannesburg
1933	South Africa	11–0	Port Elizabeth
1933	Australia	4–15	Bloemfontein
1937	South Africa	9–5	Sydney
1937	South Africa	26–17	Sydney
1953	South Africa	25–3	Johannesburg
1953	Australia	14–18	Cape Town
1953	South Africa	18–8	Durban
1953	South Africa	22–9	Port Elizabeth
1956	South Africa	9–0	Sydney
1956	South Africa	9–0	Brisbane
1961	South Africa	28–3	Johannesburg
1961	South Africa	23–11	Port Elizabeth
1963	South Africa	14–3	Pretoria
1963	Australia	5–9	Cape Town
1963	Australia	9–11	Johannesburg
1963	South Africa	22–6	Port Elizabeth
1965	Australia	11–18	Sydney
1965	Australia	8–12	Brisbane
1969	South Africa	30–11	Johannesburg
1969	South Africa	16–9	Durban
1969	South Africa	11–3	Cape Town
1969	South Africa	19–8	Bloemfontein
1971	South Africa	19–11	Sydney
1971	South Africa	14–6	Brisbane
1971	South Africa	18–6	Sydney
1992	Australia	3–26	Cape Town
1993	South Africa	19–12	Sydney
1993	Australia	20–28	Brisbane
1993	Australia	12–19	Sydney
1995	South Africa	27–18	Cape Town
1996	Australia	16–21	Sydney
1996	South Africa	25–19	Bloemfontein
1997	Australia	20–32	Brisbane
1997	South Africa	61–22	Pretoria
1998	South Africa	14–13	Perth
1998	South Africa	29–15	Johannesburg
1999	Australia	6–32	Brisbane
1999	South Africa	10–9	Cape Town
1999	Australia	21–27	London
2000	Australia	23–44	Melbourne
2000	Australia	6–26	Sydney
2000	Australia	18–19	Durban
2001	South Africa	20–15	Pretoria
2001	Drawn	14–14	Perth
2002	Australia	27–38	Brisbane
2002	South Africa	33–31	Johannesburg
2003	South Africa	26–22	Cape Town
2003	Australia	9–29	Brisbane
2004	Australia	26–30	Perth
2004	South Africa	23–19	Durban
2005	Australia	12–30	Sydney
2005	South Africa	33–20	Johannesburg
2005	South Africa	22–16	Pretoria
2005	South Africa	22–19	Perth
2006	Australia	0–49	Brisbane
2006	Australia	18–20	Sydney
2006	South Africa	24–16	Johannesburg
2007	South Africa	22–19	Cape Town
2007	Australia	17–25	Sydney
2008	Australia	9–16	Perth
2008	Australia	15–27	Durban
2008	South Africa	53–8	Johannesburg
2009	South Africa	29–17	Cape Town
2009	South Africa	32–25	Perth
2009	Australia	6–21	Brisbane
2010	Australia	13–30	Brisbane
2010	South Africa	44–31	Pretoria
2010	Australia	39–41	Bloemfontein

BRITISH ISLES

Played 46   Won 23   Lost 17   Drawn 6   PF 600   PA 516

Year	Winner	Score	Venue
1891	British Isles	0–4	Port Elizabeth
1891	British Isles	0–3	Kimberley
1891	British Isles	0–4	Cape Town
1896	British Isles	0–8	Port Elizabeth
1896	British Isles	8–17	Johannesburg
1896	British Isles	3–9	Kimberley
1896	South Africa	5–0	Cape Town
1903	Drawn	10–10	Johannesburg
1903	Drawn	0–0	Kimberley
1903	South Africa	8–0	Cape Town
1910	South Africa	14–10	Johannesburg
1910	British Isles	3–8	Port Elizabeth
1910	South Africa	21–5	Cape Town
1924	South Africa	7–3	Durban
1924	South Africa	17–0	Johannesburg
1924	Drawn	3–3	Port Elizabeth
1924	South Africa	16–9	Cape Town
1938	South Africa	26–12	Johannesburg
1938	South Africa	19–3	Port Elizabeth
1938	British Isles	16–21	Cape Town
1955	British Isles	22–23	Johannesburg
1955	South Africa	25–9	Cape Town
1955	British Isles	6–9	Pretoria
1955	South Africa	22–8	Port Elizabeth
1962	Drawn	3–3	Johannesburg
1962	South Africa	3–0	Durban
1962	South Africa	8–3	Cape Town
1962	South Africa	34–14	Bloemfontein
1968	South Africa	25–20	Pretoria
1968	Drawn	6–6	Port Elizabeth
1968	South Africa	11–6	Cape Town
1968	South Africa	19–6	Johannesburg
1974	British Isles	3–12	Cape Town
1974	British Isles	9–28	Pretoria
1974	British Isles	9–26	Port Elizabeth
1974	Drawn	13–13	Johannesburg
1980	South Africa	26–22	Cape Town
1980	South Africa	26–19	Bloemfontein
1980	South Africa	12–10	Port Elizabeth
1980	British Isles	13–17	Pretoria
1997	British Isles	16–25	Cape Town
1997	British Isles	15–18	Durban
1997	South Africa	35–16	Johannesburg
2009	South Africa	26–21	Durban
2009	South Africa	28–25	Pretoria
2009	British Isles	9–28	Johannesburg

CANADA

Played 2   Won 2   Lost 0   Drawn 0   PF 71   PA 18

Year	Winner	Score	Venue
1995	South Africa	20–0	Port Elizabeth
2000	South Africa	51–18	East London

ENGLAND

Played 32   Won 19   Lost 12   Drawn 1   PF 661   PA 491

Year	Winner	Score	Venue
1906	Drawn	3–3	London
1913	South Africa	9–3	London
1932	South Africa	7–0	London
1952	South Africa	8–3	London
1961	South Africa	5–0	London
1969	England	8–11	London
1972	England	9–18	Johannesburg
1984	South Africa	33–15	Port Elizabeth
1984	South Africa	35–9	Johannesburg
1992	England	16–33	London
1994	England	15–32	Pretoria
1994	South Africa	27–9	Cape Town
1995	South Africa	24–14	London
1997	South Africa	29–11	London
1998	South Africa	18–0	Cape Town
1998	England	7–13	London
1999	South Africa	44–21	Paris
2000	South Africa	18–13	Pretoria
2000	England	22–27	Bloemfontein
2000	England	17–25	London
2001	England	9–29	London
2002	England	3–53	London
2003	England	6–25	Perth
2004	England	16–32	London
2006	England	21–23	London
2006	South Africa	25–14	London
2007	South Africa	58–10	Bloemfontein
2007	South Africa	55–22	Pretoria
2007	South Africa	36–0	Paris
2007	South Africa	15–6	Paris
2008	South Africa	42–6	London
2010	South Africa	21–11	London

FIJI

Played 2   Won 2   Lost 0   Drawn 0   PF 80   PA 38

Year	Winner	Score	Venue
1996	South Africa	43–18	Pretoria
2007	South Africa	37–20	Marseille

FRANCE

Played 38   Won 21   Lost 11   Drawn 6   PF 764   PA 568

Year	Winner	Score		Venue
1913	South Africa		38–5	Bordeaux
1952	South Africa		25–3	Paris
1958	Drawn		3–3	Cape Town
1958	France		5–9	Johannesburg
1961	Drawn		0–0	Paris
1964	France		6–8	Springs
1967	South Africa		26–3	Durban
1967	South Africa		16–3	Bloemfontein
1967	France		14–19	Johannesburg
1967	Drawn		6–6	Cape Town
1968	South Africa		12–9	Bordeaux
1968	South Africa		16–11	Paris
1971	South Africa		22–9	Bloemfontein
1971	Drawn		8–8	Durban
1974	South Africa		13–4	Toulouse
1974	South Africa		10–8	Paris
1975	South Africa		38–25	Bloemfontein
1975	South Africa		33–18	Pretoria
1980	South Africa		37–15	Pretoria
1992	South Africa		20–15	Lyon
1992	France		16–29	Paris
1993	Drawn		20–20	Durban
1993	France		17–18	Johannesburg
1995	South Africa		19–15	Durban
1996	South Africa		22–12	Bordeaux
1996	South Africa		13–12	Paris
1997	South Africa		36–32	Lyon
1997	South Africa		52–10	Paris
2001	France		23–32	Johannesburg
2001	South Africa		20–15	Durban
2001	France		10–20	Paris
2002	France		10–30	Marseilles
2005	Drawn		30–30	Durban
2005	South Africa		27–13	Port Elizabeth
2005	France		20–26	Paris
2006	France		26–36	Cape Town
2009	France		13–20	Toulouse
2010	South Africa		42–17	Cape Town

GEORGIA

Played 1   Won 1   Lost 0   Drawn 0   PF 46   PA 19

Year	Winner	Score	Venue
2003	South Africa	46–19	Sydney

IRELAND

Played 20   Won 15   Lost 4   Drawn 1   PF 401   PA 236

Year	Winner	Score	Venue
1906	South Africa	15–12	Belfast
1912	South Africa	38–0	Dublin
1931	South Africa	8–3	Dublin
1951	South Africa	17–5	Dublin
1960	South Africa	8–3	Dublin
1961	Ireland	24–8	Cape Town
1965	Drawn	6–9	Dublin
1970	South Africa	8–8	Dublin
1981	South Africa	23–15	Cape Town
1981	South Africa	12–10	Durban
1998	South Africa	37–13	Bloemfontein
1998	South Africa	33–0	Pretoria
1998	South Africa	27–13	Dublin
2000	South Africa	28–18	Dublin
2004	South Africa	31–17	Bloemfontein
2004	South Africa	26–17	Cape Town
2004	Ireland	12–17	Dublin
2006	Ireland	15–32	Dublin
2009	Ireland	10–15	Dublin
2010	South Africa	23–21	Dublin

ITALY

Played 10   Won 10   Lost 0   Drawn 0   PF 533   PA 129

Year	Winner	Score	Venue
1995	South Africa	40–21	Rome
1997	South Africa	62–31	Bologna
1999	South Africa	74–3	Port Elizabeth
1999	South Africa	101–0	Durban
2001	South Africa	60–14	Port Elizabeth
2001	South Africa	54–26	Genoa
2008	South Africa	26–0	Cape Town
2009	South Africa	32–10	Udine
2010	South Africa	29–13	Witbank
2010	South Africa	55–11	East London

NAMIBIA

Played 1   Won 1   Lost 0   Drawn 0   PF 105   PA 13

Year	Winner	Score	Venue
2007	South Africa	105–13	Cape Town

NEW ZEALAND

Played 81   Won 33   Lost 45   Drawn 3   PF 1261   PA 1514

Year	Winner	Score	Venue
1921	New Zealand	5–13	Dunedin
1921	South Africa	9–5	Auckland
1921	Drawn	0–0	Wellington
1928	South Africa	17–0	Durban
1928	New Zealand	6–7	Johannesburg
1928	South Africa	11–6	Port Elizabeth
1928	New Zealand	5–13	Cape Town
1937	New Zealand	7–13	Wellington
1937	South Africa	13–6	Christchurch
1937	South Africa	17–6	Auckland
1949	South Africa	15–11	Cape Town
1949	South Africa	12–6	Johannesburg
1949	South Africa	9–3	Durban
1949	South Africa	11–8	Port Elizabeth
1956	New Zealand	6–10	Dunedin
1956	South Africa	8–3	Wellington
1956	New Zealand	10–17	Christchurch
1956	New Zealand	5–11	Auckland
1960	South Africa	13–0	Johannesburg
1960	New Zealand	3–11	Cape Town
1960	Drawn	11–11	Bloemfontein
1960	South Africa	8–3	Port Elizabeth
1965	New Zealand	3–6	Wellington
1965	New Zealand	0–13	Dunedin
1965	South Africa	19–16	Christchurch
1965	New Zealand	3–20	Auckland
1970	South Africa	17–6	Pretoria
1970	New Zealand	8–9	Cape Town
1970	South Africa	14–3	Port Elizabeth
1970	South Africa	20–17	Johannesburg
1976	South Africa	16–7	Durban
1976	New Zealand	9–15	Bloemfontein
1976	South Africa	15–10	Cape Town
1976	South Africa	15–14	Johannesburg
1981	New Zealand	9–14	Christchurch
1981	South Africa	24–12	Wellington
1981	New Zealand	22–25	Auckland
1992	New Zealand	24–27	Johannesburg
1994	New Zealand	14–22	Dunedin
1994	New Zealand	9–13	Wellington
1994	Drawn	18–18	Auckland
1995	South Africa	15–12	Johannesburg
1996	New Zealand	11–15	Christchurch
1996	New Zealand	18–29	Cape Town
1996	New Zealand	19–23	Durban
1996	New Zealand	26–33	Pretoria
1996	South Africa	32–22	Johannesburg
1997	New Zealand	32–35	Johannesburg
1997	New Zealand	35–55	Auckland
1998	South Africa	13–3	Wellington
1998	South Africa	24–23	Durban
1999	New Zealand	0–28	Dunedin
1999	New Zealand	18–34	Pretoria
1999	South Africa	22–18	Cardiff
2000	New Zealand	12–25	Christchurch
2000	South Africa	46–40	Johannesburg
2001	New Zealand	3–12	Cape Town
2001	New Zealand	15–26	Auckland
2002	New Zealand	20–41	Wellington
2002	New Zealand	23–30	Durban
2003	New Zealand	16–52	Pretoria
2003	New Zealand	11–19	Dunedin
2003	New Zealand	9–29	Melbourne
2004	New Zealand	21–23	Christchurch
2004	South Africa	40–26	Johannesburg
2005	South Africa	22–16	Cape Town
2005	New Zealand	27–31	Dunedin
2006	New Zealand	17–35	Wellington
2006	New Zealand	26–45	Pretoria
2006	South Africa	21–20	Rustenburg
2007	New Zealand	21–26	Durban
2007	New Zealand	6–33	Christchurch
2008	New Zealand	8–19	Wellington
2008	South Africa	30–28	Dunedin
2008	New Zealand	0–19	Cape Town
2009	South Africa	28–19	Bloemfontein
2009	South Africa	31–19	Durban
2009	South Africa	32–29	Hamilton
2010	New Zealand	12–32	Auckland
2010	New Zealand	17–31	Wellington
2010	New Zealand	22–29	Soweto

NEW ZEALAND CAVALIERS

Played 4   Won 3   Lost 1   Drawn 0   PF 96   PA 62

Year	Winner	Score	Venue
1986	South Africa	21–15	Cape Town
1986	NZ Cavaliers	18–19	Durban
1986	South Africa	33–18	Pretoria
1986	South Africa	24–10	Johannesburg

PACIFIC ISLANDS

Played 1   Won 1   Lost 0   Drawn 0   PF 38   PA 24

Year	Winner	Score	Venue
2004	South Africa	38–24	Gosford

ROMANIA

Played 1   Won 1   Lost 0   Drawn 0   PF 21   PA 8

Year	Winner	Score	Venue
1995	South Africa	21–8	Cape Town

SAMOA

Played 6   Won 6   Lost 0   Drawn 0   PF 316   PA 65

Year	Winner	Score	Venue
1995	South Africa	60–8	Johannesburg
1995	South Africa	42–14	Johannesburg
2002	South Africa	60–18	Pretoria
2003	South Africa	60–10	Brisbane
2007	South Africa	35–8	Johannesburg
2007	South Africa	59–7	Paris

SCOTLAND

Played 21   Won 16   Lost 5   Drawn 0   PF 518   PA 237

Year	Winner	Score	Venue
1906	Scotland	0–6	Glasgow
1912	South Africa	16–0	Edinburgh
1932	South Africa	6–3	Edinburgh
1951	South Africa	44–0	Edinburgh
1960	South Africa	18–10	Port Elizabeth
1961	South Africa	12–5	Edinburgh
1965	Scotland	5–8	Edinburgh
1969	Scotland	3–6	Edinburgh
1994	South Africa	34–10	Edinburgh
1997	South Africa	68–10	Edinburgh
1998	South Africa	35–10	Edinburgh
1999	South Africa	46–29	Edinburgh
2002	Scotland	6–21	Edinburgh
2003	South Africa	29–25	Durban
2003	South Africa	28–19	Johannesburg
2004	South Africa	45–10	Edinburgh
2006	South Africa	36–16	Durban
2006	South Africa	29–15	Port Elizabeth
2007	South Africa	27–3	Edinburgh
2008	South Africa	14–10	Edinburgh
2010	Scotland	17–21	Edinburgh

SOUTH AMERICA

Played 8   Won 7   Lost 1   Drawn 0   PF 210   PA 114

Year	Winner	Score	Venue
1980	South Africa	24–9	Johannesburg
1980	South Africa	18–9	Durban
1980	South Africa	22–13	Montevideo
1980	South Africa	30–16	Santiago
1982	South Africa	50–18	Pretoria
1982	South America	12–21	Bloemfontein
1984	South Africa	32–15	Pretoria
1984	South Africa	22–13	Cape Town

SPAIN

Played 1   Won 1   Lost 0   Drawn 0   PF 47   PA 3

Year	Winner	Score	Venue
1999	South Africa	47–3	Edinburgh

TONGA

Played 2   Won 2   Lost 0   Drawn 0   PF 104   PA 35

Year	Winner	Score	Venue
1997	South Africa	74–10	Cape Town
2007	South Africa	30–25	Lens

UNITED STATES OF AMERICA

Played 3–Won 3–Lost 0–Drawn 0–PF 145–PA 42

Year	Winner	Score	Venue
1981	South Africa	38–7	Glenville
2001	South Africa	43–20	Houston
2007	South Africa	64–15	Montpellier

URUGUAY

Played 3   Won 3   Lost 0   Drawn 0   PF 245   PA 12

Year	Winner	Score	Venue
1999	South Africa	39–3	Glasgow
2003	South Africa	72–6	Perth
2005	South Africa	134–3	East London

WALES

Played 25   Won 23   Lost 1   Drawn 1   PF 698   PA 351

Year	Winner	Score	Venue
1906	South Africa	11–0	Swansea
1912	South Africa	3–0	Cardiff
1931	South Africa	8–3	Swansea
1951	South Africa	6–3	Cardiff
1960	South Africa	3–0	Cardiff
1964	South Africa	24–3	Durban
1970	Drawn	6–6	Cardiff
1994	South Africa	20–12	Cardiff
1995	South Africa	40–11	Johannesburg
1996	South Africa	37–20	Cardiff
1998	South Africa	96–13	Pretoria
1998	South Africa	28–20	London
1999	Wales	19–29	Cardiff
2000	South Africa	23–13	Cardiff
2002	South Africa	34–19	Bloemfontein
2002	South Africa	19–8	Cape Town
2004	South Africa	53–18	Pretoria
2004	South Africa	38–36	Cardiff
2005	South Africa	33–16	Cardiff
2007	South Africa	34–12	Cardiff
2008	South Africa	43–17	Bloemfontein
2008	South Africa	37–21	Pretoria
2008	South Africa	20–15	Cardiff
2010	South Africa	34–31	Cardiff
2010	South Africa	29–25	Cardiff

WORLD TEAMS

Played 3   Won 3   Lost 0   Drawn 0   PF 87   PA 59

Year	Winner	Score	Venue
1977	South Africa	45–24	Pretoria
1989	South Africa	20–19	Cape Town
1989	South Africa	22–16	Johannesburg

INTERNATIONAL TOURS TO SOUTH AFRICA 1891–2010 (excluding tours where only test matches were played)

Year	Tour	Captain	Tour matches	Tests	Total matches	Won	Lost	Drawn	Points for	Points against	Tries for	Tries against
1891	British Isles	WE Maclagan (Scotland)	16	3	19	19	0	0	224	1	89	1
1896	British Isles	JF Hammond (Cambridge University)	17	4	21	19	1	1	310	45	64	10
1903	British Isles	MC Morrison (Scotland)	19	3	22	11	8	3	231	138	49	29
1910	British Isles	T Smyth (Ireland)	21	3	24	13	8	3	290	236	68	54
1924	British Isles	R Cove-Smith (England)	17	4	21	9	9	3	175	155	45	26
1928	New Zealand	MJ Brownlie (Hawke's Bay)	18	4	22	16	5	1	339	144	70	23
1933	Australia	AW Ross (New South Wales)	18	5	23	12	10	1	299	195	67	29
1938	British Isles	S Walker (Ireland)	20	3	23	17	6	0	407	272	79	43
1949	New Zealand	FR Allen (Auckland)	20	4	24	14	7	3	230	146	43	8
1953	Australia	HJ Solomon (New South Wales)	23	4	27	16	10	1	450	413	92	68
1955	British Isles	RH Thompson (Ireland)	20	4	24	18	5	1	418	271	94	39
1958	France	M Celaya (Biarritz)	8	2	10	5	3	2	137	124	26	17
1960	Scotland	GH Waddell (Cambridge University)	2	1	3	2	1	0	61	45	13	9
1960	New Zealand	WJ Whineray (Auckland)	22	4	26	20	4	2	441	164	75	23
1961	Ireland	AR Dawson (Wanderers)	3	1	4	3	1	0	59	36	8	6
1961	Australia	KW Catchpole (New South Wales)	4	2	6	3	2	1	90	80	15	16
1962	British Isles	AR Smith (Scotland)	20	4	24	15	5	4	351	208	62	37
1963	Australia	JE Thornett (New South Wales)	20	4	24	15	8	1	303	233	46	28
1964	Wales	DCT Rowlands (Pontypool)	3	1	4	2	2	0	43	58	5	6
1964	France	M Crauste (Lourdes)	5	1	6	5	1	0	117	55	18	4
1967	France	C Darrouy (Mont-de-Marsan)	9	4	13	8	4	1	209	161	30	23
1968	British Isles	TJ Kiernan (Ireland)	16	4	20	15	4	1	377	181	55	21
1969	Australia	GV Davis (New South Wales)	22	4	26	15	11	0	465	353	78	54
1970	New Zealand	BJ Lochore (Wairarapa)	20	4	24	21	3	0	687	228	135	23
1971	France	C Carrere(Toulon)	7	2	9	7	1	1	228	92	42	9
1972	England	JV Pullin (Bristol)	6	1	7	6	0	1	166	58	23	4
1974	British Isles	WJ McBride (Ireland)	18	4	22	21	0	1	729	207	107	16
1975	France	J Fouroux (La Voulte) & R Astre (Beziers)	9	2	11	6	4	1	282	190	41	20
1976	New Zealand	AR Leslie (Wellington)	20	4	24	18	6	0	610	291	89	27
1977	World Team	WJ McBride (Ireland)	2	1	3	0	3	0	76	142	13	23
1980	South America	H Porta (Argentina)	5	2	7	4	3	0	174	134	23	16
1980	British Isles	WB Beaumont (England)	14	4	18	15	3	0	401	244	47	27
1980	France	J-P Rives (Toulouse)	3	1	4	3	1	0	90	95	13	12
1981	Ireland	JF Slattery (Blackrock College)	5	2	7	3	4	0	207	90	30	10
1982	South America	H Porta (Argentina)	12	2	14	12	1	1	448	179	62	25
1984	England	JP Scott (Cardiff)	5	2	7	4	2	1	156	145	19	18
1984	South America & Spain	H Porta (Argentina)	5	2	7	4	3	0	146	140	17	20
1986	New Zealand Cavaliers	AG Dalton (Counties)	8	4	12	8	4	0	275	229	33	16
1989	World Team	P Berbizier (France)	3	2	5	1	4	0	100	130	14	20
1992	New Zealand	SBT Fitzpatrick (Auckland)	4	1	5	5	0	0	167	79	20	6
1992	Australia	NC Farr-Jones (New South Wales)	3	1	4	4	0	0	130	41	15	4
1993	France	J-F Tordo (Nice)	6	2	8	4	2	2	169	159	14	12
1994	England	WDC Carling (Harlequins)	6	2	8	3	5	0	152	165	11	13
1994	Argentina	MH Lofreda (Buenos Aires)	4	2	6	3	3	0	216	216	27	28
1995	Western Samoa	P Fatialofa (Auckland, New Zealand)	2	1	3	0	3	0	38	104	4	12
1995	Wales	MH Humphreys (Cardiff)	1	1	2	0	2	0	17	87	1	10
1996	Fiji	J Veitayaki (King Country, New Zealand)	1	1	2	1	1	0	62	80	7	9
1996	New Zealand	SBT Fitzpatrick (Auckland)	4	3	7	5	1	1	190	139	24	14
1997	British Isles	MO Johnson (England)	10	3	13	11	2	0	480	278	56	32
1997	Tonga	L Katoa (Siutaka)	3	1	4	2	2	0	77	149	9	23
1998	Ireland	PS Johns (Saracens, England)	5	2	7	2	5	0	126	214	11	26

Year	Tour	Captain	Tour matches	Tests	Total matches	Won	Lost	Drawn	Points for	Points against	Tries for	Tries against
1998	Wales	R Howley (Cardiff)	4	1	5	0	5	0	94	224	9	32
1999	Italy	M Giovanelli (Narbonne, France)	2	2	4	0	4	0	30	267	3	40
2000	England	MO Johnson (Leicester)	3	2	5	4	1	0	183	105	20	6
2001	Italy	A Moscardi (Benetton Treviso)	1	1	2	0	2	0	25	102	2	14
2002	Argentina	A Pichot (Bristol, England)	1	1	2	0	2	0	65	91	7	11
2002	Samoa	S Sititi (Borders, Scotland)	2	1	3	1	2	0	75	117	9	15
2003	Argentina	G Longo (Narbonne, France)	1	1	2	0	1	1	55	56	6	5
2009	British Isles	PJ O'Connell (Ireland)	7	3	10	7	2	1	309	169	34	15
			555	144	699	457	202	40	13461	9150	2188	1187

SPRINGBOK TOURS 1906–2010 (excluding tours where only test matches were played)

Total matches	Won	Lost	Drawn	Pts for	Pts against	Tries for	Tries against
28	25	2	1	553	79	130	19
27	24	3	0	441	101	103	22
23	19	2	2	327	119	74	21
26	23	1	2	407	124	86	23
26	24	2	0	753	169	161	29
31	30	1	0	562	167	120	26
29	22	6	1	520	203	108	31
34	31	1	2	567	132	132	25
5	0	4	1	37	53	7	8
30	22	8	0	669	285	144	42
6	5	1	0	84	43	12	5
24	15	5	4	323	157	59	23
13	13	0	0	396	102	76	11
9	8	1	0	170	74	23	10
6	6	0	0	376	78	66	8
17	14	2	1	535	190	81	16
13	8	5	0	297	236	30	16
12	9	3	0	527	147	75	15
6	5	1	0	243	152	32	11
14	10	3	1	445	241	58	22
13	11	2	0	375	151	50	12
10	8	2	0	367	205	53	19
7	5	2	0	276	155	40	16
8	7	1	0	290	92	42	6
9	6	3	0	253	219	30	20
4	2	2	0	93	76	9	8
2	2	0	0	18	3	2	0
2	1	1	0	39	34	6	5
5	1	4	0	95	91	10	5
5	3	2	0	110	104	10	10
444	359	70	15	10148	3982	1829	484

SPRINGBOK MATCH RECORDS

Highest scores

134–3 v Uruguay East London 2005
105–13 v Namibia Cape Town 2007
101–0 v Italy Durban 1999
96–13 v Wales Pretoria 1998
74–10 v Tonga Cape Town 1997
74–3 v Italy Port Elizabeth 1999
72–6 v Uruguay Perth 2003
68–10 v Scotland Edinburgh 1997
64–15 v USA Montpellier 2007
63–9 v Argentina Johannesburg 2008
62–31 v Italy Bologna 1997
61–22 v Australia Pretoria 1997
60–8 v Western Samoa Johannesburg 1995
60–14 v Italy Port Elizabeth 2001
60–18 v Samoa Pretoria 2002
60–10 v Samoa Brisbane 2003

Biggest wins

131 v Uruguay (134–4) East London 2005
101 v Italy (101–0) Durban 1999
92 v Namibia (105–13) Cape Town 2007
83 v Wales (96–13) Pretoria 1998
71 v Italy (74–3) Port Elizabeth 1999
66 v Uruguay (72–6) Perth 2003
64 v Tonga (74–10) Cape Town 1997
58 v Scotland (68–10) Edinburgh 1997
54 v Argentina (63–9) Johannesburg 2008
52 v Western Samoa (60–8) Johannesburg 1995
52 v Samoa (59–7) Paris 2007
50 v Samoa (60–10) Brisbane 2003

Most tries scored

21 v Uruguay East London 2005
15 v Italy Durban 1999
15 v Wales Pretoria 1998
15 v Namibia Cape Town 2007
12 v Uruguay Perth 2003
12 v Tonga Cape Town 1997
11 v Italy Port Elizabeth 1999
10 v Scotland Edinburgh 1997
10 v Ireland Dublin 1912

Most points conceded

55–35 v New Zealand Auckland 1997
53–3 v England London 2002
52–16 v New Zealand Pretoria 2003
49–0 v Australia Brisbane 2006
45–26 v New Zealand Pretoria 2006
44–23 v Australia Melbourne 2000
41–20 v New Zealand Wellington 2002
41–39 v Australia Bloemfontein 2010
40–46 v New Zealand Johannesburg 2000
38–27 v Australia Brisbane 2002
36–38 v Wales Cardiff 2004
36–26 v France Cape Town 2006
35–32 v New Zealand Johannesburg 1997
35–17 v New Zealand Wellington 2006

Biggest defeats

50 England (3–53) London 2002
49 Australia (0–49) Brisbane 2006
36 New Zealand (16–52) Pretoria 2003
28 New Zealand (0–28) Dunedin 1999
27 New Zealand (6–33) Christchurch 2007
26 Australia (6–32) Brisbane 1999
23 Australia (3–26) Cape Town 1992
21 Australia (23–44) Melbourne 2000
21 New Zealand (20–41) Wellington 2002
20 New Zealand (35–55) Auckland 1997
20 Australia (6–26) Sydney 2000
20 England (9–29) London 2001
20 France (10–30) Marseilles 2002
20 Australia (9–29) Brisbane 2003
20 New Zealand (9–29) Melbourne 2003
20 New Zealand (12–32) Auckland 2010

Most points by a player

35 PC Montgomery v Namibia (1t, 12c, 2p) Cape Town 2007
34 JH de Beer v England (2c, 5p, 5dg) Paris 1999
31 PC Montgomery v Wales (2t, 9c, 1p) Pretoria 1998
31 M Steyn v New Zealand (1t, 1c, 8p) Durban 2009
30 T Chavhanga v Uruguay (6t) East London 2005
29 GS du Toit v Italy (2t, 8c, 1p) Port Elizabeth 1999
29 PC Montgomery v Samoa (2t, 5c, 3p) Paris 2007
28 GK Johnson v W Samoa (3t, 5c, 1p) Johannesburg 1995
26 JH de Beer v Australia (1t, 6c, 3p) Pretoria 1997
26 PC Montgomery v Scotland (2t, 8c) Edinburgh 1997
26 M Steyn v Italy (2t, 5c, 2p) East London 2010
25 JT Stransky v Australia (1t, 1c, 6p) Bloemfontein 1996
25 CS Terblanche v Italy (5t) Durban 1999

Most tries by a player

6 T Chavhanga v Uruguay East London 2005
5 CS Terblanche v Italy Durban 1999
4 CM Williams v W Samoa Johannesburg 1995
4 PWG Rossouw v France Paris 1997
4 CS Terblanche v Ireland Bloemfontein 1998
4 BG Habana v Samoa Paris 2007
4 JL Nokwe v Australia Johannesburg 2008
3 EE McHardy v Ireland Dublin 1912
3 JA Stegmann v Ireland Dublin 1912
3 KT van Vollenhoven v B Isles Cape Town 1955
3 HJ van Zyl v Australia Johannesburg 1961
3 RH Mordt v New Zealand Auckland 1981
3 RH Mordt v USA New York 1981
3 DM Gerber v South America Pretoria 1982
3 DM Gerber v England Johannesburg 1984
3 GK Johnson v W Samoa Johannesburg 1995
3 JH van der Westhuizen v Wales Cardiff 1996
3 AH Snyman v Tonga Cape Town 1997
3 PWG Rossouw v Wales Pretoria 1998
3 BJ Paulse v Italy Port Elizabeth 1999
3 DJ Kayser v Italy Durban 1999
3 JH van der Westhuizen v Uruguay Perth 2003
3 MC Joubert v New Zealand Johannesburg 2004
3 JH Smith v Namibia Cape Town 2007
3 SWP Burger v Namibia Cape Town 2007

Most conversions by a player

12 PC Montgomery v Namibia Cape Town 2007
9 PC Montgomery v Wales Pretoria 1998
9 AD James v Argentina Johannesburg 2008
8 PC Montgomery v Scotland Edinburgh 1997
8 GS du Toit v Italy Port Elizabeth 1999
8 GS du Toit v Italy Durban 1999

Most penalty goals by a player

8 M Steyn v New Zealand Durban 2009
7 PC Montgomery v Scotland Port Elizabeth 2006
7 PC Montgomery v France Cape Town 2006
7 M Steyn v Australia Cape Town 2009
6 GR Bosch v France Pretoria 1975
6 JT Stransky v Australia Bloemfontein 1996
6 JH de Beer v Australia London 1999
6 AJJ van Straaten v England Pretoria 2000
6 AJJ van Straaten v Australia Durban 2000
6 PC Montgomery v France Johannesburg 2001
6 LJ Koen v Scotland Johannesburg 2003
6 M Steyn v Australia Bloemfontein 2010

Most drop goals by a player

5 JH de Beer v England Paris 1999
4 AS Pretorius v England London 2006
3 HE Botha v South America Durban 1980
3 HE Botha v Ireland Durban 1981
3 JNB van der Westhuyzen v Scotland Edinburgh 2004

Scored all points in a test (>15)

31* M Steyn v New Zealand Durban 2009
25 JT Stransky v Australia Bloemfontein 1996
21 JH de Beer v Australia London 1999
18 AJJ van Straaten v England Pretoria 2000
18 AJJ van Straaten v Australia Durban 2000
17 AJJ van Straaten v England London 2000
World Record

Scored in all four ways in a test

22 JT Stransky (22 pts–1t, 1c, 4p, 1dg) v Australia 1995
18 AS Pretorius (18 pts–1t, 2c, 2p, 1dg) v New Zealand 2002
21 DJ Hougaard (21 pts–1t, 5c, 1p, 1dg) v Samoa 2003

Most points by a player against SA

29 SA Mortlock, Australia (2t, 2c, 5p) Melbourne 2000
27 CR Andrew, England (1t, 2c, 5p, 1d) Pretoria 1994
27 JP Wilkinson, England (8p, 1d) Bloemfontein 2000
27 G Merceron, France (1t, 2c, 6p) Johannesburg 2001
27 CC Hodgson, England (1t, 2c, 5p, 1d) London 2004
25 CJ Spencer, New Zealand (1t, 4c, 4p) Auckland 1997
25 DW Carter, New Zealand (2c, 7p) Wellington 2006
24 MC Burke, Australia (8p) London 1999
23 DW Carter, New Zealand (1t, 3c, 4p) Christchurch 2007
23 DW Carter, New Zealand (1c, 6p, 1d) Dunedin 2008

Most tries by a player against SA

2 HS Sugars (Ireland) Belfast 1906
2 JL Sullivan (New Zealand) Christchurch 1937
2 IST Smith (New Zealand) Auckland 1965
2 B Dauga (France) Bordeaux 1968
2 JJ Williams (British Isles) Pretoria 1974
2 JJ Williams (British Isles) Port Elizabeth 1974
2 J–L Averous (France) Pretoria 1977
2 PV Carozza (Australia) Cape Town 1992
2 A Penaud (France) Lyon 1992
2 JS Little (Australia) Brisbane 1993
2 JW Wilson (New Zealand) Pretoria 1996
2 FE Bunce (New Zealand) Johannesburg 1997
2 BN Tune (Australia) Brisbane 1997

2 CM Cullen (New Zealand) Auckland 1997
2 JW Roff (Australia) Brisbane 1999
2 CM Cullen (New Zealand) Pretoria 1999
2 SA Mortlock (Australia) Melbourne 2000
2 CM Cullen (New Zealand) Christchurch 2000
2 CM Cullen (New Zealand) Johannesburg 2000
2 JF Umaga (New Zealand) Johannesburg 2000
2 CE Latham (Australia) Brisbane 2000
2 WJH Greenwood (England) London 2000
2 JT Rokocoko (New Zealand) Pretoria 2003
2 DC Howlett (New Zealand) Pretoria 2003
2 S Sivivatu (Pacific Islands) Gosford 2004
2 GL Henson (Wales) Cardiff 2004
2 MJ Giteau (Australia) Sydney 2005
2 JT Rokocoko (New Zealand) Dunedin 2005
2 V Clerc (France) Cape Town 2006
2 MJ Giteau (Australia) Brisbane 2006
2 T Croft (British Isles) Durban 2009
2 SM Williams (British Isles) Johannesburg 2009
2 MJ Giteau (Australia) Perth 2009
2 JD O'Connor (Australia) Pretoria 2010
2 G North (Wales) Cardiff 2010

Most conversions by a player against SA

5 SA Mortlock (Australia) Brisbane 2006

Most penalty goals by a player against SA

8 MC Burke (Australia) London 1999
8 JP Wilkinson (England) Bloemfontein 2000
7 AP Mehrtens (New Zealand) Pretoria 1999
6 JP Wilkinson (England) London 2000
6 G Merceron (France) Johannesburg 2001
6 DW Carter (New Zealand) Dunedin 2008
6 DA Parks (Scotland) Edinburgh 2010

Most drop goals by a player against SA

2 G Camberabero (France) Johannesburg 1967
2 P Bennett (British Isles) Port Elizabeth 1974
2 JP Wilkinson (England) Perth 2003

SPRINGBOK SEASON RECORDS

BY THE TEAM

Most conversions

62 17 tests 3.7 per game 2007
54 13 tests 4.2 per game 1997

Most penalty goals

46 14 tests 3.3 per game 2010
42 12 tests 3.5 per game 2009
41 17 tests 2.4 per game 2007
40 13 tests 3.1 per game 1996

Most drop goals

8 13 tests 1999

Most consecutive wins

17 August 1997 to November 1998

Most consecutive defeats

7 July 1964 to August 1965

Most consecutive matches without conceding a try

5 1999

Most consecutive matches without scoring a try

4 1891 to 1896 & 1972 to 1974

BY A PLAYER

Most points

219 PC Montgomery in 14 tests (5t, 52c, 30p) 2007
185 M Steyn in 13 tests (3t, 24c, 40p) 2010
158 PC Montgomery in 12 tests (1t, 24c, 32p, 3d) 2005
154 PC Montgomery in 11 tests (1t, 28c, 31p) 2004
137 M Steyn in 12 tests (1t, 12c, 31p, 5d) 2009
136 AJJ van Straaten in 11 tests (2t, 12c, 34p) 2000
120 LJ Koen in 11 tests (15c, 28p, 2d) 2003
112 JT Stransky in 9 tests (2t, 12c, 23p, 3d) 1995
111 PC Montgomery in 12 tests (2t, 25c, 17p) 1998
102 JH de Beer in 6 tests (18c, 16p, 6d) 1999
102 AS Pretorius in 10 tests (2t, 22c, 15p,1d) 2002

Most tries

13 BG Habana in 11 tests 2007
12 BG Habana in 12 tests 2005
10 PWG Rossouw in 11 tests 1997
9 CS Terblanche in 12 tests 1998
9 J Fourie in 12 tests 2007
8 JT Small in 7 tests 1993
8 CM Williams in 6 tests 1995
8 PC Montgomery in 10 tests 1997
8 JH van der Westhuizen in 12 tests 1998
8 JH Smith in 13 tests 2007

Most conversions

52 PC Montgomery in 14 tests 2007
28 PC Montgomery in 11 tests 2004
25 PC Montgomery in 12 tests 1998
25 M Steyn in 13 tests 2010
24 PC Montgomery in 12 tests 2005
23 HW Honiball in 12 tests 1997
22 AS Pretorius in 10 tests 2002

Most penalty goals

40 M Steyn in 13 tests 2010
34 AJJ van Straaten in 11 tests 2000
32 PC Montgomery in 12 tests 2005
31 PC Montgomery in 11 tests 2004
31 M Steyn in 12 tests 2009
30 PC Montgomery in 14 tests 2007

Most drop goals

6 HE Botha in 9 tests 1980
6 JH de Beer in 6 tests 1999
5 HE Botha in 6 tests 1981
5 AS Pretorius in 6 tests 2006
5 M Steyn in 12 tests 2009

SPRINGBOK CAREER RECORDS

Most test match appearances

105 V Matfield 2001–2010
102 PC Montgomery 1997–2008
102 JW Smit 2000–2010
89 JH van der Westhuizen 1993–2003
80 JP du Randt 1994–2007

77 MG Andrews 1994–2001
72 JP Botha 2002–2010
69 JH Smith 2003–2010
69 CJ van der Linde 2002–2010
68 BG Habana 2004–2010
67 J de Villiers 2002–2010
66 AG Venter 1996–2001
64 BJ Paulse 1999–2007
63 SWP Burger 2003–2010
62 J Fourie 2003–2010
55 PF du Preez 2004–2009
54 A-H le Roux 1994–2002
54 DJ Rossouw 2003–2010
52 JC van Niekerk 2001–2010
51 PA van den Berg 1999–2007

Most appearances in all Springbok matches

111 JH van der Westhuizen 1993–2003
109 V Matfield 2001–2010
104 PC Montgomery 1997–2008
103 JW Smit 2000–2010
90 MG Andrews 1994–2001
87 FCH du Preez 1961–1971
85 JP du Randt 1994–2007
79 JFK Marais 1963–1974

Most points in all Springbok matches

906 PC Montgomery (104 matches) 1997–2008
485 HE Botha (40 matches) 1980–1992
329 JT Stransky (36 maches) 1993–1996
322 M Steyn (25 matches) 2009–2010
294 AJJ van Straaten (27 matches) 1999–2001
293 GH Brand (46 matches) 1928–1938
280 JH van der Westhuizen (111 matches) 1993–2003
258 AJ Joubert (49 matches) 1989–1997
240 PJ Visagie (44 matches) 1967–1971
201 K Oxlee (48 matches) 1960–1965

Most tries in test matches

38 JH van der Westhuizen (89 tests) 1993–2003
38 BG Habana (68 tests) 2004–2010
30 J Fourie (62 tests) 2003–2010
26 BJ Paulse (64 tests) 1999–2007
25 PC Montgomery (102 tests) 1997–2008
21 PWG Rossouw (43 tests) 1997–2003
20 JT Small (47 tests) 1992–1997
19 DM Gerber (24 tests) 1980–1992
19 CS Terblanche (37 tests) 1998–2003
19 J de Villiers (67 tests) 2002–2010

Most tries in all Springbok matches

56 JH van der Westhuizen (111 matches) 1993–2003
44 JP Engelbrecht (67 matches) 1960–1969
39 BJ Paulse (74 matches) 1999–2007
38 BG Habana (70 matches) 2004–2010
32 JH Ellis (74 matches) 1965–1976
31 JL Gainsford (71 matches) 1960–1967
30 J Fourie (64 matches) 2003–2010

Most penalty goals in test matches

148 PC Montgomery (102 tests) 1997–2008
71 M Steyn (25 tests) 2009–2010
55 AJJ van Straaten (21 tests) 1999–2001
50 HE Botha (28 tests) 1980–1992

Most drop goals in test matches

18 HE Botha (28 tests) 1980–1992
8 JH de Beer (13 tests) 1997–1999
8 AS Pretorius (31 tests) 2002–2007
6 PC Montgomery (102 tests) 1997–2008
5 JD Brewis (10 tests) 1949–1953
5 PJ Visagie (25 tests) 1967–1971
5 M Steyn (25 tests) 2009–2010

Most drop goals in all Springbok matches

27 HE Botha (40 matches) 1980–1992
8 BL Osler (30 matches) 1924–1933
8 PJ Visagie (44 matches) 1967–1971
8 JH de Beer (14 matches) 1997–1999
8 AS Pretorius (33 matches) 2002–2007

Most test match appearances against SA

30 GM Gregan (Australia) 1994–2007
23 SJ Larkham (Australia) 1996–2007
22 JW Marshall (New Zealand) 1995–2005
22 GB Smith (Australia) 2000–2009
21 JM Muliaina (New Zealand) 2003–2010

Most drop goals in tests against SA

4 AP Mehrtens (New Zealand) (16 tests) 1995–2004
3 JP Wilkinson (England) (9 tests) 1998–2007
3 RJR O'Gara (Ireland) (6 tests) 2000–2010

SPRINGBOK MISCELLANEOUS RECORDS

Most test match appearances in each position

Fullback PC Montgomery[1] 87
Wing BG Habana[2] 67
Centre J de Villiers[3] 53
Flyhalf AD James 36
Scrumhalf JH van der Westhuizen 87
Prop JP du Randt 80
Hooker JW Smit 87
Lock V Matfield 105
Flank SWP Burger 61
Eighthman GH Teichmann 42
Captain JW Smit 76*

1. Also made nine appearances as a centre, five as flyhalf and one as a wing.
2. Also made one appearance as a centre.
3. Also made 14 appearances as a wing. Also made three appearances as a centre and one as a fullback. Also made two appearances as a replacement wing. Also made two appearances as a replacement prop and 13 as a prop in the starting 15. Also made two appearances as a No 8.
*World record

Most consecutive test match appearances

By position

Fullback PC Montgomery (1997–1999) 24
Wing PWG Rossouw (1997–1999) 24
Centre JL Gainsford (1961–1967) 23
Flyhalf BL Osler (1924–1933) 17
HE Botha (1980–1982) 17
JNB van der Westhuyzen (2004–2005) 17
Scrumhalf PF du Preez (2004–2006) 21
Prop A–H le Roux (1998–1999) 25
Hooker JW Smit (2003–2007) 46
Lock V Matfield (2008–2010) 28
Flank RJ Kruger (1995–1997) 22
Eighthman GH Teichmann (1996–1999) 39
Captain JW Smit (2004–2007) 43

Most consecutive test match appearances

46 JW Smit (hooker) 2003–2007
39 GH Teichmann (eighthman) 1996–1999
28 V Matfield (lock) 2008–2010
26 AH Snyman (centre/wing) 1996–1998
26 AN Vos (eighthman/flank) 1999–2001

Most test match tries in each position

Fullback 18 PC Montgomery *87 tests
Wing 38 BG Habana *67 tests
Centre 26 J Fourie *51 tests
Flyhalf 6 PJ Visgaie 25 tests

6 JT Stransky *21 tests

Scrumhalf 38 JH van der Westhuizen *87 tests

Prop 5 AC Koch 22 tests

5 JP du Randt 80 tests

5 GG Steenkamp 31 tests

Hooker 5 J Dalton 43 tests

5 BW du Plessis *35 tests

Lock 12 MG Andrews *75 tests

Flank 11 SWP Burger *61 tests

11 JH Smith *59 tests

Eighthman 7 PJ Spies *35 tests

*Excludes tests played in other positions

Longest international career

14 seasons JP du Randt (1994–2007) 13 years, 12 days

13 seasons HE Botha (1980–1992) 12 years, 202 days

13 seasons DM Gerber (1980–1992) 12 years, 27 days

13 seasons BH Heatlie (1891–1903) 12 years, 14 days

13 seasons JM Powell (1891–1903) 12 years, 7 days

Most test matches as a replacement   Total tests

	Total tests
43 A–H le Roux	54
31 CJ van der Linde	69
29 PA van den Berg	51
28 R Pienaar	47
19 DJ Rossouw	54
18 JC van Niekerk	52

Oldest living Springboks*

P Malan b 13/02/1919 91 years, 321 days

WHM Barnard b 07/08/1923 87 years, 146 days

C Moss b 12/02/1925 85 years, 322 days

MT Lategan b 29/09/1925 85 years, 93 days

RP Bekker b 15/12/1926 84 years, 16 days

*Age as at 31/12/2010

Most appearances as a test match combination

Fullback/wings PC Montgomery, CS Terblanche & PWG Rossouw
   (1998–1999) 13

Centre pair J de Villiers & J Fourie (2005–2010) 22

Halfbacks JH van der Westhuizen & HW Honiball (1993–1999) 24

Locks V Matfield & JP Botha (2003–2010) 60*

Front row EP Andrews, JP du Randt & JW Smit (2004–2006) 14

Loose forwards AG Venter, RJ Kruger & GH Teichmann (1996–1997) 14

AG Venter, J Erasmus & GH Teichmann (1997–1999) 14

*World record

Springboks sent off in tests (7)

Player	Opponent	Referee	Venue	Date
JT Small	v Australia	EF Morrison (England)	Brisbane	1993
J Dalton	v Canada	DTM McHugh (Ireland)	Port Elizabeth	1995
AG Venter	v New Zealand	WD Bevan (Wales)	Auckland	1997
B Venter	v Uruguay	PL Marshall (Australia)	Glasgow	1999
MC Joubert	v Australia	PD O'Brien (New Zealand)	Johannesburg	2002
JJ Labuschagne	v England	PD O'Brien (New Zealand)	London	2002
PC Montgomery*	v Wales	SJ Dickinson (Australia)	Cardiff	2005

*Montgomery's first yellow card was subsequently dismissed by a disciplinary commission
and his red card rescinded.

Players sent off in tests against South Africa (3)

Player	Team	Referee	Venue	Date
R Snow	Canada	DTM McHugh (Ireland)	Port Elizabeth	1995
GL Rees	Canada	DTM McHugh (Ireland)	Port Elizabeth	1995
GR Jenkins	Wales	J Dumé (France)	Johannesburg	1995

South Africa's affiliated rugby unions and their early clubs

Western Province Rugby Football Union 1883
Hamilton Rugby Club 1875
Diocesan Rugby Football Club 1875
Villagers Rugby Club 1876
Stellenbosch Rugby Club 1880
Gardens Rugby Football Club 1882
SA College Rugby Football Club 1882

Griqualand West Rugby Football Union 1986
Kimberley Rugby Football Club 1870s (records of matches
and tours exist but no firm date of establishment)
West End 1872/73 (first match played 1873)
De Beers 1883
Pirates Rugby Club 1884
Beaconsfield 1886

Eastern Province Rugby Union 1888
Olympics 1880
Crusaders 1887
Uitenhage Swifts 1892
Albany 1893

Natal Rugby Football Union 1890
Wanderers (Pietermaritzburg) 1890
Savages (1889, but as an Association/Rugby Club)
Dragoons 1890
Hussars 1891
Wasps 1891
Berea 1891

Border Rugby Football Union 1891
Alberts RFC 1878
Buffalo 1880
Queenstown Swifts 1882
Pirates 1889

Transvaal RFU 1889
Potchefstroom Dorp 1885
Rand Wanderers 1887

Pirates 1888
Pretoria 1888
West Rand 1892
Diggers 1893

Orange Free State and Basutoland RFU 1895
No records of establishment dates exist. However, matches
were played in the late 1870s, and in the 1880s Pirates,
Bloemfontein (later Ramblers) and Railways were the
apparent leading clubs. They competed with St Andrew's
(initially) and later Grey College.

South Western Districts Rugby Union 1899
Swellendam (possibly 10 years older than Hamilton,
officially regarded as South Africa's first club. Records of
the Swellendam Club were destroyed in a fire in 1865.)

Unions established after 1900
Western Transvaal Rugby Union 1920
Northern Transvaal Rugby Union 1938
Boland Rugby Union 1939
Eastern Transvaal Rugby Union 1947
Northern Free State Rugby Union 1968
South Eastern Transvaal Rugby Union 1969

Rhodesia and South West Africa (SWA) were also affiliated
to the SA Rugby Football Union.

SWA affiliated as the Damaraland RFU in 1922. Their first
Springbok was wing Sias Swart in 1955 while flank Jan Ellis
is the best-known rugby player from SWA and represented
South Africa in 38 tests – a record until the 1990s.

Rhodesia (including Northern Rhodesia which is now
Zambia) produced a number of players who represented
South Africa as Springboks, including Des van Jaarsveldt
who captained the Springboks in 1960.

(Also see chapter 4 for the early black rugby clubs that were not part of
these rugby unions)

CURRIE CUP SEMI-FINALS

Year	Winners		Losers		Venue
1954	Northern Transvaal	9	Free State	8	Free State Stadium, Bloemfontein
1956	Natal	11	Western Province	10	Newlands, Cape Town
1969	Western Province	13	Boland	11	Newlands, Cape Town
1970	Northern Transvaal	24	Natal	8	King's Park, Durban
1971	Transvaal	23	Natal	10	Ellis Park, Johannesburg
1972	Free State	19	Western Province	15	Newlands, Cape Town
1973	Northern Transvaal	20	Rhodesia	7	Loftus Versfeld, Pretoria
1974	Transvaal	30	Eastern Province	6	Ellis Park, Johannesburg
1979	Northern Transvaal	16	Eastern Province	6	Boet Erasmus, Port Elizabeth
	Western Province	20	Griqualand West	15	De Beers Stadium, Kimberley
1980	Northern Transvaal	49	SE Transvaal	6	Loftus Versfeld, Pretoria
	Western Province	21	Eastern Province	13	Boet Erasmus, Port Elizabeth
1981	Northern Transvaal	36	Northern Free State	12	Loftus Versfeld, Pretoria
	Free State	28	Eastern Transvaal	15	Pam Brink Stadium, Springs
1982	Western Province	47	Natal	18	Newlands, Cape Town
	Northern Transvaal	24	Northern Free State	21	North West Stadium, Welkom
1983	Western Province	7	Natal	3	King's Park, Durban
	Northern Transvaal	32	Northern Free State	15	Loftus Versfeld, Pretoria
1984	Natal	26	Free State	15	King's Park, Durban
	Western Province	53	Eastern Transvaal	0	Newlands, Cape Town
1986	Transvaal	18	Natal	4	King's Park, Durban
1987	Transvaal	12	South West Africa	9	National Stadium, Windhoek
1988	Western Province	26	Northern Free State	9	North West Stadium, Welkom
1989	Western Province	71	Western Transvaal	9	Olën Park, Potchefstroom
1996	Natal	35	Free State	20	King's Park, Durban
	Transvaal	31	Northern Transvaal	21	Loftus Versfeld, Pretoria
1997	Western Province	38	Lions	18	Newlands, Cape Town
	Cheetahs	40	Natal	22	King's Park, Durban
1998	Western Province	27	Griqualand West	11	Hoffe Park, Kimberley
	Blue Bulls	31	Natal Sharks	17	Loftus Versfeld, Pretoria
1999	Lions	81	SWD Eagles	21	Ellis Park, Johannesburg
	Natal Sharks	45	Cheetahs	8	King's Park, Durban
2000	Natal Sharks	29	Cheetahs	15	Absa Stadium, Durban
	Western Province	43	Lions	22	Newlands, Cape Town
2001	Western Province	40	Cheetahs	18	Newlands, Cape Town
	Natal Sharks	16	Lions	9	Absa Stadium, Durban
2002	Lions	43	Cheetahs	29	Vodacom Park, Bloemfontein
	Blue Bulls	22	Natal Sharks	19	Absa Stadium, Durban
2004	Blue Bulls	40	Lions	33	Loftus Versfeld, Pretoria
	Cheetahs	17	Western Province	11	Newlands, Cape Town
2005	Cheetahs	16	Western Province	11	Newlands, Cape Town
	Blue Bulls	31	Lions	23	Loftus Versfeld, Pretoria
2006	Blue Bulls	45	Western Province	30	Loftus Versfeld, Pretoria
	Cheetahs	30	Natal Sharks	14	Vodacom Park, Bloemfontein
2007	Lions	19	Sharks	12	Absa Stadium, Durban
	Cheetahs	11	Blue Bulls	6	Vodacom Park, Bloemfontein
2008	Sharks	29	Lions	14	Absa Stadium, Durban
	Blue Bulls	31	Cheetahs	19	Loftus Versfeld, Pretoria
2009	Cheetahs	23	Sharks	21	Absa Stadium, Durban
	Blue Bulls	21	Western Province	19	Newlands, Cape Town
2010	Sharks	16	Blue Bulls	12	Absa Stadium, Durban
	Western Province	31	Cheetahs	7	Newlands, Cape Town

CURRIE CUP WINNERS

Various league systems from 1892 to 1936

Season	Winners		
1892	Western Province	Tournament	Kimberley
1894	Western Province	Tournament	Cape Town
1895	Western Province	Tournament	Johannesburg
1897	Western Province	Tournament	Port Elizabeth
1898	Western Province	Tournament	Cape Town
1899	Griquas	Tournament	Kimberley
1904	Western Province	Tournament	East London
1906	Western Province	Tournament	Johannesburg
1908	Western Province	Tournament	Port Elizabeth
1911	Griquas	Tournament	Cape Town
1914	Western Province	Tournament	Durban
1920	Western Province	Tournament	Bloemfontein & Kimberley
1922	Transvaal	League	
1925	Western Province	League	
1927	Western Province	League	
1929	Western Province	League	
1932	Border/Western Province	League	
1934	Border/Western Province	League	
1936	Western Province	League	

Finals from 1939 (with two exceptions*)

1939	Transvaal	16–6	Western Province	Newlands
1946	Northern Transvaal	11–9	Western Province	Loftus Versfeld
1947	Western Province	16–12	Transvaal	Newlands
1950	Transvaal	22–11	Western Province	Ellis Park
1952	Boland	11–9	Transvaal	Boland Stadium
1954	Western Province	11 8	Northern Transvaal	Newlands
1956	Northern Transvaal	9–8	Natal	King's Park
1957–59*	Western Province	League	Decided over two seasons (1957 and 1959)	
			Thereafter no Currie Cup until 1964	
1964*	Western Province	League		
1968	Northern Transvaal	16–3	Transvaal	Loftus Versfeld
1969	Northern Transvaal	28–13	Western Province	Loftus Versfeld
1970	Griquas	11–9	Northern Transvaal	De Beers
1971	Transvaal	14–14	Northern Transvaal	Ellis Park
1972	Transvaal	25–19	Eastern Transvaal	PAM Brink
1973	Northern Transvaal	30–22	Orange Free State	Loftus Versfeld
1974	Northern Transvaal	17–15	Transvaal	Loftus Versfeld
1975	Northern Transvaal	12–6	Orange Free State	Free State Stadium
1976	Orange Free State	33–16	Western Province	Free State Stadium
1977	Northern Transvaal	27–12	Orange Free State	Loftus Versfeld
1978	Northern Transvaal	13–9	Orange Free State	Free State Stadium
1979	Western Province	15–15	Northern Transvaal	Newlands
1980	Northern Transvaal	39–9	Western Province	Loftus Versfeld
1981	Northern Transvaal	23–6	Orange Free State	Loftus Versfeld
1982	Western Province	24–7	Northern Transvaal	Newlands
1983	Western Province	9–3	Northern Transvaal	Loftus Versfeld

1984	Western Province	19–9	Northern Transvaal	Newlands
1985	Western Province	22–15	Northern Transvaal	Newlands
1986	Western Province	22–9	Transvaal	Newlands
1987	Northern Transvaal	24–18	Transvaal	Ellis Park
1988	Northern Transvaal	19–18	Western Province	Loftus Versfeld
1989	Northern Transvaal	16–16	Western Province	Newlands
1990	Natal	18–12	Northern Transvaal	Loftus Versfeld
1991	Northern Transvaal	27–15	Transvaal	Loftus Versfeld
1992	Natal	14–13	Transvaal	Ellis Park
1993	Gauteng Lions	21–15	Natal	King's Park
1994	Gauteng Lions	56–35	Orange Free State	Springbok Park
1995	Natal Sharks	25–17	Western Province	King's Park
1996	Natal Sharks	33–15	Golden Lions	Ellis Park
1997	Western Province	14–12	Free State Cheetahs	Newlands
1998	Blue Bulls	24–20	Western Province	Loftus Versfeld
1999	Golden Lions	32–9	Natal Sharks	King's Park
2000	Western Province	25–15	Natal Sharks	Absa Stadium
2001	Western Province	29–24	Natal Sharks	Newlands
2002	Blue Bulls	31–7	Golden Lions	Ellis Park
2003	Blue Bulls	40–19	Natal Sharks	Loftus Versfeld
2004	Blue Bulls	42–33	Free State Cheetahs	Loftus Versfeld
2005	Free State Cheetahs	29–25	Blue Bulls	Loftus Versfeld
2006	Free State Cheetahs	28–28	Blue Bulls	Vodacom Park
2007	Free State Cheetahs	20–18	Golden Lions	Vodacom Park
2008	Natal Sharks	14–9	Blue Bulls	Absa Stadium, Durban
2009	Blue Bulls	36–24	Cheetahs	Loftus Versfeld
2010	Sharks	30–10	Western Province	King's Park

CURRIE CUP FINAL RECORDS

Scores of more than 30 points

56 Transvaal v Orange Free State, 1994 final score 56–33*
42 Blue Bulls v FS Cheetahs, 2004 final score 42–33
40 Blue Bulls v Sharks, 2003 final score 40–19
39 Northern Transvaal v WP, 1980 final score 39–9
36 Blue Bulls v FS Cheetahs, 2009 final score 36–24
33 Free State v WP, 1976 final score 33–16
33 Free State v Lions, 1994 final score 33–56
33 Sharks v Lions, 1996 final score 33–15
33 FS Cheetahs v Blue Bulls, 2004 final score 33–42

*The match aggregate of 89 points is also a finals record

Five tries or more

7 Lions v Orange Free State 1994
6 Blue Bulls v Cheetahs 2004
5 Blue Bulls v WP 1980
5 Lions v Sharks 1999
5 Blue Bulls v Sharks 2003

20 points or more by a player

26 Derick Hougaard, Blue Bulls v Lions 2002
    (1 try, 5 penalties, 2 drop goals)
25 Patrick Lambie, Sharks v WP 2010
    (2 tries, 3 conversions, 3 penalties)
24 Naas Botha, Blue Bulls v Lions 1987
    (4 penalties, 4 drop goals)
    Braam van Straaten, WP v Sharks 2001
    (1 try, 2 conversions, 5 penalties)
21 Gavin Johnson, Lions v Free State 1994
    (6 conversions, 3 penalties)
    Morné Steyn, Blue Bulls v FS Cheetahs 2009
    (3 conversions, 4 penalties, a drop goal)
20 Thierry Lacroix, Natal v WP 1995
    (6 penalties, 1 conversion)

Six conversions by a player

6 Gavin Johnson, Lions v Cheetahs 1994

Six penalty goals by a player

6 Thierry Lacroix, Natal v WP 1995

Four drop goals by a player

4 Naas Botha, Northern Transvaal v Transvaal 1987

40 points or more in finals

138 Naas Botha 1t, 10c, 20p, 18dg 1977-1991
 62 Willem de Waal 7c, 16p 2004-2010
 54 Morné Steyn 6c, 12p, 2dg 2005-2009
 45 Calla Scholtz 1t, 4c, 9p, 2dg 1983-1988
 44 Derick Hougaard 1t, 3c, 8p, 3dg 2002-2006
 41 Joel Stransky 1c, 13p 1990-1995

Three tries in final

4 Ettienne Botha Blue Bulls 2003-2004
3 Neil Burger WP 1982-1985
3 Edrich Krantz FS & Tvl 1976-1980

CURRIE CUP MATCH RECORDS

More than 110 points

147 Blue Bulls v SWD (147-8) Pietersburg 1996
113 Cheetahs v SWD (113-11) Bloemfontein 1996
111 Pumas v SWD (111-14) Witbank 2001

Wins by 100 points

139 Blue Bulls v SWD (147-8) Pietersburg 1996
106 Cheetahs v NFS (106-0) Bloemfontein 1997
102 Cheetahs v SWD (113-11) Bloemfontein 1996
102 SWD Eagles v NFS (102-0) George 1999

16 tries

23 Blue Bulls v SWD (147-8) 1996
18 Western Transvaal v E.OFS (103-9) 1988
16 Transvaal v Far North (99-9) 1973
16 SWD Eagles v NFS (102-0) 1999
16 Pumas v SWD Eagles (111-14) 2001

35 or more points by a player

46 Jannie de Beer (3t, 14c, 1p) FS Cheetahs v NFS 1997
40 Casper Steyn (2t, 3c, 8p) Blue Bulls v SWD 2000
38 Henry Honiball (4t, 6c, 2p) Sharks v Boland 1996
    Lance Sherrell (2t, 14c) Blue Bulls v SWD 1996
37 Casper Steyn (2t, 3c, 7p) Pumas v FS Cheetahs 2003
36 Gerald Bosch (1t, 13c, 2dg) Tvl v FN 1973
    Eric Herbert (3c, 9p, 1dg) NFS v Valke 1997
    Casper Steyn (1t, 7c, 7p) Blue Bulls v Pumas 2000
35 Jacques Olivier (7t) Blue Bulls v SWD 1996
    Kennedy Tsimba (1t, 9c, 4p) FS Cheetahs v Griquas 2003
    Braam Pretorius (2t, 11c, 1p) Pumas v Valke 2009

Six tries by a player

7 Jacques Olivier N Tvl v SWD (147-8) 1996
6 Buks Marais Boland v NED (33-3) 1952

14 conversions by a player

14 Lance Sherrell N Tvl v SWD 1996
14 Jannie de Beer FS Cheetahs v NFS 1997
14 Nel Fourie Pumas v SWD Eagles 2001

Nine penalty goals by a player

9 Eric Herbert NFS v Valke 1997
9 Derick Hougaard Blue Bulls v WP 2002

Five drop goals by a player

5 Naas Botha N Tvl v Natal 1992

50 conversions

62 Louis Koen WP 1997
55 Jannie de Beer FS Cheetahs 1997
54 Braam Pretorius Pumas 2009

40 penalties

50 Willem de Waal WP 2010
48 Gavin Lawless Lions 1996
45 Lance Sherrell WP 1991
    Johan Heunis N Tvl 1987
    Cameron Oliver Transvaal 1989
42 Cameron Oliver Transvaal 1990
    Andre Joubert FS 1989

20 drop goals

20 Naas Botha N Tvl 1985

CURRIE CUP SEASON RECORDS

750 points

792 Natal 15 matches 1996
783 Northern Transvaal 13 matches 1996

100 tries by a team

112 Natal Sharks 15 matches 1996
102 Northern Transvaal 13 matches 1996

250 points by a player

268 Johan Heunis N Tvl 1989
263 Gavin Lawless Transvaal 1996
252 Casper Steyn Blue Bulls 1999

15 tries

21 Bjorn Basson Griquas 2010
19 Carel du Plessis WP 1989
19 Colin Lloyd Leopards 2006
18 Ettienne Botha Blue Bulls 2004
18 Alistair Kettledas Pumas 2009
16 Jan-Harm van Wyk FS 1997
16 Ryno Benjamin Boland 2006
15 Philip Burger FS Cheetahs 2006

CURRIE CUP CAREER RECORDS

100 matches

142 Helgard Müller FS 1983–1998
141 Rudi Visagie
     FS, Natal, SE-TVL 1980–1996
136 Chris Badenhorst FS, Natal, SE-TVL 1986–1999
128 Burger Geldenhuys N Tvl 1977–1989
     Ollie le Roux FS & Natal Sharks 1993–2007
126 André Joubert FS & Natal Sharks 1986–1999
125 Eric Herbert NFS & FS Cheetahs 1986–2001
123 Naas Botha N Tvl 1977–1992
118 Willie Meyer EP, FS, Lions 1989–2002
115 AJ Venter FS Cheetahs, Lions & Sharks 1997–2008
114 Piet Krause Lions, GW, BB, Valke 1996–2007
     Bevin Fortuin SWD, FS Cheetahs 2000–2010
     Louis Strydom Griffons, Blue Bulls,
     Valke, Lions, FS Cheetahs 2001–2010
113 Skipper Badenhorst Valke, Pumas, Sharks, FS Cheetahs 2000–2010
112 Stefan Terblanche Boland, Sharks 1996–2010
112 Louis Moolman N Tvl 1974–1986
111 Jacques Botes Pumas, Sharks 2002–2010
     Willem de Waal Leopards, FS Cheetahs, WP 2003–2010
110 Justin Peach EP, Boland 2001–2010
108 Eddie Fredericks Leopards, FS Cheetahs, NFS 1998–2010
106 Gavin Passens Griffons, Pumas, Blue Bulls,
     FS Cheetahs, Griquas 1999–2010
     Kabamba Floors SWD, FS Cheetahs 2003–2010
     Martiens le Roux FS 1973–1986
     De Wet Ras FS & Natal 1974–1986

104 Gerrie Sonnekus FS 1974–1985
103 Uli Schmidt N Tvl & Tvl 1983–1994
     Albert van den Berg GW & Sharks 1996–2009
102 Adolf Malan N Tvl 1983–1992
     John Daniels Boland, Lions 1998–2008
     Adi Jacobs Valke, Sharks 2001–2010
101 Gysie Pienaar FS 1974–1987
     Hendro Scholtz FS Cheetahs 1999–2010

1000 points

1699 Naas Botha N Transvaal 1977–1992
1433 Willem de Waal FS Cheetahs, WP 2002–2010
1402 Eric Herbert NFS, FS Cheetahs 1986–2001
1210 De Wet Ras FS & Natal 1974–1986
1165 Andre Joubert FS 2& Sharks 1986–1999
1017 Calla Scholtz Boland & WP 1980–1989

Most tries

77 John Daniels Boland, Lions 1998–2008
70 Breyton Paulse WP 1996–2007
65 Chris Badenhorst FS 1986–1999
58 André Joubert FS, Sharks 1986–1999
56 Stefan Terblanche Boland, Sharks 1994–2010
53 Eddie Fredericks WP, NFS, FS, Leopards 1998–2010
52 Egon Seconds WP, Griquas 2001–2009
51 Gerrie Germishuys FS, Transvaal 1971–1985
    Carel du Plessis WP, Transvaal 1980–1989
    Neil Burger WP 1982–1991
    Jan-Harm van Wyk FS, Pumas 1996–2001
50 Fabian Juries EP, FS Cheetahs, NFS 2001–2009

17 points or more in a final

26 Derick Hougaard, Blue Bulls v Golden Lions 1 try, 2 drop goals,
    5 pen 2002
24 Naas Botha, N-Tvl v Transvaal 4 drop goals, 4 pen 1987
24 Braam van Straaten, Western Province v Natal Sharks 1 try, 2 con,
    5 pen 2001
21 Gavin Johnson, Golden Lions v Free State 6 con, 3 pen 1994
21 Morné Steyn, Blue Bulls v FS Cheetahs 3 con, 4 pen, 1 drop goal 2009
20 Thierry Lacroix, Natal v Western Province 6 pen, 1 con 1995
19 Naas Botha, N-Tvl v Western Province 2 con, 3 pen, 2 drop goals 1980
19 Willem de Waal, FS Cheetahs v Blue Bulls 5 pen, 2 con 2005
18 De Wet Ras, Free State v Western Province 3 con, 3 pen,
    1 drop goal 1976
18 Henry Honiball, Natal Sharks v Golden Lions 3 con, 4 pen 1996
17 Gerald Bosch, Transvaal v E-Tvl 1 con, 2 pen, 3 drop goals 1972

CURRIE CUP MOST DROP GOALS

Career

135 Naas Botha, N-Tvl
69 De Wet Ras, Free State, Natal

Season

20 Naas Botha, N-Tvl–1985
19 Naas Botha, N-Tvl–1987

Final

4 Naas Botha, N-Tvl v Transvaal–1987
3 Gerald Bosch, Transvaal v E-Tvl–1972
3 Naas Botha, N-Tvl v Western Province–1985

Non-final match

5 Naas Botha, Northern Transvaal v Natal 1992
4 Len Rodriquez, Western Province v Griqualand West 1950
4 De Wet Ras, Natal v Western Province 1979
4 Giepie van Zyl, Eastern Province v Transvaal 1981
4 Naas Botha, N-Tvl v Golden Lions 1985
4 Naas Botha, N-Tvl v NFS 1985
4 Naas Botha, N-Tvl v Golden Lions 1987 (at Loftus)
4 Naas Botha, N-Tvl v Golden Lions 1987 (at Ellis Park) NFS 1985

CURRIE CUP MISCELLANEOUS

Fastest try after kick-off

20 seconds: Chris Jack, 11/7/2009 WP v Natal Sharks: Newlands
29 seconds: Gerrie Britz, 2/8/2003 FS Cheetahs v Pumas: Puma Stadium
39 seconds: Paul de Koker, 5/10/2002 Griquas v Blue Bulls: Absa Park
40 seconds: Dale Heidtman, 20/7/2002 Pumas v EP, EPRFU Stadium
46 seconds: Juan de Jongh, 10/10/2009 WP v Lions: Coca-Cola Park
54 seconds: Riaan Swanepoel, 17/7/2009 Natal Sharks v Boland: Absa
    Stadium

Fastest drop goal after kick-off

22 seconds: Willem de Waal 22/9/2007 FS Cheetahs v WP: Newlands

Fastest yellow card after kick-off

43 seconds Derick Kuün, Blue Bulls v Sharks, Loftus Versfeld 5/7/2008
58 seconds Bakkies Botha, Blue Bulls v WP, Newlands 17/10/2009

Youngest winning captain in a final

22 years 217 days: Naas Botha Blue Bulls 1980

Winning captain, manager and coach in finals

Naka Drotské, FS Cheetahs captain 2005 manager 2006 coach 2007

Most successful coaches

Brig. Buurman van Zyl, Northern Transvaal: 9 wins & 2 draws 1968-1981
Dawie Snyman, Western Province: 5 consecutive wins, 1982-1986
Ian McIntosh, Natal/Natal Sharks: 4 wins 1990-1996
Heyneke Meyer, Blue Bulls: 3 consecutive wins, 1 draw 2002-2006

Youngest winning coaches

32 years 351 days: Rassie Erasmus 5/11/1972, FS Cheetahs 22/10/2005
33 years 89 days: Dawie Snyman 5/7/1949, Western Province 2/10/1982

Club with most players in a final

Shimlas (Free State v Western Province, 1976): 13 players:
Gerrie Germishuys, Joggie Jansen, Dirk Froneman, Edrich Krantz, De Wet
Ras, Barry Wolmarans, Wouter Hugo, Martiens le Roux, Theuns Stofberg,
Klippies Kritzinger, Ross van Reenen, Eben Jansen (injured Jansen
replaced by Gerrie Sonnekus during the match).

Currie Cup individual records

Most Currie Cup matches as referee
135 Jonathan Kaplan Saru
100 André Watson Saru

Most finals

11 Burger Geldenhuys Northern Transvaal
11 Naas Botha Northern Transvaal
9 Louis Moolman Northern Transvaal
8 Hennie Bekker Free State & Western Province
8 Tommy du Plessis Northern Transvaal
8 Thys Lourens Northern Transvaal (on the winning side in every final,
     four times as captain)
8 Uli Schmidt Northern Transvaal & Transvaal
7 Jannie Breedt Northern Transvaal & Transvaal
7 Carel du Plessis Western Province & Transvaal
7 Pierre Edwards Northern Transvaal
7 Willie Kahts Northern Transvaal
7 Ollie le Roux Free State & Natal Sharks & FS Cheetahs
7 Adolf Malan Northern Transvaal
7 Heinrich Rodgers Northern Transvaal & Transvaal
7 Theuns Stofberg Free State (win 1976), Northern Transvaal (share
     with WP in 1979, win 1980) and Western Province (win in 1982 and
     1983)
6 Daan du Plessis Northern Transvaal
6 Michael du Plessis Western Province & Transvaal
6 Gerbrand Grobler Northern Transvaal & Transvaal
6 Martiens le Roux Free State
6 Rob Louw Western Province
6 Shaun Povey Western Province
6 Divan Serfontein Western Province
6 James Small Transvaal & Natal & Western Province
6 Henning van Aswegen Free State & Western Province
6 Pedrie Wannenburg Blue Bulls
5 Mark Andrews Natal
5 Wahl Bartmann Transvaal & Natal
5 Darius Botha Northern Transvaal
5 Gary Botha Blue Bulls
5 Fourie du Preez Blue Bulls
5 Robert du Preez Northern Transvaal & Natal
5 Pote Fourie Northern Transvaal
5 John Knox Northern Transvaal
5 Johann Lampbrecht Northern Transvaal
5 Hennie le Roux Transvaal
5 Victor Matfield Blue Bulls
5 Dick Muir Natal & Western Province
5 Jan Oberholzer Northern Transvaal
5 Gavin Passens Blue Bulls (2002, 2003, 2004) and Cheetahs (2006,
     2007) – on the winning side in every final
5 Francois Pienaar Transvaal
5 De Wet Ras Free State
5 Danie Rossouw Blue Bulls
5 Pieter Rossouw Western Province
5 Calla Scholtz Western Province
5 André Skinner Northern Transvaal & Transvaal
5 Gerrie Sonnekus Free State
5 Toks van der Linde Western Province
5 Moaner van Heerden Northern Transvaal
5 André van Staden Northern Transvaal
5 Christo Wagenaar Northern Transvaal

Select bibliography

Bath, Richard. 2008. *The British and Irish Lions miscellany*. London. Vision Sports Publishing.

Bishop, John. 2000. *MAC: The face of rugby*. Cape Town. Don Nelson.

Burger, Gerhard & Van der Berg, Wim. 2008. *The Lions Tale – 120 Years of the Red and White*. Johannesburg. Online Communications.

Carmichael, Shelley (editor) and various authors, 2003. *112 Years of Springbok Rugby, Tests and Heroes*. Cape Town. Published by Highbury Monarch Communications for the South African Rugby Football Union.

Claassen, Wynand. 1985. *More than Just Rugby*. Johannesburg. Hans Strydom Publishers.

Colquhoun, Andy. 2007. *Hennie Muller: Die Windhond*. Cape Town. Don Nelson.

Craven, DH & Jordaan, Piet. 1955. *Met die Maties op die Rugbyveld, 1880–1955*. Kaapstad. Nasionale Boekhandel.

Craven, DH. 1949. *Ek Speel vir Suid-Afrika*. Kaapstad. Nasionale Pers Bpk.

Craven, DH. 1964. *Springbok-annale/Springbok Annals 1891-1964*. Published by the SA Rugby Board as part of their jubilee celebrations. (Uitgegee deur die SA Rugbyraad as deel van sy jubileumfees.) Johannesburg. Mimosa Publishers (Pty) Ltd.

Craven, DH. 1980.*Die Groot Rugbygesin van die Maties.1980*. Cape Town. Galvin and Sales.

De Villiers, Steve. 1989. *Kaviaar vir ʾn Kameraad*. Johannesburg. Perskor.

De Villiers, Steve. 1990. *Kaviaar vir ʾn Kanniedood*. Johannesburg. Perskor.

Difford, Ivor D. 1933. *History of South African Rugby Football* . Wynberg, Cape. The Speciality Press of SA, Ltd.

Dobson, Paul. 1889. *Rugby in Suid-Afrika: ʾn Geskiedenis, 1861–1988*. Kaapstad

Dobson, Paul. 1990. *Bishops Rugby – a History*. Cape Town. Don Nelson.

Dobson, Paul. 1996. *Rugby's Greatest Rivalry*. Cape Town Human and Rosseau.

Ferreira, JT; Blignaut, JP; Landman PJ & du Toit, JF. 1989.*Transvaal Rugby Football Union: 100 years*. Johannesburg. Published by TRFU.

Gerber, Hennie. 1982. *Craven*. Cape Town. Tafelberg.

Gouws, Leon. 1971. *Frik du Preez, Rugbyreus*. Honeydew. Janssonius & Heyns.

Greyvenstein, Chris. 1977. *Springbok Saga*. Cape Town. Don Nelson Publishers and Toyota SA.

Greyvenstein, Chris. 1989. *Naas Botha, Rugby's Golden Boy (SA Sporting Greats)*. Cape Town. Don Nelson.

Grieb, Eddie & Farmer, Stuart. 2009. *Springbok Miscellany*. Johannesburg. Jonathan Ball Publishers.

Heenop, Albert. 2001. *Team of the 90s*. Durban. Mundell Media.

Herbert, Alfred. 1980. *The Natal Rugby Story*. Pietermaritzburg. Shuter and Shooter.

Howitt, Bob. 2005. *Sanzar Saga*. Johannesburg. Jonathan Ball Publishers.

Jooste, Graham K. 1995. *South African Rugby Teams*. London. Penguin.

Le Roux, Herman. 1998. *Sportpourri*. Pretoria. JL van Schaik.

Luyt, Louis. 2003. *Walking Proud: the Louis Luyt Autobiography*. Cape Town. Don Nelson.

Medworth, CO. 1964. *Natal Rugby, 1870–1964*. Cape Town. Howard Timmins.

Parker, AC. 1983. *WP Rugby Centenary 1883–1983*. Cape Town. Published by the Western Province Rugby Football Union.

Partridge, Ted. 1991. *A Life in Rugby*. Halfway House. Southern Book publishers.

Rugby in Suid-Afrika: 'n geskiedenis, 1861–1988. 1989.

SA Rugby Annuals. 1950–2011. Various publishers, sponsors and printers.

SA Rugby Football Union, 1995. Cape Town. Royston Lamond International.

SA Rugby publications. Various years, publishers, sponsors and printers.

Shippey, Kim. 1971. *The Unbeatables. Springboks in Australia*. (No reference to publishers, printers, distributors.)

Shnaps, Teddy. 1989. *A Statistical History of Springbok Rugby*. Cape Town. Don Nelson Publishers.

Smit, John with Mike Greenaway. 2009. *Captain in the Cauldron*. Durban. Highbury Safika Media.

Smit, Kobus. 2007. *The Complete Book of Springbok Rugby Records*. Cape Town. Don Nelson.

Sweet, Reg 1956. *The Kiwis Conquer*. Cape Town. Howard Timmins.

Sweet, Reg. 1990. *Natal 100 – Centenary of Natal Rugby Union*. Durban. Published by Natal Rugby Union.

Van der Berg, Wim & Burger, Gerhard. 2008. *Blue Bulls: 70 years of glory*. Johannesburg. Penguin.

Van der Berg, Wim. 2010. *Greatest Currie Cup moments*. Johannesburg. Penguin.

Van Rensburg, Frikkie. 1986. *Die Ontstaan van Griekwaland-Wes-Rugby, 1886–1986*. Kimberley. Noordkaaplandse Drukkers.

Van Zyl, MC (editor) and various authors, 1988. *Noord-Transvaalrugby 50*. Published by Northern Transvaal Rugby Union, Pretoria.

Volschenk, Johan. 1977. *Die Ligbloues*. Pretoria. TRI-Uitgewers.

White, Jake with Craig Ray. 2007. *In Black and White: The Jake White Story*. Cape Town. Zebra Press.

OTHER SOURCES

Archives and magazine cuttings

Blou – Official magazine of the Bulls and Blue Bulls

Blue Bulls Rugby Union

Golden Lions Rugby Union archives

Griqualand West Rugby Union archives

Herman le Roux. Brochures and newspaper and magazine cuttings from the collection of Herman le Roux, former sports editor of *Volksblad* and *Beeld*

Raiders Rugby Club Museum

Transvaal Independent Rugby Football Union literature

Websites

http://bleacherreport.com/articles
http://myfundi.co.za
www.absa.co.za
www.bluebull.co.za
www.classicclashes.co.za
www.genslin.us/bokke
www.irb.com
www.johnsmit.co.za
www.lionsrugby.co.za
www.planetrugby.com
www.rugby365.com
www.rugbyvaria.com
www.sarugby.co.za
www.sasahof.co.za
www.sharksrugby.co.za
www.sport24.co.za
www.superrugby.com
www.supersport.co.za
www.tagrugby.co.za
www.trinationsrugby.net

Index

Abass, Abdullah (Dullah) 52–3, 67, 72–3, 77–8
Ackermann, Chris 126–7
Ackermann, Dawie 98
Adams, Heini 79
Afrika, Cecil 153
Alberts, Willem 101
Alexander, Mark 63
Anderson, Biddy 29
Anderson, Henry 29
Andrews, Eddie 79
Andrews, Mark 5, 7, 12, 225
Andrew, Rob 8
Antelme, Mike 169
Aplon, Gio 152
Atherton, Steve 133

Babrow, Louis 91, 150, 168
Badela, Mono 67
Badenhorst, Chris 223–4
Badenhorst, Skipper 223
Bands, Richard 136
Barnard, Willem 217
Bartmann, Wahl 123, 128–9, 225
Basson, Bjorn 223
Basson, Carl 126–7
Basson, Stefan 153
Bastard, Ebbo 91
Beast see Mtawarira, Tendai
Bedford, Tommy 55
Behardien, Gasant Ederoos (Gamat) 78
Bekker, Daan 162
Bekker, Dolf 162
Bekker, Hennie 70, 104, 116–18, 225
Bekker, Jaap 162, 163, 169
Bekker, Martiens 162
Beneke, Izak 125
Benjamin, Ryno 178, 213
Bentel, Jenny 144
Bezuidenhout, Gert 113, 126–7
Blair, Robbie 150
Bobo, Gcobani 76
Bosch, Gerald 106, 113–14, 213, 222, 224
Boshoff, Leon 133
Bosman, Meyer 136–7
Botes, Jacques 223
Botha, Bakkies 108, 136, 144, 160, 198, 225
Botha, Bernardo 154
Botha, BJ 18
Botha, Darius 225
Botha, Ettienne 136, 222–3

Botha, Gary 137, 224
Botha, Naas 11, 68, 105–7, 110, 116–19, 121, 123, 125, 134–5, 163, 172, 224–5
Botha, PW 53
Brand, Gerry 215
Breedt, Jannie 119, 121–2, 125, 128, 225
Brewis, Hannes (Hansie) 95–6, 98, 169, 216
Brink, Robby 12
Brits, Ockert 103
Britz, Gerrie 150, 224
Brooks, Freddie 41
Brümmer, Francois 145
Brüssow, Heinrich 137–8, 150, 152, 191–2, 195
Brynard, Gert 162, 169
Burger, Chris 103, 116, 165
Burger, Freek 126–7
Burger, Jan 97
Burger, Neil 118, 222, 224
Burger, Philip 164, 223
Burger, Schalk 6, 18, 102, 171, 177, 192, 196, 198, 213, 215–17
Burger, Thys 117, 164, 172
Burmeister, Ralph 98, 126–7

Cadwallader, HG 45
Calitz, Ben 112, 126–7
Carden, Daddy 43, 46
Carstens, Cassie 126–7
Chavhanga, Tonderai 76, 152, 213
Christie, Kitch 2, 9, 12, 14, 50, 57, 105–6, 128–9
Cilliers, Gert 150
Claassen, Jannie 124
Claassen, Wynand 118, 170–1
Cocks, Tim 157
Coetzee, Allister 198
Coetzee, Danie 136
Coetzer, Gerrit 150
Collins, Willie 34
Colquhoun, Andy 179
Conradie, Bolla 79
Coombe, Bowden 126, 127
Cousins, RL 45
Craven, Danie 33, 35, 40, 43–4, 48–53, 55–6, 58–9, 73, 78, 83, 88, 90, 94, 98, 105, 116, 130, 149, 157, 166, 168–9, 174–5
Cronje, Geo 16
Currie, Sir Donald 36, 45, 84
Cushe, Morgan 70, 75

Dalton, James 2, 5, 12, 183, 210, 217
Daniel, Keegan 101
Daniels, John 224
Dannhauser, Gert 97
Dannhauser, Toy 34
Davids, Nicky 70
Davids, Quinton 16, 79
Dazel, Renfred 153
De Beer, Jannie 15, 18, 222–3
De Bruyn, Tewis 138
De Jongh, Juan 79, 152, 224
De Klerk, FW 52
De Klerk, Kevin 113, 171
De Klerk, Moffie 114
De Kock, Con 96
De Kock, Kockie 53, 88
De Koker, Paul 224
De Villiers, Dawie 52, 109, 162, 171
De Villiers, Dirkie 96
De Villiers, HO 109, 111
De Villiers, JD 49
De Villiers, Jean 18, 21, 197, 215–17, 226
De Villiers, Justice Willem 59
De Villiers, Peter 61–2, 70, 160, 179, 185, 187, 191, 193, 195–7
De Villiers, Pierre 90
De Vos, Dirk 114, 162
De Waal, Willem 106, 136–8, 222–4
De Wet, Piet 91, 150
Delport, Gerard 162
Delport, Tertius 162
Delport, Thinus 133, 162
Delport, Willem 162
Denton, Robert 175
Dercksen, Bennie 113
Dippa, JM 72
Dlulane, Tim 76
Dobbin, Uncle 87
Drotské, Naka 12, 150, 225
Dry, Chris 154
Dryburgh, Roy 96, 99, 117
Du Plessis, Bismarck 101, 150, 186
Du Plessis, Carel 14, 16, 68, 105, 117, 119, 163, 183, 223–5
Du Plessis, Daan 116, 201, 225
Du Plessis, Felix 165
Du Plessis, Jannie 101, 186
Du Plessis, Michael 105, 117, 163, 225
Du Plessis, Morné 2, 12, 56, 74, 103, 105, 116, 121, 150, 156, 165, 173, 201
Du Plessis, Piet 113
Du Plessis, Tommy 115, 225

Du Plessis, Willie 68, 105, 163
Du Preez, Branco 154
Du Preez, Fourie 18–19, 108, 139, 159, 195, 197–8, 225
Du Preez, Frik 109, 111–12
Du Preez, Robert 225
Du Preez, Wian 150
Du Rand, Salty 41, 94, 104, 110
Du Randt, Os 12, 14, 215–17
Du Toit, Apies 128
Du Toit, Gaffie 212–13
Du Toit, Pikkie 114
Du Toit, Tobias 113
Du Toit, Wouter 146
Duke of Edinburgh 91
Duvenhage, Floris 91
Dwesi, Alfred 67, 70

Edwards, Pierre 225
Ehlers, Koos 128
Ellis, Jan 218
Eloff, Fritz 53, 55, 135, 175
Els, Jannie 117
Engelbrecht, Jannie 34, 167
Engelbrecht, Kobus 133, 216
Erasmus, Rassie 130, 134, 137, 225
Erasmus, Trens 146
Esterhuizen, Johan 113

Fleck, Robbie 132
Floors, Kabamba 79, 137, 152, 181, 223
Fortuin, Bevin 79, 136, 223
Fourie, Jaque 21, 195
Fourie, Nel 223
Fourie, Pote 225
Frames, Percy Ross 33, 40, 43–5, 104
Fredericks, Eddie 223–4
Frederickson, Dave 114
Froneman, Dirk 225
Fry, Dennis 96
Fry, Stephen 91, 94–5
Fuls, Heinrich 150
Fynn, Etienne 79

Gainsford, John 169, 216
Gamat see Behardien, Gasant Ederoos
Garvey, Adrian 133
Geffin, Okey 97, 166, 168–9
Geldenhuys, Burger 105–6, 223, 225
George, Mluleki 59
Gerber, Danie 68, 105, 163, 213, 215, 217

Gerber, Len 114–15
Germishuys, Gerrie 105, 115, 157, 163, 224–5
Gidane, Aubrey 75
Gous, Riaan 119
Gouws, Johan 126–7
Gradwell, Dudley 113
Greenaway, Mike 173
Greyling, Piet 41, 113
Grobler, Freddie 154
Grobler, Gerbrand 124, 225
Grobler, Kleintjie 115

Habana, Bryan 18–20, 79, 108, 152, 189, 191–2, 198–9, 213, 215–16
Hargreaves, Alistair 101
Harris, Tony 91, 168
Heatlie, Barry (Fairy) 46, 83, 85, 217
Heidtman, Dale 223
Hendricks, McNeil 79
Hendriks, Pieter 2, 4–5, 10, 12, 128, 180
Henkes, Albie 126–7
Henning, Tappe 127
Herbert, Eric 222–4
Heunis, Johan 105, 163, 223
Heymans, Piet 20, 180
Heyneman, John (Jack) 47
Hoffman, Steve 97–8
Hofmeyr, Eddie 126–7, 169
Hofmeyr, Koffie 90
Honiball, Henry 14, 131–7, 170, 215, 217, 222, 224
Horak, Att 150
Horn, Frankie 153
Hoskins, Oregan 55, 61–3, 171, 193
Hougaard, Derick 101, 135–7, 191–3, 222–4
Hougaard, Francois 108, 190, 198
Hugo, Wouter 225
Hurter, Marius 12

Jackson, Petro 103, 165
Jacobs, Adi 79, 101, 224
James, Butch 19, 191
Jamieson, Craig 123
Jansen, Eben 157, 225
Jansen, Joggie 157, 170, 225
Jantjes, Conrad 79
Jantjies, Elton 79
Januarie, Ricky 79
Jardine, Bill 59
Johnson, Ashley 79, 178
Johnson, Gavin 2, 4, 12, 129, 222, 224
Johnson, Martin 14
Jonas, Lillee 70
Jones, Eddie 7
Jordaan, Norman 79
Jordaan, Paul 149, 153
Joubert, André 2, 5, 7, 8, 12, 123, 131–3, 215, 223–4
Joubert, Craig 126–7, 171, 198
Joubert, Marius 126–7, 213, 217
Julies, Wayne 16, 79
Juries, Fabian 153, 224

Kahts, Willie 114, 117, 225
Kankowski, Ryan 101, 152
Kaplan, Jonathan 126–7, 225
Kayser, Deon 16, 79, 213
Kebble, Guy 123
Kennie, H 78
Kettledas, Alistair 223
Khomo, Grant 73, 147
King, Jomo 128
Kipling, Bert 49
Kirchner, Zane 79, 198
Kirkpatrick, Ian 111
Knox, John 225
Koch, Bubbles 97
Koch, Chris 97, 217
Koch, Willem 97
Koen, Louis 213–14, 223
Kondile, Dumile 67
Koornhof, Piet 52, 73, 78
Krantz, Edrich 117, 222, 225
Krause, Piet 223
Krige, Corné 17, 19, 41, 60
Krige, Japie 86
Kritzinger, Klippies 225
Kruger, Gert 97
Kruger, Hendrik 106
Kruger, Ruben 7, 8, 12, 132, 150, 216–17
Kruger, Werner 198
Kuün, Derick 198, 225

Labuschagne, Jannes 217
Labuschagne, Lappies 94
Lacroix, Thierry 6, 129–30, 222, 224
Lamani, Xhanti 67
Lambie, Patrick 36, 101–2, 139, 222
Lamprecht, Johann 225
Lategan, Connie 162
Lategan, Tjol 217
Lawless, Gavin 131, 223
Lawless, Mike 131
Lawrence, Mark 127
Lawton, Tom 123
Le Roux, Hennie 12–13, 180, 215–17, 225
Le Roux, Jannie 113
Le Roux, Martiens 70, 223, 225
Le Roux, Ollie 150, 223, 225
Lerm, Danie 153
Linee, Thinus 69
Lloyd, Colin 223
Lobberts, Hilton 79
Lochner, Flappie 168
Lochner, Hennie 146
Lock, Jan 103
Loristen, Cuthbert 52, 72–3, 77–8
Lotz, Jan 91, 96
Loubser, Bob 85–6
Lourens, Johnny 96
Lourens, Thys 74, 105–6, 110, 114, 116, 157, 225
Louw, Boy 90–1, 94, 126–7
Louw, Fanie 90–1
Louw, Francois 95
Louw, Rob 70, 225
Luck, Aubrey 94

Ludeke, Frans 193
Luther, Chris 112–13
Luyt, Dick 163
Luyt, Fred 163
Luyt, John 163
Luyt, Louis 2, 7, 9, 11, 13, 44, 51, 53–7, 59–60, 67, 104, 121, 128–30, 132, 135, 149
Lyster, Pat 91

Macdonald, Ian 128
Madiba see Mandela, Nelson
Mains, Laurie 128, 132, 188
Majola, Eric 67
Maku, Bandise 76, 178, 198
Malan, Abe 174
Malan, Adolf 224–5
Malan, Avril 70, 172, 174
Malan, Ewoud 70
Mallett, Nick 6, 9, 14, 16–17, 149, 183–5
Malotana, Kaya 16–17, 76
Manana, Thando 76
Mandela, Nelson 3–4, 12–13, 53, 54, 59
Marais, Buks 97–8, 223
Marais, Charl 132, 150
Marais, Hannes 52, 130, 165, 174, 215
Markgraaff, André 14, 60, 130, 167
Markötter, Oubaas 83, 88, 95
Martin, Henry 150
Masimla, Herman 149
Matfield, Victor 21, 136, 144, 159–60, 171, 186, 189–90, 193–4, 196–9, 215–17, 225
Mboto, Michael 75–6
Mbovane, Tshotsho 153
McDermott, Dale 20
McDonald, Andre 88, 90
McHardy, Boet 150
McIntosh, Ian 2, 9, 57, 124–5, 128–9, 132–3, 225
Mcleod, Charl 101
Mdyesha, Curnick 67, 73
Mehrtens, Andrew 3, 8, 11, 214, 216, 223, 225
Meiring, Koos 109
Mellish, Frank 50
Menter, Alan 109
Meyer, Hanne 70
Meyer, Heyneke 62, 134, 142, 182, 187, 190, 193, 197, 225
Meyer, Willie 223
Mhlaba, Solomon 70, 75
Millar, Billy 87, 163
Milton, William H 27
Minnie, Derek 128
Montgomery, Percy 1, 17–19, 186–7, 191, 212–17
Moolman, Justus 126–7, 150
Moolman, Louis 114–15, 157, 223, 225
Mordt, Ray 9, 105, 128–9, 163, 172, 213
Morkel, Andrew 98, 163
Morkel, Boy 86–7, 98, 163, 164
Morkel, Dougie 86–7, 98, 163

Morkel, Gerhard 98, 163
Morkel, Harry 98, 163
Morkel, Henry 98, 163
Morkel, Jacky 87, 98, 163
Morkel, PK 98, 163
Morkel, Royal 98, 163
Morkel, Sommie 86, 98, 163
Moss, Cecil 94, 217
Msuki, Andrew 75
Mtawarira, Tendai (Beast) 76, 101, 194
Muir, Dick 225
Mujati, Brian 76
Mulder, Japie 12
Mulder, Koos 113
Muller, Gert 109
Müller, Helgard 131–2, 150, 223
Muller, Hennie 91, 95–7
Müller, Pieter 125, 129
Murray, TK Sir 38
Murray, Waylon 79, 191
Mvovo, Lwazi vii, 76, 101
Myburgh, Mof 109, 111–12
Myburgh, Ryk 30

Naude, Tiny 170
Ncate, Sydney 70, 75
Ndungane, Akona 76, 152
Ndungane, Odwa 76, 101
Neethling, Stef 127
Nel, JP 137
Nel, Marijke 164
Nel, Philip 164, 168
Nel, Pieter 124
Newham, Charlie 91
Niels, Johnny 78
Nkanunu, Silas 53–5, 59–60, 67, 74
Nkonki, Timothy 70, 74–5
Nkumane, Owen 69, 75–6
Noakes, Tim 6, 179
Nokwe, Jongi 76, 152, 213
Norwood, Simon 113
Nyondo, Amon 67, 74

Oberholzer, Jan 225
Oberholzer, Rian 9, 60
O'Cuinneagain, Dion 152
Oelofse, Hansie 98
Ogilvie, George 23–6, 30, 38
Oliver, Cameron 223
Olivier, Eben 162
Olivier, Eric (Jnr) 162
Olivier, Eric (Snr) 162
Olivier, Jacques 222, 223
Olivier, Wynand 197–8
Oosthuizen, Coenie 150, 184
Osche, Chum 96
Osler, Bennie 58, 90, 168, 216
Oxlee, Keith 169, 172, 215

Pagel, Garry 12
Passens, Gavin 79, 223, 225
Patel, Ebrahim 44, 53, 55, 60
Patricios, Jon 142–3
Paulse, Breyton 16, 79, 187, 213, 215–16, 224
Paulse, Louis 70

Payne, Shaun 133
Peach, Justin 223
Pelser, Martin 169
Pelser, Pa 98, 128
Pickard, Jan 94–5, 98, 117
Pienaar, AJ (Sport) 47–51
Pienaar, Francois 3, 12–14, 128, 130, 167, 171, 180
Pienaar, Gysie 12, 105
Pienaar, Ruan 138, 150, 217
Pienaar, Theo 48, 164
Pietersen, JP 18, 79
Pilditch, Gerald 34
Plaatje, Halley 72
Plumtree, John 101–2, 138
Poro, Arthur 70
Potgieter, Dewald 198
Potgieter, Jacques-Louis 198
Povey, Shaun 225
Powell, Jackie 217
Pretorius, André 213–16
Pretorius, Braam 222–3
Pretorius, Fatty 91
Pretorius, Jaco 152, 198
Preuyt, Jan 146, 147

Qeqe, Dan 66–7, 74

Ralepelle, Chiliboy iv, 76
Ras, De Wet 115, 223–5
Raubenheimer, Davon 79
Reinach, Jaco 150
Rens, Natie 97–8, 122
Rhodes, Cecil John 77
Richards, Alf 83
Richter, Adriaan 4, 12
Robbertse, Piet 126–7
Robbie, John 119
Roberts, Adrian 41
Rodgers, Heinrich 225
Rodriquez, Len 224
Roos, GJ 91
Roos, Paul 34, 43, 46–7, 83, 86–8, 93, 162, 174
Rose, Earl 79, 137, 152
Rossouw, Chris 5, 12
Rossouw, Danie 19, 21, 197–8, 215, 217, 225
Rossouw, Pieter 170, 213, 215–17, 224–5
Roux, Bees 198
Roux, Francois (Lucky) 98
Roux, Johan 12
Roux, Mannetjies 111–13, 169

Santon, Dale 79
Sauerman, Meyer 146
Sauerman, Theo (Sakkie) 113
Sauls, Eric 148
Schlemmer, Alfred 33, 103
Schmidt, Barry 97
Schmidt, Uli 107, 129–30, 224–5
Schoeman, Marius 153
Scholtz, Calla 222, 224–5
Scholtz, Christiaan 12
Scholtz, Hendro 224
Schreiner, William (Bill) 47, 68
Schwartz, Buddy 112

Searle, W 23
Seconds, Egon 224
Sephaka, Lawrence 76
Serfontein, Divan 70, 104–5, 117–18, 163, 225
Serfontein, Hentie 172
Serfontein, Nico 135, 153
Sherrel, Lance 222–3
Shields, Hennie 70, 74
Shields, Turkey 70
Simkins, WV (Bill) 44, 46–7
Sinclair, Des 97
Singapi, Norris 67
Sithole, Sibusiso 154
Skinstad, Bob 14, 41, 60, 152, 183
Small, James 12, 133, 225
Smethurst, Horace 165
Smethurst, Norman 165
Smit, FC 125
Smit, John 17, 20, 160, 173, 175, 196, 213, 215–17
Smit, Roxane 173
Smith, Juan 18–9, 159–60, 213, 215, 217
Smith, Luke 129
Smith, Nelie 171
Smith, Peet 112–3, 122
Smith-Belton, Jimmy 126–7
Snyman, André 213, 216
Snyman, Dawie 117–18, 128, 130, 137, 150, 156, 165, 225
Snyman, Jackie 130, 150
Sonnekus, Gerrie 224–5
Sonto, Bridgman 70
Speechly, Evan 12
Spies, Johan 150
Spies, Pierre (Jnr) 18, 197–8, 217
Spies, Pierre (Snr) 114–15, 124
Stander, Ben 113
Stander, Rampie 103
Stanton, Reg 150
Stapelberg, Willem 109
Steenkamp, Gurthrö iv, 79, 198, 217
Stegmann, Anton 86, 162
Stegmann, Deon 150, 198
Stegmann, Ebbie 162
Stegmann, Jan 162, 213
Stewart, Christian 5
Stewart, Dave 5
Steyn, Casper 222–3
Steyn, Frans 138, 150, 192
Steyn, Morné 108, 137, 139, 159, 191, 193–5, 197–8, 212–16, 222, 224
Steytler, Herman 88
Stick, Mzwandile 153
Stofberg, Theuns 117, 150, 225
Stofile, Makhenkesi 62
Stofile, Mike 61–3
Stoll, Billy 86
Straeuli, Rudolf 6, 12, 16, 20, 60, 129, 133, 185
Stransky, Joel 4, 8, 11–13, 124, 130, 180, 212–15, 217, 222
Strasheim, Bertie 126–7
Strauss, Adriaan 101, 150
Strauss, Andries 101, 150

Strauss, Johan 167
Strauss, Sarel 150
Strauss, Tiaan 130, 171
Strydom, Hannes 12, 128
Strydom, Louis 145, 223
Strydom, Piet 124
Strydom, Popeye 150
Strydom, Steve 114, 126–7, 150
Strydom, Wynie 190
Styger, Johan 150
Swanepoel, Riaan 224
Swanepoel, Werner 150
Swart, Balie 12
Swart, Sias 218
Symons, Tommy 113

Teichmann, Gary 14, 16, 41, 125, 129–33, 166–7, 173, 184–5, 216–17
Terblanche, Stefan 212–13, 215, 217, 223–4
Thomson, Jeremy 131
Tobias, Errol 68–70, 75, 79
Treu, Paul 148–9, 151–3
Truscott, Andries 150
Tshwete, Steve 56, 59
Tsimba, Kennedy 222
Tudhope, Edgar 50
Turner, Freddie 91, 168
Tyamzashe, Mthobi 59
Tyibilika, Solly 76

Uys, Piet 109, 111, 172

Van As, Hugo 128
Van Aswegen, Henning 225
Van Aswegen, Jannie 113
Van Broekhuisen, Herman 150
Van den Berg, Albert 192, 215, 217, 224
Van den Berg, Mauritz 90
Van den Heever, Gerhard 198
Van der Linde, CJ iv, 150, 215, 217
Van der Linde, Toks 225
Van der Merwe, Alfie 90
Van der Merwe, Bertus 97
Van der Merwe, Flip 150, 198
Van der Ryst, Franz 97–8
Van der Schyff, Jack 169
Van der Vyver, Fonnie 126–7
Van der Westhuizen, Cabous 129
Van der Westhuizen, JC 90
Van der Westhuizen, Joost 7, 12, 14–17, 130, 132, 136, 173, 183, 213, 215–17
Van der Westhuyzen, Jaco 136, 213, 216
Van Deventer, Jannie 109, 113
Van Dyk, Schalk 98
Van Graan, Barend 188
Van Heerden, Attie 91
Van Heerden, Goggie 119
Van Heerden, Izak 50, 122, 175
Van Heerden, Moaner 114, 117, 225
Van Heerden, Wikus 18
Van Jaarsveldt, Des 41, 218
Van Niekerk, Joe 186, 215, 217
Van Niekerk, Johann 162

Van Niekerk, Otto 91
Van Reenen, George 49
Van Reenen, Ross 225
Van Rensburg, Theo 124
Van Rooyen, Brian 53, 55, 57, 59–62, 199
Van Rooyen, George 90
Van Staden, André 225
Van Staden, Fancy 97
Van Straaten, Braam 134, 213–16, 222, 224
Van Vollenhoven, Tom 213
Van Wyk, Basie 97–8
Van Wyk, Jan-Harm 131–2, 223–4
Van Zyl, Ben-Piet 98
Van Zyl, Buurman 104–6, 108, 110, 115, 117, 130, 225
Van Zyl, Giepie 224
Van Zyl, Hennie 98, 169, 213
Van Zyl, Hugo 98
Van Zyl, Piet 98
Veldsman, Shaun 127
Venter, AJ 133, 223
Venter, André 60, 215, 217
Venter, Brendan 2, 12, 14, 217
Vermaak, Jano 137
Vermeulen, Riaan 145
Versfeld, Loftus Robert 32–3
Verster, Frans 12
Verwoerd, Hendrik 51–3, 170
Viljoen, Harry 6, 128, 149, 185
Viljoen, Joggie 112
Viljoen, Riaan 145
Visagie, Piet 111–12, 215–16
Visagie, Rudi 223
Visser, De Villiers 70
Visser, Jan 97
Vorster, John 52–3
Vos, André 60, 216

Wagenaar, Christo 114–15, 225
Wahl, Ballie 96
Waldeck, Koos 112
Wannenburg, Pedrie 198, 225
Waring, Frankie 90
Watson, André 126–7, 131–2, 198, 225
Watson, Cheeky 62, 63
Watson, Luke 63
Watson, Tony 124–5
Wepener, Willie 137
Wiley, JR 23
Willemse, Ashwin 79
Williams, Avril 69, 79
Williams, Charles 70
Williams, Chester 2, 5, 10, 12, 69, 79, 132–3, 151–2
Williams, Dai 90
Williams, John 114
Williams, Tobias Pompies 70
Wolmarans, Barry 225
Wrentmore, GG 23

Zimerman, Morris 90